THE DHARMA TYPES

THE DHARMA TYPES

Secrets of the Five Ancient Castes That Will Transform Your Life!

Simon Tony Chokoisky
With Illustrations by Vijay Murtikar

UpayaPublications

Copyright © 2012 Simon Tony Chokoisky
All Rights Reserved

All rights reserved. No part of this publication may be reproduced or transmitted in any form or by any means, electronic or mechanical, including photocopying, recording, or by any information storage and retrieval system, without permission in writing from the author or publisher. Reviewers may quote brief passages.

Illustrations by Vijay Murtikar

ISBN 978-0-9848859-1-6

Upaya Publications
www.spirittype.com
siddhadeva@yahoo.com

My grateful acknowledgment to Mantriji, Dr. Vasant Lad, Hart de Fouw, and all keepers of ancient wisdom the world over.

Special thanks to my wife, Ventzi, for her love and support, without which this book would never have come to fruition!

CONTENTS

Introduction/*Self Test* 3
Matter & Spirit/ Why Vedic?/ Be Yourself/ Dharma/ The Search for Home
Self Test 1 & 2

Part I

1. Merchant Society and the Dharma Type 21
Four Types/ Four Ages/ Past & Present

2. Educators: *Enlighten Others* 41
Instant Karma/ Surrender/ Money/ Path to Integration-Disintegration

3. Warriors: *Protect Others* 57
Teamwork/ The Three C's/ The Fight for Dharma/ War & Warriors
 Path to Integration-Disintegration

4. Merchants: *Clothe, Connect, and Animate Others* 69
Merchants & Ritual/ Shakti/ The Social Merchant/ Charity
Path to Integration-Disintegration/ Saints

5. Laborers: *Nourish and Serve Others* 85
Inferiority/ Path to Integration-Disintegration

6. Outsiders: *Innovate, Rebel, and Free Others* 95
Who's to Blame? Keys to Self Realization/ Unique Expression
Self-Awareness: Overcoming Deceit/ Overcoming Anxiety
Path to Integration-Disintegration/ Summary of the Types: Homework

Part II

7. Five Paths to Wellness 121
Anatomy/ The Brain/ Body Type/ Diet, Exercise, and Fitness
Special Cases: Laborers & Merchants

8. The Social Conscience of the Types 153
The Circle of Duty: Discipline/ Persuasion/ Priority Avatars: a story from the Circle of Life/ Government: Political Myths/ Homework

9. Element, Taste, and Season 181
Special Applications

10. Intelligence, Speech, and Secret Fear 209
*Language/ Men & Women/ Educator-Laborer Speech Dynamics
Laborers & Preachiness/ Warriors & Harshness/ Language & Educators*

11. Music, Myth, and Poodles 231
Outsider Heroes/ Modern Myths/ Homework/ The Value of Myth/ Pets

12. Sport, War, and Warriors 257
*Sport as Metaphor/ Sport in Practice/ Play/ Sport & Dharma Type
Team & Community/ War & Warriors: Post-Traumatic Stress Disorder
PTSD- Prevention/ Yoga/ Homework*

13. Money and Profession 277
*Money & The 5 Dharma Types/ Lessons from the Labor Type
Cautions for the Merchant/ Earning Power and Consumption of Luxury
Rules of the Game/ Dangers of the Game/ Warriors & Wellness/ Homework*

14. The Life Cycles 307
*Summary of the Cycles/ Integration-Disintegration/ Homework
The Outsider Life Cycle/ Special Conditioning: 5 Types
Cycles Within Cycles/ The Merchant Life Cycle/ Neutral Dynamics*

Part III 334
Appendices
*Appendix I: Skills, Strength, & Weakness/ Season, Yoga Body, Intelligence, Element, Duty, Priority/ Yama, Niyama/ Gross & Subtle Anatomy
Circle of Duty & Priority/ Negative & Positive Emotion/ Veda & Upaveda
Type of Stress & Nature/ Summary of the Types
Appendix II: East/West Wisdom: Author's Picks*

Index 343

PREFACE

This work is a practical manual intended to help you attain fulfillment in your personal, social, and spiritual life. It is not a treatise on religion, philosophy, or academics— which offer relative truths to a specific culture, age, and environment. Instead, it is distilled from all of the above to present universal truths pertinent to humanity in the modern age. In today's global society, where mankind's understanding of reality is muddled by distinctions of race, color, and creed, it is ever so difficult to find one's place. The mundane world is a cacophony of sound, and the song of the spirit is difficult to discern for the multitude of contrary voices pulling us this way and that. This guide is intended to help you find *your* voice in the chorus of the many, and perhaps more importantly, to develop your *ear*, that you may better hear and harmonize yourself with the world about you. It is designed to help you know your Purpose, and understand that of others, and by doing so, to live in the world in a way envisioned by our most cherished prophets and mystics.

By fulfilling your destiny you empower others to do the same and, when another fulfills her destiny, you are benefited in turn. This is the basis for mutual respect, sharing, and responsibility, and these are foundations that pave the way to wisdom. May this be a useful guide to such wisdom and of service to all who use it!

NOTE:
This is not a translation, but an original work that makes use of Sanskrit terms with no real English equivalents. Where appropriate, these have been plainly spelled out, rather than transliterated. This is for two reasons. First, readers new to the material may find it cumbersome to decipher transliterations along with the plethora of new vocabulary and concepts. For those who are inspired to continue learning, sources for learning proper Sanskrit, Ayurveda, Jyotisha, and other Vedic arts and sciences are listed in Appendix II. Second, readers who are already familiar with diacritical marks or even conversant in Sanskrit, should know the proper spelling and pronunciation of these words. Thus, no great need is served by introducing transliteration here.

INTRODUCTION

Dharma kshetre Kuru kshetre...[1] begins that well-known and beloved classic of spiritual wisdom, the Bhagavad Gita. In India's Vedic tradition, it was customary to open an important work with an auspicious word. This served to both set the tone as well as to give readers an idea of its content. With *dharma* at its fore, we can understand the *Gita* to be a treatise on Purpose, Duty, and Natural Law. Dharma is also the subject of this book. In the West we are familiar with terms like *karma*, but there is less understanding of *dharma*, our Purpose in the world. Life without Purpose is meaningless. Our modern Merchant society tries to provide meaning by giving us wealth and possessions to strive after, but material things cannot answer those most basic questions—*"Who am I?"* and, *"Why am I here?"* Material objects can sustain us on our quest— but what we have come to do remains a mystery.

The *Gita* tells us that we must embrace dharma, our Purpose, in order to find happiness in life. But how can we do this if we do not know what our Purpose is? How are we to walk the path of fulfillment without a map to show us the way?

It is the role of society to organize people in such a way as to foster their optimal self-expression. Over the last several thousand years, mankind has tried to invent and reinvent social structures that befit the free expression of our destinies, but our inventions are limited in scope and knowledge. As Paul writes in Corinthians, *we know in part, and we prophesy in part.* What is needed is something that addresses our core essence to align us with the Natural Laws of the universe. Myth and Archetypes do that very thing.

> *"That which is beyond even the concept of reality, that which transcends all thought— the myth puts you there all the time, gives you a line to connect with that mystery which you are."*
>
> **-Joseph Campbell from** *The Power of Myth*

If you do not think that myths are important, consider that we pour ourselves into mythic moulds every day without realizing it. Fashion, movies, sports, family and social dynamics all

---

[1] "On the battlefield of Destiny, on the battlefield of the *Kuru* clan..." BG 1:1

furnish different identities, casting us into roles like 'boss,' 'parent,' 'chic girl,' or 'Lakers fan,' thereby affecting how we behave and what we expect from life. But most of these roles are poor complements to the fullness of who we really are. The Dharma Types, on the other hand, are personal myths that have existed since time immemorial and will continue to be useful so long as mankind exists, because they are the unseen matrices that guide how human beings express their destinies. Though invisible, their effects can be readily determined: a Warrior behaves like a Warrior and a Merchant like a Merchant, in organized, predictable patterns.

Matter & Spirit

A person's archetype is like an Operating System, the internal software that runs a computer. Regardless of the color, size, or manufacture date of its *hardware*, it is the OS that gives a computer its most basic expression and instructs it to work. Likewise, the Dharma Type informs every human being regardless of race, sex, age, or nationality. In this book we shall consider five Dharma Types, or Operating Systems, and how they affect us in specific ways. To get the most out of the systems we were born with, we must become familiar with how they work. To that end, this is an instruction manual detailing the inner workings of each type in practically every area of life, from how to maintain *Health*, to how to make *Money*. In later volumes, we will also explore *Romance* and *Religion*— compatibility between the types and how they best express their spiritual impulses, for these require more space than the present volume affords.

The Dharma Types are Individual Archetypal Myths, the "I AM" identity inside that guides each of us in subtle but definitive patterns. Today we associate the word *myth* with something 'unreal' or 'untrue.' But to our ancestors myths spoke to an enduring truth that lay beyond the ken of the senses. Consider that our everyday world is in perpetual flux— coming into being, changing form, and dying. In Sanskrit, the ancient language of India, this was termed *samsara*, 'constant movement, constant change.' But myth is eternal, driven by the intelligent blueprint that underlies the mundane world of name and form.

Our ancient ancestors thought in mythic terms not because they were primitive, but because in many they were advanced. They understood that what would survive their bodies, societies, and even civilizations, was not made of earth and stone, but of something more subtle and permanent. Their personal myths helped them to find Purpose and obtain an everlasting life beyond the

Introduction

parenthetical existence of the human body, for the Dharma Types are alive today even as they lived 5,000 years ago, here for us to access if we only know how.

Like the laws of gravity or flight, archetypes existed before they were harnessed by the conscious mind, and have been around as long as the universe itself. Accordingly, they are considered *apaurusheya*, a Sanskrit word that means '*not invented by the mind of man.*' And to this day, though it may be impossible to localize one's 'Warrior' or 'Philosopher' genes, (perhaps because no one has looked for them) these continue to influence our lives in every sphere from the most mundane— such as relating to a lover— to the most spiritual— such as relating to God.

In this context, spirituality does not equate to religiosity. Myths delve deeper than religion, and *spirituality* here simply means that:

1. *There is Purpose to life,*
2. *There is order and justice in the world,* and
3. *There is more to it than material existence.*

These three points, in Sanskrit called *Dharma*, *Karma*, and *Duhkha*, separate the ordinary believer, or the materialist, from the true spiritual seeker.

Duhkha means '*suffering,*' and suggests that it is impossible to have lasting peace from physical existence alone because of the difficulties inherent to balancing the material needs of life. *Ayurveda*, the Vedic science of holistic healing, illustrates this by depicting three bodily humours constantly vying to pull us out of balance, and states that health is tantamount to skillfully juggling them to minimize their effects. Physical *duhkha* is evident in how much cleansing, movement, nourishment, rest, and maintenance the body requires. Without attentive daily care it breaks down into disease—and even careful maintenance only prolongs the inevitable. Nothing is permanent in the physical world, nothing endures; change is the only constant. *Duhkha*.

The next concept is *karma*, or universal justice. Nobody, no thing escapes the laws of cause and effect; knowing this, a wise person practices the Golden Rule— *do unto others as you would have them do unto you*— not out of some pious obligation, but from an earnest desire to have an optimal life experience, and ultimately, to free oneself of *samsara*. Everything you do, rubs off on you. *Karma*.

> *"A certain order prevails in our universe. This order can be formulated in terms of purposeful activity"*
> —Max Planck

Finally, *Dharma* is the sense that there is Purpose to life. Without Purpose there is only chaos and entropy in the universe. Without *dharma* life is a series of random moments ungoverned by any sense of Natural Order. The eventual question that a self-inquiring person asks themselves is *"Do I live in an orderly universe, or in a world of random chance?"* Our ancient ancestors were secure in their belief that there was more to life than the transitory material (*duhkha*), that it was governed by inextricable laws (*karma*), and that these laws were organized to serve the purpose of our evolution (*dharma*). These three elements of spirituality, tripod of all Vedic philosophy, are developed throughout this book and its subsequent volumes.

Why Vedic?

From Norway to Nigeria, from the 'Indians' of the Americas to the Indians of the Asian subcontinent, archetypes are universal human attributes. They do not belong to any culture or religion any more than the earth's atmosphere belongs to one country. Nonetheless, some traditions have nurtured them longer and more successfully than others. This work is based on the Vedic lineage of India. The Dharma Types do not belong to India, though it has done much to develop and, in the modern age, corrupt them. We shall see the reasons for this in the following chapter, and explore the pure essence of these types, divested of its cultural dogma.

The word 'Vedic' here is used not in an academic sense, tied as that is to historical timelines and geo-political considerations, but rather to describe a living tradition that, while rooted in India, has spread its branches across time and territory to offer its fruits to the modern Western world. *Vedic* refers not to an individual tree planted in antiquity along the skirts of the Sarasvati (an ancient river in northern India), but to the lush garden that has flourished from its fortunate seed and continues to grow, though the waters that fed it have long disappeared from the earth. Today, the Vedic lineage is evident in the fruits, flowers, and even weeds that comprise the culture of the Indian subcontinent. Its branches are known to anyone who has taken a yoga class or who practices meditation. From healing Herbology to Vedic Astrology, the implications of Vedic thought have spread around the world and common words like *nirvana, guru,* and *pundit* have become part of our lexicon.

Introduction

The West appreciates function when it sees it, and the litmus test for success in a capitalist society is the ability to generate money. From religion to relaxation, Vedic imports like yoga and meditation are multi-million dollar industries in America, which is all the more astounding since they are essentially free in India! But beyond their economic success, there is a reason that Vedic transplants have found a rich soil in the West, and a people hungry for their harvest. That is because they offer an unbroken link to our ancestral past, and beyond that, to our divine roots. Therein lies the difference between modern personality measurements and the Vedic archetypes, between systems based in the last century and those with roots that probe deeper into the reaches of time: the latter recognize one's connection to a sacred Self that is primordial, ancient, and unseen, though very much governed by Natural Laws.

Many self-help strategies exist today that cover some portion of the human experience, but none have the breadth and depth of the Dharma Type. None go so deep into the spiritual component of existence, or trace their lineage back as far into the ancient past. They are recent inventions of an industrialized world. Archetypes and myth on the other hand, have been around forever, and speak to a more lasting aspect of man's being: his dharma.

The introduction of the Vedic *Vidya*, or *body of knowledge*, to America in the 1800s began a process of seeding this knowledge into new earth, and since then has made the place that gave it birth appreciate it anew: Indians are taking a fresh look at their own cultural treasures since these sprouted in America. Yoga, Vedanta, and Ayurveda enjoy an ever-increasing popularity today because people find in them something deep and real, an unbroken connection to the past that brings them in contact with their authentic selves.

> *Love, Prosperity, and God are on your path; find it, and you find them all!*

Be Yourself

It is painful to be anything but yourself. *It is better to be bad at what you do, than good at what is bad for you,*[2] warns Krishna in the Bhagavad Gita. The *dharma* of another is fraught with anxiety, and it is no wonder people today are overwhelmed and dis-eased. Life is stressful and empty when we discard our destinies, for no amount of wealth, food, or entertainment can fill us like a tiny grain of Purpose. The Vedic tradition asks, *why chase after different destinies, when*

---

[2] *Shreyan svadharmo vigunah, paradharmat svanushthitat.* Bhagavad Gita 3:35

it is hard enough to find your own? Helping people find their Purpose was crucial in ancient cultures, and it is a multi-billion dollar industry in today's global Merchant society. From self-help books and seminars, to religion— the original self-help methodology— everyone seems to have a different answer. But the truth is deceptively simple: Love, Prosperity, and God are **on your path**: find **that**, and you find them all! We are so busy looking for these things, we ignore that they are synchronous with our journey. Our job is simply to anchor ourselves to our *dharma*; everything follows therewith.

> *Relationships are the test and temper of any person, philosophy, government, or religion.*

People pray for what they think will make them happy, like a certain amount of money, a certain job, or a certain partner. But how do we know that what we pray for is indeed our highest good? Even if we get what we desire, how much of our time is wasted yearning for things that do not pertain to our highest destiny, or worse, that distract us from our paths? When we follow dharma we are assured not only of our own prosperity, but the good of everyone around us. The more one obtains to one's Purpose in the world, the more one lifts up others in the process. There is more than enough fulfillment to go around for everyone on the planet, because fulfillment is not a material resource like coal or water, but a limitless side effect of dharma. Spiritual treasure is not tied to the rules of natural selection and competition: the more one gives of it, the more one obtains.

If fulfillment were based on limited resources there would always be haves and have-nots: those who hold the resources and those who do not. Great misery is tied to this belief, especially when people do not know another way. The Dharma Types state that everything you need is already inside you. Your dharma is wired in you just as the oak is present in the seed; it needs only to be watered and guided by the hand of an able gardener; Nature takes care of the rest. There is no need to step on others to get to where we want to go. Competition now comes out to challenge and inspire people, rather than dominate them. Imagine relating with someone without needing to *get* anything from them. Imagine relating to people not as obstacles, but as allies, helping each other obtain fulfillment.

Relationships are the test and temper of any person, philosophy, government, or religion. How we behave towards others reflects our evolution and refinement. We may be great at balancing our checkbooks or have mastery of the latest NLP technique, but if in our daily life we cannot do something as simple as treating others as we treat ourselves—the Golden Rule—then we are really only compartmentalized beings, not whole — unholy. Improving relationships with others begins by improving the relationship with ourselves. This entails understanding the dharma of the individuated self, and ultimately merging it with the larger Self, the Self of All. Love dawns when you know yourself, and Compassion begins when you know the Self of All. When your "i am" becomes the I AM of everyone, all conflicts cease and misunderstanding fades like darkness before a torch.

'Self-Improvement' in the Vedic sense is really Self-actualization; the Self is already perfect and cannot be improved upon. It is a question of realizing that essence, which in reality has no distinctions, the silent, pure witness living in the present moment. It is devoid of labels like Dharma Type, Man/Woman, Human Being. It simply Is. Abiding in that, one has no need for a book like this. But books like this offer pointing instructions to help you find your essence. Aligning with your Purpose makes it easier to be yourself. And being oneself translates into Being. One. Self. And that is the goal of spirituality, no matter what system you use. All that changes is the words— from Georgia Baptists to Greek Orthodox Christians; from Theravada to Tantric Buddhists, and from Kashmir Shaktas to Krishna Bhaktas, the goal is the same: to know that one Self by knowing which all things can be known.

Once you understand that the Self is the doer, and you in fact do nothing, then what else is left to do? The answer is—your dharma, that which is required by virtue of your birth. Every being that is born is constrained to act. From breathing, talking and eating, to moving and even thinking, action is incumbent on us as a Natural Law. These are general actions germane to the species. But there are actions specific to your individual nature that must be done, performing which one receives the maximum of desirable karma and minimizes undesirable karma. What these are and how they are to be performed is the subject of the remainder of this book.

The Search For Home

Whether by secular or sacred paths, the human mind is always searching for its source. People look for this connection in their genetic heritage, their country, and their religion, among other things. This search for belonging is evidenced by our attachment to everything from sports teams, to ethnic cuisine, to the vernaculars we speak. We may love Italian food because somewhere in our genes our Mediterranean ancestors desire to be fed. Something latent inside wants us to remember who we are and whence we came. People want to be connected to their own kind, and even within one country, a state, city, or neighborhood differentiates itself from its neighbor streets, cities and states in order to carve out its identity.

When this search for belonging becomes perverted, it turns into racism, prejudice, and ethnic cleansings. When our search for Purpose is derailed and we cannot find who we really are, we become attached to our race, profession, social status, and other temporary labels. In fact it is important to honor our genetic traditions; we owe much to the body we use, and the physical inheritance it brings us through gender, race, and cultural heritage. Part of our duty on this planet is to discharge the karma of our forefathers, to fulfill the dharma of our sex, and abide by the customs and traditions of our clan and country. These are all obligations we must deal with if we want to survive and prosper. But even above these, the Dharma Type offers us a way out of mere survival into an expression of our true selves, and a relationship with the world that is based on the ecumenical principle of unity.

Ecumenical means *"of worldwide scope, universal, concerned with establishing unity among churches or religions."* It comes from the Greek word *oikos*, which means *home*.[3] Our home lies in the unity of our species by the understanding that we are related by the dharmas we share. More expressive than the role of 'parent,' and deeper than gender, profession, or race, is your archetype. In that, all Merchants are brothers, regardless of the expanse of language, custom, or geography that separates them. All Warriors share the common bond of their dharma, no matter how it expresses in the world. Today, through DNA mapping, people are exploring their genetic heritage many generations into the past to discover their roots, to find their country of origin. But in the modern world where nations and borders come and go and national identities change, the role of the Dharma Type remains constant. This is the real meaning of the root *dhri*, from which *dharma* comes: *'to remain fixed, constant, centered in reality.'*

It is that fixity we all seek when we jump to identify ourselves with our sports team, our local restaurant, or our favorite song. But as we know, these things lose their meaning and grow stale in time, and the search for belonging continues. But one who is fixed in the eternal dharma of her archetype remains at home wherever she goes.

---

[3] The word *catholic,* which means *liberal, universal, of interest to all,* also contains the same root.

Introduction

Discover Your Dharma Type!

So let us now discover your Dharma Type. In Self Test 1, choose one answer that describes you best, though you can pick up to four for each multiple choice question if you are unable to decide. Next, read the paragraphs in Self Test 2 and choose two that describe you *best*. Not all of their qualities have to fit, though they should at least elicit a gut reaction of *"yeah, that's me"*— even if you don't necessarily like them! There are two paragraphs for each type. If it is difficult to decide, you may pick as many paragraphs as you like, and narrow the results later. Check the Answer Keys at the bottom of the tests to tally your choices. The type that receives the most answers is most likely your Dharma Type.

Another way to find your type is to consult your Vedic Life Map. An accurate birth-time and place are required for this, though it is often possible to use general information, such as 'around 10 am'. This special technique not only zeroes-in on your Dharma Type, but also the sequence of Life Cycles. Though our Dharma Type remains unchanged, our basic nature can take on different qualities as we travel through life and assume different roles and karmas. These are called Life Cycles, and the Vedic Life Map is the easiest way to map them.[4] They are covered in detail in Chapter 14.

The final way to determine your type is simply to read the descriptions that follow in this book, and make sense of them in light of your own life experience. Ultimately, it is useful to have friends or relatives help us with the tests and descriptions. Often we see ourselves differently from how the rest of the world perceives us. We may also be in Life Cycles that make it difficult to access our essential Dharma Type. Life Cycles can tint our basic expression like different-colored lenses. Some enhance our light while others sometimes diffuse it. Therefore, take your whole life into consideration when reading the following descriptions, and have a friend or relative help you in the process. Look at your self—childhood to now—to get a complete portrait. That should determine your type, or at least narrow it down sufficiently to make a determination when you read the descriptions in Part I of this book. *Enjoy!*

---

[4] You can find a Dharma Type practitioner near you by visiting www.spirittye.com

SELF TEST I

Circle the answers that best apply to you. You may choose more than one answer for each question if applicable. Try to think of qualities that are permanent in you—how you have always been—rather than how you are at times or during recent changes in your life. Tally them up at the end to determine your Dharma Type.

1. Circle the word that means the most to you or describes you best.
    a. Freedom
    b. Loyalty
    c. Wisdom
    d. Honor
    e. Prosperity

2. Circle the phrase that means the most to you or describes you best.
    a. Independence and Bliss
    b. Love and Devotion
    c. Worldliness and Knowledge
    d. Discipline and Perfection
    e. Entertainment and Fun

3. Circle the phrase that means the most to you or describes you best.
    a. I love being alone. Sometimes I hate people, sometimes I like them, but they usually don't understand me.
    b. I don't mind being alone as long as I have something constructive and productive to do.
    c. I love being alone. I like people, but I need time to spend by myself for quiet contemplation and rejuvenation.
    d. I don't mind being alone, as long as I have a goal to accomplish.
    e. I hate being alone. I prefer the company of people, even if I don't know them.

Introduction

4. Circle the phrase that means the most to you or describes you best.

   a. I like strange, dark, or wild places, remote places no one has ever thought of or been to.

   b. (circled) I like the plains and wide expanses of earth. I like living close to the ground, on ground floors rather than high-rise apartments.

   c. I like high and remote places. I like upper floors, high-rise buildings, and living above others looking down.

   d. I like challenging places. Places that are high, but not so high as to be remote. I like fortified and strong places.

   e. From the Beverly Hills to gently rolling slopes, I like places where the action is; places that are easy to get to, but also exclusive. I like living in the middle ground, not too high, not too low, where there is activity and access to the world.

5. Circle the sentence that describes you best:

   a. I am the rebel or black sheep of my family. As a parent, I give freedom to my kids and let them individualize themselves from others.

   b. I am deeply bonded with my family. As a parent, I nurture my kids by making sure they are well-fed, healthy and content.

   c. **I tend to teach my family and urge them to improve themselves. As a parent, I make certain my kids learn how to think for themselves, get a good education, and understand the world.**

   d. I am the strong one in my family. As a parent, I lead by example, and earn my kids' respect with discipline and order.

   e. I actively support my family with shelter and resources. As a parent, I provide for my kids, and make sure they understand the value of money, self-effort, and making your way in the world.

6. In religion, I *most* value the following:
   a. Going my own way ✓
   b. Faith and Devotion ✓
   c. Study and Scripture
   d. Penance and Discipline ✓
   e. Rituals and Observances

7. In marriage I *most* value the following:
   a. An unconventional spouse, one who understands my particular quirks and desires.
   b. A dutiful spouse, who is loyal and provides for me: a woman who cooks and cleans/ a man who brings home the bacon. ✓
   c. A sensitive, intelligent spouse.
   d. A challenging spouse with whom I can do activities.
   e. A beautiful spouse.

8. I mainly watch TV for:
   a. Horror, alternative political and spiritual viewpoints, science fiction... the Sci-Fi, FX, Indie and Alternative channels.
   b. Family, Drama, History, and Community programs like soap operas, Reality TV, daytime shows, cartoons, entertainment gossip, and re-runs.
   c. Educational, thought-provoking, human-interest stories and entertainment... National Geographic, PBS, Sci-Fi, and Documentary channels. ✓
   d. Sports, Action, News & Politics, Adventure stories and entertainment... ESPN, CNN.
   e. Fun programs, drama, music, comedy, game shows, financial and motivational stories and entertainment... HBO, Comedy Channel, Spike. ✓

9. Under stress I tend to...
   a. bend the rules or lie to get my way, feel invisible, and self-deprecate
   b. become lazy, closed-down in my own space, and worry a lot
   c. be scatterbrained, feckless, and wishy-washy
   (d.) become anger-prone, inattentive, and reckless
   (e.) be moody/depressed, loud, and restless

10. At my best I am:
    a. A Revolutionary, an Inventor, a Genius
    b. A Devoted Friend, a Hard Worker, a Caregiver
    c. A Counselor, a Teacher, a Diplomat
    d. A Leader, a Hero, a Risk-Taker
    e. An Optimist, a Self-Starter, a Promoter, an Adventurer

Answer Key:

Tally up your answers now; the most selected letter likely reflects your **Dharma Type**. For confirmation you should now move on to **SELF TEST 2**.

A. Outsider |
B. Laborer | | | |
C. Educator | | | |
D. Warrior | | | |
E. Merchant | |

SELF TEST II

Select TWO paragraphs that describe you best. Refer to the answer key at the end to determine your type.

1. Sometimes I think no one really understands me, and no one ever will. I love freedom, and need to feel independent and free most of all. Although I can fit into many crowds, I never really feel a part of any of them. I wear many hats but none of them defines me. People may see me as secretive or mysterious, but I am just the way I am~ different. By fate or choice, I am attracted to foreign lands, cultures, religions, and values, and have embraced some of these. I have talents and abilities that are not always recognized, and it can be hard to make a living if I do not compromise with my society. My ambitions are somewhat unique, and I have a quirky way of seeing the world. Sometimes I feel lost— I don't know what my true purpose is, but when I look at others I am reminded what it is not: I can't conform to somebody else's lifestyle just for the sake of security, even though I may have not found my own.

2. I have often dreamt of owning my own business and being financially independent. From an early age I have felt a need to provide and be provided for. I have a strong sense of the value of money and I don't mind working long hours to generate security for myself and family. I don't pay much attention to my body, unless it is part of my business, or I have the leisure time. I like giving and the feeling that it creates, but in this competitive world it is most important to secure my own and my family's needs first. I have a good practical sense and know how to take care of mundane obligations. I believe that anyone can make it in today's society if they're willing to apply themselves. I am motivated and self-driven, and can't understand idealistic or so-called 'spiritual' people who deny the importance of financial security.

3. I like to protect those who cannot protect themselves. I believe in standing up for a good cause, whether it is social, environmental, ecological, etc. Money is less important to me than securing justice in the world. I have strong convictions and character, and people often look to me for leadership. I have an inner strength that drives me to achieve. I can usually outperform others by sheer force of will. I have an eye for deception and can tell when someone is lying. I admire wisdom, and like to associate with smart and educated people, though I may not have the time or opportunity to cultivate these qualities in myself. I can be highly disciplined, and therefore acquire skills quickly. At my best I am courageous, noble, and self-sacrificing, but can also be distracted, anger-prone, and judgmental.

4. I love the camaraderie of working with others to construct something useful. I am handy, skilled, practical, and not averse to work. I am devoted to friends and family, and though not an intellectual, I have a good sense about things, though I can't always explain it in words. My needs and tastes are simple: it doesn't take a lot to make me happy: good food, good company, and a solid roof over my head are the essentials in life. I like being of service and feeling needed. Being useful to someone is more important than how much money I make, though I don't like to be cheated. I believe in hard work and don't understand lazy people. I can be superstitious, and have deep-seated beliefs about things that often stem from my childhood, and cannot be easily rationalized.

5. I prefer intellectual work to physical labor. I can be idealistic, and focus on concepts and philosophies rather than living in the 'real' world. I become disheartened by the ugliness and injustice of life and often lack energy to change it. I have always been smarter and more perceptive than most of my peers, though not inherently practical. I like to counsel others, though I don't always practice what I preach. I have a knack for encouraging and finding the best in people, and as a result people come to me for advice. I don't have a 'killer instinct' and that's a disadvantage if I try to compete in physical or other 'cutthroat' professions. I like to live in a peaceful environment, rather than the hustle and bustle of the busy world. I often know what needs to be done, but don't necessarily have the energy or skills to do it. It is often easier for me to 'tell' others what to do, rather than to do it myself.

6. I set strong standards for myself, and expect to live up to them. I love competition, debate, and testing my limits. I even compete with myself when others are not around. I have a huge heart, and my generosity sometimes gets me in trouble. I like to lay down the law in my family and with others. From early on, I was blessed with physical and mental strength, though I often abuse these by pushing too much—I play hard and party hard. I like to care for those who cannot fend for themselves: the innocent, the elderly, and the underprivileged.

7. I hate constricting social, religious, and moral institutions, and I feel it is my right to speak and act out against them. I also feel justified in flouting an unjust law and not conforming to artificial regulations. I am physically, emotionally, and/or spiritually different from others, and because of this I find it hard to fit in. I can see through people's bullshit, and that makes me want to run away from society. Sometimes I resent 'normal' people, who were born with opportunities that I don't have. I would rather overthrow the status quo to allow fresh growth, than try to patch things up piece by piece. I respect an authority that allows me to be who I am, and understands the gifts I have to offer.

8. I am a devoted, loyal, and patriotic person, and have a deep connection to the things that are dearest to me: my family, friends, God, and country. I believe it is important to abide by the codes and principles of my country, church, and society. I love to build community. I guess you could say I'm sentimental about the things I value. A dutiful worker, I believe in getting a job done right, and am faithful to my word. I am also very good at what I do, and specialize in well-developed skills. I secretly admire widely-read and cultured people, and wish I were a bit more like them, but I just don't have the time to waste on that, and prefer to be better at what I do, than to know a lot of trivia. I have to touch, see, hear, or feel something otherwise it is not real for me.

9. I love attention and being the life of the party. I am quick and clever, and find it easy to get along with others. I can be very likable, though I don't necessarily like other people: I am more attached to the few people I can really trust—my self and my family. I am naturally glib and gregarious, and

Introduction

people tend to believe what I say. I have good taste and appreciation for the finer things in life, things that have beauty and value. However, I sometimes feel an emptiness that I have to fill with outside things, though it is never really filled until I give or do something for others. Sometimes I feel that I am not worth anything, and that if people really knew me, they wouldn't like me. Because of this, I respect those who have raised and supported me, and I work hard to pay back their love in return. I am also very emotional, and can go to extremes of depression and elation. This volatility may cost me in relationships and in my health, and I sometimes like to numb it with drugs, sex, and entertainment. I enjoy all sorts of fun, from performing for people and being the center of attention, to watching others do the same.

10. I consider myself a rather cultured, mild-mannered person. I don't tolerate vulgarity or crass behaviour. I have special food preferences and daily regimes that require me to be alone for parts of the day so I can tend to my rather delicate constitution. I tend to be more solitary in my personal habits, and prefer losing myself in a book over engaging in the hustle and bustle of the world. I like the realm of ideas and concepts though I am rarely able to embody them in the real world. I don't have abundant physical energy though I enjoy sports, games, and being in Nature for their recreational and inspirational value.

Answer Key

1&7: Outsider Type
2&9: Merchant Type
3&6: Warrior Type
4&8: Labor Type
5&10: Educator Type

1
MERCHANT SOCIETY AND THE DHARMA TYPE

From Celts to Polynesians, from Nordic to Vedic lands, different cultures in different climes have stamped and coined their unique version of the Dharma Type—but the archetypal gold from which it is made remains universal, valuable in the steppes and the cities, the marshes and marketplaces of the world. Unfortunately, we have left behind the gold standard of the archetype for the paper currency of believing that our Jobs, Education, Possessions, or the changing Fashions of society define us, rather than the other way around. Ancient cultures recognized that people have unique personality types that inform every facet of their individual expression. Nowadays, the homogenization of society has blended distinctions between people to such a degree that it has become increasingly difficult to distinguish ourselves from people around us. Information and cultural exchange make it easy for anyone to access the trends of popular culture. We are increasingly becoming members of a consumer-driven global society, and while this has encouraged integration among nations and neighbors, it is also more difficult to find our own destinies amidst the many choices that beckon us in different directions. More choice brings less certainty, and less certainty makes people confused about how they are supposed to live.

More choice has made casual relationships easier, but lasting union more elusive; it has made money more available, but diminished the satisfaction it brings; it has made food plentiful, but good health a rarity. As illustrated by the panoply of dating, employment, and health and wellness websites, we have a greater choice in partners, professions, and even diets, but studies show that divorce rates, poverty, and health are no better than they were 50 years ago, and are, in fact, worsening. We need a map to help us navigate the ever-increasing avenues of choice to their purported end— happiness and prosperity. If we are ever to reach that hallowed place, romanticized by phrases like 'The American Dream,' or 'The End of the Rainbow,' we must have direction, a navigation system to lead us there. The ancient Dharma Types are just such a system, more useful now than ever, to help us reach our destinations and steer us away from the storms and ill winds that threaten to divert us from our course.

Four Types

In the ancient world, our ancestors sought to condense the variety of natural phenomena into underlying principles that described the whole of creation in concise yet profound categories. In a way, this is evidenced today in Newton's laws of motion, or Einstein's $E = MC2$, seemingly simple formulations of Natural law that yet have had a profound influence on our lives, from microwave ovens to rocket travel. One of the many ways the ancients classified the world of matter and energy was according to four great Elements: Earth, Water, Air, and Fire. These described matter in its solid, liquid, gaseous, and transformative states, and helped us understand the world by condensing its amazing variety into four irreducible principles. There are other categories of four in Vedic philosophy, such as the Four Seasons of life, Four Aims of life, Four great Ages, and Four Vedas, all of which are discussed in this book. In fact, the number "4" relates to stability and solidity and was often used in the ancient world to categorize material reality.

Four right angles make a square, the most stable man-made shape according to the Vedic practice of arrangement called Vastu Shastra:[5]

Corresponding to the four perceptible Elements are four basic archetypes: The Laborer, Merchant, Warrior, and Educator:

---

[5] *Vastu Shastra,* like all Vedic Vidyas, or bodies of knowledge, is best learned from authentic practitioners and teachers of the material. Visit the Appendices in the back for more resources.

Chapter 1: Merchant Society and the Dharma Type

AIR EDUCATOR	WATER MERCHANT
EARTH LABORER	FIRE WARRIOR

Not surprisingly, just as these types relate to an Element, they also correspond to one of the four aims of life, in Sanskrit called *purusharthas*.

AIR EDUCATOR **FREEDOM**	WATER MERCHANT **ENJOYMENT**
EARTH LABORER **SECURITY**	FIRE WARRIOR **PURPOSE**

The reasons any living creature acts or does anything in this world were categorized by the Vedic seers into four basic drives:

> 1. *Dharma:* The drive to live according to the Natural Law of one's being, and obtain to one's rightful *Purpose* in the world. Dharma, sometimes called 'natural destiny,' is the foundation of any Vedic philosophy and the cornerstone of this book.

2. *Artha:* The drive to win *Security* and sustenance for self and family. From plants to human beings, all creatures have a built-in desire to secure their existence.

3. *Kama:* The drive to obtain *Enjoyment* resulting from one's attainment of Purpose and Security.

4. *Moksha:* The drive to gain *Freedom* from any type of bondage or restriction.

Though they bear Sanskrit names, these principles are universal and express themselves at all times and places in the world. They were mirrored in the Declaration of Independence as *"Life, Liberty, and the pursuit of Happiness."* Life, Liberty, and the pursuit of Happiness correspond to Artha, Moksha, and Kama, three of the aims of life the Vedic seers deemed vital to mankind. Yet conspicuously absent from the Declaration is the concept of *dharma.* Though in formulating his masterful civic document Thomas Jefferson drew heavily on Enlightenment philosophy, he did not have a tradition to describe dharma and how to ensure it for all people. Perhaps as a result, American society to this day continues to live out the legacy of slavery while its citizens struggle to find their rightful place in society. America, though arguably the most Secure, Free, and Enjoyable country in the world, nevertheless lacks its rightful Purpose, which is perhaps why it is both loved and hated by its global neighbors. Dharma inspires trust, leadership, and confidence. Lack of dharma inspires anxiety, stress, and fear. Like a person, a society inspired by dharma knows where it stands and has clear direction; one infiltrated by *adharma*— its opposite— lives on the edge of fear and stress, grabbing its enjoyments where it can while living in a dog-eat-dog reality. It is rarely sustainable for very long and inevitably crumbles under the weight of its own irresponsibility and self-indulgence.

However, it is not just America that lacks an internal compass; America is conspicuous only because of its prominence in today's world. Most other countries fare no better, and often do worse when it comes to defining a standard of dharma for their people. Countries like France and Brazil that emphasize Kama (enjoyment), or cultures like Japan or Germany that idealize economic welfare all miss the mark when it comes to defining a standard of Dharma. Perhaps Bhutan comes closest to this aim by taking pains to guide its citizens along lines of Purpose and Natural Law, even ensuring a "Gross National Happiness" index. There is a lesson in this for other nations, for Happiness does not come about through the pursuit of Enjoyment and Security

Chapter 1: Merchant Society and the Dharma Type

alone, but through the development of all four aims of life, particularly Dharma.

Though every creature expresses these four drives, each Dharma Type has an affinity with one of the aims of life. For example, life on earth is impossible without food, shelter, and security, what John Locke called 'the right to property,' a founding principle of any enlightened society. These are the drives and talents of the Labor type. On the other hand, even with Security, life is dull and depressing without beauty, joy, and laughter. Sharing these is the drive of the Merchant type. Enjoyment without proper respect for Natural Law and order loses its Purpose and turns to pain in the end. Preventing this anarchy of lawlessness is the purview of the Warrior. Finally, life without an understanding of the freedom inherent to the Self can never realize its full potential, and has no context or higher inspiration. The desire to evolve into something higher, something better, to release oneself from the restrictions of a base existence, is represented by Wisdom, and the Air Element. Teaching this Wisdom, which is the key to personal freedom, is the drive of the Educator type.

These categories of four were used to describe much of the physical world in ancient times. The Greeks used them to formulate everything from personality types to four physiological humours. Yet in borrowing from the older Vedic culture, much was lost in translation. A prime example: though four Elements effectively describe the physical world, a fifth exists, Space, which is not discernible by the senses. This is akin to the difference between Newtonian and particle physics: one admirably describes the function of material reality, but breaks down when confronting subtler realms of existence. Just so, a fifth archetype exists that, like Space, encompasses the other four: the Outsider. Five is the number that takes the stable categories of Four (four cardinal directions, four discernible Elements) and spiritualizes them, by introducing *the unseen* into the equation.

Space is imperceptible and difficult to quantify. It is both the most subtle *and* most abundant Element... which makes it mysterious—a quality it shares with the Outsider type, whom it typifies. While not traditionally part of the four-fold Vedic social hierarchy, the Outsider is particularly relevant in the modern age and must be understood if we are to adapt this system to modern usage. The great yogi Vivekananda said that we must revise *smriti* and reinterpret *shruti*. We must adapt man-made laws to our time and place, and reinterpret eternal laws in light of present need. Like the fifth Element, Outsiders are the most subtle, pervasive, and influential type in today's world precisely because they are also the most abundant, a fact that we will explore in the chapters that follow.

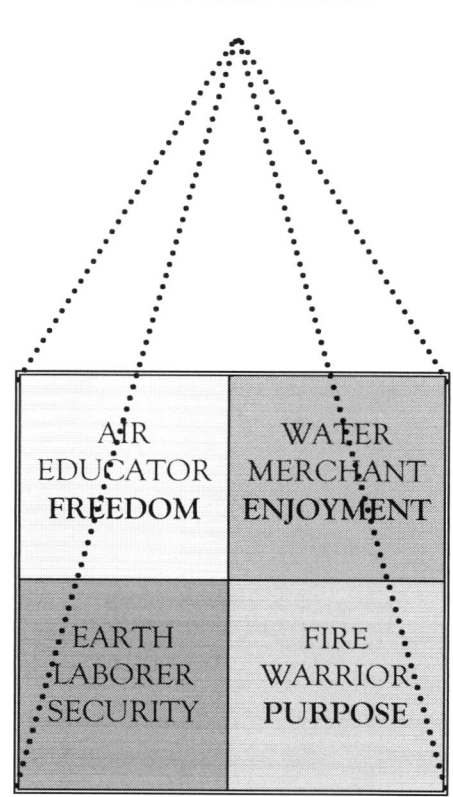

---

[6] Though Air is the most *free* of the four traditional Elements, Space ultimately represents *Freedom,* or *Moksha,* best, since Space is not bound by the rules that govern the Air Element. Thus, Educators become more indicative of Wisdom and Self-Awareness, and Outsiders Freedom and Liberty, as we shall see when we discuss the symbolism of the Elements in Part II.

Chapter 1: Merchant Society and the Dharma Type

The Four Archetypes Through Time

Elements	Air	Fire	Water	Earth (Space)
Dharma Types:	Educator	Warrior	Merchant	Laborer (Outsider)
Plato	Philosopher	Scientist	Artisan	Guardian
Aristotle	Ethical	Dialectical	Hedonic	Proprietary
Galen*	**Melancholic**	**Choleric**	**Sanguine**	**Phlegmatic**
20th century:				
Adickes	Dogmatic	Agnostic	Innovative	Traditional
Spranger	Religious	Theoretical	Esthetic	Economic
Kretschmer	Hyperesthetic	Anesthetic	Depressive	Hypomanic
Fromm	Apollonian	Promethean	Dionysian	Epimethean
Keirsey	Idealist	Rationalist	Hedonist	Traditionalist

* The typologies of Galen and Hippocrates before him (400 B.C.) refer to the four Elements differently than presented here. They also relate to a purely biological origin for the types, which comes perhaps from an older Ayurvedic classification, Vata, Pitta, Rakta, and Kapha. In Vedic tradition these were used generally for medicinal purposes, to treat illness and restore health, while the Dharma Types had broader applications.

Western thinkers from Plato to Jung have used and modified the four basic archetypes over the ages to suit their needs and levels of understanding. However, few philosophers or psychologists knew the source of these types and the context in which they were fashioned. Some people today confuse the Ayurvedic classification of mind/body types (Vata, Pitta, and Kapha) with the Dharma Type. The first are physiological humours used almost exclusively for treating diseases of the body and mind, while the latter have far wider applications, like fulfilling the four aims of life. Thousands of years before Jung and even Plato, these four archetypes enjoyed a lively existence in Vedic society, and more than gauging temperament or even healing, were designed as beacons of dharma. Failing to understand this, we relegate them to a mere remedial function, like turning an I-Pod into a paperweight, and sit in silence when we could be dancing to the rhythms of our lives.

However, while many societies have used a version of the Dharma Types to celebrate the soundtrack of humanity, their recordings over time have become denatured, and none survive today untainted. Even the Vedic archetypes, though produced in the spirit of harmony, were over time remixed into the discordant caste systems of modern day.

Although in Latin *castus* means *pure*, societies in the current age have strayed from the original intent of that word. We cannot say that one type is better than another anymore than we can claim water superior to air: both nourish us in different ways. In fact, living creatures all require Food, Water, Light or Warmth, Air, and Space to survive. These are represented respectively by the Earth, Water, Fire, Air, and Space Elements. Likewise every Dharma Type nourishes society with separate but equally valuable contributions. Society works best when it accounts for and accepts all five personality types by delegating appropriate duties to each. This way, it helps to productively channel their natural, inborn talents. But when stratification becomes a source of discrimination, it can degenerate into tyranny. What we have seen in the world's caste systems over the last few thousand years is just such a deterioration. India is not alone; examples of caste degradation can be seen in every culture that has tried to uphold this system in modern times. In Hawai'i, for example, commoners were regularly required to debase themselves before the *ali'i*, or ruling Warrior caste.

> "The Satya (Golden Age) was the age in which righteousness was eternal, when duties did not languish nor people decline. No efforts were made by men, the fruit of the earth was obtained by their mere wish. There was no malice, weeping, pride, or deceit; no contention, no hatred, cruelty, fear, affliction, jealousy, or envy. The castes (Dharma Types) alike in their function fulfilled their duties, were unceasingly devoted to one deity, and used one formula, one rule, and one rite. Though they had separate paths, they had but one Veda and practiced one duty"
>
> From *The Mahabharata*

Ultimately, neither Indian nor Polynesian society is to blame for this: it is a function of the current age that these systems are so corrupted by *literalism* and *materialism*— a fundamentalist adherence to precepts we no longer understand and do not know how to apply. The aim of this book is to wipe away the false accretions of prejudice, intolerance, and control, and reveal the spirit of a system that embraces both equality *and* individuality, freedom *as well as* righteousness— and far beyond just social categories, that portrays the complete destinies available to each type regardless of race, culture, or sex. Understanding requires radical re-vision: seeing the vibrant truth again behind the grimy veil of time and depredation. This is what we have attempted to do with the Dharma Types, in anticipation of a New Age of wisdom and justice.

In a moment we shall take a look at the types in detail, not just as members of a social class, but as **personality types** with destinies uniquely their own. But before we do, let us observe the archetypes through the lens of Sacred History and see how they have devolved over time. This is a view of the world over thousands of years that describes a cycle of Golden, Silver, Bronze, and Iron ages, and is less concerned with dates and battles, than with the changing of mores in earth society. In Sanskrit it is called the *chaturyuga*, the four great ages.

The Four Ages

Today we consider ourselves at the apex of a human history that dates back in a straight line to our ape-like ancestors and beyond— all the way into the primordial peptide pools where evolution began. Many sacred societies, however, propose a different view of history. They not only provide a cosmology connecting mankind's origins to a sacred divine source, but view time itself as a cyclical, non-linear event. They describe a sequence of great ages that come and go in intervals governed by Nature, intervals that witness the growth as well as destruction of civilization as mankind moves from age to age. They propose a **sacred history that is radically different from the standard scientific model**. We can still find hints of this mysterious history in the implacable faces of the megalithic structures some of these civilizations left behind. From the pyramids of Egypt and the Americas, to Stonehenge, cosmic signposts still survive today that provide an insight into our ancient ancestors, and suggest that these structures were built by civilizations that were far from primitive. However, despite our best estimations, we can only guess at why these monuments were placed and what they are really trying to say.

The living lore of the Vedic tradition has preserved vital records of previous civilizations in a sacred history that dates back into the mists of our origins— records carved not of stone, but etched into the minds of vessels fit to carry them over the ocean of time. This history states that world cycles are inextricably tied to the Dharma Type, and show not only how the Dharma

Type describes the lifespan of individual personalities, but the lifespan of the earth itself over ages that range from thousands to millions of years. It describes a gradual *devolution* of civilization that is marked by the higher and lower qualities of the four basic types. For example, the Silver Age is associated with the higher Warrior qualities of Truth and Honor, while the Bronze Age takes on the Warrior's lower qualities of Violence and Power.

While the spirit of the archetypes states that everyone is created equal, the Vedic record informs us that there is a natural cycle of ages during which each type successively becomes important in dictating the tenor of the age by virtue of its relevance to society. For example, during the first, or Golden age, there is an emphasis on peace, harmony, and spirituality. Societies are small, and Educators take an active role in creating and organizing an idyllic order. In a Golden age, Educators rise to prime importance, though every Dharma Type tends to follow its dharma, and there is little conflict, misunderstanding, or jealousy. Instead, people lift up and support each other by the natural dispensation of their duties. Everyone is anchored to their Purpose and works together to attain the highest personal, social, and spiritual virtues. This is a Garden of Eden in which man walks hand in hand with his Creator, and Educators are revered for their ability to interpret the word of Spirit for the benefit of all.

In a Golden age people are longer-lived, healthier, and more tuned-in to spiritual values. From the Bible to the Vedas, we see references to a distant past in which people lived for hundreds, even thousands of years, in communion with Spirit and Nature. Yet the actual duration of these ages is hotly debated. For example, from 4,800 to 1,728,000 years are allotted to the Golden Age by different sources.[7] And though there is a case to be made for each of these, we propose the figures in the chart below as most useful to the purposes of the Dharma Types. That is not to say that larger or smaller timelines are not correct, but that a reckoning in the millions of years describes events that are beyond the scope of this book to detail. By moving the decimal point two places, we get a timeline that is more relevant to the human experience on this

---

[7] The former figure comes from Dr. David Frawley, via Sri Yukteshwar, guru of the famous Paramahamsa Yogananda. The larger is the more readily accepted number referenced in Sanskrit texts. However, for our purposes it is less than ideal, since cycles of millions of years hardly describe the human career *as we know it*, and are difficult to relate to on a modern human scale. Our figures move the decimal point two places to make them relevant to a discussion of the Dharma Types, thus maintaining the numerological essence of the figures (9) while adapting them to our proximal history. Thus, 1,728,000 years become 17,280 years. For more on Dr. Frawley's unique reckoning of the ages, visit www.vedanet.com.

planet. Most authorities agree that today we are in the Iron, or Dark Age, in Sanskrit called the *Kali Yuga*. This Yuga is said to have begun in the third millennium BCE... remarkably close to the beginning of another now well-known cycle— the Mayan calendar.

AGE	SANSKRIT NAME	D. TYPE QUALITIES
Golden Age	*Satya Yuga*	Higher Educator Qualities: Peace, Religiosity 17,280 years duration
Silver Age	*Treta Yuga*	Higher Warrior Qualities: Justice, Organization, Law 12,960 years duration
Bronze Age	*Dvapara Yuga*	Lower Warrior and Merchant Qualities: Dominion, Power 8,640 years duration
Iron, or Dark Age	*Kali Yuga*	Lower Merchant, Labor, and Outsider Qualities: Materialism, Greed, Depravity 4,320 years duration

Total length of one Great Cycle= 43,200 years. After this time, the ages repeat again, thus after Kali Yuga, the Golden Age, or Satya Yuga, begins anew.

Though they last for thousands of years, every age must end and give way to its successor, as cycles of time bring about a revolution in human consciousness. It should be noted that though these cycles describe the movement of human mores through history, they are also closely connected to the earth's movement through space. It is likely that the great ages are caused by the earth's relationship to its greater galactic home, and reflect cosmic as much as personal phenomena. As the earth moves through its 'cosmic shadow' it becomes successively darker and darker, until it re-emerges into the light of another Golden Age. As the saying goes, *as above, so below*. Ultimately, the full story that links what is above and below is only known to those ancient Rishis who passed down the *chaturyuga* concept to mankind. Time and space are mysteries that become fully-realized only in the consciousness of the enlightened seer.

It was these seers, or Rishis, who organized society in a distant Golden Age many thousands of years ago. That is the role of the Educator: to teach, inspire, and guide, while seeking inspiration from above. But as societies grow and become increasingly complex, and able hands are needed to keep public order, Warriors gradually step forward to seize the reins from Educators. This is the dawn of the *Silver Age*, when divinely-appointed Warrior heroes take control of an ever-growing culture whose complexity is beyond the Educator's energy to manage. Truth, Honor, and Purity become ideals, and, though the Educator still commands respect, it is the kings and heroes of the world who take center stage. Educators prefer to give maxims to people and remove themselves from the fray. In the Silver Age, they appoint Warriors as their successors to justly enforce order and carry out the precepts of Natural law. Educators pass down their supernal wisdom and the right to rule to Warrior kings. Here is the myth of the ideal king and his guru, like Rama and Vashishta, or Arthur and Merlin, the pure-hearted knight and his erudite counsel. Whatever the tradition and geography, Silver Ages are ruled by Warrior types whose job is to sacrifice themselves for the good of the community they are sworn to protect.

In the period that follows, *The Bronze Age*, Warriors continue to rule, but instead of Honor and Virtue, their ideal becomes Power and Possession. As societies become ever more wealthy and materialistic, Warriors are challenged to hold on to their power by the increasing strength of the Merchant class. Warriors are not naturally inclined to making societies profitable; their role is to protect people and enforce justice. When the complexity of society exceeds their ability to keep up, they are tempted to seize power by the only means they know—force. Thus, in a Bronze age, we see a struggle between Merchants and Warriors, with the latter prevailing as dictators and tyrants. Now, instead of exalting the divine right of kings, petty Warriors succumb to the lure of greed and enact through violence a revolution of 'might is right.' Kings make good their claims to kingship by violence, not wisdom. And though vestiges remain of the Silver age, great valor and terrific exploits go hand in hand with terrorism and murder as warlords become the rulers of the Bronze age. The Vedic epic *Mahabharata* recounts the events of the last war of the Bronze age, and how all the rules of conduct in battle were abrogated by both sides in order to attain victory. This is a foreshadowing of the current age in which dharma is least protected, and the virtues of good conduct are all but forsaken.

The selfish thirst for name, fame, and possessions naturally degenerates into the final period, the *Dark,* or *Iron Age,* in which Merchants finally overtake Warriors, and all hell breaks loose upon the earth. In the Iron Age, Merchant

Chapter 1: Merchant Society and the Dharma Type

clout overwhelms Warrior might and money prevails over brute strength to rule. But because Ruling and Organizing Society is not the dharma of a Merchant type, the other classes also revolt, and their lower traits become evident, as materialism, greed, and profanity become the norm. Since its inception, these qualities have ruled the Kali Yuga, but with the advent of the Industrial era in the last two centuries, there has been a rapid acceleration of *production* and *commerce*, increasing the importance of the Merchant to the world. As a result, the past century has

> *"In Kali Yuga property alone will confer rank; wealth will be the only source of devotion; Passion will be the sole bond of union between the sexes ... and women will be objects merely of sensual gratification."*
>
> **From the *Vishnu Purana***

generated a powerful Merchant society, whose values are primarily **economic**, not **ecumenical**. With Possession (Wealth) as the foremost virtue, social order has become skewed to favor any concept that has profit potential and reject such goods and information as do not. While this has favored a few, most people have had to conform themselves to a system that does not promote their highest good. William Blake, living at the inception of the Industrial era, cried,

One law for the lion and the ox is oppression[8]

In Chapter 13 we will discover what promotes personal growth for each type in its Profession. For the Merchant, fulfillment comes from enjoying and sharing the resources of the world with others, including wealth and luxury. These are fine goals that serve the Purpose of the Merchant, who works very hard to attain them, but when they are systematically imposed on every type, a kind of tyranny is born out of which only a few find happiness, while the rest struggle to adapt and survive. Unlike the tyranny in the age before, this does not emanate from one person, a king, but is systemized throughout society. From the South Pacific to the Americas, its effects can be seen in aboriginal societies where "work" used to take up no more than four to five hours of the day. The rest of the time was devoted to self-development, family, leisure, and rest. Perhaps that is one reason that aboriginal cultures—those anchored to older sacred traditions— have had a hard time integrating into Merchant society. Such hours are almost laughable today, and hardly make up a part-time schedule, no less an adequate schema for full-time employment.

---

[8]From William Blake's *The Marriage of Heaven and Hell*

Today, between paying the mortgage and feeding their kids, the Merchant System is designed to keep most people occupied with securing their welfare, and taking their rest when they can, rather than promoting self-study, play, and family time. That is perhaps why we are so fierce about our entertainments in today's America. From the biggest of big-screen 3-D, HD, LCD TVs to the most outrageous displays of weekend party-heartiness, it is almost as if we were trying to catch up on the leisure and self-cultivation we miss, by stuffing it into the few remaining hours we have. That is why we like weekend seminars and quick-fixes: we don't have time for anything more. And although we are rewarded with many entertainments as a release from the stress of the long days we slog to provide for our families, these must also be paid for, which restarts the cycle of spending and earning, earning and spending.

> *The only problem with capitalism… is the capitalists.*
> -Herbert Hoover

While the Merchant system is not inherently evil, it is ill-suited to the just rule of people and society. When it becomes inextricably woven with government, as discussed in Chapter 8, iniquities are born that provoke environmental and humanitarian calamities. What promotes profit does not necessarily encourage safe working conditions; what improves productivity does not advance personal freedoms; in fact, it is usually the contrary. As a result, Merchants do not make the best political leaders. This is not out of any deficiency—in fact, Merchants are the great material benefactors of society when well-Integrated—but a system built to maximize profit and production does not see the need to optimize human rights, environmental sustainability, and equitable relations with its neighbors. We have but to look at the wars and abuses that essentially owe their existence to issues of ownership as proof of this. The lust for sugar, diamonds, oil, and gold… and now paper money, has drained the blood and sweat of billions, yet this thirst remains unquenched.

The Vedic system takes another road. It shows separate avenues of fulfillment for each of the 5 types. What's more, it allows each one to express freely without detracting from the others. It teaches how society must be run for the optimal integration of its constituents. When each type is Integrated, it becomes a boon to its neighbors. This way, the competition for resources that characterizes the material world becomes obsolete as there is enough of money, success, truth, happiness, and excitement to go around for every type, according to its nature.

Past and Present

Wisdom, Justice, Power, and Greed reflect the four *yugas*. But just because the Golden Age is more pure than the Silver does not make Educators superior to Warriors, Warriors to Merchants, and so on down the line. The reader should not construe the sequence of the ages as a hierarchy of one type over another. When a Dharma Type expresses itself at the highest level, it enacts qualities of the Satya Yuga regardless of where and when in history it might be. Later, we'll explore how everything from music styles to political systems correlate with individual archetypes. For now, we have matched them with the *yugas* because their lower and higher qualities best reflect the tenor of their age.

> *'Educator' is a universal term, and it belongs as much to India as to Indiana, to Amritsar as to America: what makes one a given Dharma Type is one's natural disposition thereto, not her cultural or familial milieu*

Whatever we decide about their duration, the ages eventually revolve so that after the Kali Yuga there again follows another Golden Age of truth and wisdom—though it may be preceded by a time of great tribulation: there is always upheaval before regeneration, death before rebirth. When such a period is likely to recur is a matter of debate. Experts differ on the timing of Sacred History and some even believe that such changes are due in our lifetime. Whatever the case, it is the purpose of the Dharma Types to align us with our higher destinies, that when such periods come we are ready to receive them, and even should nothing change, we continue to live our highest truth.

Conclusion

Here is a summary of each type: **Educators** are the designated teachers, though they are not really meant to rule or enforce policy. They are also referred to as **Sages**, **Priests**, or **Philosophers**. In India they are called *Brahmins*, though to call an Educator a Brahmin is to limit him or her to the socio-political caste system of India, and the abuses that go along with it. 'Educator' is a universal term, and it belongs as much to India as to Indiana, to Amritsar as to America: what makes one a given Dharma Type is one's natural disposition thereto, *not* her cultural or familial milieu. Likewise, the other members of this system, the *kshatriya, vaishya, shudra,* and *mleccha* castes, are regional designations that correspond to, but do not define, the remaining four types. Therefore, we do not use these terms to describe the Dharma Types, though the Dharma Types draw much of their livelihood and original spirit therefrom.

These archetypes differ from the caste systems of India and the world primarily because they are not *hierarchical* or *inherited*. The intermixture of people in a modern global society makes it impossible to determine Dharma Type by heredity or to class a person above or below another. At one time, heredity influenced Dharma Type. Blood succession was important in the Golden and Silver ages, when being born to a Warrior assuredly made one a Warrior. However, in the ages that followed, heredity became less and less of an indicator, and more of a liability in determining the Dharma Type. These days, with people mixing freely in democratic societies, it is almost absurd to believe that simply being born to a Laborer *has* to make one a Laborer. Bloodlines have 'thinned,' and what makes one a particular type is more complicated than simply looking at his or her parents. People carry the genetics of many generations, and therefore the possible influence of many Dharma Types.

The rules that applied to the Golden or Silver ages do not work in the Iron age. From the bible to the Vedas, injunctions that applied 5,000 years ago may no longer be relevant today. While the spirit of Natural Law remains the same, its exercise must be modified to fit the times we live in: we have to recognize what is useful and reject what no longer works. The Dharma Types differ from their correlates in older societies in the following ways:

1. *Non-heritable*

    Your Dharma Type is set at birth, and remains with you for the rest of your life, but is *not* indicated by your parents. It can be deduced from your Vedic Life Map [9] or the self-test in the Introduction of this book. A person's individual karma is the reason he or she is born a particular type, and in the current age that does not have to match the parental archetype.

2. *Non-hierarchical*

    All Dharma Types have equal rights as citizens, though each has a unique path to tread in living out its destiny. No restrictions,

---

[9] Visit www.spirittype.com for complete information on Vedic Life Map readings.

discrimination, or prejudice with regard to profession, marriage, religion, etc. are consistent with this system, though some types 'match' better in love and business, a topic explored in Volume II: *Sex, Love, & Dharma* Enlightenment is available to everyone and joy, life, and happiness are as much birthrights of Educators as Outsiders. No one has a stranglehold on Truth, and no one controls the means to self-realization and fulfillment. Educators are born in slums as in palaces; Laborers can deck the halls of the White House as well as the charnel house.

3. *Non-transferable*

One cannot, through work alone, become a different Dharma Type (see number 1, above). The quality and quantity of your work can determine how well you live out the dharma of your type, but it cannot change it into another. Some of us, especially in America where opportunities abound, think that with enough effort, anything is possible. While this may be true, effort must be tempered with wisdom to produce really desirable results. Knowledge of your Dharma Type is the foremost of such wisdom, as it is *Self-Knowledge*. 'Know thyself!' is the first directive, following which, all things can be known.

Karma determines the Dharma Type; how well one fulfills one's destiny depends on free will and personal merit; it is not subject to advantages or disadvantages gained by being a specific archetype. We all start at pole position, at different places on the line. It is how we drive the race that determines our position at the end. It is one's inherent talents that dictate who she is, not her socio-economic status, birthplace, sex, or race, though all of these color her expression. What makes one a superior person is the degree to which she has actualized herself within the constructs of her Type. There are excellent as well as despicable Educators, Merchants, Warriors, Laborers, and Outsiders alike.

This must be true if we are to have any respect for the system— and for it to work today. Prejudice, bigotry, and the dominance of one class over another are perversions of ancient wisdom that cannot stand if these archetypes are to be used in their true spirit. In fact, they serve to *eliminate* bigotry by cultivating knowledge and respect for everyone. To fully integrate your type, you must understand the others, and allow them to integrate themselves. This symbiotic system mirrors the vital operations of nature, in which one entity feeds another, which feeds the first in turn. Just as plants nourish us by dying, and we feed them upon our deaths, and just as we breathe their oxygen while exhaling carbon dioxide for them to breathe, so one type promotes the success of another by its natural operation. *It is not a question of competition, but cooperation.*

To conclude then, the **Warrior** class rules, protects, and dispenses law and order. **Merchants** enjoy growing society and directing the flow of goods and services, while the **Labor** class produces and consumes these goods and services. The **Outsider** completes the picture as the social misfit and most able commentator on society's ills. Also called the **Rebel,** the **Innovator,** or the **Revolutionary,** he is the shadow side of every type and is not bound by rules in the way his Dharma Type brothers and sisters are. Now let us take a look at them in detail, as we explore the permutations of what it means to be a Dharma Type in today's world.

Chapter 1: Merchant Society and the Dharma Type

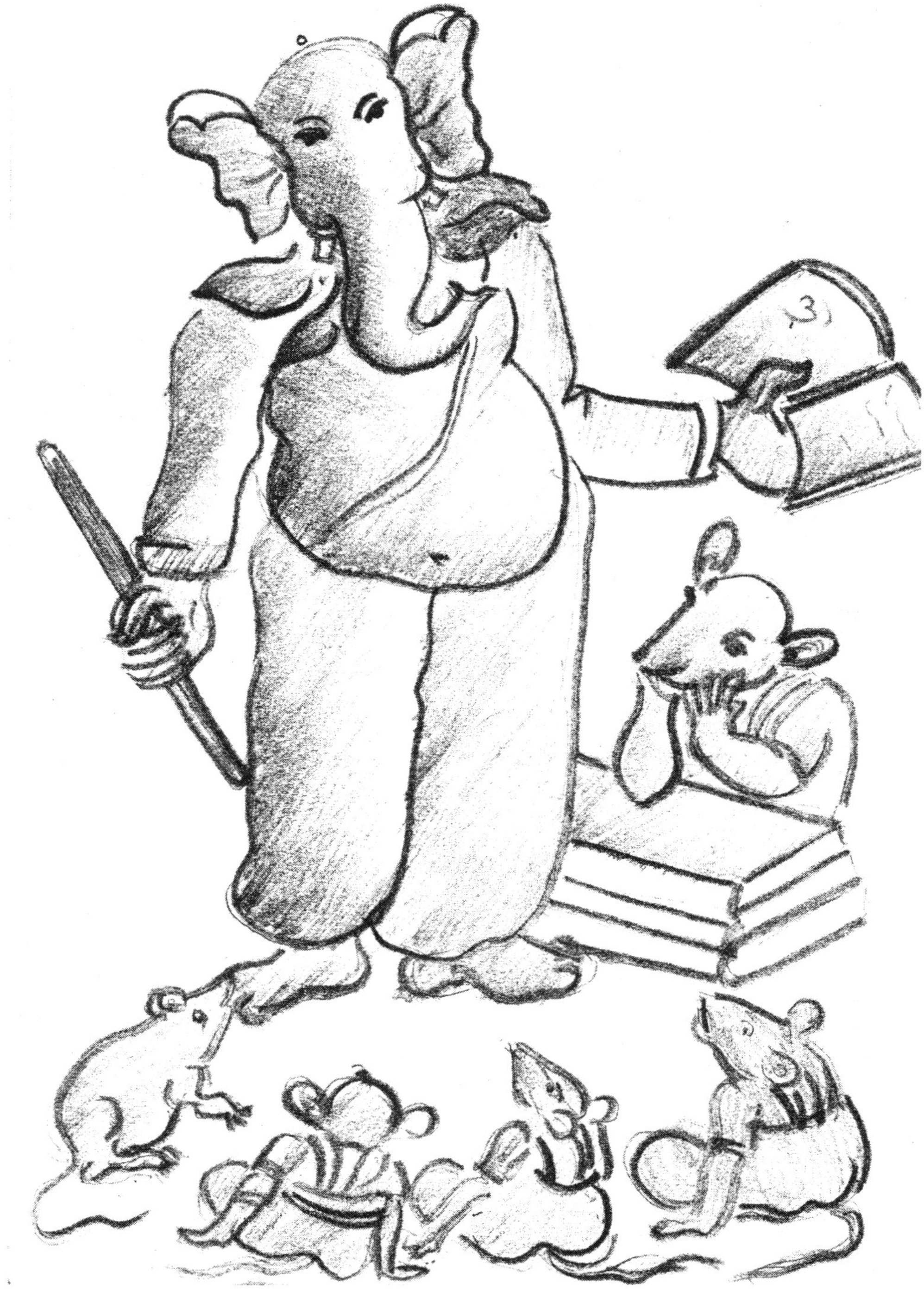

2
EDUCATOR:
"Enlighten Others"

*Compassion * Wisdom * Self-Control*

Educators, as the name implies, make the best teachers. Whatever their professions, they have a natural inclination to transfer information and enrich people with knowledge. It is also their role to give meaning and purpose to life, and inspire others with wisdom and good counsel. They do not have to be actual teachers to do so; famous Educators teach the public about their individual causes from the platform of their celebrity. From nonviolent protests to environmental causes and world peace, they spread education through their medium each in their own unique way.

The most intellectually curious of the types, Educators like to read and learn about the world. Their curious minds are always at work, and they also delight in games and pastimes to keep them sharp. From Scrabble and Sudoku, to crossword puzzles and chess, Educators love games that challenge and occupy their brains.

They may also quench their curiosity by learning a little bit about many things. At the root of this desire to learn is a strong interest in Self Help- improving their condition as well as the conditions of those around them. Whether investigating Newton's physics or New Age philosophy, Sages (Educators) seek ways to better themselves and their world. Because they are also more sensitive than other types, they tend to live for ideals, and are driven more by *ideas* than *money*, seeking *sophistication* rather than *security*. At the root of the word *sophistication* is the Greek for *to become wise*. Ultimately,

---

Famous Educators

Joan Allen
Woody Allen
Richard Dean Anderson
Alexander Graham Bell
Michael Bolton
Joseph Campbell*
Julia Child
David Copperfield
Albert Einstein
Mohandas Gandhi
Billy Graham
Geena Davis
Robert Dole
Bob Dylan*
T.S. Eliot
Gustave Flaubert
Judy Garland
Bill Gates*
John Irving
George Lucas*
Marilyn Manson
Alanis Morissette*
Moses
Barack Obama
Parasurama
Louis Pasteur
Carl Sagan
Martin Sheen
Sir Philip Sidney
Tiger Woods

Names followed by an asterisk are Outsiders finding their best expression playing another type. More on this in the Outsider chapter.

their inner wisdom benefits society, as the fruits of their labor eventually come out to serve humanity. Louis Pasteur is an example of an Educator whose research led to the upliftment of mankind.

> *Like the air that gives us life, the Educator lends breath to the endeavors of every type, by filling them with knowledge and wisdom.*

Without meaning, life perishes, but with purpose and hope, man can survive life's hardships and embrace its blessings. It is the Sage's role to find and share that meaning and inspire hope in others. Educators are not physically imposing, but their counsel can be a powerful force. Merchants cannot sell, Warriors fight, Laborers work, or Outsiders rebel, if they don't know what they are living, fighting, working for, or rebelling against. In whatever guise, be he astronomer or philosopher, the Sage's gift is to help others fulfill their dharmas. From Carl Sagan, who taught a whole generation to look up and wonder at the mysteries of the Cosmos, to Julia Child, who encouraged millions to discover the joy of cooking, like the air that gives us life, the Educator gives breath to the endeavors of every type, by filling them with knowledge and wisdom.

Every class excels in certain areas, but no type is as well-rounded as the Educator. They tend to know a little bit about everything and are the Renaissance men and women of the Dharma Type family. Educators also represent the civilizing force of society and their contributions come as much from philosophy as from politics, from science as from science fiction. Their liberality of experience makes them able teachers, and provides an ideal model for education.

In order to learn, children must have optimal stimulation through various channels, including kinesthetic (sport), artistic (music, art, theater), linguistic (language), and reasoning (math, science) media. This allows all of the learning channels of the human mind to be tuned to receive universal wisdom. When we shut ourselves down to one or two modes of learning, we become as limited and boring as that old television with the rabbit-ear antennae. Education systems that do away with music and art, or sports and leisure in schools, deprive students of the developmental benefits these activities afford. This is particularly true for children under age 10, whose minds are particularly malleable and benefit from a wide range of learning stimuli.

Even though children under age 10 have the best chance of learning languages and skills that become second nature, our learning really never stops. Modern research shows that the brain has remarkable abilities to repair itself and continue forging new links analogous with learning well into old age. Therefore it is as vital to form the young to take the right first steps in life as it is to show the old how to make their final steps with grace, through an integrated education that includes every available and effective form of learning, from youth to maturity and well into old age.

Vedic societies developed these methods into their ultimate forms of expression. Sanskrit, the ancient Vedic language, literally means 'perfected, polished,' and represents an optimal arrangement of sound and meaning that orders the consciousness of the person who studies it. It literally teaches a person *to think*. In much the same way, Hatha Yoga and classical dance arrange the subtle and gross pathways of the body for maximal *physical* integration, teaching the body how *to move*. Ayurveda, Sthapatya Veda, Gandharva Veda,[10] and the many other sciences of the Vedic canon also instruct us how to taste, see, hear, and function in the world, by ordering the sense pathways employed in studying them. It is important for any civilized culture to have an educational matrix that fosters well-rounded development. Societies lacking this show low respect for Educators and what they stand for, and ultimately doom themselves to ignorance and rigidity.

Yet while no one is better at teaching than the teachers, Educators do not always follow what they preach. They can become poor role models when they fail to walk the walk and do as they say. Perhaps because it is so easy for them to grasp concepts *intellectually*, they do not take the time to master and own them in their core. As a result, they may espouse grand ideals but still be at odds with their animal passions. They may hold others to standards they themselves cannot keep. Here is a case for a priest who, despite his great work on the pulpit, succumbs to lust and fornication A politician whose efforts for peace are tainted by shady deals and bribes. A coach who cannot perform the tasks he asks of his athletes, or a general who cannot stand up to the same standards as his soldiers. We see this all too often in media exposes of our stars and senators alike. From Woody Allen to Tiger Woods, Educators often fall from grace because of sexual impropriety. The seemingly reserved Sage holds a powerful

---

[10]The art and science of Health, Architecture and Placement, and Music, respectively. Sacred cultures around the world teach forms of dance and movement, such as Hula (Polynesia) or belly dance (in the Near East), but none are as systemized and profoundly developed as the Vedic traditions.

sexual center that needs to be properly channeled if he is to remain an exemplar of virtue. How this is done is further discussed in Volume II, *Sex, Love, & Dharma*, which details the love lives of the five types, and describes how each experiences optimal fulfillment in everything from Sex to Soulmates.

When the Educators we trust to embody high character fail us, they not only disappoint themselves but the world they are supposed to inspire with purpose and meaning. Instead of enlightening people, they darken their own reputations.

A Vedic story expresses this poignantly. When Brahma, creator god and Educator archetype of the Vedic pantheon created the universe, he marveled at its beauty, but was unable to articulate its many marvels. To do so, he created the goddess Sarasvati, patron of speech, language, art, and culture. So breathtaking was she, that he became infatuated with her beauty, growing four heads in order to behold her in each direction. Deeming his lust inappropriate for a patriarch, she rebuked him, cursing him as an inadequate object of worship for having succumbed to longing and desire. As a result, Brahma to this day has only two temples in all of India, whereas even minor deities enjoy dozens, hundreds, even thousands of shrines! This is a cautionary tale for Educators everywhere, who when they descend into lust, lose the respect of those they serve, and their rightful place in society.

> *Conscience is strong in Educators; they must turn it into Consciousness in order to prevent transgressing in the first place.*

Instant Karma

Students cannot learn from someone they do not trust. As priests and counselors of the Dharma Type family, Educators naturally inspire respect in others; people feel they can confide in Educators, and see a seriousness in them that makes them trustworthy. They may not be *cool*, or *entertaining*, but when it comes to matters of importance, people turn to Educators for help. This sometimes even escapes Educators themselves, though they would do well not to make light of the trust and esteem with which people hold them. A telling characteristic of the Educator is that when he *does* transgress, his karma usually follows instantly. He is likely to suffer the consequences of actions quickly, and to experience extreme remorse for them. From stepping on a snail to sleeping with another's spouse, many Educators subject themselves to extreme punishment for their missteps, even going to the point of suicide. Conscience is strong in Educators; they must turn it into Consciousness in order to prevent transgressing in the first place. Being constantly aware of their natures, and of their place in society as the standard bearers of virtue and trust, they must learn to express their passions appropriately.

> *Be it God, or just third-grade math, the Educator must convey Truth by getting out of the way of the message.*

Lacking the natural decisiveness of the Warrior type, Educators are not meant to rule over others, but to advise and cultivate harmony in themselves and the world. "Give peace a chance" is an Educator mantra. However, they can make excellent leaders in times of need, though with great power comes temptation. When Educators co-opt their authority for selfish purposes they lose out in the long run, and never attain the high peaks to which they aspire, but suffer the pits of infamy and shame for subverting their dharmas. The best Educators are those who surrender their own agendas to promote the values for which they stand. Like Gandhi or Moses, classic Educators, they are governed by a higher truth, so that even when they lead it is not of their own bidding, but of a supernal authority that supersedes them. Their role is to set the codes and standards in society, and to live by them as well. They accomplish this by the sincere pursuit of Surrender.

Surrender

No one understands the value of surrender better than the Educator. Surrender to the creative forces of the universe is a key element to the Educator's growth, and the means by which he or she is able to teach others. From surrender comes a deep level of detachment from material desire. Detachment allows the Educator to bear the burdens of her karma without recourse to fight. Instead, their fight is internal, to open up and appeal to the inner Self for help and sustenance. This practice requires sincerity, as in the process of going within, the Educator is faced with her failings and impure desires, all of which must be transcended if she is to succeed in becoming a model for society.

The Educator must surrender her own life to allow Truth to flow through her. Like a vessel that delivers clear water to the thirsty, she must be empty in order to fulfill her purpose. Educators are uniquely equipped to do this. A grade-school teacher surrenders her needs for adult company in order to teach when she steps through the door of her classroom. She lives her life for her pupils. One cannot be a teacher by letting personal priorities, desires, or fixations get in the way of one's primary purpose, which is to enlighten. Surrender is the means whereby Educators become vehicles for Natural Law. Be it God, or just third-grade math, the Educator must convey Truth by getting out of the way of the message.

Information contrived by the small self, the individual mind, is inferior to what is inspired from above. The greatest art, science, and knowledge materialize when our petty needs are set aside for a moment. Whether in the shower, in meditation, or at a mountain retreat, those instants when our mind steps away to graciously allow the higher Self to speak are truly divine, and result in betterment for everyone. The same surrender that makes the Educator meek has the potential to inspire armies and change history. The same surrender that allows Educators to do with little, can sustain a civilization. Though a fortuitous array of words and notes on paper, a poem or a song can move and inspire millions. In the same way, the Educator, though dependent on others for her survival, can support the species by feeding it knowledge, truth, and wisdom.

Every type relies on its skills for protection in early life. The Laborer has toughness, the Merchant cleverness, the Warrior strength, the Outsider adaptability. But the Educator's usefulness only grows apparent with time. Because they must study in order to teach, a great part of their life is dedicated to learning. Therefore, Educators begin slowly and only mature in the mid and later part of their lives, when learning has led to wisdom, and wisdom begins to emanate from them like charm from Merchants, or power from Warriors. In the beginning of life they are fragile, lacking the skills of the other types to protect them. Even when they appear robust and healthy, they are usually not so, being sensitive and vulnerable physically, save that knowledge is their power, and wisdom their strength. Like the printed word that is quick to perish, the Educator's body fades with time, but her *message* can sustain the world for centuries.

Emmet Fox describes the Educator's path of Surrender as

> *"A combination of open-mindedness, faith in God, and the realization that the Will of God for us is always something joyous and interesting and vital, and much better than anything we could think of for ourselves."*[11]

---

[11] Emmet Fox, *The Sermon on the Mount* (Harper Collins 1989)

This does not mean that all Educators are God-fearing. In fact, what some call God others term Science, Justice, Humanity, Truth—ideals that govern and inspire the Educator's life and never cease to fill her with wonder, appreciation, and the drive to know more. Carl Sagan struggled to understand this by searching the mysteries of outer space. Joseph Campbell, an Outsider playing an Educator, did it by exploring the myths that move our *inner* lives. At their best, Educators are uniquely capable of tapping into higher thought, and teaching dharma to the masses. This can express itself through any medium, and applies to atheists and evangelists alike. Some pursue Truth through Science, others through Art, still others through Social Causes, Medicine, Academia, and so on. Truth has many faces, and speaks in many voices.

The key to determine whether we have been successful in Surrendering, is the effect this has on us. Are we able to demonstrate greater compassion and wisdom, or do we just play the part of a meek Educator while harboring petty envy, pride, and anger inside? The circumstances of our lives tell. Are we better able to relate with our loved ones and contribute more in work? Do we have an undeniably beneficent effect on people and places around us? Do we leave people with more of wisdom, compassion, and peace after knowing us, than before? If the answer to these questions is 'Yes!' then we are indeed on our path as Educators. In every way and in every moment, the Educator is an exemplar of virtue: what virtue we model depends upon our evolution, integration, and wisdom.

Money

Merchant society does not value wisdom as highly as goods and services. People prefer to be Entertained rather than Educated; that is why Educators usually earn less than Merchants. Teachers, scientists, and clergy are paid a moiety of what salesmen and business types make. Unless his wisdom is particularly useful to the Merchant society, it is not the Educator's lot to be wealthy. The Educator's goal is not *emolument*, but *enlightenment*. He must be content with what is given to him in a Merchant world without haggling or fighting for it. If he is rewarded with wealth for wisdom, ducats for dharma, that is a blessing he must accept; but money for its own sake is not the best pursuit for Educators.

In fact, Educators often begged for their food in ancient societies. Things are not so different today when we consider that scientists and scholars beg for grants, public radio and television hold pledge drives to stay on the air, priests pass the collection plates to feed their ministry, and teachers hold bake sales to raise funds for their projects and field trips. It is natural for an Educator to earn her keep by the strength of her wisdom and the charity of the public that it benefits. Their cause earns them their emolument. *Take nothing for the journey except a staff—no bread, no bag, no money in your belts*[12]. This has always been the Educator's dharma, and remains so even to this day.

Mutually Disintegrate	**Mutually Integrate**
Warrior-Merchant	Warrior-Educator
Laborer-Educator	Merchant-Laborer
Outsider-All	Outsider-All

Path to Disintegration: *Laborer*

One of the ways to get the most out of your type is to follow its point of Integration and avoid its point of Disintegration. This basic relationship outlines the path of evolution for each type, as well as its *devolution*, and shall be called upon often in this book. Therefore it is important to memorize the Integration/Disintegration pairs in the chart above.

For example, Educators do well to take on qualities from the Warrior and to avoid qualities from the Labor type. Merchants do well to adopt Laborer traits and avoid going down the Warrior's track. Every type evolves into one type and devolves into another. Points of Integration and Disintegration show us *the path* each type must follow for optimal fulfillment. Thus, Educators fall apart when they follow the Laborer's road, and Laborers likewise Disintegrate when they adopt the Educator's dharma. The same is true of Warriors and Merchants. The Outsider has a special path, which we'll explore in a moment. These designations will become clear as we take a look at how they work below.

Educators Disintegrate when they become 'stuck' in a way of being. Fixity and endurance are qualities of the Laborer, and are good for the malleable Merchant personality that benefits from structure, but when an Educator sacrifices her eclectic nature to become dogmatically fixated on anything, she Disintegrates, losing inspiration and multiplying frustration. Sitting too long in front of a research paper, a math problem, or a religious conundrum only

---

[12] Mark 6:8

increases stagnation of the body and mind. By incorporating the Warrior's *movement*, she revitalizes her mind and energy, and returns to face her problems with new solutions. Stagnation breaks down her body; movement *inspires* and *heals* it.

> *"One's own dharma, even devoid of merit, is preferable to the dharma of another though well-performed. Even death in the performance of your dharma brings blessedness; another's dharma is fraught with anxiety."*
>
> Bhagavad Gita 3:35

Educators need to move, play, and be inspired so that they in turn can inspire the world. But sometimes they are forced to get 'real jobs' in order to pay the rent and survive in Merchant society. Where this restricts their ability to move freely, it eventually results in a decline in the ethics by which society itself lives, because the people best-fitted to teach and inspire them are busy doing jobs they were not meant to do. This is not to say that Educators cannot benefit from integrating practical skills into their daily lives, but that preoccupation with non-dharmic activity detracts from their basic purpose. And when Educators are deprived of meaningful employment, everyone to whom Educators give meaning is also detrimented. In short, when Educators Disintegrate, all society suffers.

When the Educator becomes a salesperson or a day laborer, she still benefits by learning from and serving others—but these activities do not represent the full complement of her talents: her best qualities remain dormant. We must make full use of our inborn faculties, or risk short-selling ourselves the success we deserve. Besides, Educators are usually not as good at manual professions as other types. Physical dexterity and endurance are not strong suits of the Educator type, and employers generally do not get what they pay for when they hire Educators for these jobs. In the words of Wayne Dyer, Educators should 'get paid by the idea, not by the hour.'

Being the Renaissance men or women of the Dharma Type family, Educators *need* to learn a little bit about everyone, but when they move too far in the direction of the Labor personality they begin to lose their objectivity. When an Educator localizes herself, by her education, upbringing, or culture, believing that she is her PhD, her job position, or her ethnicity, she loses creativity, and begins to stagnate. When her credentials become a source of pride, and her accomplishments subject to monetary reward, she can become part of the 9 to 5 Merchant machine that seeks only what's best for itself, when the true mark of the Educator is not her ability to climb the social ladder, but to elevate the culture of her world and enrich society with knowledge. It is in how much she can help others, not herself, that the Educator is recognized by her peers, and the quality of the person, not the paper that her name is printed on, that makes her indispensable.

> *"Science is a wonderful thing if one does not have to earn one's living at it."*
> -Albert Einstein

Merchant society has pushed the Educator to *sell* knowledge in order to survive, and while this has made some Educators fabulously rich and free to pursue their *dharmas*, it has made information itself a commodity subject to the highest bidder. Where this goes wrong is easy to see when we examine the ease with which people can acquire potentially dangerous knowledge, such as how to blow up buildings or hijack airplanes. Knowledge in the wrong hands can lead to disaster. We have seen this even in the subversion of simple spiritual teachings by our major religions: when people do not understand sacred principles, and wisdom fails to erase ignorance, we see the birth of Inquisitions and Holy Wars, ethnic cleansings and the rape of society. A little knowledge is a dangerous thing; it becomes even more so when it is put up for sale.

Traditionally, higher teachings were only imparted to those deemed fit to receive them. Like a weapon, information is dangerous in the hands of those not morally and intellectually equipped to handle it. In older societies every class held its proprietary secrets and passed them on to the next generation of Craftsmen, Reformers, Soldiers, Priests, and Merchants. This was not so much to hide valuable insights from others, but to protect the naïve from inflicting harm to themselves and their environment. Today, one need only look at the internet to see examples of inappropriate information commodity.

Another danger of prostituting information is more subtle, but just as pernicious. A preoccupation with marketing and self-promotion in the interest of purveying information leads to attachment and greed, and can distract Educators from their purpose, which is not to maintain fiscal solvency, but to increase knowledge and awareness in the world. Galileo was a respected

Educator, but could barely make ends meet until he invented the telescope. Educators are often forced to create out of their wisdom something valuable to the Merchant culture in order to survive. This is okay as long as it supports their work, but when an Educator begins to devote inordinate amounts of time to prospering himself, he begins to Disintegrate and move away from his Purpose.

Educators prefer the ivory tower to the hustle and bustle of the market bazaar. They need alone time in meditation in order to 'download' higher information for their society. They may toil in isolation or oblivion for long stretches until the fruits of their wisdom see the light of day. Bill Gates opted for his own garage over the lofty Harvard halls when it came to the pursuit of his ideas. Albert Einstein preferred his post at the Swiss patent office to a teaching position at university, for university life, as he said, would have kept him busy churning out trivial papers and teaching a rigid curriculum that inspired only mechanistic thinking. This was anathema for the free-spirited thinker for whom *ideas* were more valuable than *grades*, and who regularly skipped class in order to pursue his thought experiments.

Einstein detested the regimentation characteristic of schools in Germany, and the tyranny of one system for every student. Good teachers know that they must adapt their lessons to the learning styles of their students. Such rigid, mindless discipline may appear to be a Warrior quality but is in fact an example of an Education model restricted by Labor mentality. This is good for Merchants, as we'll see below, for Merchants *Integrate* into Labor types, but not so where matters of education and ideas are concerned. Thoughtless discipline ignores the needs of people and inspires repression; thoughtful discipline encourages evolution and expression. A mindless adherence to the letter of the law is an example of Educator-Laborer Disintegration. A vigorous and judicious interpretation of the spirit of a law is an example of Educator-Warrior Integration.

Path to Integration: *Warrior*

Educators Integrate into the Warrior Class because the Warrior's self-motivation and pursuit of excellence are qualities Educators do well to emulate. Like them, Warriors are not primarily motivated by money, though in many respects, Warriors and Educators are also opposites, attracting those traits in each other that balance them and make them better. For example, the

Educator's ability to Surrender is contrasted by the Warrior's never-say-die attitude; the Educator's compassion is juxtaposed to the Warrior's forcefulness.

Sometimes it is hard for Educators to behave in a way consistent with their own ideals. They know the rules, but don't always feel the rules apply to them. They *know* better, but succumb to depravity nonetheless. Warriors, on the other hand, have the discipline and character to follow and obey orders. That's why Educators do best to integrate certain core Warrior traits into their personalities. It is easy for them to slip up and succumb to temptation. Money, Sex, and Power constantly beckon the Educator, whose greatest challenge is to control his senses and overcome the lure of baser instincts. He must rise up to take his place as a leader of virtue by example. His great calling is to inspire the masses—with words and ideas, certainly— but ever more than these, *by his own comportment*. The Educator's *behavior* sets the standard for society. Those who cannot understand his ideas, can see by his actions what needs to be done. Those who cannot hear his words, can yet observe his life, and model their own according to its example. Those who do not have the time to learn his ideology, can nonetheless respect his exploits by learning about *him*. Gandhi is one such example. Stories of people living and dying for their principles sometimes inspire more than the principles themselves! Such is the Educator's gift, and it is served by Integrating with the Warrior type.

> *It is a brutal, but patent fact for the Educator that earning and learning rarely mix successfully*

Educators can sometimes be too smart for their own good. Because they grasp concepts more quickly than others, they can become bored, lazy, and never learn the value of work. Being too smart can lead to a poor work ethic, wherein Educators learn to rely on their intellect rather than self-effort. They can lose heart quickly when they encounter obstacles, or become heartless towards others. But when they Integrate the Warrior's courage and self-deterministic attitude, they become not only idealists, but effective instruments of virtue.

When Educators become locked into a socially acceptable "good boy" or "good girl" persona at the cost of denying their sensual impulses, they can become polarized: their outward social image may become more and more distant from their inner passions and desires. When their vital energies, including their sexual impulses, are not allowed to properly express, they become repressed. Over time, **repression** turns to **perversion**. To counter this, involvement in

Warrior activities like yoga, dance, sport, and other forms of guided movement allows the Educator to express passion without turning it into perversion. Then, the priests and senators of the world become exemplars of virtue, not polarized personalities who express one persona on the surface while harboring an altogether different character in secret.

In Chapter 7 we will learn about the different forms of exercise appropriate to each Dharma Type. For the Educator, exercise is a vital component of a comprehensive approach that integrates movement, leisure, meditation, work, and study. When physical stimulation is taken out of the equation, Educators lose out on the inspiration this provides and become stuck in their intellect, fantasy, and ideas. When whites first arrived in Australia, aborigines saw them as 'walking heads,' disengaged from their bodies and disconnected from the earth. This is a lesson for Educators, who need to exercise in order to circulate their vitality and get in touch with their bodies. The rewards they reap are an improved ability to think and a well-grounded energy that allows them to transmit their ideas and effectively relate with others. Movement and exercise promote better self-awareness and can be a blessing indeed for the sometimes clumsy and socially-challenged Educator— in fact, so good is the effect on their bodies, that some Educators can make their whole lives about sport, becoming coaches, trainers, and even world-class athletes!

Educators also need to continually improve their knowledge. Keeping current with the world around them can take the form of reading the daily paper, listening to news radio, or watching the Documentary channel. Whether searching for political solutions, or finding the newest way to teach algebra, the Educator's insight and love of learning make him a valuable asset to students and employers alike.

In fact, Integrated Educators are all about self improvement. *If you're not getting smarter, you're getting dumber. If you're not learning, you're forgetting.* This is a mantra for the Educator type. One is either improving or backsliding, there is little room in between. The evolved Educator is constantly engaged in questioning, discovering, and otherwise improving. She frequents the Self-Help aisles at bookstores, and is up to date on the latest theories in her field. Hers is the quest for knowledge, and the greatest knowledge is self-knowledge. Her obstacle is balancing mundane life with her self-improvement aspirations. But earning and learning do not go together: when the Educator takes on the destiny of the Labor type, and devotes her time to just making a living, she misses the mark in a couple of ways. First, she deprives others who *need* to work from opportunities to do so by taking their place in the work force. Next, she fails to develop her inherent talents, thereby depriving the world of her real gifts.

It is a brutal, but patent fact for the Educator, that earning and learning rarely mix successfully, and he needs to decide to dedicate himself to his destiny, or succumb to sub-par expectations. This is not as hard as it sounds, though it does require an effort of surrender. *Effort* and *Surrender* may seem like contradictory terms, but there is enormous willpower that goes into surrendering to your real Nature. Fortunately, Educators are uniquely equipped to do this, as it entails the use of their in-born faculties and eventually leads them to their highest destiny.

Chapter 2: Educator: Enlighten Others

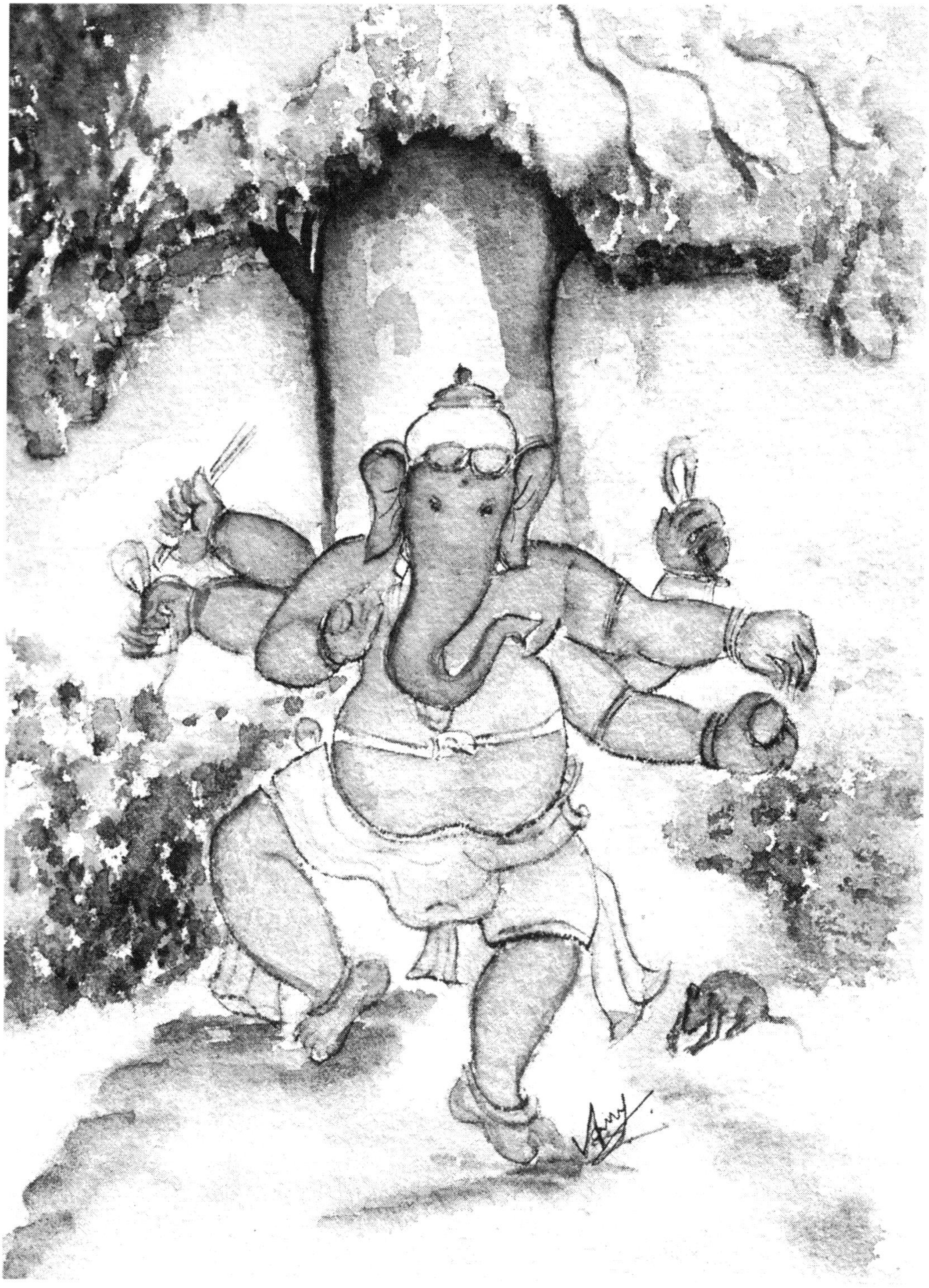

3
WARRIOR: "Protect Others"

*Courage * Discernment * Strength*

Because of their focus, drive, and discipline, Warriors can become the most skilled of all the Dharma Types. They can master practically anything they set their minds to. They are self-starting, self-determining people who believe in making their own fortune in life through struggle and effort. They are fighters, and from Madonna to Arnold Schwarzenegger, their decisive leadership instinct inspires others to follow them. Warriors are leaders, and can become ambitious and relentless in their quest for power. Yet they may also embody this ethic in surprising ways. From a single mother fighting to feed her children, to a human-aid worker fighting for the rights of hungry kids around the world, their battles take place as much on the global stage as in their own backyards. Whatever their causes, evolved Warriors take the side of the innocent, those who cannot fend for themselves. Amongst celebrities, Angelina Jolie does this as a peace ambassador for the U.N. while Robert Redford fights for the rights of independent filmmakers.

The Warrior nature naturally seeks to abide by high ideals and codes of conduct in its search for self-perfection. Warriors like to test themselves and push the boundaries of their endurance. From physical competition, to mental and even spiritual challenges, Warriors set and reset the bar on what's possible. Their

Famous Warriors

Arthur Ashe
Fred Astaire
Boris Becker*
John Belushi
Chuck Berry*
Candace Bergen*
Silvio Berlusconi
Joe Biden
Richard Burton
Buddha
George Clooney*
Michael Crichton
Anderson Cooper
James Dean
Celine Dion
Robert Downey Jr.
Wayne Gretzky
Justine Henin
Adolf Hitler
Angelina Jolie
Kris Kristofferson*
Matt LeBlanc
John McCain
Paul Newman
Rama
Robert Redford
Arnold Schwarzenegger
Robert Shapiro
Sylvester Stallone*
William Shatner
George Washington*
Venus Williams

social role is to protect the weak, the innocent, and the helpless. They are also charged with punishing the guilty: those who willingly flout the codes and standards that Warriors embody and enforce. Not surprisingly, modern-day Warriors take to professions in the Armed Forces, Justice Administration, Law Enforcement, and Politics. They also make great Firemen, Doctors, and Athletes. Traditionally, leaders and kings came from this class, naturally designed as they were to command and rule in the name of a perfect ideal. However, when Warriors are harnessed to a system designed to promote *profit*, not *perfection*, their ideals may become perverted, and their talents enslaved to selfish ends rather than common good. This is spiritual hell for a Warrior, whose highest ideals are Justice and Self-Sacrifice, the willingness to give her life for a greater purpose. Not uncommonly, good people entering into law and politics to better society become corrupted by this Merchant system, whence the popular association of lawyers and politicians with 'sharks' and 'snakes'—predatory creatures perceived to have only their own interests in mind. Consequently, Warriors may become mercenaries, bought and sold by the highest bidder, rather than self-respecting models of integrity in action. More than any other type, they may also become embittered at the ways of the world, succumbing to cynicism and a dog-eat-dog mentality by observing what the world does to those who cannot fend for themselves.

> *For Warriors to excel as leaders, they must inspire a palpable team spirit in the people they lead, a sense of common purpose that they not only work for, but themselves embody in everything they do*

Teamwork

That is why it is important for Warriors to have a support system of fellow Warriors and Educators to keep them from descending into cynicism and becoming mercenaries. Warriors gravitate to sports and the armed forces for this reason: there is a camaraderie and cohesiveness generated when like-minded people are subjected to extreme circumstances together. Whether on the basketball court or the battlefield, a special bond is created when Warriors band together for a common cause. This bond is a synergistic force stronger than the sum of its parts; it makes the members collectively stronger than they could ever be individually.

Teamwork is evident even when Warriors are leaders or solitary functionaries. A sniper may work alone, but he does so within the greater system of a trained unit, and the even greater cause of his fellow countrymen and country. A president may the 'Commander in Chief,' but he or she cannot enforce policy without a huge support system of trained equals. In fact, for Warriors to excel as leaders, they must inspire a palpable team spirit in the people they lead, a sense of common purpose that they not only work for, but themselves embody in everything they do.

Teamwork invariably helps Warriors to become more than they can ever be alone. Warriors benefit from wisdom and counsel, and the best way to receive this is through interaction with their peers. Michael Jordan was a standout superstar, but he couldn't win a championship until he was paired with a coach and fellow teammates who provided him a structure through which to achieve greatness. A few championships later, Jordan was first to acknowledge that he could not have done it without the special bond shared with his coach and teammates. This drive for personal excellence *combined with* a teamwork ethic epitomizes the Warrior spirit... as well as what it is to be a Man.

While there may be as many female as male Warrior types in society, the Warrior path has special relevance for men, regardless of their individual Dharma Type, because at a primal, biological level, *all men are Warriors*, just as *all women are Laborers*. From the standpoint of evolutionary biology, men express their masculinity as *protectors*, and women their femininity as *nurturers*. Men thrive on having challenges to overcome and a purpose to fight for, while women profit from cultivating *shakti*, their feminine energy, which often expresses in the world as nurturing, devotion, and the creation of community. These qualities of Warriors and Laborers represent a basic level of development germane to each gender. Beyond them, of course, lies the higher destiny of the Dharma Type. Nonetheless, every boy must at some time learn to express his inner Warrior if he is to actualize himself as a man; likewise, every girl should cultivate the Laborer's virtues if she is to fully embody her potential as a woman. This fundamental reality of biological evolution is an important part of coming-of-age rituals in sacred societies— rituals that have been lost or perverted in modern contexts into shallow and inappropriate displays, because Merchant society lacks the traditions necessary to ground and guide them. This topic is explored in further detail in Volume II, *Sex, Love, & Dharma*.

GOAL SETTING EXAMPLES

Finances……….. *Make coffee at home instead of Starbucks. Paint roof white to save on bills… Bike to work 2x week. Cut cable bill. Wash clothes during off peak hours…*

Health………… *Ride bike to work 2x week. Eat at least one salad/day, fix my tennis serve*

Family………… *Spend one day/wk with kid immunity: no yelling at kids. Play day with daughter….*

Romance……….. *Do something totally unexpected at least once a week… Leave work at work…. Take a stay-cation twice a month in the city.*

To find her Just Cause a Warrior must set goals in every area of life, from Relationships and Health, to Money, Sex, Profession, and Spirituality. Along with her goals, she must write out exactly how they will be achieved. Then, this must be placed somewhere visible and focused upon for at least 5 minutes a day. Warriors are ruled by the Fire element; Fire relates to sight, the Warrior's main instrument. Warriors are visual types, possessing great hand-eye coordination, focus, and intensity. The way to build a Warrior's positive focus is to remind her daily of her goals and the path she needs to take to achieve them. Repetition is the mother of learning, and Warriors have to SEE their truth consistently to make it a reality.

The Three Cs

Three Cs characterize Warriors. The first is **Control.** Warriors need to feel in control of themselves, their environment, and their destinies, and can become workaholics in the quest to attain mastery of everything from their finances to their golf swing. There is nothing that gets a Warrior's blood boiling more than the words, *"You can't!"* Warriors also have a natural sense for how to take over a situation in the interest of what they feel is just and right, and to lead and take control of the world around them in order to make it safer for others.

Warriors also **Correct** others when their behavior is not up to standard. Their job is to keep people in line, censure and punish wrongdoers, and restore justice in a situation, from the trivial to the most momentous. Whether in her own family as a single mom, or as a world leader, the Warrior is a functionary of law and order, and acts to enforce it with all her ability.

Warriors also need to hunt and **Chase** after, or **Capture** a goal. When they have nothing to set their minds to they can consume themselves. Like a fire, a Warrior's mind needs to be directed into something constructive lest it feed on itself or destroy others. A worthy goal is necessary to channel the Warrior's energy into an attainable outcome. Sport provides such an outlet, and Warriors are often, though not always, athletic and capable with their bodies. Sport is about *intention*: the strength of an athlete's intention overcoming the obstacles that prevent its realization. *The more powerful the intention, the greater the athlete.* That is why it is important for Warriors to write out worthy goals that remind them of their intentions. Lacking the direction and drive that a powerful intention provides in their lives, Warriors may become lazy, unfocused, and ineffectual, resorting to gambling, drinking, and dissipation in search of challenge and meaning in the world. Robert Downey Jr. was an example of a Warrior sidetracked by the seduction of drugs and entertainment, and the lack of a Just Cause in his life.

Written goals also serve to focus a Warrior's mind on his Just Cause. Every Warrior has a Just Cause by following which he becomes an instrument of dharma. Educators help Warriors find their Just Cause by steering them in the right direction. This is akin to the athlete-coach scenario in sports. With a coach's guidance, Warriors can scale the peaks of perfection, breaking through records, obstacles, and opponents in the process. The best athletes in the world use coaches to continue improving. Michael Jordan upped his game even after reaching the apex of his sport with coaches who guided practically every aspect of his play, from fitness and health, to psychology, nutrition, and recovery. Every martial artist has a sensei, a soldier a captain, a king his minister: Educators are instrumental in guiding Warriors in every step of their lives. Downey Jr. noted that key to his resurgence to the top of Hollywood's A-list was his continued one-on-one therapy, exemplifying the idea of counseling and guidance to keep Warriors on their path.

A continued respect between Warrior and Educator types exists where each keeps vigilance over the other to prevent regression into their respective failings, particularly *Pride* and *Lust*. Pride is an easy lure for high-achieving

Warriors and Educators help to keep them focused on *goals* rather than *achievements*, always pushing them to better themselves. On the other hand, from Gandhi to Tiger Woods, Lust is a common denominator many Educators must struggle with. Warriors and the Warrior ethic help to guide and keep them honest. Refer to the previous chapter for more on Lust and Educators.

This guidance also comes when a Warrior takes on Educator qualities on his own. A personal pursuit of wisdom keeps a Warrior's tendency to Pride in check, through constant self-questioning and introspection. It also keeps him in line with the Just Cause of his life. Though the passion to win and conquer is ever inside him, and cannot be turned off by social niceties or political correctness, he can learn to guide his drive and energy into constructive uses by incorporating Educator traits.

> *From reading books to attending seminars, or hanging around Integrated Educator types, Warriors whet the sword of discernment upon the Philosopher's stone of wisdom.*

Path to Integration: *Educator*

The Warrior's evolution consists in linking himself with a Just Cause, a powerful Intention in his life. Educators help furnish that by teaching Warriors *viveka*, discernment. Ultimately, correct discernment is a Warrior's greatest weapon. It is not strength in arms or mental fortitude that make him great, but the ability to *judge rightly* in any situation. At such a point, a Warrior knows when to speak up and when to shut up; when to fight and when to parlay, when to kill and when to heal. He understands the Just Cause of his life and is able to throw the full weight of his considerable talents behind it.

A Warrior without a Just Cause is like a sports car without a steering wheel. Powerful but without direction, it blindly ploughs through obstacles and people until it stalls or runs out of gas. Knowing his Just Cause, a Warrior aligns his life with his deepest mission, and everything from *diet* to *dating* comes out to serve his highest Purpose. He drives straight to his destination and reaches his goal directly. Finally, when he has achieved a goal, apt reward is instrumental in keeping him going forward. Positive reinforcement creates better momentum for Warriors than negative feedback. Even small accomplishments should be rewarded, as they promote greater follow-through and the desire to achieve more and more.

Educators and Warriors complement each other because one lacks what the other has in abundance. In the Warrior lies the courage, discipline, and drive to which the Educator aspires, and in the Educator, the wisdom, tranquility, and Just Cause that Warriors long to possess. Warriors are realists, and lean towards cynicism when unbalanced. Educators are idealists, and become naive when they lose touch with reality. Warriors keep Educators real and grounded, while Educators inspire Warriors out of their dog-eat-dog mentality with good counsel and motivation.

Just as bygone kings were well-advised by their ministers, so the modern-day Warrior must perfect himself through higher counsel and instruction. From reading books to attending seminars, or hanging around Integrated Educator types, Warriors whet the sword of their discernment upon the Philosopher's stone of wisdom. The same complementarity exists for Laborers and Merchants, which is characterized by *steadiness in character* on one side, and *mercurial dynamism* on the other. The *'what's in it for me?'* attitude of the Merchant finds balance in the *'let's do it right!'* approach of the Laborer, whereby each type benefits. We will see this in the next two chapters as we explore Merchant and Labor types.

The Fight for Dharma

In Sanskrit, there are three terms which describe the Warrior's Integration: *jnana, dharma,* and *viveka,* or Knowledge, Purpose, and Discernment.

These can be broken down into three steps:

1. Jnana— Obtaining Knowledge, the weapon of wisdom
2. Dharma— Having obtained Knowledge, donning the armor of the Just Cause, or life Purpose.
3. Viveka— Having obtained to a Purpose, riding out and enacting it with good Judgment and without fear in the knowledge that a Warrior is protected by the mantle of the Just Cause he serves.

It is easy for Warriors to follow orders once they know the right path. First they must arm themselves with enough wisdom to understand themselves and how they are best suited to give their gifts to the world. Knowing this, they must choose a special dharma, or Just Cause to devote their lives to. There are infinite levels of dharma, therefore this does not have to be one thing.[13] For example, a mother has an obligation to her children, her spouse, her own physical, mental, and spiritual well-being, her parents, her society, and so on. Knowing how to live in harmony with Nature and fulfilling these levels of basic dharma is crucial, and Vedic texts like the Charaka Samhita and the Yoga Sutras of Patanjali have been devoted to getting the most out of our relationships with ourselves and the world. But there is a special dharma, the Just Cause that a Warrior must embrace above and beyond these to make her life truly remarkable. There are no books that detail how to do this, and perhaps that is why the guru-disciple relationship has been so important in Vedic societies through the ages.

> *Viveka: the ability to tell the difference between what is real and unreal; what serves your highest good and what serves only temporary desire*

Most of our obligations to the world are automatic: being born in a body implies certain duties. Like having a license to drive, having a license to live means abiding by the basic laws of embodied life: exercising proper self-maintenance, fulfilling your obligations to family, and learning to live with your environment. But beyond these basic levels of dharma, there is a higher purpose to your life that you must find and embrace if you are to become fully Integrated as a Warrior. Once this is found, the final step lies in using your refined discernment to become an effective weapon of dharma in the world.

Viveka, or discernment, is the ability to relate any decision back to the measuring stick of dharma. For example, let us say that a Warrior has chosen to fight illiteracy in her neighborhood. Knowing this, when requested to teach math at a wealthy school outside of her precinct, she must ask herself, "does doing this serve my fight for literacy?" If the answer is "no!" she must refuse—it is that simple. Knowing your dharma in any area of life, you can weigh your decisions and ask yourself, "does this serve my highest purpose, or detract from it?" That is Viveka, the ability to tell the difference between what is real and unreal; what serves your highest good and what serves only temporary desire. And Viveka comes about from hanging around Educators and cultivating Educator virtues in oneself.

---

[13] The three main levels of dharma, karma, and duhkha are explored in Volume III: *The Spiritual Types*.

War and Warriors

When a soldier fights a righteous battle he is ensured of victory whether he wins or loses. But when his leaders are corrupted, and force him to commit adharmic acts (actions that go against dharma), a soldier must stand up for what is right, even if it means going against the grain of his orders. This helps to prevent the scourge of Post Traumatic Stress Disorder and other afflictions that haunt soldiers upon returning home (details on how to cope with and understand PTSD are found in Chapter 12). Warriors first and foremost fight to protect dharma. Whatever interferes with that must be challenged, even if it is their country, their family, or even their own body and mind. *If your right hand causes you to sin, cut it off.*[14] A true Warrior constantly fights the inner fight in order to win justice... *dharma kshetre kurukshetre... on the battlefield of the world, on the battlefield of dharma.* (Bhagavad Gita 1:1)

And recall from the Introduction that the battlefield is both within and without us. It is in the spaces of the mind as in the terrains of the wild. In order to fight the fight, a Warrior must know what dharma is and how to protect it. Yet the world does not have to be at war for Warriors to be effectual. In fact, most of a Warrior's dharma is enacted during peacetime. Warriors do not lack for causes to fight for at home. They simply need to arm themselves with Knowledge, don the protective cloak of their Cause, and put their skills and good Judgment into action.

> *When a Warrior is seduced by Merchant life, his Power becomes anger, his Vitality lust, his Glory pride.*

When Warriors fail to develop *Jnana, Dharma, and Viveka*—Wisdom, Purpose, and Discernment, they become distracted, lazy and addicted to sensations. The restless thrill seeker, the inveterate gambler, the alcoholic: these are some negative patterns of a Warrior lacking his Just Cause. Disintegrated Warriors seek artificial stimulation, which is a substitute for the exhilaration they feel when they are aligned with their Purpose. But embracing the Just Fight, Warriors are replenished and filled in a way that frivolous activities cannot fill them. They become calm, centered, and at peace with themselves while ever in dynamic motion, like the eye of a hurricane that remains tranquil even as violent winds swirl around it.

---

[14] Warrior teachings from the New Testament (Matthew 5:30).

Path to Destruction: *Merchant*

> *Cynicism is as unrealistic as idealism, and more negative for Warriors... but* **Heart** *and* **Generosity** *are hallmarks of the evolved Warrior. To lose these is to lose himself.*

When a Warrior Disintegrates, he becomes prideful, anger-prone, and arrogant. He may still be a great fighter, but being a Warrior is not only about fighting, but being an agent of justice. To know justice he must have judgment, and that is what he loses when he descends into anger and pride. Only by Integrating into the Educator does he acquire judgment. And when the types Integrate, they begin to look like each other; when the Warrior evolves into the Educator, he becomes settled, calm, and self-possessed. He may even appear meek, though he is still a tiger inside. In the same way, Educators appear athletic, virile, and capable when they evolve into Warriors. Integrated types are easily mistaken for each other!

But when a Warrior begins to assign too much value (Merchant) on his strength (Warrior) he Disintegrates into pride, and a disdain for weakness. This is deadly because it leads him to lose those very qualities he cherishes most: respect from his peers and ultimately power and authority. Warriors also devolve when they give their lives over to the pursuit of money. In Merchant society, money is power. Because Warriors naturally gravitate to power, they can become easy prey to money's lure. The assumption that they can *buy* security and protection can lead them to the misguided pursuit of financial resources to the exclusion of ethical considerations. But the Warrior's security does not come from wealth. While money facilitates many things, it cannot buy Perfection and Purpose, which is what Warriors truly seek. This is only achieved through self-cultivation. By second-guessing their ideals in the name of profit, Warriors fail to honor their basic purpose on earth and descend into a personal hell.

As a result, they can become cynical, resigning themselves to believe that the way of the world is cruel and unforgiving, belonging to those with power. But there is a fine line between realism and cynicism. Realism is the ability to see things as they are. *Cynicism is as unrealistic as idealism,* and more negative for Warriors, as it can lead them to lose heart and turn bitterly against others. But *heart* and *generosity* are hallmarks of the evolved Warrior. To lose these is to lose himself. It is not in harming others but in protecting them that a Warrior wins acclaim. It is not in his anger and resentment that people see nobility, but in his even-handedness and humility.

When the Warrior, disabled by ignorance, mistakes petty spoils and treasure for true glory, he gives away his power and enslaves himself to Pride, Lust, and Greed. We have seen this through the devolution of the ages as Warriors fell from being the upholders of morality in the Silver Age to tyrants and murderers in the Bronze and Iron ages. When a Warrior enacts brutality upon the weak he suffers a Warrior's hell for the disservice of his gifts for selfish ends. Warriors are entrusted with the protection of their people just as Merchants are made to feed, Laborers to serve, and Educators teach. When they prostitute their gifts for selfish ends Warriors become no more than mercenaries. Krishna's advice to his friend in the *Bhagavad Gita* comes to mind:

> *Karmani eva adhikaaras te maa phaleshu kadaachana ...*
>
> Devote yourself to action, never to the fruits thereof...

The Merchant path is not bad for everyone: in fact, it is great for Laborer Dharma Types. However, when a *Warrior* is seduced by Merchant life, his Power becomes *anger*, his Vitality *lust*, his Glory *pride*.. Lust is an attachment to sensuality; Pride is a fixation on one's own name and fame, and Anger is a loss of judgment. The Merchant life beckons the Warrior into a false sense of glory; one built not on merit and honor, but on power and dominion. It takes a real Hero, guided by wisdom and temperance, to wield power and not be a tyrant; to rule, but not oppress. No one type or lifestyle is better than another; knowing where you Integrate and Disintegrate can help you become the best you can be while avoiding the pitfalls relevant to your Dharma Type.

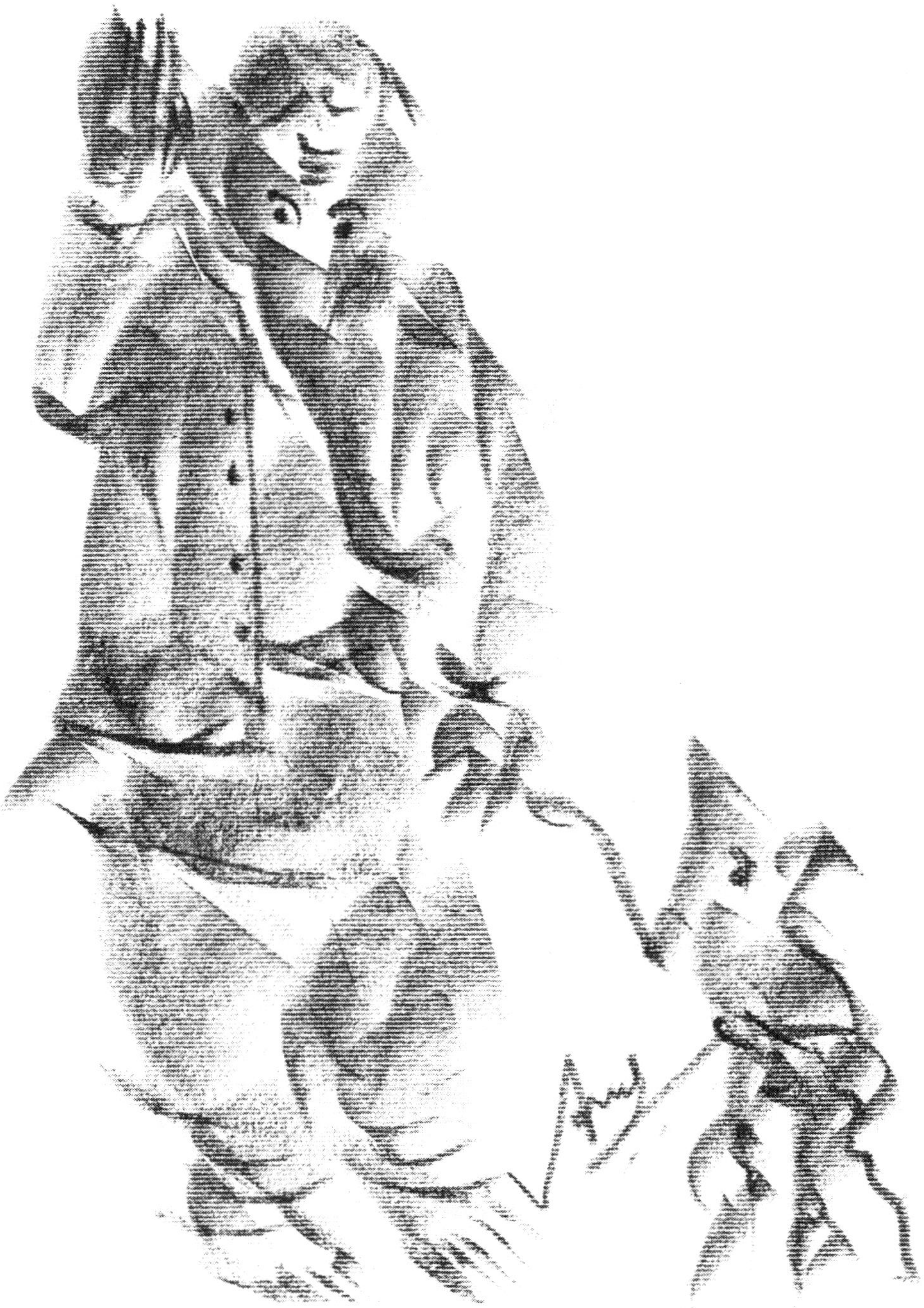

4
MERCHANT:
"Clothe, Connect, and Animate Others"

*Personality * Charity * Energy *

Merchants are go-getters, scrappers, and make-something-out-of-nothing types. They can talk themselves—and others—into accomplishing anything, which is why they can be great motivational speakers and achievers... or liars and con men, depending on their Integration or Disintegration. Merchants have an entrepreneurial and pioneering streak that typifies the best of the 'American Spirit,' which is why the United States of America is a Merchant nation.[15]

Merchant types learn from an early age the value of a dollar and never forget it. They put their family's security first—partly because they have felt real hunger at some point in their lives—and partly because they also *hunger* for the good things in life.[16] They see others who have, and they work hard to have as well. In the end, as we shall see below, their circle is completed by giving back.

Just as the Educator's goal is to provide spiritual sustenance, the Merchant's natural talents lie in

Famous Merchants

Muhammad Ali
Ammachi
Tori Amos
Harry Belafonte
Warren Beatty
Mike Bloomberg
William F. Buckley Jr.
Jimmy Carter
Charlie Chaplin
Chevy Chase
Bill Clinton
Kurt Cobain
Sean Connery
Miles Davis
Leonardo DiCaprio
Kirk Douglas
Alexandre Dumas
Fabio
Tom Hanks
Hugh Hefner
Paris Hilton
Julio Iglesias
Dwayne Johnson
Jim Jones (cult leader)
Krishna*
Marilyn Monroe
Sean Penn
Michelle Pfeiffer
Brad Pitt*
Elvis Presley
Anthony Quinn
Frank Sinatra
Oskar Schindler
Percy Bysshe Shelley
Britney Spears*
Rick Springfield
John Travolta
Tina Turner

---

[15] Countries, like people, have personality types, which will be discussed in later sections.

[16] Among bodily functions, Merchants relate to digestion and assimilation, what Ayurveda terms *samana vayu*. Anatomy and the Dharma Types is covered in Chapter 7.

sustaining, sheltering, and providing for the material needs of people. Thus, Merchants work well in any profession that caters to the masses, be it in non-essential goods such as fashion and entertainment, or day to day necessities like food, hospitality, clothing, and drugs. Their natural ability to network and manage material resources also makes them masters of trade, commerce, and banking. Sales is a natural profession for Merchants, as they have the ability to evoke and shape strong emotions in others. Since most of us are led by our emotions, Merchants generate success by attaching their products to the positive feelings people want to have. This ability is also supremely useful in the entertainment industry, where they excel at creating, performing, and producing popular music, art, and movies, and otherwise entertaining people. Of all the types, Merchants know best how to have a good time!

However, Merchants are not limited to sustaining the masses by their professions. In fact, most of the time their professions are simply about making money, not directly contributing to society. Merchants are the only type with free rein to make money for its own sake, because they can later turn this money to benefit society. An Engineer (Laborer), Doctor (Warrior), Teacher (Educator), and Inventor (Outsider) benefit others by the daily operation of their duties. They earn their keep by contributing to society. Bankers, Investors, and other Speculators, on the other hand, benefit only themselves by their professions. However, this is okay if these Investors are Merchant types, for Merchants need to cultivate prosperity in order to give back to the world, as **wealth is an instrument for the performance of their dharma**. Merchants show us how comfortable life can be. Where Educators teach and Warriors enforce *dharma*, (purposeful living), Merchants are masters of *kama*, Enjoyment. Like no other type, they show us how to *live*, in the Las Vegas sense of that word! Ironically, they also work harder, putting in more hours, more inspiration, and more cunning than any other type in order to earn their enjoyments.

> *Merchants are the only type with free rein to make money for its own sake*

Time is money for the Merchant. Knowing this, they tend to sleep less and do more in their day than other people, though they can also be extremely lazy when Disintegrated. Whether filling their time with entertainment or discovering the newest internet business strategies, Merchants are always thinking, scheming, and developing ideas. They may not act on all of them, but usually have enough on their plate to keep them busy 25 hours of the day. That is why they are so fierce about their enjoyments, because they take their work *and* play very seriously! In fact, leisure is an important part of a Merchant's routine. They become imbalanced if they cannot have *some* down time during their week, which usually comes through some form of social ritual.

> *Merchants can just as easily become moody as motivated, depressed as well as dynamic.*

Merchants and Ritual

Merchants love rituals. Social rituals like courtship and parties, or spiritual rituals like religious ceremonies, have strong appeal for the Merchant archetype. Laborers also enjoy rituals, but more as spectators than performers: they prefer to be the audience, while Merchants enjoy being center stage. Merchants are also masters of tension. Building, guiding, and diffusing tension at the appropriate moment for maximal effect is a gift that suits them well in everything from selling cars to selling themselves to an audience on stage. This mastery of tension makes them captive storytellers, and from the boardroom to the boardwalk, they rarely fail to emotionally hook an audience when they have something to say.

We shall explore in depth the Yogic technology of the 5 bodies in later chapters, but the Merchant's affinity for the Sensate body, or *manomayakosha*, makes them especially sensitive to the emotional highs and lows of the human experience. They can just as easily become moody as motivated, depressed as well as dynamic. They are both susceptible to and masters of the body's emotion cocktail, and can use it to soar to the heights of ecstasy, or bottom out in the depths of despair. One word for emotion in Sanskrit is *rasa*, which also means 'juice,' or 'flavor.' Merchants are masters of life's juiciness, and can go to extremes to extract flavor from their experiences, even becoming *rasa* addicts.

Do not be afraid of these italicized Sanskrit words for they stand for things we experience every day, but don't have words for in English. In the Vedic worldview, as in chemistry, emotions are *material* things. *Rasa* is a physical experience; in our bodies, chemicals and neuropeptides are carriers of emotion, and the proof is that we can manipulate them through drugs, diet, and exercise. The Merchant's mastery of these most valuable of material resources, our very feelings and sensations, gains him an impressive edge when dealing with others. This is because, when asked their desires in life, most people say that they "*want to be happy.*" As an average person's experience of happiness is tied to their emotional state, the Merchant's innate understanding of emotion allows him to fulfill these needs... and profit tremendously thereby!

People can get fired up and inspired, or deeply moved and even carried away by Merchants. They must be careful, however, not to feel let down when the experience is over, because there is an inevitable drop after the 'Merchant Moment' has worn off. This is the buyer's remorse that people experience after dealing with Merchant types. For their part, Merchants need to contain and channel their enthusiasm so they don't misrepresent themselves. Later, in the *Speech* section of Chapter 10, we will see how Merchants get carried away and overstate things, or even blatantly lie, in order to get their point across. They need to rein this in for their own benefit and good health.

That is because what you work with becomes who you are. To protect their own reputations, and improve their social standing in the long run, they need to learn to control their emotions and their speech. In business, entertainment, or with family and friends, the karma of what you do to others inexorably rubs off on you, which is why *karma yoga*, compassionate and conscious action and living is a particularly suitable spiritual path for Merchants.[17]

Warriors live and die by the sword, Educators by the pen. Merchants, who are used to riding an emotional roller coaster, can become worn down by its highs and lows. The process of purveying *rasa* can drain their own. As a result, they may search out experiences that numb them to the world, such as drugs, food, and entertainment. They may also require more and more stimulation to feel pleasure and pain, and become willing to push the envelope of accepted social norms to get it. In the fall of Rome we saw a Merchant society taken to debauchery in its search for the extremes of *numbness* and *excitement*, *stimulation* and *fulfillment*. Rome was a *rasa*-addicted society. This took shape in the savage combat spectacles of the Coliseum as in the excesses of the marketplace and the bathhouse, not to mention the exploitation of other cultures through the rape of their people, wealth, and resources. Yet more abundance and variety of food and luxury cannot satisfy a Merchant society, and its ever-increasing girth, like a person's waistline, expands into ill-health and eventually self-destruction.

The road of excess leads to the palace of wisdom[18] is a slogan appropriate to the Outsider, *not* the Merchant, who suffers from the karmic repercussions of too

---

[17] The spiritual paths most appropriate to each type are discussed in Volume III: *The Spiritual Types*.
[18] William Blake, *The Marriage of Heaven and Hell*

much food, sex, and drugs. Instead of filling up, she needs to *lighten up*, by shedding excess material, which can take the form of losing extra pounds or cleaning her closets and giving away outdated clothes. Charity does for the soul what diet does for the body, and in giving what comes natural to her, the Merchant shares her gifts with the world while receiving in turn what money can't buy... gratitude.

Charity & Shakti

Charity is more than donating *things*. It is giving your attention and life-energy to others. It is offering something, rather than taking it, with no attachment to the outcome. The biblical injunction that it is better to give than to receive is an ironic truth for the Merchant type, for the more they give the more they get. By being attentive and solicitous to their fellow man, Merchants become indispensable, which in turn increases their value. It is a no-brainer equation that makes perfect business sense: by offering to help, to assist a friend or stranger without thought for reward, a Merchant grows her network of friends, a network that repays her a thousand times over during her lifetime, for it is better to have people *owe* you, than to be in *debt* to them. Once Merchants learn this basic rule of karma and human relations, they are on their way to super-stardom in life!

Whether offering a compliment or an article of clothing, Merchants get back in return the medicine they need most, gratitude— especially when they offer these things with no thought of reward. Giving comes naturally to Integrated Merchants, and Merchants who wish to Integrate must learn how to do it effectively. The secret is to begin by **giving things that do not diminish you in any way**: a piece of fashion advice, the phone number of a business associate, or things you no longer use that someone might find indispensable. Sometimes a smile, a joke, or a heart-felt compliment are enough! These can be invaluable to a person whose spirit needs lifting, and they do not detract from your well-being—in fact, they increase your value in the eyes of others by motivating and energizing them.

'Energy' in Sanskrit is called *Shakti*. Merchants love to both work with and worship *shakti*, as it is a way to obtain *rasa*, the positive emotions they want to feel. In Sanskrit *shakti* is a feminine noun that can mean *energy*, *power*, or even *money*, and like *shekhinah*, a Hebrew word for *God's energy*, *shakti* is associated with the Feminine Divine. It is the radiance of divinity, personal charisma, the power of electricity, or even the wave of warm vibes at a concert. Every Dharma Type possesses its own unique form of *shakti*:

Educator-	*Mantra Shakti,*	The Power of Good Counsel
Outsider-	*Ananda Shakti*	The Power of Bliss and Freedom
Laborer-	*Prema Shakti*	The Power of Love and Devotion
Warrior-	*Prabhava Shakti*	The Power of Majesty and Strength
Merchant-	*Utsaha Shakti*	The Power of Effort and Desire

Shakti is present in every Dharma Type, though Merchants are the most covetous of it. From performing temple rituals to singing on stage, they crave *shakti* in the form of attention and adulation, but also best radiate it in the form of charisma and energy. As a result, Merchants tend to be the most famous and remembered people in society. Muhammad Ali made his living by the sting of his wit no less than the fury of his punches. He also revolutionized boxing by making it a big-money sport through his gift of gab and self-promotion. In India the great personality Krishna, an Outsider playing the part of a Merchant, was known as Bhagavan— the noun *bhaga* means *fortune,* or *wealth*. A Bhagavan is one possessed of great glories, including fame, personal magnetism, and prosperity, among others.

> *Merchants are essentially investors, reaping magnified returns on the investment of their time and energy.*

Shakti is also money, the most prominent and material form of *shakti* in the world today. Less spiritually-inclined Merchants may worship it exclusively because it in turn buys other sources of *shakti* and *rasa*, such as sex, food, and luxury. In fact, anything that is *material* and *valuable* is the purview of the Merchant type.

Merchants are guardians to the most valuable things in life because they know how to attract and keep them. From a beautiful painting to a rare *vidya*, or body of knowledge, they work hard to earn and hold the treasures of the world. As a result, they are irritated by freeloaders who feel entitled to their charisma or prosperity. Merchants work hard to earn what they have, though it may not always appear so. Sometimes a Merchant is born with gifts in abundance, which is the result, perhaps, of hard work in another life. What people do not understand, though, is that Merchants are willing to put all their *shakti* on the line in order to generate more. Investors risk their capital for the chance to create exponential returns. Entertainers pour their hearts out on stage for a return in *shakti*, in the form of adoration, applause, money, and fame. Spiritual seekers invest their *shakti* into a ritual practice in order to culture the mind to such a degree as to earn the blessings of that ritual. *Merchants are essentially investors, reaping magnified returns on the investment of their time and energy.*

As a result, they are wary of people who want to reap the fruits of their insight and ingenuity without investing their own. They can grow mistrustful of others... except perhaps Laborers. Merchants feel safe around Laborers, who are usually not out to get anything from them. Laborers have the simple and unique desire to be with Merchants and to be like Merchants *without* the need to leech their energy. Laborers in fact *invest* energy into Merchants, which is why Merchant types are usually more than glad to reciprocate. Merchants are willing to give their energy to those who give something in exchange. By contrast, Educators spread their knowledge to all who want to hear, and Warriors are happy to give their life and breath for someone without expectation of return... but Merchants have to charge money for their gifts.

The Social Merchant

Keenly aware of social rules and rituals, Merchants are often status-driven creatures who crave the good things in life— as much for their inherent value as for what these things say about them. Merchants buy with an eye for value and luxury, rather than form and function. A typical Merchant appreciates a luxury car more for its caché than its performance; she buys a purse because of the status it confers, rather than its inherent usefulness. Because of their appreciation for social hierarchies, Merchants attempt to 'buy' their way up the social ladder using their charm, wit, money, and other talents to get ahead. In the process, they set the standards for what is *in* and what is not, what is *cool* and what is passé. Merchants are the mavens of fashion, beauty, and entertainment.

Like the *Sanguine* type in medieval physiology, at her finest a Merchant's *shakti* is incomparable. Merchants can have bright smiles, alluring energy, and an open, gregarious air. They are able to harness the power of attraction unlike anyone else, and are the most popular and likeable of the Dharma Types. Merchants are movers and shakers of energy, creating the rituals and customs of our world, from pop music to popular New Age philosophies like *The Secret*. They are the artists, entertainers, and media moguls who control what we see, hear, wear, and even think. In doing so, they can be outgoing and garish, but also quietly controlling, working behind the scenes to create and accumulate *shakti* in the form of money, power, and influence.

But this desire for attention hides a core emptiness, a sense of inadequacy or *not-enoughness* that can only be filled when Merchants Integrate into the Labor type. The same emptiness that makes them hate to be alone can drive them to fill their lives with abundance and help others by providing resources and opportunities for people, for it is only in giving that Merchants become ultimately fulfilled. Merchants cannot stand to be alone, and their inner void can become so painful that they search out anything to numb it. But material things are temporary anodynes: money, booze, luxury and entertainment are only sedatives that wear out when their novelty is gone. The permanent cure for their loneliness is Charity.

The Gift That Keeps on Giving

No amount of attention-seeking or contrived, paid-for companionship can fill a Merchant's soul to the depths like creating merit through action—karma yoga—which in turn ensures future blessings and continued enjoyment of the good things in life. The good will and gratitude created by karma yoga heal a Merchant's loneliness better than any drug can, and are freely given by those who have benefited from a Merchant's generosity. The grateful love of a full belly and a warm sheltered body offer more to the Merchant than any currency can buy.

> *"Ah! what a divine religion might be found out if charity were really made the principle of it instead of faith."*
>
> -Percy Shelley

What happens when a Merchant has everything he wants? He still feels empty, anxious, and unfulfilled. Having possessions leads to more worry and anxiety. Merchants crave the beautiful things in life, but upon obtaining them, enjoyment comes hand in hand with worry over losing, breaking or diminishing their value. A Merchant with a beautiful spouse or a new BMW is more likely to keep a jealous eye out for trouble than someone without these things, and become more anxious and stressed-out as a result. This stress can force a Merchant to find ways to numb out. But better than winding down after a hard day's work with alcohol, drugs, and mindless entertainment is going to the local homeless shelter and spooning out soup to the hungry, or handing out

> *It is better to have people owe you, than to be in debt to them. Once Merchants learn this basic rule of karma and human relations, they are on their way to super-stardom in life!*

clothes to the needy. This is a permanent cure for what ails the Merchant, and the feeling of giving can even become addicting— the sense of wholeness and gratitude can itself become a sort of positive *fix* that healthy Merchants begin to crave!

Giving releases a Merchant from anxiety. By providing for others, he practices letting go, which leads to greater serenity. And the best part for the Merchant is that he simply has to apply his natural ingenuity to part with things he no longer needs. For example, every year before the Super Bowl, t-shirts are printed proclaiming each team Super Bowl champion. Since one has to lose, half of the shirts become immediately unsellable once the game is over. But to people in developing countries who have little to wear, such leftovers are very useful indeed, and a welcome blessing. A company that donates rather than discards what it cannot use becomes both profitable *and* charitable, earning at once material and spiritual merit.

By applying their natural ingenuity, Merchants can make the most of what they have, and find mutually beneficial ways to prosper others. Those who own restaurants, instead of throwing away food, can feed the hungry and poor. Those who have clothing can give clothes, those who have opportunities give opportunity ... it is giving that is important, not what is given. Some donate millions to charity, thereby ensuring their long-term success as Merchant types. But giving may mean simply devoting your time and expertise to show others how to prosper themselves. Muhammad Yunus won the Nobel prize for developing Microlending, a system that pairs people in Western countries with those in undeveloped parts of the world, giving them micro-loans of $20 to $50 to promote self-sufficiency through business and entrepreneurship. What is throwaway money for many Westerners can become a lifeblood for others; what a Merchant might blow on lunch can be used to feed a family for years to come when properly channeled. Merchants understand giving in order to receive, whether it is investing in the stock market or investing in their emotional and spiritual prosperity. By caring for the material needs of their fellow types, they ensure a continued return for their investment in the form of inner peace and serenity.

The difference between Merchants and Laborers is that Laborers are completed by family and community, whereas Merchants feed off the gratitude of strangers. It is enough for Laborers to nourish their families: Merchants must nourish the world. They must move beyond the circle of their blood and community to find fulfillment, though this can be difficult to do. Like Labor types, Merchants value their blood ties. From an early age, they are driven to win security for themselves and family. Unfortunately, less Integrated types do not ever look past this, to helping others outside of their inner circle. Because they sometimes mistrust people's motivations, they are especially close to those who have invested energy and resources into them, and spend their lives working to prove worthy of this support. In fact, one of the Merchant's hang ups is her sense of worth, and she may go through life trying to provide it by reaching for material objects. And though the antidote is easily available, it is not found in these things.

> *"He who sees a need and waits to be asked for help is as unkind as if he had refused it."*
> -Dante

Like any skill, giving must be practiced. *It is good to give when you are asked; it is better to give before you are asked* is an injunction from Vedic times that has special relevance for Merchant types, who keep saving and hoping that one day when they are secure enough they will be able to give back. The problem is, that day never comes. In English, the phrase is *the road to hell is paved with good intentions*. Anyone can provide for their family- even animals do it- it is another thing to give wholeheartedly to strangers, especially when it is unbidden. This generates a blessing exponentially superior to the value of the thing given, and in a karmic sense further multiplies the Merchant's wealth and abundance. In essence, it is a great deal for the Merchant type, because he always gets back more than he gives. And, by practicing his skill, he is rewarded with further opportunities to do so.

Path to Integration: *The Laborer*

The Laborer's natural attention to detail, workmanship, and quality offers a model of Integration for the Merchant type. Because Laborers are intimate with how much work goes into crafting something, they are less likely to take shortcuts or to step on their fellow workers to achieve their ends, things Merchants may do when Disintegrated. Laborers enjoy work; when a Merchant tunes into the pleasure of the creative process, he gains an appreciation for what he makes and the hard work that goes into it. He also learns to value and authentically relate with people.

When a Merchant Integrates into the Labor type, she gains the serenity characteristic of the Laborer; feeling contented, loved, and connected to her community. Her behavior goes from attention-seeking and overblown to confident and affable. Her compliments come out of genuine appreciation, rather than surface flattery. She *makes friends*, rather than *closing deals*, creating lifelong, ongoing relationships based on caring, rather than using people for short-term gain. This produces long-term returns on her investment of time and energy: returns that are infinitely greater than when she treats people as a means to an end. Even in sales, people want to give their money to a *friend*, or someone they can trust: making friends is real selling.

Laborers teach Merchants contentment and gratitude. Gratitude from others, and their own contentment and gratitude for what they possess open up Merchants to a wealth of blessings. Laborers also show them how to savor the little things in life and get the most out of their possessions. But even more importantly, they teach Merchants the real meaning of Community. By learning to expand their definition of 'family,' Merchants begin to see not just their relatives, but their neighborhood, city, and eventually the world as their own extended family. Then, their potential for good becomes boundless. When the Merchant lays down the *"what's in it for me?"* and takes up the *"giving feels better than getting"* mantra, she enriches not only the world with her talents, but ultimately herself. She earns a wealth of blessing and cheer that is beyond the purveyance of money and goods. It is amazing how a Merchant's inadequacies disappear in the wake of a grateful smile or hug from someone she has touched!

Sometimes a Merchant has to suffer before she can find a way to help others.

In Chapter 11 we will cover Myths and the Dharma Types. The Scrooge myth is a Merchant cautionary tale that demonstrates the importance of 'family.' As mentioned earlier, the Merchant's drive to win security begins at home, usually at an early age. Unfortunately once this objective is fulfilled, her inclination to nourishment can turn to greed and overindulgence for lack of anyone with whom to share her bounty. That is, once the Merchant has secured her family's needs, she seeks little beyond her definition of that term. And when her family is no more, she begins to hoard wealth, ignoring the obvious needs of those around her. That was the case of

Ebenezer Scrooge, who had no one with whom to share his abundance, or so he thought. However, his epiphany opened him up to a world where he was not only instrumental in benefiting others, but in healing himself.

As is the case with many Merchants, he responded better to *fear* than to *politeness*: it can take a traumatic event such as a brush with death to set a wayward Merchant on the right path. Sometimes he has to get and beat cancer before realizing that health-care needs to be reformed. Sometimes he falls upon hard times before realizing the plight of the poor. Sometimes a Merchant has to suffer before he can find a way to help others. In Part II we will discuss the Circle of Life and the role that Warriors play in keeping Merchants in line so that they abide by their dharma without recourse to such extreme incentives. Merchants need and respect a strong hand to keep them in line. An everyday example is a Warrior doctor warning his Merchant patient that if he continues his high-stress, no-rest life, he must surely die of a heart attack. The result? A smart Merchant learns to take a vacation, get a massage... and write off the expenses!

> *From heart surgery to gastric bypass, from Valerian to Viagra, Merchants believe heavily in doctors and drugs as miracle fixes to keep them going*

Path to Destruction: *The Warrior*

Merchant types like to make noise. If they are the loudest, they will get the most attention, or so they believe... and they are usually right. The squeaky wheel does indeed get the grease. The problem is, the squeaky wheel makes noise because it is not well, and Merchants act up and make spectacles of themselves because they feel empty inside. They love the energy that attention gives them, and when they get used to getting it, attention seeking becomes habitual. However, it does not address the inherent flaw, which is the Merchant's loneliness.

Merchants love to be loved. They enjoy being the center of attention. People are drawn to the sparkling personalities of the Merchant type. When their luster and sparkle is backed by real value, they enrich the world with their energy, humor, and vitality. When the glitter is just a surface show, as when the Merchant is on a Path of Destruction, then it quickly fades to reveal an empty setting; under pressure, the golden sheen peels off to reveal a dull interior. When Merchants Integrate into the Labor type, they gain a level of *profundity* that only the Laborer can give them. They become solid, dependable, able to

Merchants are lovers and fighters, but given the chance, they prefer the former

back their words with actions. There is substance to their speak, depth to their dialogue. They are real and approachable. But when they are all talk and no substance, they only think of themselves, and cannot be a real friend to anyone. Such a Merchant *competes with* (Warrior) rather than *accepts* people (Laborer).

Merchants do not like to face the consequences of their actions. Unlike Outsiders, who run because they desire freedom, Merchants run away because they desire luxury: the luxury of having their cake and eating it too. The overeater is not concerned about heart disease and diabetes; the binge drinker is not worried about cirrhosis of his liver, and the fornicator does not like to think about child support and alimony. These things are not a 'good deal' for them, and instead of the *buzz kill* of dealing with the effects of their actions directly, they try to bargain or even cheat their way around them. At this level, the Merchant believes he can even cheat death, given the right opportunity.

Instead of diet and exercise, he elects the quick fix of surgery. From heart surgery to gastric bypass, from Valerian to Viagra, Merchants believe heavily in doctors and drugs as miracle fixes to keep them going. Instead of taking more responsibility in relationships, they seek to buy their way out with gifts, threats, flattery, or even rituals, turning religion into a *drive-thru pit stop* to redemption. Instead of looking at the emptiness within, they project their problems on others, eating through people in a stream of empty friendships that leave them worn out and hung over. And when Merchants cannot get what they want with guile and persuasiveness, they descend into Warrior tactics of force and intimidation.

When they channel their bluster and vivacity into anger, Merchants can be noisy and intimidating. But this is not good for them. When the Merchant's natural skill for manipulation is channeled into aggression and a lust for power, the results are usually disastrous for themselves and the world. Because Merchants do not possess the principled discipline of a Warrior, they can take shortcuts to obtain what they want, often at the expense of others— thus going against the basic grain of their type, which is to feed and clothe (provide for) the masses. One of the differences between Merchant and Warrior societies is that Warrior kings of yore proved themselves through extreme trials of fortitude and purity before assuming power. They rode first into battle, dying to defend their people. Such trials were put in place by Educators and Warriors as test and temper of their character. Can you imagine today's political leaders, many of them Merchants posing as Warriors, fighting for their ideals on the battlefield? Would their rhetoric be the same if they had to put their lives on the line to stand behind it? Merchants make great leaders of industry where their drive and talent makes them excel, but they are not meant to lead society.

Merchants are Lovers and Fighters, but given the choice, they prefer the former. Love is a Labor game, and Death is the Warrior's domain. Merchants do well to stay with their point of Integration and spread love and cheer rather than conflict in the world. Many are given a choice in life between sports and sales, army or entertainment, and most rightly choose sales and entertainment, as these are closer to their point of Integration. Sean Connery, the well-known man's man of the silver screen, dropped out of the Navy because of stomach ulcers. He took up drama, taking acting lessons and learning his craft, and went on to portray his iconic masculinity in roles like *James Bond*. Merchants do better *playing* Warriors than *being* Warriors.

Merchants are volatile and temperamental, and sometimes mistake their Volatility for Violence. But they are not good Warriors because war does not serve their highest good, which is to benefit the body, not destroy it. They also lack the Warrior's ability to follow orders, and the judgment to determine who needs to be punished, and when. Therefore, Merchants must keep to their own dharma, and not get entangled and destroyed by the Warrior's path.

And though Merchants *can* make their careers in the military or sports, more often than not these Warrior pursuits are cut short for some reason. Merchants may become injured, sick, or otherwise unable to continue their careers, or like Muhammad Ali, suffer debilitating consequences later in life. Dwayne 'The Rock' Johnson began by playing football before an injury forced him into WWF wrestling, and eventually into movies and entertainment. Julio Iglesias was a soccer player before he turned his Merchant skills to serenading the world. WWF Wrestling, cinema, and song are more entertainment than competition, and better suited to Merchant personalities, which goes to show that, even when we choose to go in one direction, fate often chooses otherwise for us— such is the power of dharma!

Saints

There are enlightened sages from every Dharma Type. Ammachi, the modern-day "hugging saint" of Kerala, is an example of a Merchant Dharma Type who has inspired an organization that helps hundreds of millions of people from all walks of life. From the creation of hospitals and homes, to the building of schools and libraries, her Merchant ability to organize and galvanize people with her limitless *Shakti* has little equal, in either the spiritual or secular worlds.

Merchants are essentially brokers— of people, food, things, and ideas. Ammachi, with a few of hours of sleep per night and tremendous good cheer, has transmitted the virtues of *charity* and *selfless service* to the West in a way never before imagined. Not surprisingly, her most cherished exemplars of divine consciousness are Devi/Shakti (the feminine divine) and Krishna (the mischievous Merchant personality of the Vishnu avatar).

The Dharma Types key how we all express our unique gifts— even enlightened sages. Ramakrishna Paramahamsa was a Laborer Type, and as we shall see in the following chapter, Laborers are devotional, grounded, and self-effacing. Even though he embodied the highest states of Samadhi, spiritual consciousness, he remained ever humble and true to his roots. Swami Yogananda was another Laborer Type, whose devotion and love for his teachers saturate his seminal book, *Autobiography of a Yogi*.

Ramakrishna's chief disciple, Vivekananda, is an example of an enlightened Educator. Because relationships between Educators and Laborers can be rocky, it took Vivekananda time to truly recognize his guru. Educators and Laborers essentially speak different languages, and think with different Intelligences (discussed in depth in Chapter 10, *Intelligence, Speech, & Secret Fear*). Nonetheless, after acknowledging his spiritual master, Vivekananda went on to express his dharma in typical Educator fashion: by writing, lecturing, and educating the masses. It is because of Vivekananda that we know the terms *yoga*, *vedanta*, and *dharma*.

> *"Caste is good. That is the only natural way of solving life. Men must form themselves into groups, and you cannot get rid of that. Wherever you go there will be caste. But that does not mean that there should be these privileges. They should be knocked on the head. If you teach Vedanta to the fisherman, he will say, I am as good a man as you, I am a fisherman, you are a philosopher, but I have the same God in me as you have in you. And that is what we want, no privileges for any one, equal chances for all; let everyone be taught that the Divine is within, and everyone will work out his own salvation."*
> -The Complete Works of the Swami Vivekananda, III 246

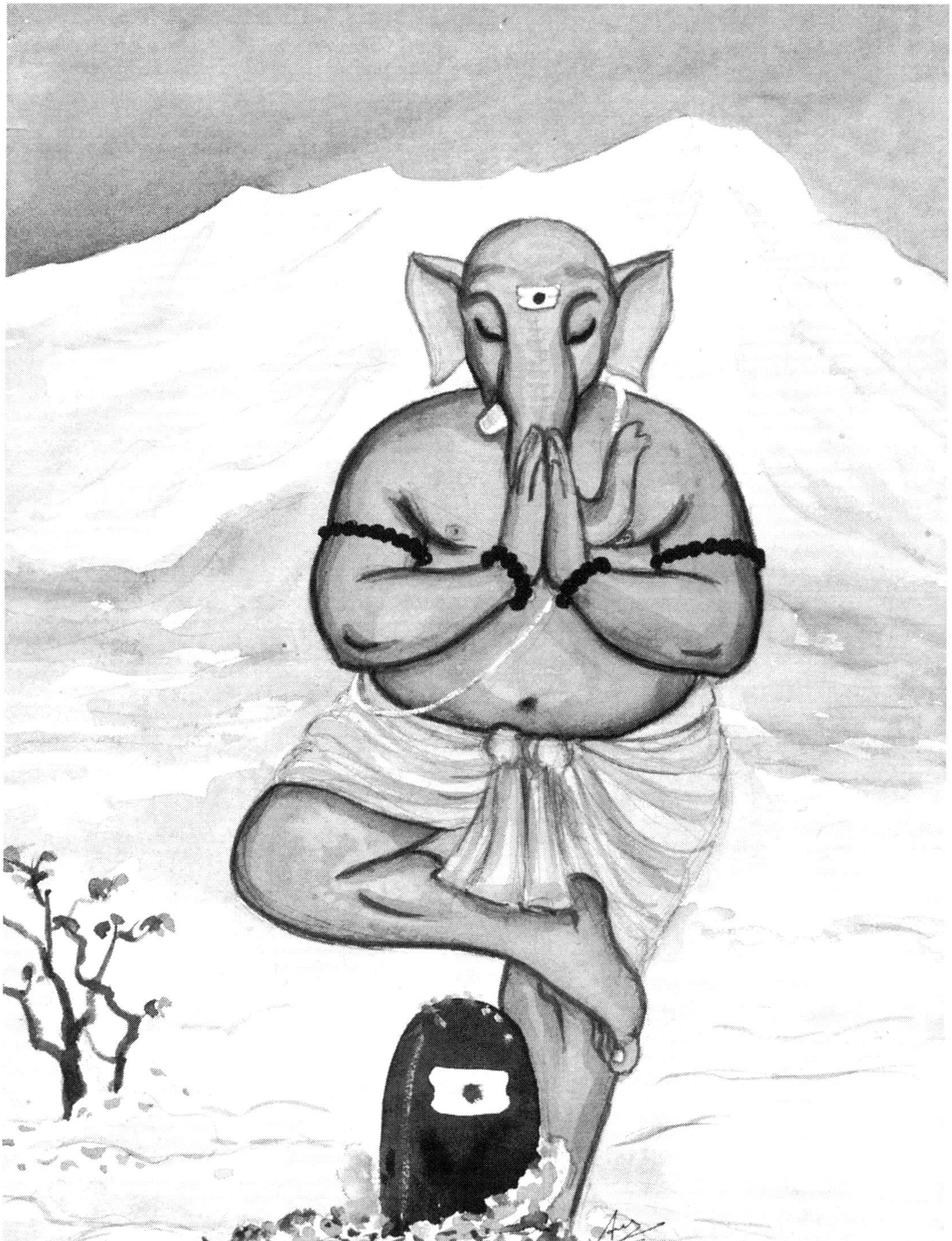

5

LABORER: "Nourish and Serve Others"

*Devotion * Work * Perseverance*

Sometimes people take the test and say, '*I hope I'm not a Laborer, or an Outsider!*" which underscores the hierarchical mindset and belief that one type is better than another. The truth as we have seen is that all types are equal, with different roads to happiness. But if any type were to be considered fully equipped with the tools to enjoy life, it should be the Laborer. Merchants lack self-esteem and tend to overcompensate for it; Educators are awkward, clumsy, and take a long time to develop wisdom; Warriors need guidance and direction, and Outsiders have to play many roles before they find their own unique expression. But Laborers come *ready to go* from the starting gate. Though they also mature, gaining wisdom and respect with age, they have less of a learning curve than other types, and require less reward to feel gratified.

Laborers don't need much from the world to make them happy. The warm touch of a loved one, a place they can call their own, and a way to use their talents to create something worthwhile is enough to make a Laborer content. Loving and serving, qualities that come naturally to Laborers, are mainstays of their expression. They express love by creating and growing family; and they serve by giving the gift of their hard work. When Oprah Winfrey or Mother Teresa donate to

Famous Laborers

Marlon Brando
Maria Callas
Johnny Carson
Deepak Chopra
Saint Catherine
Dick Cheney
Alice Cooper
Willem Dafoe
Clint Eastwood
Harrison Ford
Al Gore
MC Hammer
George Harrison
Katherine Hepburn
Benny Hill
Larry King
Kevin Kostner
Rush Limbaugh
Paul McCartney
Dean Martin
Martina Navratilova
Chuck Norris
Shaquille O'Neal
Sidney Poitier
Roy Orbison
Al Pacino
Luciano Pavarotti
Franklin D. Roosevelt
Bruce Springsteen
Mother Teresa
Bruce Willis
Oprah Winfrey

charity or care for their community, they do so out of a natural sense of service. And when Laborers Integrate Merchant qualities, as we'll see below, they become a force of love and nourishment in the world. In fact, when Laborers and Merchants Integrate, they begin to look a lot like each other.

Every type receives something by the natural operation of its talents. In protecting others, Warriors gain fame and power. From enriching people the Merchant gets money and gratitude. By enlightening the masses, the Sage earns respect, and by shaking up society, Outsiders find their own unique expression. But Laborers have no such agenda. For Labor types, the act of serving is its *own* reward. They need no gratitude, esteem, power, or soul-searching: they already have everything inside them. In that sense, they are the most complete type, being able to give of themselves without requiring anything in return. This does not mean, however, that they should work for nothing. In fact, by Integrating into the Merchant type, they increase their earning power and learn the true value of their work. It also does not mean that they are not insecure. When the Laborers Disintegrate, as we all do at times, they doubt their own intelligence and knowledge about the world.

But generally, Laborers feel called to service because they have so much of themselves to give without expectation of reward. Subtle remnants of this ethic exist in the service and hospitality industry where waiters and valets work on 'tips'—voluntary gifts for service well done. A true Labor type finds fulfillment in her work and extra money is an added bonus, not an end in itself—though in Merchant society tipping has become the norm.

The Laborer loves and feels deeply, though one would be hard-pressed to get him to say it. He expresses love through deeds. He does what he says and says what he does, and has the strength to stick to his word and follow through with his promise. He lives by principles that, though simple, are far from simplistic:

Loyalty—though easy to explain, is something especially tough to carry out in practice.

Truthfulness—a person is only as good as their word, and what they say, they must do.

Work—a person earns his bread by the sweat of his brow, and the quality of his work speaks to the quality of the person

Love— is difficult to express and hard to feign, and the sum of the previous three. In effect, the Laborer shows his love by his loyalty, plain speaking and hard work. Where these are present in abundance, there is no need for words.

The Laborer enjoys bringing people together and sharing community with others. She loves barbeques, pow-wows, and gatherings centered around food, believing that *the way to the heart is through the stomach* and that it is easier to get to know somebody over a meal and a drink than in hours of stuffy conversation. She is also the most caring of the types, and gravitates to industries and professions that succor, nourish, or otherwise tend to the needy, making a great social worker, nurse, or therapist, and can often be found working 'in the trenches' as the first contact with people she serves.

Laborers also excel at professions of skill and manual dexterity. They are masterful at manipulating material resources, and make the best craftsmen, artisans, and engineers. They are usually highly talented in their area of expertise, though not necessarily well-rounded, and gravitate to the Service and Trades industries, again working in the front lines of their field. Thus, while a Merchant type may own a restaurant and work the door, the Labor type would enjoy building, cooking, and serving there. Where the Merchant owns a medical business, the Laborer is the EMT first responder, anesthesiologist, X-Ray tech or nurse who cares for patients.

The Labor type is a creature of habit and enjoys his daily rituals. Routine and simplicity are far more satisfying than the hustle and bustle of busy life. In later years, Laborers may yearn for the ways of the past and hearken to a day when *life was more simple*. They are also the most superstitious of types, believing things with an ingrained faith that is hard to budge. Getting them to change their beliefs is like pulling teeth. But when they do change, they are likely to be as staunch in their new credo as they were in their old, even if it is the opposite of what they used to think!

Path to Destruction: *The Educator*

When Laborers Disintegrate into Educators they become literal-minded, oversensitive, and dogmatic. They take slight at little things and carry grudges to their graves; sometimes taking offense if people do not rub them the right way and never speaking to them again! When they Disintegrate they tend to over think things, and become stuck in a mental loop from which they cannot get out. They become 'fixed,' or rooted in a style of thinking or belief. Here is the Classic Rock junkie who cannot get out of the 60s, or the televangelist who cannot accept other faiths. Here is the over-possessive mother who cannot let her children go, but meddles in every aspect of their lives. These problems are remedied by the Laborer's Integration into the Merchant type.

Merchants are gregarious while Laborers tend to be closed. Merchants introduce Laborers to a wide world of sensations, concepts, and new experiences. They are go-getters while Laborers tend to run on inertia. Laborers are phlegmatic, traditional types who prefer security over extravagance, and when they Disintegrate, tend to fall into an Animal Realm psychology that is territorial, resentful, and aggressive if challenged. Like a junkyard dog, they remain guardians of their private domain without ever venturing to see what lies beyond its borders. They become prisoners of their own knowledge and beliefs, becoming closed in and parochial. They may also misuse knowledge to the point of becoming obsessed with an idea. Obsession means possession, and Laborers can become fixated on a person, place or thing to the point of being unable to see anything else.

> *"Pavarotti could not read or write music, but oh, could he sing!"*

When he takes on Educator values, the Labor type begins to assume that he knows it all, and this can lead to fundamentalism that tries to convert others to its cause. There is a narrowness of vision to the Laborer that doesn't work well with issues that require a broad perspective and the willingness to see different sides of a story. Because he also tends to mix emotion with reason, sentimentality with logic, he may come to conclusions that *feel right* to him, but often have no objective value. For this reason, politics, law, religion, and philosophy are areas where the Laborer is disadvantaged. Ironically, when he Disintegrates, he becomes interested in just such topics. And while the result is that he converts many to his cause for his tireless work and good intentions, the cause itself will be diminished in the long run for his lack of liberality.

Laborers are heart-based, feeling deeply whatever they believe. When a Disintegrated Laborer misconstrues fact and feeling the result can be catastrophic for the world, as in oppressive political ideologies, fundamentalist religious sects, and petty, bigoted philosophies. By nature, Laborers tend to be conservative, in the sense that they have a deep appreciation for past traditions. William F. Buckley Jr., one of the pioneers of modern conservatism, defined it as the *"tacit acknowledgment that all that is finally important in human experience is behind us."*[19] When this love of the past embraces life-affirming traditions, it preserves the best of civilization. When it indiscriminately clings to the past over progress, it risks embarrassing the Laborer with wrongheaded thinking.

Progress is the hallmark of a liberal mindset. *Webster's* defines liberalism as, *"a political philosophy based on belief in progress, the essential goodness of man, and the autonomy of the individual and standing for the protection of political and civil liberties."* While not every Educator is liberal, and not every Laborer is conservative, these strains of *progress* (Educator) and *tradition* (Laborer) tend to run strong in these two types. In the final analysis, they both need each other, as new ideas cannot be built without the foundation of the past. Tradition cannot be maintained without embracing the progress that allows for the improvement of our daily lives, be it through indoor plumbing, or the recognition of the civil rights of all races, genders, ages, and physical abilities. Both inclinations, both types need to recognize the value of the other. But when they Disintegrate, they both become stuck, unable to move from their positions.

The Laborer thinks he knows; the Educator thinks he can. This is another mantra for these types when they Disintegrate. On the one hand, the Labor type believes that she is sufficiently informed to be righteous and dogmatic about a cause. On the other, the Educator thinks he has the skill to create and maintain projects that require manual dexterity, endurance, and perseverance. In fact, the Educator has none of these in sufficient quantities, nor does the Laborer possess the quality of information to make judgments on matters of political, philosophical, or religious relevance. The problem with the Disintegrated type is that it believes it has enough of another's attributes to be successful in its work. Reality, however, does not bear this out, and the Educator's work quality, even his body, suffers from the stress of Disintegration. The Labor type's accumulation of fact and feeling suffices to build a box that closes in around and chokes him.

The Vedic view of personal dharma is simple: *it is hard enough to do what you were born to do... why complicate it by trying to be someone else? Why take away another's livelihood when it is so difficult to find and follow your own?* This is the gist of the Integration and Disintegration points. One path leads us to our dharma; the other away from it. These observations are not value judgments, or

---

[19]*Up From Liberalism,* William F. Buckley Jr.

imprecations on the intelligence, decency, or moral character of the types. We find PhD candidates among Laborers just as we find craftsmen among Educators. In fact, it is not the *quantity*, but the *quality* and *specificity* of intelligence that is at question here.[20] The point is that, all factors being equal, Educators are bound to possess a liberality and worldliness that Labor types lack. For specialists like accountants or rocket scientists, these may not be considerations, and Laborers are qualified to perform these professions. Where laser-like focus and specificity is required the Laborer is advantaged; where wide-ranging knowledge of language, customs, and policies is required, as in, say, diplomacy, the Laborer is detrimented. In much the same way, the Educator is at a deficit when it comes to the cleverness and application of manual skill and mundane duties. While he may know the perfect recipe in theory, it will not taste as good as the Laborer's creation, because of the latter's indelible instinct for its real-life preparation, seasoning, and presentation.

> *It is hard enough to do what you were born to do... why complicate it by trying to be someone else?*

Inferiority

Another instance of the Laborer's Disintegration is a feeling of inferiority and overwhelm when confronted with too much information. The Labor type can become anxious and closed-down if he feels that he is not smart enough in a given situation. He begins to doubt himself, even to the point of not trusting what has worked for him for years. Oprah Winfrey, a well-Integrated Labor type, has commented on her diffidence in front of certain audiences that make her doubt her own wisdom. A famous story illustrates the concept...

Once there was a Tibetan farmer who was visited by a young itinerant monk. The farmer welcomed the monk with great reverence and sincerity, offering him shelter, food, and, of course, butter tea. Impressed with this genuine display of devotion, the monk asked the farmer about his spiritual practice. The farmer smiled sheepishly and said that he only knew one mantra, but that he practiced it faithfully every day while he was tilling the fields. Curious, the monk asked to hear it.

As the farmer began to recite, a peaceful smile washed across his face, the sun came out from behind the clouds, rainbows appeared in the sky, and birds in the valley began to sing. Impressed, the monk said to the farmer, "You have done well, but you are

---

[20] Refer to Chapter 10 for more on the Intelligences specific to each type.

Chapter 5: Laborer: Nourish and Serve Others

> *To Laborers, the essence of a rose is always more important than its name, and confusion sets in when they try to replace pure experience with its linguistic counterpart.*

mispronouncing it." With this, he instructed the grateful farmer on the mantra's proper usage, and, thanking him for his food and board, left to pursue his journey.

A year passed, and the monk happened again through that valley, but now it appeared dark and desolate, a shadow of its former self. When he came across the farmer he asked, "What happened? This field was once so green and full of life!" The farmer bowed respectfully and said, "Ever since I changed the mantra, my life has been falling apart: there are no crops, no animals, and no food in the valley."

Incredulous, the monk asked, "Then why didn't you change back to the way you used to recite it?" Shaking his head, the farmer replied, "I could not, for fear that I would displease you, God, and the holy order of monks. But it's okay, maybe God intends for me to suffer this karma for my highest good."

Saying this, he smiled resignedly and turned to go. The monk now realized his mistake, and, embarrassed by his own hubris, begged the farmer to resume his mantra the old way, whereupon the valley re-blossomed with abundance and cheer.

Laborers possess a natural devotion and humility that is beyond the artifice of superficial information. To them, the essence of a rose is always more important than its name, and confusion sets in when they try to replace *pure experience* with its linguistic counterpart. That is not to say that they should not learn or study, but that information should be subordinate to experience. Pavarotti could not read or write music, but oh, could he sing! An experience is always more than the sum of its parts; the chemical constituents of a flower cannot explain how it makes you feel to smell and see it; notes on a page are nothing until they have been amplified by the tenor's heart and soul. **The *linguistic* is the realm of the Educator, while the *experiential* belongs to the earthy Labor type. When one tries to take over the function of the other, confusion and misunderstanding ensue.**

Path to Integration: *The Merchant*

By taking on qualities of the Merchant type, Laborers begin to see boundaries not as borders but as meeting places— not a way to keep people out, but a place to welcome and communicate with neighbors. By incorporating movement and music in their lives they stir the depths of their souls to new levels of expression and emotion. Music is important to Laborers, who feel it more simply and profoundly than perhaps any other type. Music styles like Blues, Country, R&B, and Traditional are staples in their lives. (More on different styles of music and their relationship with the Dharma Types in Chapter 11).

Kinesthetic sense is also strong in Laborers and they need to touch and be touched to connect to their emotions. Carbohydrate-rich food is optimal for them. Unlike Warriors, who do better on higher-protein and moderate carbohydrate diets, Laborers love carbs, which pack their muscles with energy for long bouts of physical movement. Perhaps more importantly, they also release serotonin in the brain, which encourages e-motion—the expression of feelings. This is vital for Laborers, who tend to shut down and get 'stuck' when they Disintegrate. There is no *emotion* without *motion* and anything that keeps a Labor type moving is good. From ballroom dancing to hiking and gardening, exercise is great for Laborers, especially in nature. Laborers think and feel deeply, and can become depressed if they begin to obsess on negative thoughts. Distracting themselves with Music, Massage, and Movement is a way to re-frame their thinking.

Evolutionary Integration between Merchants and Laborers occurs when each adopts qualities of the other. As a Labor type, Johnny Carson tapped into his down-home Midwest sensibilities to reach and appeal to huge masses of people on his way to super-popularity. The entertainment industry is a Merchant business and well-suited to Laborers who can break out of their shells and relate to the public. Labor types are storytellers, but not in the same, animated way as Merchants. They love to tell jokes and anecdotes, and to share their values with the community. When they Integrate the Merchant's natural volubility and social ease, they can move audiences to tears of joy and sorrow.

Whether keeping alive the stories of their ancestors or their nation, they also make natural historians, antiquarians, and archaeologists— the latter especially for their connection to the Earth Element. Using Merchant savvy, Laborers popularized dusty professions like Egyptology by connecting the mysteries of the earth with people's natural desire to discover and learn. Laborers enjoy digging for mysteries, and combined with their one-track mind and dogged persistence they can unravel practically any detective story... even those told by hieroglyphs in stone.

For optimal Integration, the Labor type needs to think like a Merchant to receive her due in society. She needs to learn the *value* of her work, and Merchant society has done much to benefit her in this respect; agriculture, landscape, construction, and other skilled Labor professions these days are highly remunerated. Laborers also make great engineers, accountants, builders, and carpenters because their hands are golden. They can take a piece of metal and make it work in the service of mankind, like a plumbing pipe that brings clean water to a city or an automobile that drives us to and fro. They can take a piece of wood and make it serviceable to their needs either as art— as in a statue— or a work of utility, like a dresser drawer. Laborers are gifted with their hands and possess practical skill in just about any trade they choose to tackle. Being close to the Earth they prefer to live on ground floors rather than loft apartments. The heights are not for them— another reason they Disintegrate into the Educator, who prefers his high tower to the common halls.

Music and touch, along with good food and sensual enjoyment, tend to keep Laborers happy and Integrated, allowing them to express love, which is their highest Purpose. This is not the mushy sentimentalism we associate with the word today, but the tough and ever-so-practical love of a Mother Teresa who takes others' problems on her strong and steady shoulders. While Merchants may provide the *means* of support, Laborers are the *way*. That is, they are on the front line of care for those who most need it. Merchant types are responsible for providing capital and resources to build an infrastructure but Labor types are the ones who actually *work* to make it operable. Their work and service is love in action... which in Sanskrit is called *seva*. Seva is the spiritual path that best fits the Laborer's disposition. The spiritual paths befitting each type are discussed in detail in Volume III.

Merchants and Laborers, Capital and Labor, have always complemented each other, for one has what the other needs. One example is the relationship between the United States and Mexico. A Merchant nation, the U.S. contains well over 10% of Mexico's population, which comes to trade its labor for increased financial opportunities. On the other hand, many Americans willingly trade their capital for the dream of a relaxed, worry-free life as portrayed by tourist hubs like Cabo San Lucas and Cancun, in search of the simple pleasure of margaritas and the beach. In fact, Merchant types in America have made Mexican exports like beer and tequila staples of American weekend rituals. This is one of many examples illustrating the mutual Integration between these types, an Integration that goes beyond just personal evolution, into the nature of relationships, government, and even spiritual realization... themes explored in the chapters that follow.

6
OUTSIDER:
"Innovate, Rebel, and Free Others"

Empathy Freedom* Innovation*

"Foxes have holes and the birds of the air have nests, but the son of Man has no place to lay his head."[21]

Such is the fate of the Outsider, who is a traveler, a searcher on a quest, blending in everywhere, fitting in nowhere. He is a rebel, a radical, an enigma to himself. While most people have well-outlined dharmas, the Outsider's destiny is loosely sketched and mostly a masterpiece of his own creation. His role is that he has no role; the purpose of his life is to find his Purpose. His is the double-edged sword of freedom and confusion, who is equally comfortable in the clubhouse as in the slaughterhouse.

Nothing new comes into existence without the Outsider's touch. There is no innovation or revolution without the Outsider's instigation. Anything that requires radical re-thinking, leaps of imagination, and creative synthesis of many elements is the Outsider's purview. Ruled by the Space Element, there is no 'where' Outsiders cannot travel, just as there is no experience they cannot have. From the highest of the high to the lowest of the low, Outsiders trek the terrains of the wild and the inner spaces of the soul,

Famous Outsiders

Antonio Banderas
Brigitte Bardot
Roseanne Barr
David Beckham
Halle Berry
Bjork
David Blaine
Richard Branson
Yul Brynner
Tim Burton
George W Bush
Albert Camus
George Carlin
Johnny Cash
Jesus Christ
Joe Cocker
Salvador Dali
Johnny Depp
Lady Diana
Jane Fonda
Redd Foxx
Greta Garbo
Jimi Hendrix
Martin Luther King Jr.
Jackie Kennedy-Onassis
EvelKnievel
Jeddu Krishnamurti
John Lennon
Ian McKellan
Liza Minnelli
Osho/ Rajneesh
Vincent Price
Ravana (Rama's enemy)
Chris Rock
Martin Scorsese
Sting
Jessse Ventura
Denzel Washington

---

[21] Luke 9:58

reaching to depths and heights that no one else dares to follow. Laws and morals hold little power to obstruct their need for experience, and Outsiders are most creative in their interpretation of social strictures. As a result, they can just as easily fall into depravity, as soar to the heights of purity: such is the razor's edge that defines the Outsider's path. However, just as it is easy to fall off track, it is also simple for Outsiders to get back on, for they are never far removed from Redemption, though it may not seem that way to them. Examples of criminals-turned-saints abound in sacred literature, illustrating the Outsider's roller-coaster journey from truth to error... and back again.

Outsiders often feel alone, as if they are the only ones of their kind in the universe. Unlike Merchants, whose emptiness is *inside*, the Outsider's void appears all around them, making it difficult to know their place in the world, and how to relate with others. They are everyman and no-man. Although they have good reason to feel this way, it is ultimately not true: there is a community out there for even the most estranged of Outsiders, and part of their Purpose is to find it. The journey may take them to places far and away but the end is well worth the pains. In fact, Outsiders are the most populous of all the types in the Iron Age, and from breatharians living on nothing but sunlight, to 'trekkies' who live on sci-fi reruns, it is far easier to find solidarity with fellow Outsiders in the modern age of the internet.

> *Though the Outsider leaves, he must eventually return to his culture the treasures of his journeys, be they rare jewels or jewels of rare wisdom.*

Because they are searching for themselves, Outsiders are quick to identify with anything that personifies something they believe. From Egypt and her mysteries, to Vedic devotional chanting, Outsiders espouse ideologies that reflect Truth for them, the truth of their real identities. As a matter of rebellion, they often embody exotic or different beliefs in order to assert their independence from 'normal' people. They are masters of change, and when one identity no longer suits them, it is quickly shed for a new and better fit. From Rastafari chic to business casual, they change fashions with the seasons, all with the passion of their quest for unique self-expression.

Outsiders may spend the main of their lives searching for Purpose and meaning in the world, but when they find it they are potent forces for Change. Where they go during this quest for self-fulfillment none can follow— society only awaits what they bring back. For, though the Outsider leaves, he must eventually *return* to his culture the treasures of his journeys, be they rare jewels or jewels of rare wisdom. This is how he earns his place and value in the world while changing and redefining it thereby.

Outsiders have the unique ability to blend disparate entities and make a wholly new creation from their union. This is the cook who combines Asian and Western recipes to create fusion cuisine. It is the Country singer mixing gospel and blues to create rock 'n roll. It is Martin Luther King Jr. bringing Gandhi and Indian philosophy to bear upon the American social scene. This is the yogi who melds yoga and fitness to create a marketable new workout craze.

In fact, in traveling West, the Vedic *Vidya*[22] Herself has entered into an Outsider Life Cycle, the period of time characterized by great change and contact with new elements. Her exposure here lends itself to all sorts of new creations, some more successful than others. Such innovations that remain rooted in the authentic soil of Vedic wisdom prosper; those that cut themselves off from the source of their life, wither and die.

This is a lesson for the Outsider, who must never lose sight of the original society that forms the backdrop to his life. The only way to earn true freedom is to come back to the place that made you. A prophet is never a prophet in his hometown, but the best Outsiders, like Jesus, return from their journeys to face the music, and give people the unique insights of their inner and outer explorations.

> *Society is like a stew. If you don't keep it stirred up you get a lot of scum on the top.*
> —Edward Abbey

Of course, this comeback is sure to disrupt the status quo because new ideas are always unsettling. There is always upheaval in the wake of the Outsider's interactions. People are left with a new awareness, a positive or negative *state change* around them. From Salvador Dali to Bhagavan Rajneesh, Outsiders are a slap in the face of conformity. The hippie movement is an example of such values taking over the world in an Outsider Cycle that spanned the 60s and 70s. It was counter-cultural, experimental, and blended influences from other cultures into its own, an example of how just as people can travel through Life Cycles, countries and cultures also move through different periods in their evolution.

---

[22] The feminine personification of a body of knowledge. Generally, the Vedic culture.

And just as the free-love hippie revolution inspired change, it also highlighted the Outsider's glaring shortcomings, most notably his lack of self-responsibility.

Who's To Blame?

Outsiders are the 'accusers' and whistleblowers of society. When they are well-Integrated, they find what's wrong and bring it to our attention. When poorly integrated, they are blamers, lacking self-awareness and making others responsible for their shortcomings. The Space Element that rules Outsiders can cause confusion: with no direction or point of focus, it is easy to become disoriented by the limitless freedom of Space. Like ether, the chemical, Space, or the element Ether as it was once known, can cause confusion, delusion, and outright unconsciousness. But Space is also perfectly clear, allowing Outsiders to see things with unmatched perspicacity if they have proper orientation. Not even Educators can see with the same clarity, whose Air Element is a filter to perfect sight.

The Laborer is blinded by Earth (physicality), the Merchant by Water (emotionality), the Warrior by Fire (ambition), and the Educator by Air (ideology), whereas the Outsider is unfettered, free to see things as they are, provided he has a permanent fixed star by which to get his bearings. Ultimately, for the most well-integrated Outsiders, that becomes a spiritual referent, for everything in the physical world is perishable. That is why so many of the earth's saviors and prophets are Outsiders. In Judeo-Christian terms, Jesus and Satan form bookends of the Outsider model. Satan (literally, "The Accuser") stands on one end as utter darkness, like the darkness of Space: Jesus stands on the other, as the embodiment of light (Messiah- radiantly "Anointed"). Thus, the Outsider embodies both colors, black and white, colors, incidentally, that Outsiders favor in both personal fashion and outer design!

Which Outsider you become depends upon your *orientation*. Do you have an anchor, like the Dharma Type, to keep you grounded in reality? Do you have a technology and a system to keep you in check, to help you find your way when you stray? Below we will consider the paths to higher Integration, and the slippery slopes that spill us down into utter distress. Good Outsiders know when to upheave society and when to fly under the radar. But poorly-Integrated Outsiders are lawless reprobates who feel justified in destruction, but are unwilling to implement conscious awareness in the process.

Between these extremes, of course, lies the more common Outsider, who flows with society, never really fitting in, never really knowing himself, and never understanding how to optimize his considerable talents for self fulfillment. Such fulfillment is accomplished by learning and using the Three Steps to Integration, as we shall see below, and learning how to include the best aspects of every type into his own.

> *The Laborer is blinded by Earth (physicality), the Merchant by Water (emotionality), the Warrior by Fire (ambition), and the Educator by Air (ideology), whereas the Outsider is unfettered, free to see things as they are, provided he has a permanent fixed star by which to get his bearings*

Path to Integration: All—"*The Rebel With a Cause*"

Like hermit crabs moving from shell to shell, Outsiders can trade identities from time to time. An Outsider may go through a 'Warrior phase', during which she delights in Warrior-type activities, or she may immerse herself in a Labor period, taking on the Laborer personality and assuming its Integration and Destruction points. These phases may be brief, lasting a few months— or lengthy, lasting decades— depending on their Life Cycles and other circumstances. And while this is true to a degree for everyone, the other Dharma Types never really lose themselves in a Life Cycle like the Outsider does. No one is as good at blending in as the malleable Outsider, which is ironic, since no one is as good at *sticking out* when they want to, as the Outsider!

There are three ways in which Outsiders assume their identities. First, they may play one of the four types and stick to that identity all their lives. Next, they may opt to remain simply Outsiders without taking on any other roles. Finally, they may opt to change roles according to the season of their Life Cycles. This is the most common. Here are examples of each type:

> *As an Outsider, John was always athletic. His family moved from India to England when he was very young, and he quickly fell in love with soccer. Over the years, he distinguished himself with his skill and competitiveness, and went on to play semi-pro before entering law school and becoming an immigration lawyer, helping qualified foreigners obtain legal status.*

This story illustrates one of the prerequisites for being an Outsider. More often than not, Outsiders are either born different, or experience great change when they are young, such as moving from one continent, religion, or culture, into another. This does not always have to be the case, but is often true for Outsiders, who do not feel 'at home' in their place of birth. They may travel widely, or simply embrace foreign customs. Madonna, a Warrior type, moved to England and embraced Kabbalah during her Outsider Life Cycle. In this case, John is a real Outsider whose greatest fulfillment came through playing a Warrior due to his natural talents and genetic disposition. Throughout his whole life he enjoyed competition and other Warrior pursuits, eventually settling into law as his profession. Let's take a look at another example:

> *Fernando grew up on the mean streets of south-central L.A. to Hispanic parents in a Latino neighborhood. He resented authority and got into scuffles with his teachers, elders, and eventually the police. From tagging buildings and highways to breaking into homes, he felt justified in taking from the 'rich' because they had opportunities he didn't. To his mind, they didn't understand what it was like growing up in a place where every day is survival... and they never would.*

In this example, Fernando is an Outsider who has chosen not to take on another role. He remains a true Outsider. While this particular portrayal is a negative example, true Outsiders can be as benefic to society as others are destructive: the example is not a judgment of good or bad, but an illustration of how, like John above, Outsiders can emulate any type, or none of them at all.

> *Sara is a free-bird that flies with the wind. When she was young her parents brought her from South Africa to America, where she grew up feeling different from other girls. While her parents were wealthy, she never really fit in with their crowd. She went to college to study medicine, but dropped out three years later to pursue Thai massage. She married, had children, and settled into a quiet life of a dutiful housewife. When she divorced a few years later, she decided to open a Thai massage studio and soon became financially independent. Embracing East/West concepts, she grew attached to the plight of Tibetans living abroad, and began contributing to their cause by donating money, clothes, and shelter. Finally, she challenged herself to actively campaign for their rights by organizing Free Tibet protests in her city and working full time for their cause.*

Chapter 6: Outsider: Innovate, Rebel, and Free Others

Here is an example of an Outsider who goes where her Life Cycles take her. From Merchant ideas of business and prosperity, to Warrior values of protecting and fighting for the rights of others, she embraces the roles her Cycles give her, sometimes going back and forth between them. In this case, she went from studying medicine (Warrior) to practicing massage and raising a family (Laborer) to owning a business and contributing to her community (Merchant) and finally back to Warrior by becoming a civil rights advocate. Life Cycles can and do repeat. Sometimes people see just one or two Cycles, while others experience all 5 over and again across the span of their lives. These will be discussed in the final chapter.

The Outsider's Three Roles:

One fixed Identity: *Warrior, Educator, Laborer, Merchant*.	Changes identity over Life Cycle	No change of identity: remains an *Outsider*

Outsiders make the best actors because they can blend in seamlessly into any role. Thus, some play many, while other Outsiders play one dominant role during their lives. They remain Warriors if that is their dominant personality, or Educators if that best reflects their life Purpose, taking on the Integration and Disintegration points of each.

Such Outsiders would look, talk, and act like Educators, though on closer inspection their Outsider qualities would inevitably show through. They might teach foreign subjects, or study arcane lore. They may be interested in Sufi dance while living in Minnesota. They may study and speak the Inuit languages, though hailing from the deserts of Arizona. Joseph Campbell is an example of an Outsider firmly fixed into an Educator role. A self-proclaimed 'Maverick,' he revolutionized the study of myth and culture through his synthesis of world traditions. In Sara's example above, Outsider qualities were always present regardless of what role she played. As a young girl she felt different from her peers, while as a mature woman she embraced foreign causes from Thai massage to Tibetan liberation. Whatever identity she adopted, she retained some of her Outsider uniqueness.

Keys to Self-Realization

Because Outsiders are unique, free-flowing creatures, they must remain ever vigilant and self-aware so as to not fall into self-deceit and blaming others for their problems. Self-awareness is their most important tool to staying honest with themselves and *present* to the circumstances in their lives. This is the first step in their Integration. The second step lies in finding their Unique Expression. Finally, they must return and share their Unique Expression with the world. Here is what these three steps look like, as well as their obstacles:

The Outsider's Three Steps to Integration	The Outsider's Three Obstacles to Integration
Self-Awareness	Self-Deceit/Blaming Others
Finding Unique Expression	Getting lost in confused thinking
Returning and Sharing Unique Expression With the World	Fear-anxiety about being accepted/understood.

Standing in the way of the Outsider's ability to be self-aware is his propensity to lie to himself, blame others, and not take responsibility for his circumstances. Standing in the way of his ability to find his unique gift, is his confusion about who he is and how he is supposed to live. Finally, fear of being rejected and misunderstood keeps him from sharing his gifts with the world. When he can overcome these obstacles, an Outsider becomes an incomparable jewel, invaluable and rare.

For many Outsiders this may mean changing roles over their lifetime and learning the dharmas of every type before understanding their own. Like a bee hopping from flower to flower, they may need to imbibe the nectar of each Dharma Type in order to obtain its most authentic essence, and with inner alchemy create the honey of their own Unique Expression. Having to do this makes being an Outsider more difficult, but it also gives them the freedom to express themselves in ways other types can only dream of.

This change of roles is often not a conscious choice: it is a result of their evolution as human beings. Being an Educator might suit them for a while but they may later need to become Warriors, though as discussed above, some Outsiders *never* change roles. They remain in the costume of one type, or no type at all... being simply *Outsiders*. Whatever the case, Outsiders get to enjoy the dharmas of the other types as no one else can. They get to make their own road to happiness and create their own Purpose. This freedom is paid for by the work they do to understand every one of the other types and their destinies.

> *Like a bee hopping from flower to flower, Outsiders may need to imbibe the nectar of each Dharma Type in order to obtain its most authentic essence, and with inner alchemy create the honey of their own Unique Expression*

Unique Expression

Outsiders have a special gift, a Unique Expression to share with others. There is something that *they* can do differently and better than anyone else in the world. Finding *it*, Outsiders arrive at their Unique Expression, or at least one of them, for they may have many unique talents. These first steps, Self-Awareness and finding a Unique Expression, are instrumental to the Outsider's liberation. The final step is Returning to society.

Outsiders must remember that they are only Outsiders in relation to something. Therefore, they must not abandon the society that defines them, even if it defines them by not recognizing them. The ultimate freedom for the Outsider type is to return from time to time to the normal world, bringing new gifts and awareness to it while recharging, resting, and preparing for another adventure into the unknown.

An Outsider cannot be honest with herself if she leeches off people then turns around and decries them behind their backs—this is the way of criminals and thieves, the worst Outsiders. The best Outsider is fed by her community—she gets knowledge from Educators, Skill from Warriors, Wealth and Shelter from Merchants, Food and Craft from Laborers. She gives in return new perspectives on their own paths: from her explorations she brings new Philosophies, Weapons, Currencies, and Recipes for the other types to enjoy.

The Outsider's path to Integration lies in accepting that no embodied being is independent. She depends upon the food she eats, the air she breathes, and the clothes she wears. She is tied to the environment that provides these for her. We cannot totally destroy the society that gives us sustenance, no matter how wicked or depraved it may be. Few of us can live naked in the wilderness and none of us can do it alone— no one can survive without the support of Nature, for we are all embodied beings in bondage to the exigencies of food, water, shelter, sleep, and sex. In sharing these with all humanity lies the connection between Outsiders and the rest of the world.

True freedom for the Outsider comes when she acknowledges and accepts her dependence on the world. She can do nothing without the favor of Nature, society, and the other Dharma Types. When she realizes this, she understands that there is nothing to run from and nowhere to run. Wherever you go— there you are; the Outsider brings her inner demons with her wherever she turns. It is in facing and owning these that she can free herself from *herself*, and move on to fulfill her highest destiny. Running away is a form of self-deception, a way to refuse and deny what you don't want to look at. The Outsider's progress begins when she looks at her inner lies and boldly owns up to them. Let us look at this first step of Self-Awareness in greater detail.

SELF-AWARENESS: Overcoming Deceit

Outsiders have a looser concept of right and wrong than any other type. Their reality is fluid, changeable, and hard to define. They are for the 'spirit of the law,' rather than its 'letter.' As a result, Outsiders can be perceived as being untruthful, unreliable, or even masters of deceit. At their worst, they lie to themselves, unaware of their own self-deception, refusing to apply the same critical eye to themselves that they cast on the world. Unlike Educators, who feel great remorse when they fail to walk the walk, Outsiders are often ignorant of having done any wrong because they believe that the laws that apply to others don't apply to them. When they overcome this blindness and see themselves with the same eye they see the world, they can become masters of Truth. Very few Outsiders have the Ruth, Responsibility and Respect it takes to accomplish this; accordingly, few Outsiders live up to the unlimited potential of their type.

> *The greatest blessing for the Outsider is that, no matter how mottled his past, he is always an inch away from grace!*

1. **Responsibility**. Being true to yourself means taking Responsibility for everything in your life, including things beyond your control. For John, who came to England as a young boy from India, though it was not in his power to change it, it meant owning his past and making the most of it. For Fernando, it was taking responsibility for his crimes and the effects they had on his community. Responsibility is refusing to lie to self and others. This is the most difficult step, which involves delving deep into your inner demons and Confessing them truthfully. Good counsel is a must at this stage, and it is important to have trustworthy people to confide in.

2. **Ruth**. In Confession, there is a profound contrition that goes along with having revealed your darkest secrets. That is why Responsibility and Ruth go hand in hand. At this stage, Outsiders resolve to fight self-deception and blame, and to never repeat their wrongs. This is a deeply cleansing process. With Ruth also comes the resolution to do something positive with your talents, a desire to achieve a goal and change the world. As Outsiders begin to work their resolutions, an abiding respect begins to well up from inside their being: respect for others, but mostly, respect *for themselves*. In turn, this self-respect is reflected back on them by others. People begin to sit up and take notice of the person who has walked through the valley of the shadow of death... and survived. They become eager to hear what you have learned.

3. **Respect**. The Outsider's Responsibility and Ruth naturally lead others to respect her. People see the power and strength it takes to own your life, and respect is their gift. The Outsider herself feels a deep pride in having overcome her own brutalities, and self-respect is the natural outcome. It glows from the evolved Outsider, and is unmistakable to any with whom she comes into contact. This is the level at which Outsiders can create monumental changes in the world.

A story from the New Testament sketches out this process. As Jesus lies on the cross, two criminals beside him also paying for their crimes, we witness one Outsider's redemption, and another's damnation. The first robber turns to Jesus and cries, *"If you are the Christ, save yourself and us!"* Here is the blamer, who cannot convict himself for his own fate, but imputes responsibility to others. Immediately, from the other side, his fellow pipes up, *"Hey, do you not fear God? You who are yourself on the cross, do you even rail at the innocent? You and I are executed for our deserts, but this man has done no harm!"* Here is the Ruth of the noble Outsider. He owns up to his crimes, and accepts his punishment. Taking Responsibility for his soul, he entreats Jesus, *"Lord, remember me in your kingdom.*" As a result, he is forgiven immediately and given his Respect and absolution as Jesus replies, "*Even now, you are blessed with me!*"

OUTSIDER: 3 STEPS TO SELF-AWARENESS		
SELF AWARENESS Begins with: 1. **Responsibility** (Telling the truth to yourself) 2. **Ruth** (Resolving what you want to do with your life and what you will never repeat) 3. **Respect** (Developing self-respect that leads to respect from society)	**UNIQUE EXPRESSION** Begins with: Self-awareness and searching for your unique gift to the world. Finding your Unique Expression may mean blending many other things, or inventing something totally new. Every Outsider has a Unique Expression—find yours!	**RETURN TO SOCIETY** Begins with: Sharing your Unique Expression with the world. 'Returning' does not mean you ever left society: it means sharing the gifts of your nature with it.

"*Improvement makes straight roads, but the crooked roads are roads of genius.*"
--William Blake

And therein lies the great mystery of the Outsider's gift: no matter how mottled his past, he is always an inch away from grace… and this redemption is not just a religious concept. The graffiti artist who gets to paint city hall, the mugger turned respected self-defense teacher, the check defrauder teaching the FBI how to spot bad checks—these are all examples of everyday redemption, one that does not mean you do not pay for your misdeeds, but that you turn them around into respect when given the chance.

The Outsider's is not the straight path, but the path of Mystery. As far away as he may seem from redemption, a shortcut can take him there in no time.

Chapter 6: Outsider: Innovate, Rebel, and Free Others

Consider the Vedic story of Valmiki, author of the great epic, *Ramayana*, and other vagabond saints through history who spent their lives in thievery, lust, and murder. In the Christian tradition, Paul (or Saul as he was then known) was a fervent persecutor of early Christians before a beneficent vision turned his life around.

On a more prosaic level, consider the modern Freedom Writers, inner-city kids who were never given a chance until a momentous encounter with their teacher changed their lives, eventually turning them into college graduates and contributors to the community.[23]

Being a moment away from redemption does not mean Outsiders do not have to pay the consequences of their deeds—it simply preempts further suffering, bringing the Outsider closer to realizing his inner self... which is always free, always full of respect. Karma is ineluctable; even the most reformed Outsider has to pay karmic debts. Valmiki, whose name means 'anthill,' is so-named because of the power and duration of his austerities, remaining locked in meditation for so long that ants are said to have built a fortress around him. One may have to go to great lengths to pay one's debts... but redemption cannot be bought. It is free for the Outsider who takes the steps to Responsibility, Ruth, and Respect, and these in turn eventually lead to his freedom.

> *By earning their own freedom, Outsiders also free others... even the Educator's Air element is restricted to obey certain laws; only the Outsider's Space Element exists... everywhere and nowhere, unbounded and free.*

Freedom is all-important to Outsiders, and the three steps summarized above are how they ensure it for themselves and their community. By earning their own freedom, Outsiders also free others; by demanding their own rights, they ensure the rights of everyone like them. Educators enlighten—they bring wisdom and understanding to the world through their professions. Warriors protect—the environment, people, animals, objects, and ideas. Merchants enliven the world, and provide shelter to others. Laborers nourish—by feeding, raising, and caring for others. Outsiders, for their part, are ultimately responsible for *freeing* others—from physical, mental, emotional, and spiritual concepts and restrictions. Even the Educator's Air Element is restricted to obey certain laws; only the Outsider's

---

[23] See Erin Gruwell's *Teach With Your Heart,* and *The Freedom Writers Diary*

Space Element exists within and without, everywhere and nowhere, unbounded and free. Like the Space Element, Outsiders represent the freedom potential in each of us.

Consider Krishna's description of the spirit in the Bhagavad Gita:

"It exists without and within all beings, and constitutes the animate and inanimate creation as well. And by reason of its subtlety, it is incomprehensible; it is close at hand and stands afar too."-BG 13:15

Or his outreach to the most estranged Outsider:

"Even if the vilest sinner worships me with exclusive devotion, he should be accounted a saint, for he has rightly resolved. -BG 9:30

Following the Three Steps over and over, an Outsider refines her being and her ability to refresh society to such a degree, that she become indispensable to it. Repeating this three-step process is in fact crucial to the ongoing success of the Outsider type: it does not suffice to go through it once, but to do it over and again until your expression and sharing become second nature, ensuring that you never slip back into self-destruction.

Path to Destruction: All—*"To Hell with the World"*

Outsiders pride themselves on being unique, one-of-a-kind creatures. When they Disintegrate, they use their uniqueness to justify acting out, in the belief that no one understands them. But when they Disintegrate, Outsiders prove themselves quite predictable. They blame others for their problems. They run away from problems, and the hard reality of their present moment. They evade, deceive, and run... mostly from themselves.

An Outsider's Integration is predicated upon honesty— telling the truth to herself *about* herself. Outsiders can lie and cheat others, but the greatest lie they tell they tell themselves. But understanding karma, that all-important leg of the Vedic tripod (*dharma, duhkha,* and *karma*[24]) allows Outsiders to make peace with their past, accept their present, and act decisively to create their future. Karma is universal justice; it relates to actions of the past that have created the present, and actions of the present that create the future.

---

[24]*Dharma, Duhkha,* and *Karma* correspond to Purpose, Suffering, and Justice, as discussed in the Introduction, and in greater detail in Volume III: *The Spiritual Types.*

Let's take a look at how this works. It is the Outsider's own past karma (fate) that gives her the current life situations she must deal with; it is her own present karma (free will) that determines the result she reaps from them. Outsiders are the authors of their destinies and must realize that, instead of blaming others for their woeful story, they can take up the pen and write it themselves. This is the Vedic view of universal Justice, and for Outsiders to have justice in their lives, they must own up to their present situation first.

> *When we own our grief and suffering rebellion comes out to serve, not punish society*

Awareness of your karma leads to responsibility. Taking responsibility for your situation means that you acknowledge your present circumstances as a product of *your* actions, a result of *your own* behavior. Thus, there is no one to else to blame or point the finger at. When we own our grief and suffering, rebellion comes out to serve, not punish society. The best Outsiders have this orientation, and are backed by the Universe in their non-conformity. They come to be revered by the very society they decry. Chess players cannot blame others for playing poorly; likewise, we are responsible for the chess board that is our life, and the Vedas say that we have to embrace, own, and change our karmas if we are to enjoy our time on this planet. Just as *fate* gets us into this life in the first place, our own *free will* gets us out!

Western-minded Outsiders who are not as quick to embrace *karma* philosophy can find other systems emphasizing Responsibility, Ruth, and Respect, the three steps to self-awareness. These principles permeate many self-help methods, from Christianity and other religions, to Neuro-Linguistic-Programming, hypnosis, the Enneagram, and other empowering techniques.

In the Vedic view, karma is the root of all creation, and the efficient cause of the five Dharma Types. Being born an Outsider is the direct result of your own activities in previous incarnations. Far from using this as an excuse, the Vedic view squarely says that you have to own what you are because you got yourself there in the first place! Cultivated awareness is the answer to karma's proper diagnosis, integration, and discharge. Indeed, karma is the ultimate philosophy of Responsibility and Self-Respect. Arthur Ashe summed this up in his three-volume history of black athletes, *A Hard Road To Glory*, when he said:

> "At some point, each individual is responsible for his or her fate. At some point, one cannot blame history. Does the legacy of slavery explain why Mr. Jones eased into class 10 minutes late this morning?"

The Outsider's path to destruction lies in seeing herself a victim of the world, and thus stopping her own progress and growth. As victim, she feels justified in acting out because of having 'got a raw deal' in life, and because the world 'deserves' her wrath. In this case, it is not the destruction she causes that is the tragedy—because in truth Outsiders sometimes *do* get a raw deal— but the attenuation of the growth process inherent in that attitude. For the Outsider to Integrate, she must be honest with herself, which is not possible when her mind is wrapped up in lamenting its sorry situation.

Sometimes Outsiders are physically different from others. Illness, disability, and other afflictions may segregate them from society. Other not so apparent factors may also alienate Outsiders from others. These include sexual orientation, chemical imbalances, environmental sensitivities, political or social policies, and other influences. This does not mean, however, that all gays or disabled people are Outsiders. It means that all factors being equal, they experience a different reality from the average person. Blacks and other minorities have been treated historically as Outsiders in Western society, and this persists into today. As a group, African Americans have collectively been in a long Outsider period, regardless of their individual types. However, while social distinctions weigh on the Dharma Type, it is ultimately one's fixed, inherent makeup that determines who she is, not Jim Crow laws or the fashions of justice. It is one's individual karma, not her social situation, that makes her a particular Dharma Type. That is why black Warriors, Educators, Merchants, Laborers, and Outsiders will all express themselves differently, given the opportunity in a free society.

> *In survival mode, we revert to more basic archetypes: men become Warriors, women Laborers... regardless of our original Dharma Type*

Unfortunately, in many societies, men and women are not given the chance to be more than just pure survivors. In countries where slavery, oppression, war, famine, or other tragic situations exist, people are not given a chance to actuate their destinies, and must search instead to eke out a limited existence. In survival mode, we revert to more basic archetypes: men become Warriors, women Laborers. This is a deeper wiring in us that we experience in emergency situations. Whether killing

Chapter 6: Outsider: Innovate, Rebel, and Free Others

a bug that has strayed into the house, or fending off home-invaders, a man kicks into Warrior mode when his hard-wired response is activated. Women for their part transform into nurturers, workers, and supporters—they become Laborers, regardless of their original Dharma Type. Much more of this is covered in Volume II, *Sex, Love, & Dharma*, which treats on the male-female dynamic in depth.

Instead of trying to be like others, Outsiders must embrace their uniqueness. Instead of resenting 'normal' people, they must contribute their distinctive talents to the world. They will be not only valued by their peers, but will realize that they do not *want* to be 'normal' at all, for so-called normal people *are bound* by the very rules that make them normal! Remember that the Outsider's foremost desire is Freedom. He can never have it by living someone else's life. He must be grateful for the life he has, for all of its unique paths and crooked roads. Integrated Outsiders cherish their uniqueness—not as a point of rebellion—but as a valuable contributing identity to the social order. It is in fact cool to be who you are.

The other Dharma Types have a path, a boundary. The Outsider has no boundaries, and can truly make and define her own road. Because of that, however, many get lost, convincing themselves that they are right and the world is wrong. But those who refuse to lie to themselves become geniuses of society. Jesus was such an Outsider, scourging himself with scrutiny and penance before subjecting others to it, clearing the road within before imposing revolution without. Outsiders can take the best and worst qualities of every type, and he took the Warrior's penance, the Educator's wisdom, the Laborer's love, and the Merchant's charity and made them hallmarks of his ministry.

"We must become the change we desire."
-Gandhi

To become Integrated, Outsiders must have inner revolution before imposing external change: *inner evolution before outer revolution.* They must kill their own deceit before destroying others.' These values run deep in the teachings of the Christ, as evidenced in quotes like,

> *First remove the plank from your own eye, and then you will see clearly to remove the speck from your brother's eye.*

> *Whoever desires to come after me, let him deny himself, and take up his cross, and follow Me....*

Those Outsiders who do not take up their crosses to bear the burden of their karmas cannot wholly share their gifts with the world. Even Martin Luther King's revolution of values was hampered by his philandering. Those Outsiders who do not purify themselves within will never know purity without, and will ultimately fail to become the change they desire. These are Christian examples, but Purification practices are common to every spiritual tradition in the world, the details of which are explored in Volume III: *The Spiritual Types*.

Overcoming Anxiety

Outsiders tend to run anxious, and at extremes can be paranoid or even schizophrenic. They have higher anxiety levels than other types, perhaps because as Outsiders they fear the judgment or verdict of others, as they have always been stigmatized by society, whence the name 'Outsider.' To combat this, they must remember that they are now the most populous type, and have more in common with their fellow man than they suspect. Their uneasiness is more of a genetic, physiological remnant of bygone ages than an accurate response to real stress. Therefore, relaxation techniques and self-acceptance are important for the Outsider's Integration. Some of these are discussed in the Health section that follows.

Having high anxiety levels also leads them to blame others for their misfortunes. Outsiders will swerve into a lane, then scream at another driver for cutting them off; they get themselves into trouble, and imprecate others when they suffer the consequences. When Disintegrated, Outsiders implicate the world in their problems; when Integrated, they identify the problem and implicate themselves in *fixing* it. Being the troubleshooters of society, they can quickly see what's wrong—and when Integrated, work to find solutions. To his enduring credit, Martin Luther King, in addressing the issue of equality, offered real solutions to achieve it. Integrated Outsiders not only identify what isn't working, but also work to fix it. Take a look at the list of rebels and dissenters in your life and you will see a lineup of Integrated and Disintegrated Outsiders: those who create change to better the world, and those who disrupt the world so they don't have to change themselves!

Stereotypes

To conclude, let us look at what some of the negative stereotypes associated with Outsiders really mean. The degradation of caste systems and social hierarchies led to Outsiders being vilified with slurs like *unclean, unreliable, thief, liar, vagabond,* and others. Here is another way to look at these characterizations through the lens of the Dharma Type:

Unclean: Outsiders have their own, unique views on hygiene. Their tendency to extremes can lead them to become neat freaks or slobs. Whatever their orientation, Outsiders do not place as high a value on *superficial* cleanliness as they do on *inner* purity, such as they define it. More precisely, Outsiders keep pure what they value, and let go what isn't important to them. Their lesson is to find balance between the two extremes.

> *Take a look at the list of rebels and dissenters in your life and you will see a line-up of Integrated and Disintegrated Outsiders: those who create change to better the world, and those who disrupt the world so they don't have to change themselves.*

A Harley biker might polish his chrome to a bright shine, but defile his mouth with obscenities. The Rasta environmentalist might have pure thoughts about cleaning the environment, but may not shower for weeks, or may pollute her inner environment with daily pot smoking. Outsiders make their own roads and redefine cultural practices, including personal hygiene: *"Blind Pharisee, first cleanse the inside of the cup and dish, that the outside may be clean also!"*[25] cried Outsider Jesus to those who sacrificed inner purity for superficial appearance.

Thief: Because Outsiders empathize well with others, they can take on their energies to such a degree as to be perceived as *stealing* their essence. Outsiders can become anyone they desire. This can be misconstrued as copying or stealing another's identity. On another level, Outsiders who were often underprivileged were forced to steal resources in order to survive. Coupled with their looser

---

[25] Matthew 23:26

views of 'right and wrong,' this sets up Outsiders to be fall guys in society. But if Outsiders had not been marginalized, and allowed the same economic, health, and political, rights as other citizens, they would not need to resort to crime. Consider the overwhelming statistics that blacks face in America. Though supposedly living in a post-racial society, they are more than twice as likely to be poor, imprisoned, and marginalized than whites. Such is the Outsider legacy they still face. Let every minority and oppressed group heed the Outsider recommendations in this chapter in order to loosen the bonds of their oppression and transcend the petty customs that keep them in check. Every Outsider must learn the three steps in order to free herself and change the world around her.

Deviant: Outsiders have looser definitions of sexual propriety, and as a rule, require *more* and *more varied* sex than other types. When they do not get it, they are more likely to masturbate and seek to self-gratify, being less inhibited about sexual expression. People who find themselves in an Outsider period will often experience a sexual 'awakening' of sorts that may lead them to explore depths of their sexuality hitherto untapped. Deviancy truly occurs only when natural sexual impulses are repressed over time, and inappropriately expressed when they finally come out. Repression can be imposed by society, religion, family, or by one's own ideologies. In any case, Outsiders need to learn the fine line between repression and expression, deviancy and self-control. Like anything else in their lives, they walk the razor's edge that separates healthy sexual attitudes from perversion and self-destruction. Sex is covered more in-depth in Volume II.

	Negative Emotion	**Positive Emotion**
Outsider	Deception, Anxiety	Empathy/Wonder
Educator	Lust	Compassion
Laborer	Sloth, Jealousy	Love, Loyalty
Warrior	Anger, Pride	Generosity
Merchant	Greed	Conviviality, Enthusiasm

SUMMARY OF THE TYPES

Educator
Strongly idealistic, but not necessarily practical…
Noted for intelligence and grasp of abstruse concepts…
Generally not forceful, physically less resilient than other types…
Good counselor, but unable to follow his own counsel…
Motivated by truth, rather than money, but prone to indiscretions due to lack of control over his senses, i.e. anger, lust, greed.
Sanskrit terms: *jnana, dayaa, kshanti: wisdom, compassion, forbearance*

Outsider
Culture, beliefs, race, physicality, and other traits make her different from her immediate environment…
Travels to or lives in foreign lands and different or unusual places…
Absorbs and adopts foreign ideologies and concepts…
Incredibly adaptive—able to blend in and wear many hats…
Resents establishment and the 'normal' life of others…
Keenly aware of injustices in society, be they economic, educational, political, etc…
Values personal freedom over other things…
Sanskrit terms: *ananda, kaivalya, svatantriya: bliss, isolation/independence, freedom*

Warrior
Motivated by challenge to improve self and others…
Interested in protecting those who cannot protect themselves…
Responds to defiance and competition…
Values knowledge, wisdom, and innocence in others…
Sanskrit terms: *yukti, virya, viveka: skill, strength, judgement*

Merchant
Strongly motivated to secure personal and family interests…
Need to be around others, feels lonely or empty without company…
A smooth talker: likeable, glib, and socially active; highly entertaining …
Feels best when giving; at first to family, then community, and eventually the world.
Understands how the Merchant society functions and is good at taking advantage of it…
Sanskrit terms: *shakti, rasa, danam: energy, juiciness, charity*

Labor
Strong likes and dislikes…
Deep sense of community and belonging…
Emotional ties and loyalty to her 'own' things: her family, country, job, home team…
Good physical strength and endurance, and a powerful work ethic…
Capable of great service and self-sacrifice…
Strong intuition and specific intelligence, but not well-rounded…
Sanskrit terms: *bhakti, seva, dhriti: devotion/love, service, solidity/endurance*

Homework

Take a moment now to determine your type, and if you're ambitions, those of friends and family. Try to understand its individual points of Integration and Disintegration and see if you can judge how to implement these in your life. Do you remember times when you went against the grain of your nature, and later suffered for it? Or, have there been times when you pushed yourself to develop and integrate skills that ended up benefiting you immensely, so much so that you cannot see yourself living without them now? Try to learn 3 things about each type; even memorizing their Sanskrit keywords from the previous page can be invaluable to unlocking their meaning. This will benefit you as we build on them in the following chapters, showing you how to implement Dharma Type strategies in everyday life situations. But don't worry if you do not understand everything at once; the 5 types and their qualities will be developed throughout this book and its succeeding volumes, by the end of which you will be able to confidently use them in practically any situation you should encounter.

Educators

The pen is mightier than the sword, and the Educator's weapon is the modern version of his pen, the laptop. But as an Educator, you will obtain more inspiration and better ideas by moving your energy and cultivating the Warrior's gifts of Discipline, Action, and Strength, than sitting motionless in front of a computer screen all day. Therefore, take some time to discover a new form of exercise this week. From Yoga to horseback riding, take a class or hit the trails to find newfound growth and inspiration in your life!

Warriors

Warriors Integrate by learning and envisioning their Just Cause. This week, Warrior, take some time to study deeply about an issue that is important to you. Do some research, expand your mind—you just may find that you were *wrong* about something you held as certain. Next, write down your goals on a sheet of paper and how you might achieve them, as solutions present themselves. Do this for each aspect of your life, Family, Profession, Sex, Spirituality, etc. Nothing is as useful to Warriors as *seeing* their truth. Post this somewhere visible, and make it the object of your daily focus for at least 6 weeks!

Merchants

Merchants need to feel needed. There is no more useful way to fill up on pure energy than by giving to others. This week, find something you can do to benefit your community. Volunteer at a soup kitchen, donate your old clothes or appliances, or teach others new skills. Take little steps; you do not need to give away the farm. Become a part of the community that supports you, and you will find an ever-renewing source of vitality and health!

Laborers

Laborers love their routines. This week, take a new spin on your daily routines by doing them differently. From brushing your teeth with the non-dominant hand to taking in new restaurants, movies, or even a vacation, try something new this week, dear Labor type, and let yourself be inspired and distracted by the ever-changing world around you!

Being natural Detectives, Laborers love Easter egg hunts and fact-finding missions. They are also thrifty and naturally economical. One way to keep your routine lively while stimulating these skills is to check coupons in the mail or online, and use them to discover new restaurants, stores, and other places of entertainment. Go to a new place to eat, shop, or hang out each week, using the coupons in your daily paper or mailbox. Many Laborers also prefer to take *"stay-cations"*–leisurely vacations where they live. This way, they discover interesting places while staying close to home, saving money on hotel, gas, and even food. Take a look at your surroundings and see if you can discover new and exciting things to do around you!

Outsiders

Out of fear or frustration, Outsiders fail to deliver their truth to others. This week, Outsider, find a way to be relevant and share your truth with the world. In between the blank stares you might also get a few minds to light up and open to your unusual wisdom. Also, ask people that know you about your best and worst qualities. Ask them what you could do to become a better, more authentic person. The responses you get might surprise you! You do not have to do everything they say—use this exercise as a form of reflection and self-inquiry. It is often hard to see the truth about ourselves, but when it is reflected back on us by others it can be a revelation!

	Skills	Strengths	Weaknesses
Warrior	Both gross and fine motor skills; usually a combination of the two that allows for the achievement of a goal- i.e. a soccer player.	Generous and self-sacrificing. Can achieve anything in the name of a good cause.	Pessimistic, cynical, materialistic. Does not believe in saving grace, and becomes prone to a dog-eat-dog mentality.
Merchant	Fine motor skills. Less goal-oriented, more focused on refinement- i.e. a violinist.	Inspirational and charitable. Entertaining and funny. Can motivate people.	Insecurity. Needs constant validation from others to believe own worthiness.
Educator	Mental skills- possesses less motor skills than other types; often clumsy or uncoordinated.	High minded, pure, and noble. A source of wisdom and purpose to others.	Wishy-washy, feckless, no backbone. Schism between ideals and reality- especially as pertains to base emotions like Lust.
Laborer	Gross motor skills, usually applied for self-sustenance as in a trade or hobby.	Loyal and devoted. Hard working and unaffected. The backbone of functional society.	Intense jealousy. Attachment to people, things, or ideas to the point of irrationality.
Outsider	Can mimic any of the types. Usually has affinity with Labor type.	Born to free other beings. Instigates revolution, progress, and positive change.	Blame, Self-Deceit. Refuses to accept responsibility for own actions; blames the world for his problems. Cannot see own faults and shortcomings.

PART II

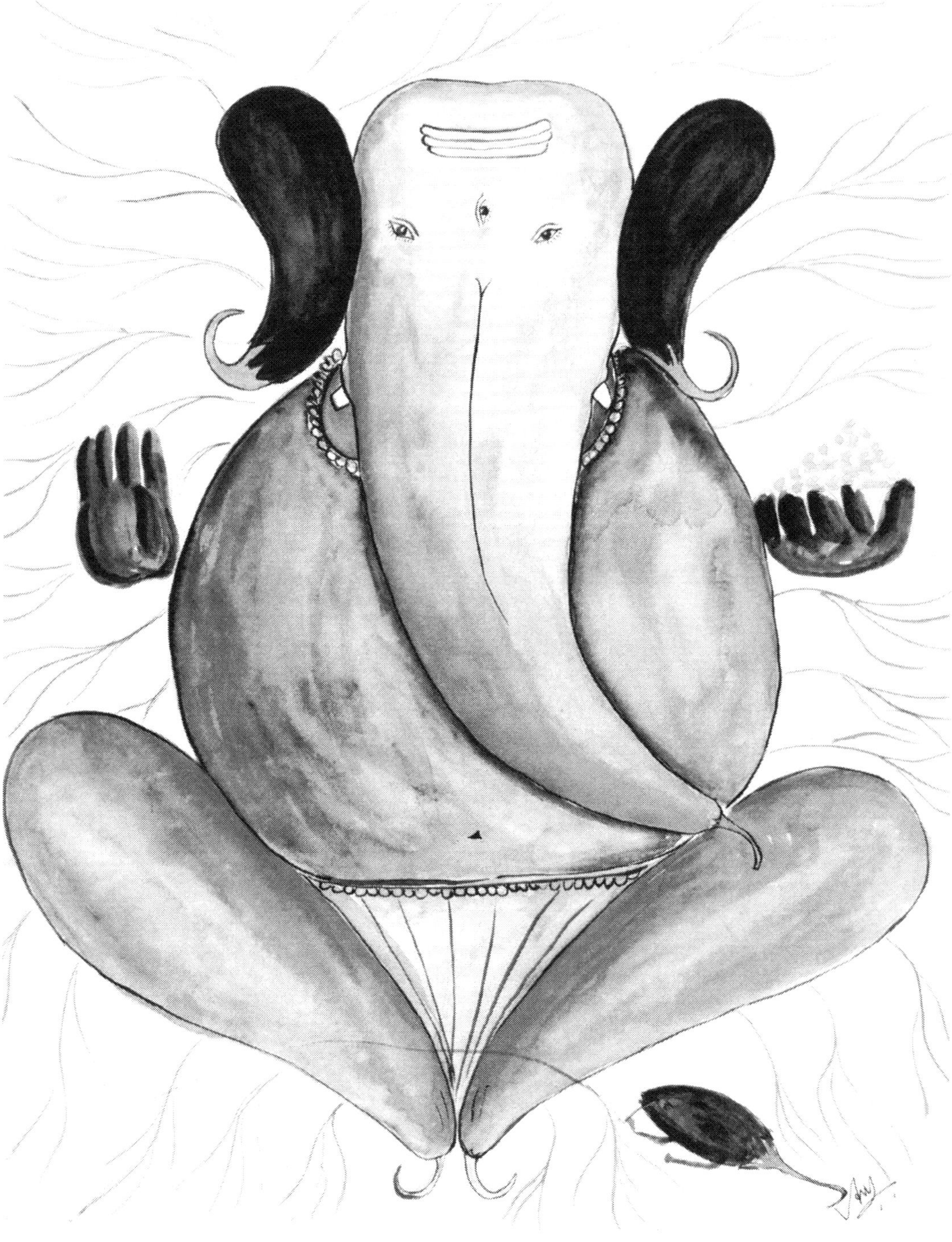

7
FIVE PATHS TO WELLNESS

The following chapters detail the mundane matters governed by the Dharma Types in an organic, sequential order. This means that, though chapters like Health, Entertainment, and Profession are discreet entities, the reader is better served by reading from beginning to end, rather than skipping through. Where the meaning of a particular topic is not outlined for Outsiders, it is implied that they are following one of the four other paths. Not every type is given equal treatment in every section, and some are emphasized in different parts. For example, Warriors get major billing under **Government**, though less press in the **Anatomy** section, and so on with the other types. Over the course of the next several chapters, however, every type is fleshed out and explained fully in different sections according to context.

Anatomy

Gross Anatomy		**Subtle Anatomy**
Outsider —	Skin	Bliss Body
Educator —	Head and Face	Wisdom Body
Merchant —	**Digestion, Legs**	**Sensate Body**
Warrior —	Heart, Blood, Arms *Prana*, Muscles	Vital/Breath Body
Laborer —	Reproduction, Bones, Feet	Food/Flesh Body

In the Rig Veda it is said, 'the Educator sprang from the mouth of God, the Warrior from His arms, the Merchant from His legs, the Laborer from His feet.' To this can be added the Outsider, who is the skin that connects them all. To eliminate even one of these renders the whole being ineffective. One can no more subjugate one class than cut off one's hands or feet: each is essential to the survival of the organism as a whole; each plays a unique role without which the entire being suffers. That is why, when one class usurps power and seeks to skew the Natural order, all society pays, as our Anatomy illustrates.

In Yoga philosophy there are five 'Bodies' that also correspond to the five types: the Food or Flesh Body, the Vital or Breath Body, the Sensate Body, the Wisdom Body, and the Bliss Body. Each of these Bodies, or sheaths, has a special Intelligence and relationship to its corresponding Dharma Type. These Yoga Bodies and their Intelligences are covered in later sections; for now, let us consider gross anatomy by examining which organs the different types use the most. For example, Educators use their brains more than any other part of their bodies. Warriors, who value physical competition and battle, need strong hearts to circulate blood and courage to the muscles. Labor types have strong bones and reproductive organs, while Merchants have an affinity with the digestive tract. Let's take a look at these below.

Outsider

Outsiders represent the skin. They live *outside* the body of society, though remaining intimately connected to it. New ideas and discoveries are their specialty: They experience new sensations first and carry them inside to be interpreted by the brain (Educator), and integrated or rejected by the body. They may tattoo or pierce their skin to set themselves apart, and though such voluntary decorations are characteristic of Outsiders, stretch marks, acne, and other skin afflictions may also distinguish them from their fellow Dharma Types. Skin is also the largest organ, and Outsiders are the largest population in the world. There are more Outsiders than any other type in the Iron age, though Integrated Outsiders are as rare as Integrated Educators, Warriors, Laborers, or Merchants.

That is to say that Outsiders who have cultivated Self-Awareness, found their Unique Expression, and Shared their gifts with the world, and continue to repeat this three-step process are few and far between. Most Outsiders stop at the first or second step, or go through it once and stop there; they find something they're good at, share it with the world, and become content to sit on their laurels. But Outsiders need to continuously expand their horizons, like the Space Element that rules them, and like the skin, which is constantly shedding, renewing, and regenerating.

Evolution is an ever turning wheel, and these steps need to be repeated to keep that wheel turning. Constant expansion ensures freedom; stagnation ensures bondage. Some Outsiders may seek destructive ways to expand their awareness, using intravenous drugs, pain, or other means of overcoming the structures that bind them. But short-term fixes only end up limiting their freedom by creating addictions, legal entanglements, and economic burdens that keep them from evolving into the people they can be.

In Chapter 6 we saw that Outsider categories come in threes. Like the layers of skin, (epidermis, dermis, hypodermis) there are also three types of Outsider: those who face away from society and the body; those who look both ways and are intermediary between society and the fringe, and those who look in, staying in society most of the time. Each type has slightly different functions. Outsiders who stay completely away from society are like the epidermis. They are the ascetics, gypsies, criminals, and off-the grid types that prefer to have as little to do with society as possible. Like the epidermis, they are not fed directly by the body of society, but by 'diffusion' from the capillaries in the dermis.

The second level, like the dermis, mediates between civilization and the wild; these Outsiders go back and forth, sharing their gifts with the world, but also taking time to retreat from it. Tattoo ink is held in the dermis, and these second-level Outsiders sometimes get tattoos to distinguish themselves from others. Finally, the third level, the hypodermis, is intimately connected to the body, and rarely if ever leaves society. These Outsiders look the most like anyone else, and assimilate better than others. Here are Halle Berry, Barbara Streisand, and David Beckham~ Outsiders intimately benefited by their society, and tied to it by their identities and professions. Because the hypodermis is 50% fat, this level of Outsider is also usually 'well-insulated,' meaning well-to-do and comfortable in the world. They do not often connect to the outside fringe, though like domesticated animals, they retain a bit of the wild within.

Another way to view the three layers is as successive degrees of integration. The first layer of Outsider is the most ordinary. He is numb to his own Nature, and has little connection to the society that feeds him; he is callused, insensitive, and disconnected. He does not look within at himself, but only sees what's wrong with others, fleeing society instead of Integrating. The second is the Outsider who has found his gifts and returned to share them with the world. Finally, the third level of Outsider has mastered himself to such a degree that Outside and Inside have no more meaning; he is as comfortable in the world as without it.

Educator

Educators are the brains of the outfit. They rely on the rest of the body to support and feed them while processing higher information and guiding the organism. They interpret Natural Law for the benefit of the body of society. From looking both ways before crossing the street to making world-changing decisions, Educators, like the brain, steer society in the direction of its highest destiny. They may do this through science, religion, politics, health or any number of disciplines, but their basic role remains the same—to teach and inspire society towards its highest good.

> *"The central nervous system... requires more energy than any other tissue of the body, including muscle... In fact, every day our brains require the equivalent of a quarter-pound of sugar to be converted into the chemical form of energy, ATP."*
> Dr. Benjamin V. Treadwell,
> *Juvenon Health Journal*
> September 2004

It is the size and function of our brains that sets us apart from lower animals. Educators likewise make the difference between an animal existence and a meaningful life by providing purpose and dharma to people. A body without a head lacks intelligence, but a head without a body is also a useless lump of matter. Therefore the Educator has to remember her place in the social order and learn humility. The brain uses up a large amount of the body's resources, and a brain that does not know how to make itself useful simply becomes a drain on the system. Also, by itself a brain is helpless, and needs the rest of the body to implement its ideas. It needs the skin and bones to protect it, legs to carry it where it needs to go, and arms to bring desirable objects to it while keeping the undesirable away. The lesson is that the body serves the brain, and the brain in turn serves the body. A teacher is without students cannot teach; a coach without players cannot win; a pastor without parishioners cannot save. Educators must remember that without the body of their students, pupils, or followers, they are useless.

There is also a special relationship between the organs that illustrates Dharma Type Integration and Disintegration For example, just as the heart pumps blood to the brain, the brain itself reciprocates by regulating the heart's function. This illustrates how, from Anatomy to Zoology, Dharma Type relationships influence our lives at the most personal and mundane levels, whether we're aware of them or not.

Laborers and Merchants benefit each other through the reproductive and digestive systems, respectively. It takes proper digestion and assimilation of nutrients to feed the reproductive system, while healthy sexual activity exercises the organs and stimulates digestion. Each organ benefits its neighbors by its normal operation, and without the function of one, the whole body suffers. Like the Dharma Types, it is not a question of competition, but of cooperation. Our individual parts, like the Dharma Types, have a symbiotic relationship that prospers the whole body when they do their jobs.

Laborer

Laborers are the feet of the cosmic man. We tread the earth with our feet, and rely on them to carry out our dharmas. Consider the consequences if everyone on earth sprained their ankles for a day. What would happen if you could not walk to the store for food, or go to work to earn money? Society would likely grind to a halt, a helpless, hobbled thing. Without feet to ground us to the earth, we could not realize the full meaning of our material existence.

Laborers also rule the generative organs. These are linked to the human creative impulse, both in the material sense of creating children as well as in artistic creativity. Laborers like to build something out of nothing. In previous ages they were the 'proletariat' whose job was to propagate the species. Though today Outsiders are the most populous type, the Laborer's instinct to raise children and cohere family, community, and country is still supremely powerful. They are the glue that holds society together, and in the body that glue is represented by the reproductive impulse.

The sexual organs are also sources of vitality and vigor. By drawing on the ancient healing traditions of the Orient, in the next volume we will further explore the correlations between sex and vitality. Briefly, these traditions state that the stronger one's reproductive function, the stronger one's constitution, because for the reproductive organs to be optimally nourished nutrition must pass through the rest of the body's tissues first. Having the most endurance and lasting-power both physically and sexually, Laborers are the longest lived of the Dharma Types, and are usually spry and sprightly well into old age. This endurance differs, however, from the Warrior's energy. Warriors are associated with ATP and the cell mechanisms that turn sugar fuel into quick-burning energy for the muscles. But Laborers are connected to the bones, the solid structures in the body that confer structural integrity and thereby longevity. Warriors are good for quick bursts of strength, while Laborers are better-suited to longer bouts of exertion. Warriors tend to burn out, while the Labor flame is long and steady.

Warrior

Because of their association with blood, Warriors have good circulation and sometimes even a 'ruddy' complexion that marks them as the action heroes of the Dharma Type family. Being the *heart* of the Cosmic Man, they also represent courage and energy. While under stress Laborers may get broken bones, stressed Warriors usually get broken hearts— problems with bleeding, circulation, even heart attacks.

Just as Educators rule the brain and nervous system, Warriors are the electricity that runs along it, carrying out its orders. One executes the commands of the other in an instantaneous dance of cause and effect. Warriors are the *chi*, *prana*, or life force that courses through the body. Like the Merchant-Laborer dynamic, the Warrior-Educator relationship is based on reciprocity. Merchants and Laborers complement each other because it takes food to nourish the reproductive impulse, as indicated above. Likewise, the heart and brain work together to coordinate the actions of the body, each giving life to the other through an orchestrated interplay of purpose and energy.

> *Without movement of the colon there is no movement in the body.*

Merchant

Merchants rule the digestive organs. It is their role to 'digest' experience in the world, and from thrills and excitement to food and drink, Merchants are the hedonists of the Dharma Type family. This is rightly so, and why Merchants are given a remarkable ability to recover from binge drinking, eating, and other excesses. Neither Educators, Warriors, nor even Laborers can endure the party hardiness of the Merchant type, and the emotional roller-coaster that sometimes characterizes their life experience. They are in constant pursuit of *rasa*, life's juiciness, and the digestive organs offer a perfect metaphor by taking in, digesting, and assimilating experience.

Like the digestive process, Merchants are responsible for moving resources/rasa in society. Without movement of goods and capital, society stagnates. Without movement of food through the intestines and colon, there is no movement in the body. Although the colon is actually a Labor organ, it is part of the digestive system, a fact that illustrates the inseparability of Merchant and Labor types. A story details the colon's importance to the body:

'Once, all the organs convened to determine who was the most important. Of course, the major players, the heart and brain, had their say, and their claims received much bluster and applause. Other organs spoke out as well, like the lungs and liver, each making its eloquent claim for supremacy. Finally, after everyone had had a turn, a tremulous voice piped up from the rear, 'what about me?' It was the colon.

'As the organs turned back to look, a round of laughter boomed through the body: 'what will you do that is greater than the heart?' said the heart. And 'what can you do that is greater than the brain?' asked the brain.

'Nothing,' replied the colon, and he turned to leave. 'I will do nothing.' And true to his word, he quit working. After a couple of days, things began to get a bit uncomfortable in the body, and after a week, all the organs were feeling sluggish from the backup of morbid elements. Finally, after two weeks, they lined up each and every one to beg the colon to resume his duties, whereupon the body gradually returned to optimal function. The very happy organs then unanimously accorded him the *honorary* title *of* 'Mr. Most Important!'

In Ayurveda, health and immunity are centered in the colon. Even modern medicine recognizes that up to 70% of the body's immunity is located in the gut. By keeping a clean and healthy digestive system, by stoking *agni* (digestive fire), and feeding the body *rasa* in the form of nourishing food and positive, sweet experiences, there is nothing that it cannot digest, and no pathogens it cannot fend off. But when we abuse our digestive systems, such as we do when we overeat, drink, or take inappropriate food combinations, our internal Merchant system suffers, and we become sluggish, slow, and sick. And like a sick society, a sick body suffers and can eventually **break down and become overrun by its enemies. Therefore, Merchants must take special care not to abuse their digestive organs and to learn proper diet,** food-combining, and supplementation. Recommended sources for doing this through Ayurveda are found in the Appendix.

The Brain

Working with the Dharma Types lends itself to endless creative applications. Just as some animals can be sub-classified according to the Dharma Type of their breed, the function of some organs in the body can be similarly broken down. For example, dogs are Warrior animals— but even within their species, there are some breeds that are Educators, like Golden Retrievers, while others are Labor types, like Bulldogs, and still others are Merchants, like Chihuahuas. In the same way, though the brain is an Educator organ, its functions can be insightfully stratified according to Dharma Type.

In his book, *Change Your Brain, Change Your Life*[26] Dr. Daniel Amen describes five brain systems that remarkably mirror the function of the Dharma Types and their Integration and Disintegration points. Reading Dr. Amen's descriptions through the lens of the Dharma Type lends itself to a deeper understanding of the brain and how it influences behavior. Below is a summary of the brain systems described by Dr. Amen, and their relationship to the Dharma Types. For more information, refer to Dr. Amen's book, or visit www.amenclinics.com.

The Deep Limbic System is the emotional center of the brain, most closely associated with the Merchant type. It is implicated in our ability to bond socially with others. Desire, passion, and libido are also strongly connected here. As discussed in previous chapters, Merchants are masters of the emotion cocktail that makes us tick, and they derive their inspiration from the thoughts they have and the emotions these create. A Sanskrit phrase puts it succinctly: *yato bhaavas tato rasa*– 'whatever your state that's your experience,' or 'where the mind goes, emotion follows.' Managing her internal state is the most important lesson a Merchant can learn. Neuro-Linguistic Programming (NLP) and other techniques (such as those popularized by Anthony Robbins) work wonders for Merchant types. According to Robbins, there are no good or bad people, only resourceful and unresourceful *states*. This can be a revelation for Merchants; when negative thoughts can be eliminated by positive states, one can escape the depression, moodiness, and unreliability common among Disintegrated Merchants.

> *"Perfect valor is to behave, without witnesses, as one would act were all the world watching."*
> -Francois, duc de La Rochefoucauld

Prescriptions for Merchant types are similar to prescriptions for the Deep Limbic System. St. John's Wort, Valerian, and other herbal remedies help to keep them emotionally steady and relaxed, and to sleep at night.

Merchants also Integrate when they take on qualities of the Labor type. Laborers are steady, loyal, and heart-based. When Merchants take the time to form deep, lasting bonds with others their Deep Limbic System tends to normalize. On the other hand, when they make only casual or superficial friends, their Limbic System becomes overactive and their inner void expands.

---

[26] Three Rivers Press, New York. 1998

When they relate authentically they form lasting relationships that fill their void and confer on them a durable fulfillment such as they cannot get through superficial contacts. Research consistently shows that marriage, especially sex with a life partner, is more deeply satisfying than fly-by-night liaisons with many partners, because there is not enough time for the Deep Limbic System to form emotional bonds during a one night stand, and this lack of connection eventually wears on the Merchant, driving her to look for more and more experiences while gaining less and less satisfaction in the process.

The Pre-Frontal Cortex is the executive part of the brain. It supervises, directs and focuses our behavior. It is responsible for goal setting and follow-through, planning as well as completion of tasks. These are Warrior functions. The PFC is also responsible for critical thinking and judgment (*viveka*), vital skills for Warrior types (see Chapter 3). When it is working properly, it promotes thoughtfulness, learning from mistakes, and applying the lessons of the past to the present. When it is out of order it leads people to repeat mistakes, have poor attention, focus, and follow-through. ADD is a result of dysfunction in the prefrontal cortex. The PFC influences self-control and the ability to act in consistent, thoughtful ways. Like well-trained martial artists who know when to act and when to step back, it confers the ability to think through and understand the consequences of actions.

Interestingly, the PFC has many connections to the Limbic System, the 'Merchant' part of the brain, sending inhibitory messages to help keep emotions under control. In the next chapter we will see this expressed explicitly in the *Circle of Life* as the Warrior's Duty to patrol and govern the Merchant type. Form follows function, and the beauty of the social relationship between the archetypes is mirrored in their physiological interactions. Different parts of the brain interact like the Dharma Types. As a result, our martial artist is able to control his primal emotions and make the right decisions in a crisis. This in turn earns him the respect and leadership of his community, which is the Integrated Warrior's natural function.

Suggestions for drug and other treatments for PFC related problems, like impulsivity, ADD, and hyperactivity can be found in Dr. Amen's book. Generally, Warriors and the PFC do well on higher-protein diets, with more fruits and vegetables as carbohydrate sources, than grains and simple sugars. Other recommendations consist basically of the Warrior's Integration into the Educator type: using *praise rather than pressure*, and incorporating Educator values of coaching and positive reinforcement. The mark of an Integrated Warrior is relaxation and self-control, not hyperactivity and impulsivity. Educator techniques that promote relaxation, like guided meditation, are excellent. Disintegrated Warriors, like people

> *Fear cannot exist where awareness lives... taking responsibility for our actions focuses awareness into every area of our lives, and vowing not to repeat mistakes brings mindfulness and meditation to our activities.*

with ADD, tend to be in constant turmoil with people around them. They seek conflict and distraction as a form of self-stimulation. While searching out distraction is okay for Merchant types it is not for Warriors, whose hallmark is focus and intensity. When they Integrate, they naturally regain focus, good judgment, and control over their brain's limbic system.

The Cingulate Gyrus is the gears of the brain. When it is out of balance, people cannot *shift* into new modes of thinking, and become cognitively inflexible. They only eat certain foods, do things a particular way, and are unwilling to try anything new. They keep their space a certain way, make love a certain way, and become upset if things are changed on them. This is how Disintegrated Labor types function. They become stuck in an 'Animal Realm' (of Buddhist Psychology[27]) that makes them territorial, confrontational, and unable to relate to people using natural, healthy boundaries. They tend to suffer from obsessive-compulsive disorder, and other OCD-related problems such as body-dysmorphic and eating disorders, autism, compulsive behavior, chronic pain, gambling, excessive and senseless worrying and other addictions. These all stem from negative repetitive thoughts that they cannot *shift* in their brains. The answer lies in the Laborer's Integration into the Merchant type.

Merchants are constantly on the go, and *movement* is key for Labor types. Physical movement, such as exercise, as well as emotional and mental stimulation keeps Laborers from getting stuck in one mode of thinking. Distraction, the Merchant's forte, is essential in re-directing negative thinking.

In a difficult work environment, it helps to sing a song as you work to make the day go easier. Stories and tales also serve that function, and Labor types make excellent storytellers. Prayer and mantras also help to reprogram negative thought-patterns into positive states. Rosary beads, which could have been invented for Labor types, serve to keep their thoughts focused on resourceful vibrations. And

---

[27] To learn more about Buddhist psychology and the Six Realms, please refer to Lar Short's excellent book, *Opening the Heart of Compassion*. Co-authored with Martin Lowenthal, Charles E. Tuttle Company, Inc, 1993.

just as they serve the Merchant's Deep Limbic System, NLP and other state-change exercises, as well as 5-HTP and natural supplements that help optimize dopamine and serotonin levels may also be useful for Laborers.

The *Basal Ganglia* are associated with the body's anxiety levels, controlling both ecstasy and paranoia. These extremes typify the Outsider personality. Outsiders often feel the world is against them, and read the worst into otherwise neutral situations. George W. Bush, an Outsider type playing a Merchant, spearheaded a campaign called *The War on Terror*, which is ironic since fighting fear with fear only builds fear, and makes it impossible to sever its vicious cycle. This politics of paranoia is a hallmark of the Disintegrated Outsider. Integrated Outsiders, however, can also soar to the heights of ecstasy. We have already mentioned Martin Luther King Jr. and his revolution of values, and the ability of the Outsider to refresh society. It all depends upon one's personal evolution, which is grounded in the three-pronged approach of Responsibility, Ruth, and Respect. Outsiders earn Respect when they have been honest with themselves and the people around them, and expressed Ruth for their past misdeeds. This is also a healing strategy for the basal ganglia, as fear cannot exist where awareness lives. Taking responsibility for our actions focuses awareness into every area of our lives, and vowing not to repeat mistakes brings mindfulness and meditation to our activities.

Problems with the basal ganglia express in negative Outsider traits: irrational anxiety, nervousness or fear, panic attacks, tendency to think the worst, tremors, tics, low motivation, and even Tourett's syndrome. Outsiders are the most likely type to turn to drugs, particularly consciousness-altering substances, to deal with their reality. From marijuana and peyote, to LSD and ecstasy, Outsiders are the psycho-nauts of the Dharma Type family, their Space Element driving them to explore the inner and outer reaches of consciousness. Ultimately, however, they must find a balance between mundane and extraordinary reality, because as many Outsider spiritual traditions relate, *the truth is where you are, here and now.*[28] Escapism and drug taking eventually corrupt an Outsider's soul. Learning to be grounded in reality, while using natural, sustainable strategies for dealing with anxiety is an individual and lifelong journey for the Outsider. Other pharmaceutical suggestions for dealing with the Basal Ganglia can be found in Dr. Amen's book.

The *Temporal Lobes* are intimately involved with understanding and processing language, complex memories, and visual and auditory recognition. Language is what

---

[28] Outsider spiritual traditions include Tantrism and Taoism. For more information, refer to Volume III, *The Spiritual Types.*

sets humans apart from other animals. Reading, speech and understanding language are higher human functions that correspond to the Educator type. Educators rely on their memory power to recite complex information; this is strongly connected to the dominant (usually left) temporal lobe. Reading facial expressions and appreciating music are connected to the non-dominant (usually right) temporal lobe. Interpreting and giving meaning to information, conviction, great insight, and the sense of truth are also attributed to the temporal lobes.

Memory is responsible for learning. We cannot learn if we cannot remember. Memory also reminds us of who we were as a family, culture, or species. Educators are wisdom keepers who connect us to our ancient roots. They write books, do research and teach in order to keep alive the lore of our forefathers. When there are problems in this part of the brain, there can be memory impairment, as well as violent thoughts, anger, and susceptibility to slights. Educators often internally entertain strong base emotions, like lust, anger, and greed. Their ability to control these is what makes them great teachers and peacemakers: they understand the inner struggle and work hard to resolve it. When they fail to do so and act out, they may become so guilt-ridden as to even resort to suicide. Whatever the case, Educators are *always* sorry when they give in to anger, lust or greed, and usually suffer the consequences of such behavior quickly. As the moral exemplars of the Dharma Type family, their karma is instant when they fail to live up to the high standard of their type.

The temporal lobes are also active during spiritual experiences, and Educators serve as mediators of the spirit for the masses. They are the priests and philosophers of the Dharma Type family. Head injuries to this area of the brain can sometimes spontaneously produce such experiences, or do quite the opposite: make it impossible for an Educator to handle her temper and rage. Natural substances which help the brain, like *gotu kola, brahmi,* and *saraswati,* are useful for Educators.

Body Type

While body types vary by genetics, race, and geography, and there is no distinctive mark that sets one Dharma Type from another, there are general characteristics inherent to different physiques that give us a clue to their Dharma Type.

Educator

Though they can be tall and burly, Educators are not usually blessed with imposing physiques and powerful personalities, because those things are reserved for athletes and salesmen, and do not endear them to the masses. In describing Jesus, Gary Wills writes,

> *"Hurt people are not drawn to the aggressively healthy, to the televangelist's plumy voice, the fire-hose gush of bonhomie"*[29]

This is true of Educators. A sensitive, truth-seeking nature essentially breeds a sensitive physical nature, as the spiritual person shies away from violent displays of strength and domination. Accordingly, as he gets older his physiology shrinks from the lack of attention, just as his psychology commensurately grows. Stephen Hawking provides a striking example of someone who has had to surrender the function of his body, even while cultivating the function of the mind.

Though Educators are archetypally gentle, there is a contingency among the Priestly class that is also large, forceful, and even imposing (at least at first glance), with a robust body and a demeanor to match. After all, Educators integrate into Warriors, and it makes sense that they should develop those traits natural to the Warrior personality— force of will and power. These types carry a certain authority and swagger that serves them on the pulpit as well as in the classroom. They are strong, articulate, and outgoing, though ultimately fraught with contradictions, as their strength is more like the Hindenberg balloon— impressive at a glance, but structurally vulnerable to calamity, disease, and physical degeneration.

> *Educators should not rely on their strength of arms to get them through life, but on their strength of wisdom.*

Why is this?

In the material world, you cannot have it all. This is particularly true of Educators, who have to Surrender some portion of their life in order to fully Integrate. Some give up sex, some money, and still others give up fame and power. Whatever their sacrifice, Educators are the most willing to surrender to life's demands. *Do not lay up for yourselves treasures on earth, but lay up for yourselves treasures in Heaven.* These exhortations from the Beatitudes are Educator sentiments.

From *What Jesus Meant* by Gary Wills. Penguin Books, 2006

Embodied life is about giving one thing up for another. This is celebrated in spiritual institutions like marriage, where one gives up lust for the many for the love of one, and in traditions like fasting, where we abstain from food in order to feast on good health and spiritual blessings. Material life is a constant trade-off: one can never have every desire fulfilled, and we must learn to make do with what we have, to Surrender to What Is. One of the ways Educators learn this is through their bodies. Experiencing the limitations of physicality, through debilitation, pain, and suffering, breeds in them compassion and the desire to help other beings.

It is the Educator's job to mentor and minister to the general welfare of his society. A solitary scientist may labor away in his laboratory with the burning desire to cure cancer because he has witnessed its ravages firsthand. A foreign aid worker may pledge herself tirelessly to end hunger, because she has herself hungered, and witnessed people die for want of food. An astronomer may plunge himself into the lake of stars to bring back pearls that inspire humanity with knowledge and wonder, because he too wonders and wants to know. Whatever his Profession, the Educator has an obligation to every type, for the scientist has an obligation to science as well as society; the Priest belongs to his people as much as to God, with one foot in the world, and one foot beyond it.

Therefore it is finally too distracting to care for his own health and appearance, whereby the Labor and Outsider types are called in to support him in their daily Duty (see the Circle of Life in the next chapter). It is his sincerity, not his good looks that make him attractive. It is the light of truth burning in his eyes that shines forth and calls people to his side, not the ripple of his muscles or the glimmer of his jewels. In short, that which is neglected fades away—and the Educator's body fades with time, just as his *presence* and *authority* grow, for that which is fed by attention becomes powerful. Einstein was great for his ideas, not his stature, nor was he disliked, but beloved of all, for being physically unassuming.

Educators are more fragile and less dynamic than the other types, except when in the full train of their dharma, as when teaching, researching, or preaching, where they take on a magnitude greater than their everyday demeanor. Like Moses in the face of Pharaoh, Educators are irresistible when they have tapped into the full force of their dharma.

Yet it is often true that you can't have brains *and* brawn. Though they would like both, on average life makes Educators Surrender and choose brains, while for their part Warriors elect brawn, as these best represent their individual dharmas. But that does not mean that Educators should give up on physical cultivation— *only attachment to the results thereof.* Educators must release any attachment to strength and force, because violence does not become them. They should not rely on their strength of arms to get them through life, but on their strength of wisdom.

One of the lessons for practitioners of Jyotisha (Vedic Astrology) is learning to live with the effects of Saturn. In a horoscope, the planet Saturn denotes those things that are difficult to change, what we in the West naively call 'karma.' Taking Saturn's lessons and transforming undesirable karma is one of the most difficult things for anyone to do because Saturn teaches us what we are not keen to learn: humility and obeisance. These qualities are present in Labor types, as Saturn is a Labor planet. However, Saturn also teaches Surrender, a quality especially important to Educators.

Warrior

Where the Educator's body is vulnerable, the Warrior's physique is made for the rough and tumble. It is resilient, self-healing, and able to withstand shocks and stresses that the Warrior personality imposes on it. After all, it is the Warrior's primary tool in the service of his mission. It is the vehicle of his Purpose, and with judgment and wisdom, he uses it to protect others from harm, while putting himself in the way of harm.

Where the Educator's eyes shine with Truth and Compassion, the Warrior's blaze with stored power—the force of will to burn through anything to achieve his ends. The lesson Warriors learn from physicality is not *Surrender*, but *Sacrifice*. Warriors learn to push through hardships and pain to achieve their goals. Accordingly, physicality presents a challenge to them, not a limitation. Their strength of character gives them the drive to break through physical barriers and triumph where others fail. As a result, they are not interested in *empathizing* with others, but in *energizing* them!

Educators inspire the soul, Warriors the body. Educators empathize, Warriors galvanize.

Warriors offer themselves as examples of what *can* be done. They charge people with energy and inspiration. Educators inspire the soul, Warriors the body. Educators empathize, Warriors galvanize. Both have their place, and neither approach works for all situations. That is why the Dharma Types complement rather than compete with each other: they all have different gifts to share with the world. Where the Educator is understanding, the Warrior is demanding. One says *'Let it be'* the other, *'Let me see...'*

Warriors have a palpable presence that makes them seem larger than life, regardless of their physical stature. There is a readiness for action that makes others take notice and tread lightly in their presence. They menace, not only physically—for violence can also take the form of words and ideas—but intellectually as well. Anyone confronting them may as well be ready to battle— in Justice Court or the tennis court— for in either arena they come to win.

That is not to say that Warriors are always about competition, for they can have gentle demeanors when Integrated. Even so, the stored potential for violence that marks Warrior personalities is always present, no matter how peaceful they may appear. This usually reflects in them as an athletic or capable physique, though they are not always 'fit.' Their ability to generate and express energy, be it kinetic, psychic, or spiritual, is second to none, and what sets Warriors apart from the other types. This affinity for expressing *chi*, or *prana* is discussed in a later section, when we return to look in greater detail at the Yogic system of 5 Bodies.

Laborer

If Warriors have an affinity with the Vital (prana) Body, the Labor type is associated with the physical, or Flesh Body. The Labor body is built for work. It may be short and stocky or long and lean, depending on genetics, racial heritage, and other factors, but its pervasive quality is a well-knit toughness that gives it ample strength and good stamina for long bouts of physical work. Because of their proclivity to family and community, Labor type women may have wider hips or a stronger reproductive system for giving birth, and Labor men have bones that are generally stronger and bigger as required to provide for a big family. Consistent with the Earth Element, Laborers are hard-headed and thick-skinned. Whether these metaphoric descriptives have an actual physical correlation is a matter for medical research, but they nevertheless describe the swarthy toughness of the Laborer body.

That does not mean that Labor types do not get sick. Laborers endure pain and suffering like anyone else, but this is usually because they overwork, and do not invest enough attention into self-care. Because they are hardy, Laborers ignore their own needs, and later suffer the effects of bad diet, stress, and poor habits. Ideally, they must pair up with a Merchant partner who can teach them the value of working smarter, not harder, or another Laborer as a spouse, who will at least nurture and take care of their needs when they come home. Laborers match up best with Merchant partners, just as Educators do with Warriors. Compatibility between the types is explored deeply in Volume II: *Sex, Love, and Dharma*.

Merchant

The Merchant's physique is the most malleable of all the types. Just as his emotions fluctuate from extremes of loneliness to conviviality, the Merchant's body can also be fit and athletic, or morbidly obese. There is a 'smoothness' to a Merchant's physique, however, that sets it apart. Muhammad Ali, even at his most fit, had a fluidity and looseness that separated him from his Warrior or Labor-type opponents. Merchant types are go-getters and self-made people. When physicality is their profession, they will care for their bodies like a business owner cares for his business. But when it is not, it has a low priority. Britney Spears, an Outsider playing a Merchant, may have done hundreds of sit-ups on her way to the top, but that fell away when it was no longer necessary to maintain her popularity.

A side note to Merchants and fitness is that, because they Disintegrate into Warriors, Merchants do not have a natural sense for discipline and training. They follow routines and diets that are less-than-scientific, and often dangerous. Popular books and trendy magazines are more inspiring to Merchants than real training expertise. As a result, they may do thousands of crunches per day, where a few well-executed Dragon Flags would work wonders.[30] They may fast on celery and soup, where a nutrition program based on their body type would serve them better. Or, they may resort to plastic surgery, where proper diet and exercise are more natural and less expensive. But of all the types, they are allowed to experiment with beauty and fashion, and benefit more than anyone else from nips and tucks and other enhancements, when done in moderation.

Outsider

Outsider bodies come in all shapes and sizes. Aside from obvious decorations like tattoos or extreme hairstyles, they do not have telltale characteristics that set them apart from others. It is precisely because of this that they sometimes seek to match their unique *internal* states with *external* decorations, such as piercings, garish outfits, or other unusual apparel. But most Outsiders just blend in nicely with everyone else, particularly the types they are emulating. Boris Becker and Sly Stallone look like typical Warriors, but they are Outsiders. Farrah Fawcett and Halle Berry appear mignon Merchant types, though they are both Outsiders. Joseph Campbell and Steven Spielberg may look like Educators, but they are Outsiders. When their integration is smooth, there are no problems, but when their ability to emulate

---

[30] Popularized by Bruce Lee, and more recently by Pavel Tsatsouline, Dragon Flags are one of the most difficult but effective abdominal exercises. More information on hard-core ab training and fitness is available from his website, www.dragondoor.com.

others is disturbed, there can be considerable fallout, as in the case of Britney Spears when she sought to regain her Outsider identity and went to great lengths to show the world more than her manufactured Merchant pop persona, even to the point of cutting off all her hair.

As a counter-culture statement, Outsiders may also adopt uniforms to mock the uniformed conformity of others. Ironically, these can create structures subject to the same conformity as the other classes: a nun and a Goth, or a soldier and a Hell's Angel, share the same attachment to their uniforms; Integrated Outsiders seek freedom from all labels while learning to abide and live within them, which is true independence.

> *Pushups are metaphorically related to pushing things away— like the dessert plate—a skill Kaphas do especially well to cultivate!*

Diet, Exercise, and Fitness

Exercise

In matters of health and exercise, Dharma Type philosophy defers to its sister sciences Ayurveda and Yoga: the first for diet and lifestyle and the second for specific exercise recommendations. While yoga is considered the perfect form of exercise in the Vedic tradition, it must be practiced along with a deep knowledge of Ayurveda and your individual *dosha*, or mind/body constitution. To determine which *dosha* is predominant in you, *Vata*, *Pitta*, or *Kapha*, you can fill out a free Mind/body type evaluation or simply visit a qualified Ayurvedic practitioner in your area.[31] Different yoga asanas (postures) and even different forms of yoga conform to each of the mind/body types and should be learned from a qualified professional. Western exercises can also be adapted to your constitution once you understand where the *dosha*s accumulate—their muscular seat. Each *dosha* has a muscular region where it collects and needs to be discharged if the body is to function optimally. Vata collects most in the largest muscles—the legs and buttocks. Vatas are *ectomorphs,* thin and small-boned people. They are characterized by constant movement and coldness in their extremities. Vatas find it difficult to sit still, especially when imbalanced, and therefore need to ground themselves to the earth. Massage, especially of the thighs and buttocks, is helpful for *Vata* types, as are squats. Properly-executed squats work

---

[31] To find out more about Ayurveda, or to consult with an AyurYoga professional, visit the Ayurvedic Institute at www.ayurveda.com. For tons of excellent information on diet, fitness, and holistic living, visit Dr. John Douillard's clinic at www.lifespa.com

wonders for *Vatas* by promoting blood-flow to the legs and massaging the colon and organs of the inner abdomen.

Legs are the roots of the body tree. They extend down to connect us with the earth below. By squatting in slow, deliberate, and weighted repetitions, Vata individuals connect to the heaviness of their bodies and the density of the earth while building strength and size in their legs, the part of their bodies most prone to Vata accumulation. This accumulation can take shape in any number of ways. Vata is dry and cold, and these qualities promote muscle loss and adhesions in the fibers. Adhesions are deleterious 'knots' in muscle tissue that reduce strength, impede muscle function, and cause pain by tying up microscopic muscle fibers into ineffective traffic jams. These jams are best relieved by warm massage, self-myofascial release, and proper exercise, the most important of which is squatting. It is important to build from no weight up to heavy weight when doing squats, while avoiding excessive joint loading and strain. The advice of a well-qualified personal trainer is necessary before embarking on any training program.[32]

The exercise best-suited to Kapha types is the chest press, whose most common form is the simple push-up. Push-ups train chest and abdomen, two areas where Kapha accumulates most. Kaphas are *endomorphs*, big-boned, heavy and naturally muscular. They are the most prone to fat accumulation, especially in the Kapha areas of the chest and stomach. Therefore vigorous exercise and push-ups help to bring blood flow to these areas and stimulate the Kapha type into action. Metaphorically, the pressing motion is also related to pushing things away— like the dessert plate— a skill Kaphas do especially well to cultivate! Kaphas benefit from learning to exercise restraint and say 'No!' to themselves and others, who sometimes abuse the Kapha's easygoing nature.

Finally, Pittas benefit from a complex exercise called the 'Snatch." This is a one or two-handed version of an Olympic lift characterized by explosiveness, control, and total-body integration. It requires the coordination of practically every muscle in the body working together as a team. Teamwork is something solitary Pittas particularly benefit from learning. The one-handed kettlebell or dumbbell snatch entails lifting a weight from below one's knees to above one's head in a single fluid acceleration. This exercise targets the muscles where Pitta accumulates most: the back, neck, and trapezius— muscles Pittas also do well to have released. Also, by opening up the body (hip extension) Pittas practice opening their chest and their hearts to the world. This is just the opposite of what push-ups do for Kaphas, which encourage slightly *closing*

---

[32] Qualified personal trainers can be found through the National Academy of Sports Medicine, the American College of Sports Medicine, and other quality sports certifying bodies.

up and pushing away the world to establish proper boundaries. Pittas already have well-established boundaries and need to learn to relate more with other types.

The properly performed one-handed dumbbell (or better yet, kettlebell) snatch is a complex skill suitable for Pitta types who like the challenge of mastering difficult tasks. It keeps their sharp and busy minds yoked to the drill's proper execution while pumping enormous amounts of blood throughout the body. Proper circulation is vital for *mesomorph* Pittas, whose blood tends to stagnate and become 'dirty,' slowing down liver function and contributing to the infamous Pitta temper. [33]

Fitness

Fitness is optimum vitality allowing for a full experience of life with health and longevity. Fitness is achieved through movement. Every Dharma Type prefers a specific kind of movement, which is intimately reflected by the 5 Yoga Bodies. Recall from the *Anatomy* section earlier in this chapter that there are five subtle Bodies, or Sheaths, that relate to each Dharma Type, as illustrated below.

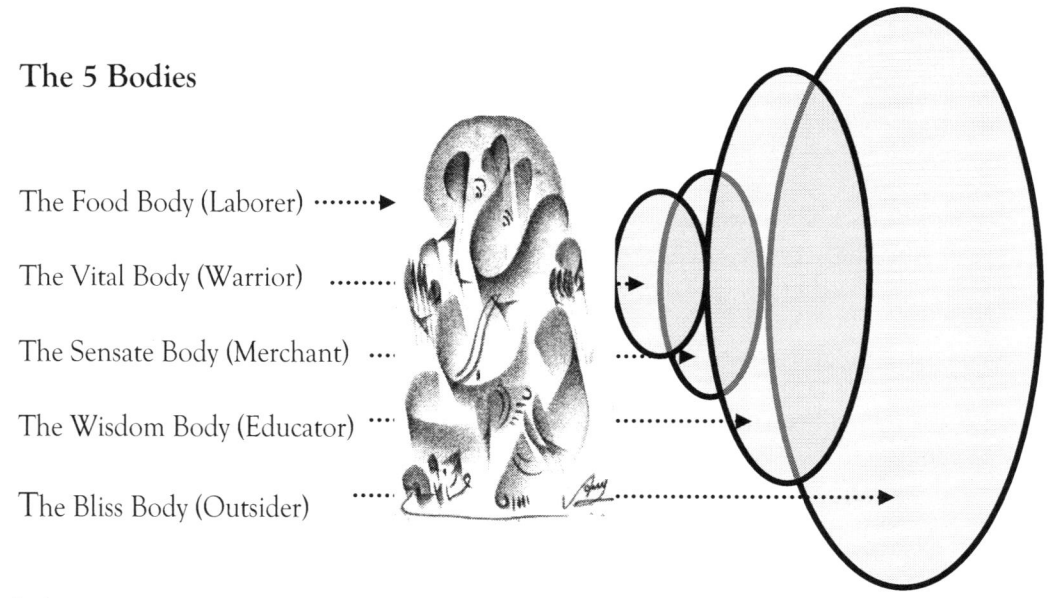

The 5 Bodies

The Food Body (Laborer)

The Vital Body (Warrior)

The Sensate Body (Merchant)

The Wisdom Body (Educator)

The Bliss Body (Outsider)

Laborer

Being tied to the Earth Element and the Food Sheath, the Labor type thrives on physical movement. His muscles and bones must flex and move if he is to feel

---

[33] More information and videos demonstrating the proper execution of the one-handed snatch are available at www.dragondoor.com

healthy and happy. Movement for the Laborer can take many forms, though it should serve some practical purpose and help support the Labor type financially if he is to adhere to it. **Exercise for its own sake is low on the Laborer's list of priorities, unless it serves a functional purpose.** Because the Labor type is fed and nourished by the physical body, he must also feed and nourish it in turn, with good food, massage, stretching and self-myofacial release, as well as relaxation using warm heat, like saunas or hot tubs, which work wonders to revitalize a sore and aching Laborer body.

The Laborer's gift is that he can access subtler realms of existence directly through his body. Spirituality, psychology, morality are all experienced by the Laborer in this way. This is also true of other types, but nowhere as intensely as for the Laborer. A thing has to be *here,* and *now* for it to be real, and nothing makes one present to immediate feedback like one's own body. A Laborer has to feel something in her gut to really get it. Consider that *half* of the body's nerve cells are located in the gut, and that the enteric nervous system (the gut) and the brain originate from one clump of tissue during embryogenesis. The brain and the gut are the two thinking centers in the body, and Laborers are expert at using the gut's Intelligence, as we shall see when we analyze Intelligence in Chapter 10.

> *Competition is the test and temper of energy-mastery. It demonstrates the degree of control and skill a Warrior has over herself.*

Warrior

To keep fit, the Warrior requires movement of breath and energy. From *chi* to electricity, energy is the intelligent movement of intention through the body. Electricity carries messages from the brain to the muscles to make them work. If harnessed sufficiently, it can cause them to contract with such power as to snap the bones that support them! Such is the potential strength in every human being. However, most of us can't access that strength, as the body has built-in fail-safes to keep energy in check. It is the Warrior's dharma to challenge these fail-safes, to develop and ride the body's natural energy systems in the service of his Just Cause. This is accomplished by practice and study, what in Yoga is called *abhyasa* and *vairagya*. In Sanskrit, *yoga* is the meaningful linking of two elements, such as the hand and the eye, foot and ball, or matter and spirit. Another Sanskrit term for this is *yukti*: skill. It takes great skill to achieve mastery. Thus, yoga is said to be skillfulness in action.[34]

---

[34]*Yogah karmasu kaushalam* Bhagavad Gita, II:50

When a person wants to accomplish any skill task, the brain directs the muscles to fire sequentially and intelligently to achieve it. In yogic terms, *prana* is the carrier of intention and energy. Warriors are best-suited to harness and direct their *prana* for a specific purpose. That is why in a boxing ring or in a courtroom, even a disadvantaged Warrior can take out a better-equipped Educator or Merchant, for he has the ability to channel his energy directly onto an opponent's weakness and destroy him.

Thus, goal-oriented activity like sports, law, or debate is preferred by Warriors, as it stimulates their need to compete and exercise the energy body. Competition is the test and temper of energy-mastery, as it demonstrates the degree of control and skill a Warrior has over herself. To keep fit, Warriors must also exert their lungs, to exchange oxygen and refresh their systems. Warriors need to run, play, or perform yogic exercises called *pranayama* in order to keep their Breath Body functioning. Experienced yogis and Chi Gung practitioners are famous for demonstrating the capabilities of the Energy Body through unbelievable exploits.

Merchant

> *"I can resist anything—except temptation."*
> -Oscar Wilde

Just as it is more difficult to control one's energy than it is one's body, it is even harder to master the mind and its senses. This is a task set to Merchant types. Earlier we said that Merchants are masters of indulgence—drinking, gambling, sex, and spending. However, Merchants have a natural sense of what is acceptable indulgence and what oversteps their ability to recover. Warriors, by contrast, because of overconfidence or pride, put themselves into unwarranted risk in these areas, which is why Warriors are traditionally prohibited from preoccupying themselves with Drinking, Gambling, Dissipation, and Wealth. Notice here that they are not prohibited from *engaging* in sex or making money, but from *undue preoccupation* with the same, for these activities lead away from the Just Cause of their lives into dissolution. It is supremely difficult to master addictions to gambling, sex, and alcohol, especially for Warriors. This, in effect, is their Achilles heel. Famous examples of virtuous Warriors or Educators who have succumbed to pride and lost themselves through intemperance abound in the world's sacred scriptures. *Yuddhishtira* is a hero famous for losing his kingdom, brothers, wife, and even his self in a game of dice in the Vedic epic, *The Mahabharata*.

That is why Merchant activities like gambling and drinking should be left to Merchants, who can enjoy sense stimulation without letting it overwhelm their personalities. Merchants require movement of the senses and emotions. They *need* to be stimulated and inspired by something. This is what leads them to try new foods, music, and other enjoyments. They become connoisseurs of culture, media, and entertainment.

What does this have to do with fitness, you say? Nothing. That's the point—Merchants need to be coaxed out of their normal routines of sense-gratification and taught to experience the sense enjoyment of a fit and healthy body. Looking good is one motivator. In fact, Merchants are largely responsible for the fads and standards in fitness and fashion. If a six pack stomach is what's in, that's enough motivation for the Merchant to get started. But because they are not primarily creatures of the Earth (physical) or Fire (energetic) Elements, exercise does not have for them the natural hold that it does for Labor and Warrior types. As a result, they need constant support and encouragement in order to keep on track, such as one gets from fitness coaches, dietitians, or other self-help gurus.

Lacking these, Merchants may turn to doctors and plastic surgeons to 'fix' them without having to expend the effort. The truth is, Merchants are so busy with other things, that exercise, diet, and wellness are just not at the top of their agenda... unless of course their careers require it, as in, say, movie stars, models, or athletes. Eventually, however, Merchants do come to a point of balance with themselves, and learn to maintain health without any help from the outside. But that process can take a long time, which is why until then they need the positive reinforcement of a health and wellness professional by their side.

Merchants work as hard as any type. They can perform physical labor and become great athletes if this leads to fortune and glory. As long as their first priority is met, which is financial security, Merchants are willing to dedicate themselves to any pursuit. Some of our greatest sports heroes are Merchant types who decided to earn money with their bodies. The difference between Merchant and Warrior athletes is that the former are more flashy, and have a greater flair for self-promotion. Their gift for gab and ability to handle the media makes their personalities bigger than the stage they play on, and often leads to fame and notoriety.

Fitness for Merchants must be associated with pleasure. It must be interesting, sensually stimulating, and fun if it is to grab their attention. Walking on a treadmill is boring; walking on the beach in Hawaii is much better. Doing endless pushups on the dirty gym floor is loathsome; doing pushups on top of your lover is exciting. Merchants and their trainers need to change up their routines and find stimulation in everything they do in order to accommodate their short attention spans. Ultimately, a Merchant sticks to a wellness program when she sees the real VALUE in it. Her motivation may be hope for gain or fear of loss— that is, she may be scared straight by her doctor, or have to learn the financial setbacks of illness in order to understand that health is a commodity at least as precious as anything else in her life. Then she can give it due attention without feeling that she is wasting her time.

Educator

Movement of Ideas is the primary 'exercise' of the Priestly class. Playing chess and solving puzzles, as well as solving real problems with their minds constitutes mental fitness for Educators. Walking, hiking, and light activity is also good, but only insofar as it stimulates mental health.

Their bodies are not made to withstand the rigors of heavy exercise, and will break down if overworked. Instead, their minds are capable of intense activity analogous to the efforts that Laborers or Warriors put forth with their bodies. Notwithstanding this caution against excessive strain, Educators must have adequate movement of their physical, energetic, and emotional systems if they are to really stimulate the intellect and be considered well-integrated persons.

According to the Yogic classification of human constitution, each Body depends on the one beneath it for optimal well-being. Thus, while the Laborer is mainly concerned with his physical being, the Warrior must train his *physical* body and *energy* systems to be optimally functional. The Merchant, in turn, must have adequate *physical*, *energetic*, and *emotional* movement in order to enable optimal fitness. He must have physical activity (work) along with proper intent and goal-orientation (energy body), and leisure entertainment in order to obtain satisfaction in his life. Remember, there is no e-motion without motion.

The Educator needs to have *physical, energetic, emotional*, and *intellectual* development to ensure his happiness. That is why Educators are often called the Renaissance men and women of the Dharma Types, because they must master, or at least become conversant with, the ways of the Labor, Merchant, and Warrior types to be useful Educators. Teachers must know their students to be good teachers. This means that they must become students for a large part of their lives if they are to learn the ways and attitudes of the world. It is only by learning from others and understanding the Physical, Energetic, Sensate, and Wisdom bodies that Educators become truly useful. When they fail to do so, they may become ineffectual, distracted, or lazy.

A balance of light activity, skill-development, emotional variety, and intellectual stimulation is necessary in order for the Educator to experience proper fitness. This is why Educators are often perceived as 'finicky,' for they have special needs that must be met for them to function optimally. Remember that Fitness is *optimum vitality allowing for a full experience of life with health and longevity.* The Educator's fitness is predicated upon movement of ideas, and ideas only move when they have well-developed Physical, Energetic, and Emotional pathways to travel upon.

Outsider

If mastering four bodies makes the Educator well-rounded, what are we to say of Outsider types, whose ownership of the *Bliss* body is contingent on mastery of *five* sheaths? They would be the real 'Renaissance Men and Women' if they subscribed to social systems that make such distinctions. But Outsiders are usually happier without restrictive labels. They value freedom above everything else—the freedom to think, say, and do what they feel. The founders of the Americas were Outsiders (though in practice the United States is a Merchant country).

The *ananda maya kosha* (Bliss Body) is the least defined and most tenuous of the five sheaths. We can feel the Flesh, the Breath, and our Emotions, and even measure our Intelligence—but there is no measure to the Bliss Body. This is the most conceptual of the five sheaths, and consequently it is up to the Outsider to define her own fitness strategy according to her experience. In doing so, she must follow the guidelines and avoid the pitfalls for her type as described in Part One. Outsiders must be allowed to roam and explore the world with their Food, Vital, Sensate, and Wisdom Bodies in order to obtain the *ananda,* or bliss and freedom promised by their own.

> *Warriors prefer to feel pain than to feel sub-par*

Practically, fitness for Outsiders consists of exercises they piece together from their explorations. They are more or less successful based on how well they understand the other 4 bodies and their requirements. Outsiders are true experimenters, and are often themselves the vessel for the experiment. Like the alchemists of yore, they combine and recombine, add and subtract different elements from different disciplines to come up with something that fits their life—something that ends up being a totally new creation in the world. From Tae-Bo to Botox, Outsider inventions are different, weird, and when they work, sometimes revolutionary!

Diet and Health

There are no specific diets related to the Dharma Types since nourishment from food is limited mostly to the Food Body, and the Food Body is tied to one's ancestry, culture, and environment more than any other identity factor. Nonetheless, long bouts of work require carbohydrates, while short bouts of strength and intensity are anaerobic and need protein for large muscles. Thus, Laborers generally prefer carbohydrate-rich diets that are also good for the Cingulate Brain system (see *Brain*, above) while Warriors do well on a high-protein regimen to fuel their muscles and the Pre-frontal cortex. Educators do well on vegan, vegetarian, or other specialized diets, while Merchants and Outsiders can eat anything: Merchants because they love pleasure, and Outsiders because they love the unknown.

We can see the different effects of diet on the Food Body simply by looking at Olympic track athletes. Those who require intense, short-lived energy, such as the 100 to 400 meter sprinters, are always larger and more muscular than those who need sustained, longer-lasting energy, like marathoners. In the Middle Ages, feudal lords knew this well and used it to control the masses by feeding their laborers high-carbohydrate/low protein diets while reserving a high-protein meat diet for their armies and themselves. This went so far as outlawing hunting and punishing poachers with death, thus ensuring the compliance of their serotonin-drunk vassals, who suffered the perils of severely low-protein intake, like poor health, lack of motivation, and a short life-span.

Things may not be much different today. Though good food and protein are abundant, much of our fast food is high-carb, low-quality processed fare made to satisfy the palate but not the soul. It is stuff that lulls the population into a drone-like existence, ensuring little resistance to longer working days and less time for self-reflection. Self-reflection nurtures rebellion and is not a high priority in a Merchant-run society. It is a quality pertinent more to the 'thinking' duo of Educator and Warrior types, whereas Merchants and Laborers are the 'feeling' duo who rely more on experience than abstract concepts. As a result, these two camps suffer different types of stress, as illustrated on the next page.

Physically, Laborers suffer long-term, chronic disorders, typically as a result of failing to take care of themselves. Laborers prefer to care for others and leave themselves last, neglecting their good health while promoting that of others. They can be lazy in their diet and self-care regimens, and as a result suffer from nutritionally-related illnesses such as diabetes and heart disease, or work-related stresses like joint pain, arthritis, and exhaustion. Because the Labor type is hardy they will not see the effects of bad diet and health choices until later in life, which makes such afflictions more difficult to treat. Consequently, Laborers along with Merchants are most likely to take prescription drugs for illnesses that have been entrenched in the body for a long time.

DHARMA TYPE	RULED BY	DURATION	REALM	WEALTH AS GOAL	SPIRITUAL SKILL*
Laborer	Emotion	Long-term	Objects	Yes	Works (Service)
Merchant	Emotion	Short-term	Objects	Yes	Works (Charity)
Warrior	Intellect	Short-term	Ideas	No	Wisdom (Judgment)
Educator	Intellect	Long-term	Ideas	No	Wisdom (Knowledge)

* The spiritual skills, or Yogas, prescribed for each type in the Bhagavad Gita and other Vedic sources, are detailed in Volume III: The Spiritual Types.

** Note that the pairs who are most like each other, Laborer-Merchant, Educator-Warrior, also Integrate into one another. For this, among other reasons, these types are considered 'compatible.'

Warriors and Educators lean less heavily on drugs than do Merchants and Laborers, as drugs are inventions of the Merchant type. Warriors especially hate taking drugs like antibiotics and pain medications unless it is a life or death situation. There are three reasons for this. First, as a matter of competitive pride, they prefer to fight their symptoms on their own... and win. Second, their energy bodies are wired like a finely-tuned machine; introducing clumsy drugs can dull their senses and make them perform at less than 100%. As a result, Warriors prefer to feel pain than to feel sub-par. Finally, drugs are an invention of the Merchant, who represents the Disintegration point of the Warrior.

Essentially, drugs work well on the body, but have side-effects that Educators and Warriors are less willing to accept. Laborers are more ready to deal with side effects if their medications are effective. While they don't mind pain, they mind not being able to work, and will do anything to keep from being useless, which is hell for a

Labor type. Merchants for their part hate pain, and rely on pain killers, antidepressants, alcohol, and recreational drugs like marijuana to keep them emotionally level and relieve tensions.

Long-term prescription drugs	**Laborers**
Short-term prescription drugs	**Merchants**
Long-term alternative medicine	**Educator**
Short-term alternative medicine	**Warrior**

It is no sin to use drugs to treat disorders of the Kali Yuga, at least as an adjunct with lifestyle modifications. The ultimate goal is to attune to the natural rhythms of Nature and the body so that we do not have to use drugs to stave off disease. Ayurveda is the healing science that teaches how to do this most elegantly, to laypersons and health professionals alike.

Ultimately, the cure is present in the disease: we must remedy the ills of the Iron Age with the tools of the Iron Age. It is not wrong to employ science to understand Nature, so long as we place our understanding in the greater context of dharma and sacred history. *Use what you have* is the mantra of Kali Yuga. And *use it wisely* is its implicit corollary.

Maintaining Balance: Laborers

Laborers and Warriors possess the most vitality of the Dharma Types. Laborers in particular are less concerned with their physical bodies, being well-knit and built to withstand enormous workloads. Aside from the normal aches and pains of work, Laborers suffer little in the way of *physical* damage save for self-neglect. However, like Merchants, they can be emotionally vulnerable, though unlike Merchants their stress results from long-term worry rather than short-term anxiety. They worry about their sons and daughters, about their parents, and about the state of the world. Little concerned for *their own* health, they make it a point to involve themselves in the affairs of others because of their selfless sense of community.

Order of Physical Hardiness:	Laborer	Warrior	Merchant	Educator
Order of Mental Hardiness:	Educator	Warrior	Laborer	Merchant

Their antidote is simply to **love**. Worry is low-level fear, while love is the opposite of fear. To love and serve, and be a constant source of devotion for friends and relatives ensures that the Laborer will be taken care of by the world. When Laborers feel the need to react, correct, or otherwise involve themselves with the affairs of others as *critics* rather than *nurturers*, they get in trouble. Instead, they should let go and allow people to make their own mistakes, while still supporting and nurturing them. That does not mean they have to endorse an action they deem unfitting, but to love another *despite* their failings and ill choices. The Laborer's mantra in this case is: "***I hate what you do, but I still love You.***"

Laborers get health complications when they *complicate* their lives— by involving themselves in politics, intrigues, plots, and schemes that block their natural ability to love. *A simple life is simply marvelous.* Untangling from their need to change others is the miracle that heals Laborers. Miraculously, by doing nothing they accomplish everything. This is the principle of *"Not my will, Lord, but Thine be done!"* Laborers are healed when they open up their hearts and share their natural loving ability with the world.

Because of their physical and emotional endurance, Laborers make great parents. Their abundant patience, devotion, and love naturally make them family patriarchs and matriarchs, and earn them the respect of their community. Patience and endurance have a strong *physical* component, as anyone knows who has raised a child. Likewise, caring for a community takes a Herculean mental and physical effort that only Labor types are ready to give. Furthermore, because Laborers integrate into Merchants, there is a certain skill and craftiness they bring to bear to get things done. Mother Theresa was not above wheeling and dealing when it came to promoting her causes. As long as her cause is based on love, devotion, and nurturing others, the world supports the Laborer. When love is present, the Laborer is advantaged in all of her dealings with the world, and becomes a true force of Nature! Love in action is Service. While the Laborer will be the last to admit that he is 'loving,' his actions, not his words, express this sentiment, and service, or seva, is compassion in motion.

Service is Love in action

Maintaining Balance: Merchants

In contrast to the Laborer's susceptibility to long-term stress and chronic-illness, the Merchant type suffers from acute, short-term dis- ease. As a result, his highly-wound nervous system responds particularly well to stress management. Merchants, whose instincts drive them to self-medicate, often go about this haphazardly by shopping, relaxing at the spa, taking pills, or using recreational drugs. However, real health begins when they incorporate wisdom in their approach and learn lifestyle adaptations from health professionals, be they practitioners of Ayurveda or allopathic medicine.

There are a number of ways for Merchants to improve their lifestyles. First, they must eliminate multi-tasking as far as possible. While this is a lofty goal for the on-the-go Merchant personality, it will improve their productivity and ability to enjoy life by keeping them healthy and stress-free. One cannot truly enjoy something unless one gives it full attention: eating and watching television while talking on the phone does not translate into an enjoyable meal, movie, or conversation. By taking the time to focus on their activities, Merchants actually get more out of life than when they rush through things.

Besides, there is little you can accomplish when you're sick and strapped to a hospital bed. Because Merchants have obligations that require their energy and attention, they allow themselves little time to relax and de-stress. But this is exactly what they need. Even if they have to take the phone off the hook, every Merchant deserves a little break; the reward is increased mental focus, productivity, and immunity.

The second thing Merchants can do is to insure they are protected. Insurance is a Merchant invention, and Life, Home, and Auto insurance are a must for Merchant types who worry about their health, property, and possessions. The more things one owns, the greater one's commitment to securing their safety. If one has beautiful objects, the stress associated with owning them can detract from the pleasure they give. Such are the paradoxes of embodied life: more wealth requires more care, which creates stress and anxiety. Perhaps this is why Jesus lamented that, *"It is easier for a camel to pass through the eye of a needle, than for a rich man to enter into the kingdom of God."*[35] Of course, the Merchant can divest himself of unnecessary things in order

---

[35] George Lamsa's translation of the Aramaic *Peshitta* reads the word *gamla* as "rope," not "camel" though the meaning is the same.

Chapter 7: Five Paths to Wellness

to reduce stress, but he will always be drawn to the precious and beautiful in life, for one can never escape one's dharma.

Ultimately, the highest form of security is spiritual certainty. Our prophets tell us not to lay up treasures for ourselves on the earth, but to secure our treasures in Heaven, which is the highest form of Self-realization. In such a state one obtains fullness from within, and does not require sustenance from without. But to get there, baby steps can be taken, whereby Merchants can learn to be happy with less material things and more spiritual attainments. In fact, the savvy Merchant can make rapid gains to self-realization by understanding that the tradeoff value of material to spiritual things will always favor the spiritual.

Here's an example from the *Devi Mahatmyam*,[36] a Sanskrit text sacred to worshippers of the feminine divine. [My paraphrase]

> *Once, a Warrior king was overthrown and exiled to a forest, where he happened upon the ashram of a holy saint. There, he met a Merchant who was also homeless and alone, having been plundered of his possessions by his greedy family. Upon meeting the sage, the king and the Merchant were introduced to the story of the Divine Mother and Her mysterious power, and each assigned their own mystical practices to invoke her. After three years of successful tapas, or spiritual austerity, the king and Merchant finally received a boon from the Divine Mother. The King asked Her for restoration of his kingship, and a very long rule. The Merchant, instead, asked for wisdom. His business instinct made him choose the most valuable prize, for more valuable than money or power is that which cannot be obtained by human effort alone. They both got what they wanted.*

This is the point to the tale, that even power to reign over the earth is as nothing when compared to the wisdom of Heaven. In the end, the Merchant was enlightened, while the king remained trapped in the cycle of worldly suffering for ages to come. The most appropriate and rapid spiritual paths for every type are detailed in Volume III: *The Spiritual Types*. It suffices here to conclude that when Merchants understand the *value* of karmic merit, compassion, and spiritual attainment, they can apply their work ethic and ingenuity to receive it in record time. This in turn reduces their stress and leads to greater health, wealth, and happiness in this world and the next.

---

[36] Like the *Bhagavad Gita,* the *Devi Mahatmyam* is part of a larger work. Also called the *Chandi Path*, it forms the thirteenth chapter of the *Markandeya Puraana*.

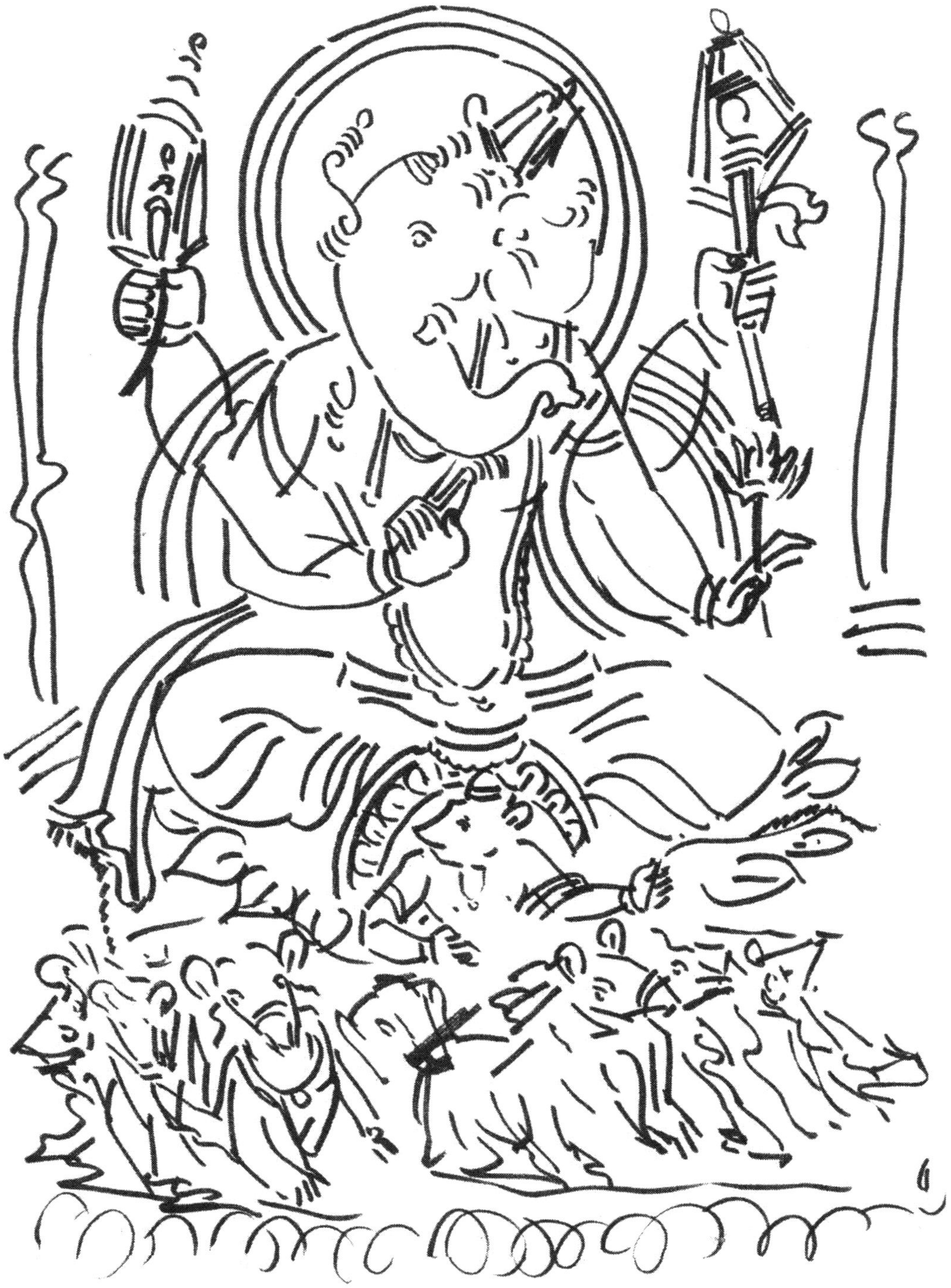

8
THE SOCIAL CONSCIENCE OF THE TYPES

Circle of Duty

The Circle of Duty, also called the Circle of Life, is the most important tool for understanding the social function of the Dharma Types. Every type has a **Duty** to another in the daily course of its existence. It is pictured below in a counter-clockwise direction. **Priority**, on the other hand, is given in times of emergency or desperate need to the adjacent type in the clockwise direction. For example, the Educator's Duty is to teach and form the Warrior class so they can better enforce the rules and principles of society. It is the Warrior's Duty in turn to attend to the Merchant, who needs the Warrior's enforcement of those rules for the well-oiled function of the economic machine. Merchants then give their Duty to Laborers and Outsiders, who share the same functions in the Circle of Life, and who are the primary consumers in society. These in turn care for the Educator, who pays only selective attention to really caring for himself.

Priority, on the other hand, flows in the opposite direction. In times of need or crisis, the Educator's Priority is to care for the Labor and Outsider classes. Embattled Outsiders and Laborers turn to the open-minded Educator to redress momentous problems such as issues with law, religion, or education. Because Educators are well-rounded and well-read they offer solutions the other types cannot. For example, immigrant workers entering the U.S. need Educators to translate, teach, and advocate for them to maintain their legal status. Once this is done, Educators and Labor types revert to their normal Duties. Thus, only in times of need or stress is one type given Priority— at other times Duty takes precedence, informing the everyday functions of the Dharma Types.

The Warrior's Priority is to the Educator, who may need the Warrior's protection in times of extreme stress. During war or conflict, it is the Warrior's obligation to protect the Educator, who represents the founding principles of society. This is the case of bodyguards 'taking a bullet' for a prime minister, or the principle of 'diplomatic immunity,' where diplomats are granted exemptions by law enforcement officials. These are **Priorities** given to Educators by Warriors. In his daily Duty, however, the Warrior is more concerned with keeping the Merchant in line and maintaining the smooth operation of civil life. Priority is always to a higher, usually more acute purpose; Duty is to a lower and more quotidian function.

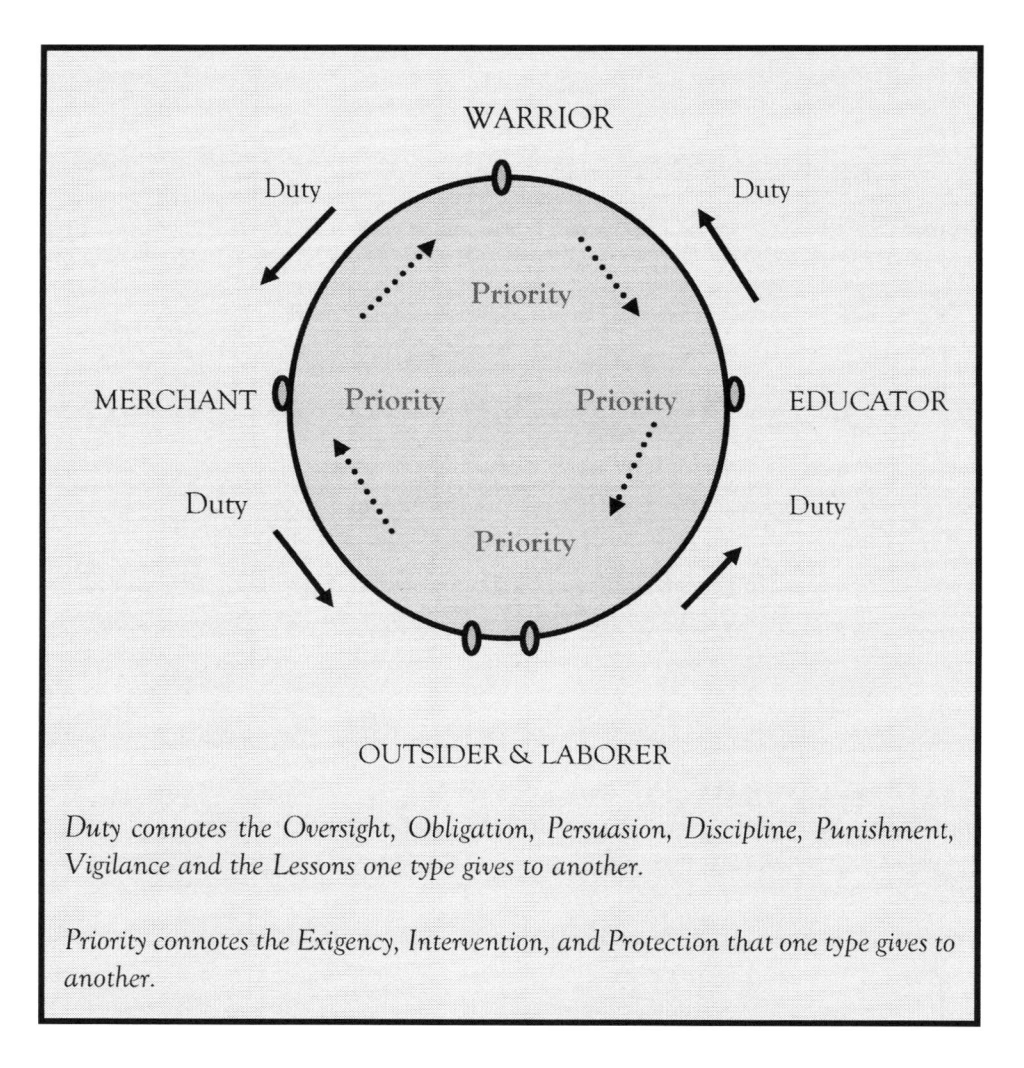

WARRIOR

MERCHANT — EDUCATOR

OUTSIDER & LABORER

Duty connotes the Oversight, Obligation, Persuasion, Discipline, Punishment, Vigilance and the Lessons one type gives to another.

Priority connotes the Exigency, Intervention, and Protection that one type gives to another.

The Merchant's Duty is to Laborers and Outsiders; to employ, pay, and shelter the biggest constituent of society. Laborers and Outsiders, being the most populous of the Dharma Types, present the largest consumer base. Therefore it is the Merchant's daily obligation to create opportunities for them and service their needs, while keeping an eye out for the Warrior class, who take Priority in times of need and crisis. Warriors may require shelter and resources in emergencies. To this day, as vestiges of feudal societies where Warriors ruled unilaterally, government retains basic rights over citizens and their land, especially in times of extreme need. Police Power and Eminent Domain—the right to seize and condemn property— are examples of such rights. Temporary confiscation of personal or real property is a dramatic illustration of the *Priority* given to the Warrior by Merchants. Warriors may need to take over a building in a hostage situation, or commandeer a vehicle in pursuit of criminals, and they can always find shelter with Merchants, who respect and fear them. In turn, Warriors give their lives as part of their Duty to protect the Merchant and other classes. This is the real meaning of the Warrior's 'line of Duty.'

Merchants will stop what they're doing to acknowledge a Warrior, though they know that their bread and butter is the Labor type. Like gazelles in the presence of a lion, Merchants react to Warriors as to a nearby predator. This is their natural sense of Priority, an instinctual reaction that may not be evident on the outside, but one that sharpens their inner senses and makes them ready to do what needs to be done in order to survive. This 'fight or flight' dynamic is hard-wired into the sympathetic nervous system, which is controlled by the hypothalamus in the brain. The hypothalamus is part of the Deep Limbic System, the part of the brain most closely associated with Merchant types. Thus, Merchants are most susceptible to these instincts, though the instincts are hard-wired in all of us. Anytime we feel stage fright, or butterflies in our stomachs, we are connecting to the Merchant part of ourselves. Some Merchants thrive off these feelings and gravitate to performance and entertainment and the emotional high that is the payoff for anxiety and fear. Interestingly enough, the parasympathetic nervous system, responsible for relaxation, is also governed by the hypothalamus; thus our bodies show the potential to display both calm and Integrated as well as stressed-out Disintegrated qualities of the Merchant type.

The Laborer's Priority is to the Merchant, who is his material benefactor, and more directly responsible for his well-being than any other type. Laborers instinctively feel it is more important to work and pay their bills than to finish their next homework assignment, except where education is directly useful for their advancement. The Merchant's *realities* hold more clout than the Educator's *concepts* for Laborers, whose concern is more practical education, like the trades, which Merchant types are better suited to give them. Grammar and philosophy are fine... but they don't pay the bills; Merchants teach Laborers how to make money and feed their families—the number one concern for Labor types. In return, they receive the Laborer's gratitude and Priority.

> *Who is there to teach the teachers? The Labor and Outsider classes demonstrate the real-world applications of the Educator's dreams and ideals*

Thus, every type has a Duty and Priority to its neighbors. What one does, all must do. What one receives, all receive: there is no question of high or low, of one type above another. Every type must swallow its pride and abide its neighbors in the daily course of its Duties. This does not mean, however, that it has to spend inordinate amounts of time with them: Warriors do not need to interact with Merchants in order to maintain the law and order that directly benefits them. Merchants do not need to be around the Laborers and Outsiders to whom they provide shelter, work, and inspiration. Educators do not need to look over the Warrior's shoulder to make sure that their precepts are followed. And for their part, Laborers and Outsiders are not required to attend to the Educator's every whim, but simply to provide him what he needs to survive.

Tithing is a practical example of a Duty that has been practiced for millennia in Judeo-Christian circles, in this case the Laborer's Duty to the Educator. Mosaic Law required farmers and land-workers to give one grain in ten, or one sheep in ten, to priests of the church who owned no such land, and raised no animals. What the Laborer has in abundance—nourishment, material goods—he must share with those who need it the most. In turn, Educators care for Laborers and Outsiders in their own way, giving them Priority in times of great need, while teaching the Warrior class in their daily Duty, who then share their natural gifts with Merchants, and so on down the line in a well-run society.

Another way to picture the Circle of Duty and Priority is to substitute Duty for what each type has to *teach* another, and Priority for how each type *protects* another. Thus, Educators *teach* Warriors the principles and ideals necessary for them to live dharmic lives. In turn, Warriors *teach* Merchants discipline and how to walk the straight and narrow with honor and respect. Merchants then *teach* Laborers and Outsiders how to prosper themselves, how to increase their work yield, and how to be happy. Finally, Laborers and Outsiders *teach* Educators the practical morality Educators need. Who is there to teach the teachers? It is the Labor and Outsider classes that demonstrate the real-world applications of the Educator's dreams and ideals.

Going in the reverse direction, Priority equates with *protection*. Warriors *protect* Educators from physical harm, while Educators *protect* Laborers and Outsiders

Relationships are the machine steered by the wheel of Duty and Priority

from forces beyond their control, such as legal, political, and social issues. Laborers and Outsiders then *protect* the Merchant class while Merchants in turn *protect* the Warrior, by providing shelter, resources, and exclusive access to them when necessary.

Discipline and Persuasion

The direction of Duty also gives us an idea of the best persuasion tactics to employ with each type, and indicates which types are best-fitted to discipline others. This can be invaluable to parents, sales professionals, corporations, and even governments. From dealing with employees to relating with your children, knowing how to guide and discipline others is key to getting the most out of your personal and professional relationships, for relationships are the machine steered by the wheel of Duty and Priority. Let's take a look at how it works.

Merchants respond to fear and intimidation, the strong hand of the Warrior. At his best, a Warrior does not need to say or do anything at all—his inner strength and *potential* for action are enough to keep even the rowdiest of Merchants in line. This is not cruel or harsh, for Merchants actually appreciate a firm hand; Merchant personalities have little respect for people they can just run over with the bluster of their words and the charm of their wit. They appreciate a strong guiding presence to keep them in line, just as children respect parents who are firm but loving, though they may whine and complain to test the limits of that firmness and love. When Warriors prove that they are strong, just, and equitable, like good parents they earn the Merchant type's respect and enjoy a profitable and mutually beneficial relationship.

However, if a Warrior succumbs to excessive force, anger, and other out of control behavior, he becomes unfit to guide the Merchant type, just as a parent who behaves this way is unfit to discipline her children. Anger and violence are actually *weaknesses* that demonstrate the Warrior's *lack* of self control. A Warrior not in control of herself cannot hope to control others. That is why she must herself be disciplined by the Educator type. Educators in their Duty are best at disciplining and persuading Warriors.

Just as Merchants respond to strength and seriousness, Warriors respond best to praise and encouragement. Educators can appear stern on the outside, but in the final analysis they are the mildest types. Warriors are already competitive by nature and do not need a mentor who gets down on them but one who lifts them up. The Educator in his natural Duty to the Warrior does this best, and appeals to the Warrior's gentle side. Thus, while an iron fist works wonders for Merchants, it is misplaced when dealing with Warriors. Taking away privileges, punishing, or otherwise berating a Warrior will only motivate him for a short while—and even then in a negative way. Instead, giving him a goal to accomplish or a prize to win is a better strategy.

For their part, Educators respond to persuasion and discipline by Labor and Outsider types. Educators have a soft spot for the ingenuousness of the Laborer and the mystery of the Outsider. Finally, Laborers and Outsiders are best disciplined by Merchants. Laborers instinctively respond to Merchant tactics of seduction, incentive, and the promise of pleasure. Merchants are also great at 'the takeaway;' refusing incentive rather than offering it. Here's an example:

"You couldn't have this even if you *did* your homework…"

"*Why?*"

"Because your teacher said you're falling behind in class…"

"I'll do it all and get an A, I promise… just let me have it!"

Merchants are masters of the takeaway, of temptation, and the promise of reward. They also steer the changing fashions in society. They dictate what's *in* and what's *out*, and their greatest consumers are Laborers and Outsiders. As a result, they get people to do what they want by associating themselves with what's *cool*, and making others *want* what they have. Thus, to get a Laborer or Outsider to toe the line, it is best to call in a Merchant type or to use Merchant tactics.

Priority

A type tends to be 'softer' to its point of Priority and harder on its point of Duty. Warriors will tend to go easy on Educators while being rough on Merchants. Educators will lend a kind ear to the Labor class while holding Warriors to more rigorous standards. Even though Educators are encouraging to Warriors, they also expect more of them. Not so with Labor and Outsider types, who have their Priority. You can sometimes see this dynamic in the way parents interact with their children. Labor children may be treated differently than their Warrior siblings, especially by an Educator parent. This does not mean that one is loved any more or less than another, but that the Educator

> *There is karmic merit to playing your role in the Circle of Life, and each type grows as a result of following its dharma. The Warrior, Laborer, Merchant, Outsider, and Educator learn things they could never learn otherwise, and mature emotionally, socially, and spiritually, into real human beings.*

parent's natural Priority is to the Labor child, though his committed Duty is to the Warrior. The bible also provides examples of this. While Jesus forgave others their debt, he held his own disciples to stricter standards and made them accountable for their actions: *Anyone who does not take up his cross and tread in my footsteps does not deserve me.* (Mat. 23) Such attitudes are typical of Educators in relation to Warriors because Warriors represent the Educator's point of Duty.

Labor and Outsider types, on the other hand, are not expected to undergo the same arduous training, and are given instant attention in times of need; Warriors, being groomed for the just fight, are subject to greater penance, and their training can take years of tutelage. In much the same way, Merchants treat Laborers and Outsiders with less delicacy than they display towards the Warrior type, just as Laborers tend to be more direct towards Educators, while being more ingratiating and 'softer' to the Merchant class. This bluntness and directness is perhaps why a type can persuade and even punish its point of Duty better than anyone else.

Priority is not always pleasant for the Educator, who Disintegrates into the Labor type, but it ultimately benefits him, as it does **every type who gives** Priority to its neighbor. There is karmic merit to playing your role in the Circle of Life, and each type grows tremendously as a result of following its dharma. The Warrior, Laborer, Merchant, Outsider, and Educator learn things they could never learn otherwise, and mature emotionally, socially, and spiritually into real human beings.

These examples of Persuasion and Priority are only some of the ways that the Circle of Duty can be used. Since Duty connotes the idea of 'vigilance' and 'obligation' it is useful in practical applications like conflict resolution. In an argument, a Merchant is better equipped to handle a Labor type than is an Educator. Likewise, Warriors prevail over Merchants better than do Outsiders. If a Labor type is being difficult, send in a Merchant to calm her down. If an

Educator is complaining, send in the Labor type to soothe him. This reflects the natural order of Duties.

However, in more intense situations that require emergency intervention, the opposite is true and Priority takes precedence. It takes a Hero to stop a rogue Educator from destroying the world. Comic books and movies are full of similar scenarios. The Educator gone wrong is only beaten by the courage of a Warrior engaged in his Priority. Likewise, the greed of the Merchant class is overcome by revolt from the working classes, whether by strikes or revolutions. Finally, Warriors gone berserk are best handled by the Merchant's cleverness. Where Educators and the other types are no match for rogue Warriors, Merchants know how to outwit and find their weak points. A historical example is found in the Roman Empire's destruction of its Germanic enemies, by burning the forests and fields that provided food and shelter for them. While inferior in hand-to-hand combat, the Merchant Roman culture nevertheless understood how to defeat its foes by attrition, deceit, and other tactics that avoided direct conflict.

There are numerous ways to use these principles, and sacred societies naturally practice the Circle of Life, though it may be called different things in different places. In India, for example, it is common to feed a *brahmana*, an itinerant Educator type. Educators often toil in anonymity for long stretches in their search for Truth. They may have little concern for mundane matters like where their food will come from or how they will dress themselves. Here, Laborers become especially important in helping Educators remain healthy by keeping them well cared-for and nourished. While other types may also lend a helping hand, such duties bubble forth naturally in Labor types, who have the love and stamina to nurture others. The devotion present in them finds an outlet in the hapless Educator, who needs the practical sense so pregnant in the Laborer, and often so barren in herself. In return, the Educator solves the problems Laborers cannot resolve themselves. Ultimately, it is a sacrilege to see people who work for Truth suffer for want, and a sacred society actively practices the Circle of Duty to promote the welfare of all its members.

Avatars: A story from the Circle of Life

All avatars (incarnations of God) are Outsiders. In Sanskrit, 'avatar' means *someone who crosses over* down to earth. But as Outsiders, avatars can play any role. Thus, Krishna behaved as a Merchant, Christ as an Educator, and Rama as a Warrior. The Buddha was born into a Warrior family, and functionally played the part of a Warrior. Upon obtaining enlightenment, he resolved that people were not ready to hear his message because of the difficulties inherent in achieving freedom from *samsara*, the cycle of suffering. However, even the Buddha could not ignore his physical karma, and the Circle of Duty that it follows. His first and last lessons were given to Merchant types.

Reportedly, as he was strolling one day through the forest, the marks of his enlightenment— the glory emanating from him— betrayed him to two Merchant travelers whose cart was trapped in a muddy road nearby. These Integrated Merchants immediately realized that something special was afoot, and took it upon themselves to discover what.

They sought him out, and understanding their Merchant dharma, offered him food and gifts in order to earn his blessing. As the story goes, the Buddha then gave them his first words of wisdom— not to ascetics and Warriors, as is commonly believed— but to the Merchants who fed him. 'Always feed a yogi,' he said, 'and you will have luck in commerce, and you will thrive and prosper.' This, of course, is the essence of the Merchant's path to merit. He also gave them a mantra to keep their travels trouble-free. Since then, Buddhism and Business have been bosom buddies, and the Buddha is considered 'lucky' by hopeful shopkeepers who rub his belly and keep his statue near at hand.

The Buddha understood his Duty to oversee the Merchant class. Over the course of his life, he gave extensive discourses and advice on practical matters such as proper business practices and fiscal management. Of course, moving in the other direction, he also attended to his Priority, gathering his yogi comrades and giving the first official sermon to these Educators, who sought him out for the more serious task of enlightenment. Thus, even though he was born a Warrior prince, and though his sermons were perceived by the brahmanical religion of his time as Outsider teachings, (Avatars always rock the boat) Buddhism to this day carries great appeal for Integrated Merchant types, who intuitively understand the idea of karmic merit, and practice compassion in action to accumulate it.

In Part I we saw how Disintegrated Merchants run away from karma. They try to avoid the 'bad deal' that is the negative consequence of their actions, be it overeating, overworking, or fornication. Disintegrated Merchants seek to buy their way out of trouble with gifts, flattery, even force. The Integrated Merchant, however, understands that there is no free lunch. Integrated Merchants are keenly aware of the laws of cause and effect and seek to tip the karmic scales in their favor through right action and compassionate livelihood, which comprise part of the Noble Eight-fold Path of the Buddhist tradition.

Ojas (splendour), *chi* (vital essence), and mystical powers accrue to the spiritual practitioner just as money, fame, and security accrue to the worldly seeker. It is simply a matter of penance and time. The worldly man obtains merit by rising early and working late, by treating others with compassion, and by sharing his wealth with the poor. The spiritual man does it by observing vows, performing rituals and mantras, and practicing charity. There is no secret to getting the things one desires from life: one must simply be willing to do what it takes. Well aware of this, the Integrated Merchant places a high price on everything that he creates out of his self-effort. As a result, he never trades anything unless it is for equal or greater value. A savvy Merchant will trade gifts and food for blessings, for gifts and food are easy to get, but real blessings are rare.[37]

Government

The roles of the Dharma Types in government flow from their natural abilities. Warriors and those in Warrior Life Cycles are best suited for executive, leadership positions. Educators and those in Educator periods serve as diplomats and legislators, writing laws and counseling leaders, while Merchants and those in Merchant periods are best suited to trade and commerce. Like their role in the body, where they assimilate and partition nutrients, Merchants are accorded the function of guiding the benevolent expansion of society through managing and overseeing its resources via food distribution, urban development, transportation, and utilities. In this function they work most closely with Labor Types, whose service as engineers, accountants, builders, laborers, and agrarians make manifest the Merchant's plans. Laborers balance a Merchant's visions of grandeur with real-life know-how. They are the *dollars and cents* reality behind the dream. The Laborer's practical ingenuity and specialization allow him to get the most out of limited resources, and to make everything work. Because he is the ultimate beneficiary of an industrialized society, the Laborer knows what is needed to hold it together, the glue that keeps cities working and functional.

---

[37] More spiritual stories illustrating the Dharma Types in action can be found in Volume III: *The Spiritual Types*.

Finally, Outsiders find their wanderlust and adaptive nature well-suited to foreign-relations, spy services, export/import, and other government positions that require secrecy, adaptability, and foreign contact. Outsiders forge a link to the outside that keeps society relevant and tests its usefulness on a global scale. Outsiders are also troubleshooters, useful for finding what doesn't work and offering solutions for how to fix it. The move towards renewable resources and environmental clean-up, as well as the awareness behind it, is spurred by Outsiders and people in Outsider periods. A case in point is Al Gore, a Labor type whose concern with the environment did not reach fever pitch until he entered into an Outsider phase, during which he won the Nobel Peace Prize for his work in bringing to the world's attention the dangers of global warming.

The Circle of Duty gives us another insight into the roles of the Dharma Types in Government. In its Duty each type is responsible for overseeing the actions of its fellow types: Educators oversee Warriors; Warriors keep check on Merchants, while Merchants oversee Laborers and Outsiders. Finally, Outsiders and Laborers are the mass moral compass that keeps Educators honest. These are not just concepts, but observations of Natural Law, which is constantly at work in the inner environment of our bodies as in the outer environments of our communities, extending even to the far reaches of the cosmos. We saw them in action in the brain as the Pre Frontal Cortex (Warrior) inhibiting the Deep Limbic System (Merchant) in its daily Duty to produce thoughtful, appropriate behavior. We shall see them again, in matters as disparate as relationships, myths, and the cycles of time.

Like good carpenters, Vedic seers used many tools to fashion their vision of the cosmos. There are many ways to approach the same issue and Vedic texts offer yet another way of looking at the natural roles afforded to each type in society. A case in point is government. Each of the four Vedas has an *upaveda*, or second science associated with it that directly correlates to government administration. For example, Ayurveda, the Science of Life, relates to the Rig Veda and the Educator type, whose aim is to teach people how to live with Nature, including daily health routines and moral values, which are foundations of a healthy society. The Yajur Veda has as its *upaveda* the science of Warfare and Martial Arts. These are Warrior virtues designed to protect society from foreign and domestic usurpers. Here is a list of the four Vedas and their *upavedas*:

VEDA	UPAVEDA	DHARMA TYPE AND MODERN CONNOTATIONS
Rig Veda	Ayurveda (Healing)	Educator. Wellness and lifestyle. The founding principles of healthy living and society.
Yajur Veda	Dhanurveda (Warfare)	Warrior. Protecting people from threats to life and livelihood.
Sama Veda	Gandharva Veda (Music and Arts)	Merchant. Inspiring, entertaining, and distracting people. Enhancing the pleasure of living through the 64 *kalaas*, including music, trades, arts, and crafts.
Atharva Veda	Artha Shastra, (Economics) Sthapatya Veda (Architecture)	Laborer. Securing people's moveable and immovable assets. Building structures and growing the wealth of society.

Government in the Iron Age

Warriors are best-fitted to leadership and rule, because like athletics, politics is largely a Warrior game. But with the corruption of rulers into warlords in the current Iron Age, the divine right of kings has been rejected for more humanistic systems such as democratic and socialist states. In the best of times, Warriors are supposed to lead society as philosopher-kings—divinely appointed incarnations of law and justice. But in the absence of such righteous lords and in the wake of the destructive history of petty Warrior tyrants, stewardships of government have been erected, the most current and successful of which is Democracy. However, rule by the masses has never been an optimal model of leadership, as few people have the requisite knowledge and experience to make educated decisions about their government. Most citizens are too busy taking care of themselves to worry about the details of running a country, especially in a Merchant society.

Consider that in the United States alone, *fifty million* adults are functionally illiterate— unable to read past a fourth grade level.[38] What kind of voting

---
[38] Source: *National Right to Read Foundation.* 42 million American adults cannot read at all; 50 million cannot read past fourth grade level. In addition, 20 percent of graduating high

> *"The opinion of 10,000 men is of no value if none of them know anything about the subject."*
> -Marcus Aurelius

decisions can one expect from such a population? Perhaps this is why it has been so easy for the savvy and the media-conscious to manipulate public opinion with sensationalism and sentimentality—emotion rather than reason—for as long as democracy has been around. Politicians readily tie ideas of *patriotism* and *moral superiority* to further their political agenda, and sway public opinion in their favor.

The principle of a ruler genuinely guided by Natural Law and the will of God also runs through the ancient world, from Israel to the Egyptian pharaohs, and from Plato to the emperors of China. Though the days of such highly-evolved leaders are gone, modern presidents and prime ministers still pretend to have *"God on our side,"* an idea that resonates in the collective unconscious of people.

In the Iron Age, divinely-appointed rulers are hard to find, and it is even more difficult to find a populace intelligent enough to elect qualified leaders. Instead, people are fooled into believing that wealth and charisma are adequate substitutes for Honor and Virtue, and we elect the leader with the widest grin or the deepest pockets, ignoring that they are ill-qualified to protect society and dharma. As a result, countries and governments are more prone to war, pestilence, and other incursions.

Even when first instituted, Democracy was a problematic solution, but the best that Educator minds could come up with in an age that lacked virtuous **Warrior** kings. In modern times, the architects of America's constitution attempted to avoid these problems by creating a Republic, a system that allowed educated representatives to make *their own* decisions, regardless of the prevailing will of their constituents. This in theory averted the sand trap of public opinion, though in practice modern politics tend to run along party lines, and are more representative of *capitalist forces, interest groups,* and *lobbies* than the free will of the people or their elected representatives. It seems to follow that, even in a democratic government, a few people tend to seize and control power while giving the masses a semblance of autonomy and freedom. The question is, are they qualified to create policy and rule, or are they better suited to stay out of government altogether.

---

school seniors are functionally illiterate at the time they graduate, and 70 percent of prisoners in state and federal systems can be classified as illiterate.

Electing Merchants to leadership posts, for example, promotes a Merchant system of government that does not suit the best expression of a society's dharma. Running a business is not the same as running a country because corporations have profit as their *raison d'etre* while countries have the protection, safety and welfare of their citizens as their primary motive. These two are incompatible and often mutually exclusive goals. What promotes profit does not promote human rights. From ancient Athens to colonial America—the cornerstones of ancient and modern democracies— we have only to consider the practice of slavery to deduce that Merchant values do not necessarily correspond with human values.

> *Running a business is not the same as running a country because corporations have profit as their* raison d'etre *while countries have the protection, safety and welfare of their citizens as their primary motive*

From factory farms that perpetrate inhumane practices on the animals we eat, to the factories that devastate the environment, profitability is often at odds with humanity. Yet Merchant society is not all to blame. It is, in effect, trying to do its dharma by providing for the masses, though on a perverted scale. Because there are so many people to feed and shelter, it becomes impossible to nurture our lifestyles without raping our resources. Few of us want to give up our lifestyles in order to allow others to live. We would rather grow sick and die than turn vegetarian. We would rather conquer more territory, than live in a smaller house. **But lifestyle modification is at the heart of any substantive change.** This is what the greatest spiritual gurus through time, including our own modern day teachers insist, when asked how to bring peace to the world.

Real, or *vertical* change, must be contrasted with *horizontal* change. Horizontal change is trading one bad habit for another; vertical change is giving up the habit altogether. Driving a more economical car is a type of *horizontal* change, like giving up hard liquor for beer. *Vertical* change is quitting drinking period, without replacing it with other vices. By trading one vice for another, perhaps a lesser one, we are making only horizontal changes, trading dollars for pesos, which does not equate to any real transformation in the final analysis. But while driving an economical car is a better alternative, walking, bicycling, or more radically, turning vegetarian is a vertical leap in personal and social evolution. This is because meat production not only makes a *moral* footprint, it

> *"As long as there are slaughterhouses, there will be battlefields."*
> -Leo Tolstoy

creates an even greater carbon footprint, causing more global warming than all the cars, trucks, ships, and airplanes in the world combined![39]

Merchant values are not compatible with the humanistic tenets of an enlightened society. That is not to say that Merchants are by nature greedy or malevolent; quite the opposite. Merchants are responsible for *sheltering* and *providing* for the masses. However, they must be governed by a Warrior-class code of ethics that ensures proper opportunities for them to do so. **Merchants cannot police themselves.** When left alone, they will revert to what seems best, which is to make society profitable. In doing this, they may ignore other equally important variables, such as the environment, equal rights, and effective, affordable health care, which are neither their duty to address, nor their area of expertise. It is asking too much of Merchants to do the jobs naturally allotted for other types.

Matters of humanity and social equality are the concern of Educators and Warriors—it is incumbent on them to fulfill the role of counselors, educators, and governors in society, which is why many turn to political activism and public service. Outsiders also play a powerful role in shaping government policy by showing the world what doesn't work. They are the conscientious objectors and rebels who work from *outside* of government to *change* government. Ultimately, it goes against dharma to take away another's right to live out her destiny. By usurping the jobs of Educators, Warriors, and Outsiders, Merchants not only lose out in the long run, but also deprive others of following their natural destinies.

It is better to live your own dream, than to fulfill the expectations and dreams of others. Merchants and Laborers enjoy greater fulfillment doing their own dharma, than doing the work of types they either Disintegrate into (Merchant-Warrior, Labor-Educator) or who are at best neutral to them (Merchant-Educator, Labor-Warrior). When they follow their path, Merchants are free to contribute to society by organizing, mobilizing and optimizing the prosperity of their fellow Dharma Types. The same is true for Laborers, who are more effective at building community, succoring, and feeding others than in running a nation. Such are the redeeming qualities of Merchants and Laborers, and they

---

[39] Statistics and studies obtained from www.peta.org. Visit their site for more information on animal cruelty, sustainability, and the effects of factory farming on the environment.

come out best when there are no complications to get in the way of their expression.

> *"Economic success needs to be redefined: instead of increasing wealth it should be increasing well-being"* -Nic Marks, New Economics Foundation

For Laborers and Merchants accustomed to working for *material benefits* (Money, Goods), running a country can be a perplexing enterprise, whereas Warriors and Educators, whose lives are dedicated to *ideas* (Justice, and Truth, respectively), are naturally more comfortable devoting themselves to public service in the name of secular and spiritual ideals.

Not surprisingly, they make more qualified statesmen, and are better able to represent the founding principles of their countries without getting bogged down in the day-to-day rat race that can exhaust and blind politicians to the ultimate purpose for their candidacy, which is *public service*, not *personal gain*. The Silver Age idea of selfless public service is so forgotten today as to seem almost naïve and impractical, the object of scorn behind the country club doors of the Washington bureaucrat. Such ideas *are* indeed impractical, to Merchant and Labor type politicians who may possess the requisite education and influence to fill leadership positions, but are not qualified as kings or presidents to fulfill and improve on man's ability to exercise his political, human, and spiritual rights.

Even well-intentioned Merchant and Laborer leaders encounter obstacles that are ultimately too big for them to handle. Arguably, the best that Bill Clinton could do as president was to balance the budget— a great achievement suited to his Merchant talents— but he became ensnared in scandals that prevented further progress. Labor-type Nixon reached out to create a global community, a noble goal for a Laborer, with Labor-country China, but his jealousy and pettiness led to his demise. He was *too small* for the post of world leader.

The Dharma Types in Government

This summary is by no means exhaustive, but meant to give an idea of the spheres in which each type operates best. You will notice that some areas overlap, as they require the talents of more than one Dharma Type. Refer also to Chapter 13, Profession, for more detailed information.

Warrior: King (Highest Executive), Military, Law and Order (Police, Justice Administration) Health Care, Transportation

Educator: Diplomat, Counselor, Advisor, Justice, Senator/Legislator, Department of Education, Health Care, Scientific Research (NASA),

Merchant: Food and Drug Administration, Housing and Urban Development, Entertainment, Lending/Credit, Investment, Federal Funding Programs— Grants and Charities, Transportation, Trade and Commerce.

Laborer: Postal Service, Civil Engineering (all levels), Accounting, Banking, Treasury, Economy, Unions, Agriculture, Construction and Works, Health Care

Outsider: Import/Export, Foreign Relations, Diplomacy, Research, Espionage

A MEMORABLE FANCY

In my talks with teachers from different traditions, I recall conversations on various topics, from Pets in America, to War and Warriors. Here is one we had on vegetarianism. My questions are in italics.

What do you think about the rise of veganism and vegetarianism in the West?

"It is funny, you know, that we Indians are preaching vegetarianism for the last 3,000 years, but who is listening? Perhaps Yoga and Meditation have come to the West to solve these problems. People like Yoga, so they are also considering other Vedic solutions, like *ahimsaa*, non-violence towards creatures, and *dharma*, how to live with the Natural laws of your body and the universe…"

Maybe one reason Americans don't like vegetarianism is that they really don't know how to do it. I mean, they don't know how to cook vegetables and what to eat.

"You are right! *(laughing)* I would not eat this food either. If I grew up here I would probably be a meat eater too! You know, this Tofu, it is not real food. I know the Japanese eat it, but it is never a main dish, you know. But you Americans are crazy when you grab something. We need to teach you how to cook so you can digest your vegetables and your tofu and not become sick from malabsorption and bad food combining. That is why you must teach Ayurveda here."

It seems that the Vedas have a lot more to teach us than spiritual values.

"Why not? It is about the total experience of living. From how to caress your wife, you know, in the Kama Sutra, to how to build your house with (the principles of) *Vastu shastra*, there is more practical knowledge coming out of the Vedic tradition than just chanting *Hare Krishna* and twisting your body into a pretzel!

"Being vegetarian is not for everybody. Some Warriors need meat to keep their bodies strong and healthy, and milk is such a wonderful food… that is why we drink it when we are young. But what we do to get these resources is the terrible thing. How we treat our animals is the terrible thing. If eating organic and humanely treated animals and dairy means we have to spend a little more, then what is the cost? We save our souls by spending a few dollars? I say it is worth it! *(laughing)*

"Vegetarians do not understand that the land that gave birth to the practice of non-violence and not eating meat has the most know-how about the topic. They don't understand that it is okay to drink milk, if it is from your own cow that you raised and loved, or from the neighbor that you trust. But these hormones and chemicals, and the violence we use on animals today just to get them onto the trucks and into the slaughterhouse… it is killing us and them. It is killing our souls by killing their bodies. That's why you must teach people Ayurveda!"

Chapter 8: The Social Conscience of the Types

Breaking it Down

The sectors in the box above can be broken down even further. There are segments in the Military, for instance, that appeal more to one type than another. Laborers are attracted to engineering, infantry, and heavy artillery, whereas Educators may prefer communications or officer training. Merchants in the Military don't do well in the long run, but Outsiders may be snipers, translators, or other special units, while Warriors make soldiers and leaders in any capacity. With a little imagination, we can see that the U.S. armed forces also correlate neatly into four branches, the Army, Navy, Air Force and Marines, corresponding to the Laborer, Merchant, Educator, and Warrior Dharma Types, respectively. The Coast Guard, CIA or FBI effectively make up the fifth faction of the armed forces, corresponding with the Outsider. Recall the table of Elements from Chapter 1:

AIR Educator	WATER Merchant
EARTH Laborer	FIRE Warrior

To this we can insert the military branches appropriate to each...

AIR Educator (Air Force)	WATER Merchant (Navy)
EARTH Laborer (Army)	FIRE Warrior (Marines)

With a little imagination, we can discover the Dharma Types everywhere... if we only have eyes to see!

Political Myths

Western political models ignore the Dharma Type, and therefore the basic nature of human beings. But governments based on an understanding of the four aims of life as well as the basic drives of the Dharma Types can prosper their citizens by allowing them to express their destinies in full. Even the founding of political systems must involve the talents of the five types.

Like making a movie, forming a government begins with a good script. Without good writing as set down by the Educator, the greatest actors and all the money in the world are wasted, as anyone knows who has seen a bad film with good actors. That is why the Constitution is revered in the halls of American government, and why good movie scripts sell for millions of dollars. Next, it takes an executive type to give life and direction to a project. This is the Warrior's leadership role as president or director. Then, funds must be secured to produce it. Here the Merchant's skill of organizing and moving people, ideas, and currency comes into play. And the actual work of building the sets or cities, overseeing the infrastructure and crunching the daily numbers is done by the Labor type. Outsiders are the final touch, as both actors and audience, the first and last consideration of any project, the people for whom the movie is made, the citizens for whom government is constructed. Outsiders represent the proletariat, the masses. They cannot become 'insiders' until they have a role to play. A people without a government are Outsiders. An actor without a project is an Outsider. When they step into their role—whether as citizens of a country or actors on a stage—Outsiders begin to embody the character of their script.

Whatever the metaphor, every type contributes to the final result, and every type benefits from the completed whole. But not all government models are built to accommodate the dharmas of every citizen. Some emphasize one, while marginalizing the roles of others. Let's take a look at some of these below.

Communism is an example of Labor-type government. While the Marxist ideal of producers sharing in the bounty they produce seems noble in theory, the inherent flaws in the system become quickly apparent in practice. The ideals of camaraderie, solidarity, and working out of love and devotion for your fellow man are typical Labor sentiments. However, the real world bears out a few unscrupulous and ambitious types taking over and perverting this ideal into tyranny. Without a system of checks and balances in place to qualify its leaders and balance their power, communism succumbs to the rule of petty dictators. Because it is set up as a Labor government, Labor (and also Outsider) types have easy access to leadership, which is evident in the profile of Communist leaders from the past century. Outsider Bolsheviks overthrew the Warrior czarist governments to ostensibly institute a rule of the people (Labor). But leadership is not the ideal dharma for these types, and such systems fail in practice, or degenerate into a form of slavery, for the inebriation of power is too heady a force for the unenlightened to handle. Educators and the intelligentsia are particularly detrimented in Laborer-Communist regimes, because the Laborer represents an Educators Disintegration point. We have witnessed this in the last century in Mao's China and the former Soviet regime, as it filled up Siberia with the bodies and minds of its best Educators and dissenters.

Capitalism, though not a form of government, is nonetheless the dictating force *behind* government in a Merchant society. Much of public policy is dictated to conform to, or at least not interfere with, capitalist markets and the rule of free trade. This is the undercurrent of today's global economy. The pitfall of capitalism is that it creates a ***government run not by the people, but by the people with money***— a narrow group of political donors for whom congressmen write policy. As long as those charged with making laws are owned by the few who stand to benefit from these laws, an unjust system is perpetuated, whereby some get ahead, while most others remain stuck in a middle and lower class that requires them to work harder and longer hours to survive. At its worst, this system promotes the corruption of society from the inside, by deadening the impulses of creativity and growth that are encouraged by leisure and introspection.

The traditions that gave us these *dharmic* archetypes specified *work* only as part of an individual's total *dharma*, and put its upper limit at about 6 hours per day, while the rest of the time was to be devoted to spiritual, social, and individual pursuits. As an upper limit, these hours are laughable by Merchant-class standards, which is one reason aboriginal peoples, who typically require only a few hours a day to meet their material needs, have had a difficult time integrating into modern societies.

Natives of the Americas, as well as Australia and other aboriginal cultures who are a throwback to more ancient, sacred societies, have particularly suffered under the global Merchant society

Nomad and hunter-gatherer societies are structured around free-flowing Outsider principles. A *reciprocal altruism* exists in these egalitarian societies in which no citizen is above another. Every member has the freedom to self-cultivate and go about as she pleases, while remaining part of the community. Freedom, movement, and responsibility are essential aspects of this lifestyle. Each member is allowed to judge what is appropriate to herself and her tribe according to her wisdom, while keeping in mind and abiding by the above three principles. Such societies tend to remain small.

Monarchy is leadership by the Warrior class. At its worst, it can take the form of oppressive dictatorships or military tyranny. At its best it is the most natural government according to sacred society and the Dharma Types. It evokes the myth of a righteous ruler guided by wise ministers, governing, almost unwillingly, at the behest of the people. King Arthur's legend exemplifies this in the West, and the story of Rama in India, where the precedent for a just monarch shows that one does not seek the crown for oneself; it is brought to you, or bestowed from above.

The tale of Arthur relates that kingship is offered to anyone who can perform a specific rite of passage, in this case wresting Excalibur from its stone. Who has set the sword thus remains a mystery, but it is certain that this is no ordinary test. Indeed, it takes more than strength or skill to pull it out, for this is a trial of character and virtue, not mere power and force. And foreseeably, the mightiest warriors fail in their effort to budge the sword. That is, until an unlikely hero gives it a try: Arthur.

The kingship is available to anyone. In previous ages, blood lines were vital, as they carried a physical component of that divine favor bestowed on certain lineages. However, in the modern age, they have become mixed to such a degree that they are no longer reliable for judging suitability and virtue on their own. This is why the Dharma Types are not *hereditary* or *hierarchical*. This is also why monarchy is no longer tenable in our age, for we lack the tests and traditions to elect eligible kings and queens.

> *The brahmana (Educator) legitimizes the kshatriya's (Warrior) authority while the kshatriya provides patronage and protection for the brahmana.. Secular power, the commodity of the kshatriya, is concentrated in the king, while spiritual power, the commodity of the brahmana, is concentrated in the ascetic*
> -Raj Balkaran, from the essay, *Legitimizing Rama*

As the legend further suggests, authority is not based on brute strength, power, or worldly influence. Instead, everything is decided by divine favor— evidenced by Arthur's ability, against all odds, to pull the sword from its place. While everyone has a shot and fails to even budge the sword, the young Arthur lifts it out effortlessly. We find same metaphor in Valmiki's *Ramayana*, the great Silver Age epic of India. Therein, Rama, the perfect king, strings and even shatters a bow that a crowd of would-be heroes fails to even lift, thereby earning his maiden, Sita's hand. Thousands of years later in the Bronze Age, Arjuna follows suit, as related in that massive compendium of Indian history, the *Mahabharata*. These powerful mythologies demonstrate the *divine right of kings* by demonstrating that, although perverted by generations hungry for wealth and power, the right to rule is really dependent on divine grace, and a *supernal*, rather than *earthly* legacy.

It has as its stewards the Priestly types who uphold the tests and traditions of that title and its rights of passage. Enter Merlin, Arthur's 'guru,' or Vasishta, the guru of Rama, both of whom know their pupils' real identities and destinies; both of whom work to guide them on the royal path of responsible kingship.

In modern times, we are faced with more concrete, if less romantic examples of just heroes who become 'kings,' usually at the behest of their people rather than through personal ambition. Cincinnatus and George Washington come up as salient examples of generals who proved their mettle not just with their skill on the battlefield, but through their character and values in daily life. They stood as embodiments of Warrior virtue, and were beloved of their people. In turn, they were called again to duty, this time as leaders of nations rather than armies, because of their record for putting God and Country before themselves.
Here are some qualities that make a Warrior fit to rule.

1. **Adherence to one's word.**

    Integrated Warriors hold their word as their bond, and would lay down their lives rather than betray a promise. As a result, they are careful and deliberate in their speech, avoiding boasting, lies, and frivolous talk. This may not seem like a huge challenge for some, but imagine the superstar athletes of today, whose prowess exceeds their prudence, trying to live by this code. It is extremely difficult when you *know* you can do a thing, to not parade it in front of others. It is too often the case that, the stronger the man, the looser his tongue, especially among Warriors who Disintegrate into Merchant-style boasting.

2. Self-Control through devotion to one life partner.

It is said in Ayurveda that the penis is the lower tongue, which we use to taste life's pleasures. Disintegrated Warriors with loose tongues also tend to lead loose lives. Though with power comes privilege, and though one can hold a harem of thousands, the Integrated king or queen keeps one spouse for life. Squandering one's energy on a harem takes away the *shakti* (energy) that a king could devote to his people. *Shakti* is cooked and refined in the secure vessel of a loving, monogamous relationship. This *shakti* in turn promotes the just Warrior's longevity, reputation, and skill. On the other hand, we need only turn to tabloids and TV to see licentiousness and lack of self-control evinced by the motley rabble of wannabe modern Warriors, who seek to squander their honor and energy at every opportunity.

3. A friend to all— the great benefactor to the world and his people.

Naturally willing to give his life in battle for others, a Warrior demonstrates this *outside* the battlefield by sacrificing his own happiness for that of his subjects. These sacrifices confirm in him the right to rule; only such a one as this passes the tests of the sword and the bow. The just king or queen is a friend to all, and does not discriminate based on race, sex, age, or social status, but judges subjects according to their hearts and deeds. Bigotry of any kind is thoroughly inimical to such a person's being, and not tolerated.

Note that power and strength are not mentioned here as prerequisites for the ideal ruler. That is because these qualities flow naturally as side effects of *honesty*, *self-control*, and *benevolence*. In effect, they generate power and strength by virtue of their existence, and, when cultivated, make their owner indefatigable and undefeatable. That is why these principles apply to Warriors of both genders. Here is another poetic account of king Dasharatha, Rama's father, which enumerates more virtues of the just ruler:

> *Dasharatha crossed a sea of mendicants by giving what was sought. He crossed a sea of knowledge by delving deep into countless books; he crossed the sea of pleasures by heartily enjoying them. He crossed a sea of enemies by destroying them with his sword.*

This snippet from the *Kamba Ramayana* succinctly describes the Warrior's path of excellence.

He crossed... means that he succeeded, passed the test, completed the task he set out to do. It is a defined, finished action that leaves no doubt about the king's ability. Warriors called to action must complete their missions in order to be respected.

A sea... is an endless, measureless challenge. The Warrior's task is never easy and his duty never ends. Just as the vast sea cannot be crossed in one day, so the king's responsibility to his people is perpetual. This is why Tests of virtue and resilience are necessary to select a proper king. Strength alone fades; power and ambition are fickle. If a Warrior lacks the necessary virtues, he will fall as king and fail his Purpose.

What was sought... is delivered to his people. Not as *he* wanted, but as *they* needed. A just king works according to the needs and desires of his people, rather than his own. A wicked king has only his own lust and greed as guides to his rule. One is lasting and sanctioned by Natural Law; the other is fleeting, and scars the world by its existence.

Delving deep... means not skimming the surface. The sea of knowledge is crossed by diving to the depths in order to snatch the pearls of wisdom that lie on the sea floor below. It takes a heroic effort of skill and self-control to find those pearls and retrieve them for future generations. In this example, discipline is inherent to the task of learning to hold and control the breath, and regular practice gradually makes one a stronger swimmer. These two qualities, *practice* and *discipline,* are the foundation of Yoga and the Warrior's creed, without which the whole structure of his life becomes unstable, and eventually topples down. The just king must have these in abundance if he is to maintain steady integrity in the face of his rule.

Heartily... not selfishly or with attachments, is the moment enjoyed. The just king takes his pleasures where they come- and they are many. He enjoys, and then leaves them when it is time to move on. There is no harboring or lamenting their loss. The wise man knows that, when he lives his best life, whatever comes to him, pain or pleasure alike, is given full attention, and released when its time is over. This does not mean that he is a **user** of things and people, but an **experiencer** of the same. *He does not hold on to anything against its will,* or against the will of his dharma, but flows along the river of his destiny with effortless skill, navigating the waters of life to reach their final destination.

Destroyed... implies finality of action (like *crossed* above). He did not just defeat his enemies, but completely finished them. He pulled the weeds from their roots, so they could never sprout again. These enemies may be anything from social injustices (like slavery), environmental evils (like greenhouse gases), or personal opponents (like foreign terrorists). Whatever the challenge, the just king walks through it knowing he has justice and divine favor on his side. Accordingly, he does not hesitate to act when action is necessary.

His sword... is the sharp, decisive weapon that connotes finality of action. It is not words, but **actions** that mark the Warrior. When diplomacy has failed, actions speak louder than words and make the Warrior an effective instrument of his people's will. A sword is sharp and cutting, getting quickly to the point. It does not cause collateral damage, but penetrates to the heart of a problem, eliminating it. The sword is also Viveka (Discernment) personified. A wise king is able to cut through delusion and lies to see people's true intentions. His trenchant faculties of discrimination serve to separate what is eternal from what is temporary, to discern between the False and True and deal with each.

It is a Warrior's connection to these noble and divine virtues that earns him respect in the world, and a lasting legacy. In modern times, they were enumerated more succinctly by another Warrior, general Douglas MacArthur in his famous speech on Sacrifice...

> *The soldier, above all other men, is required to practice the greatest act of religious training– sacrifice.*

Divine justice...
> *No physical courage and no brute instinct can take the place of the Divine help which alone can sustain him.*

and Self-Knowledge...
> *Master yourself before you seek to master others.*

Conclusions for Every Type

Every Dharma Type has personal myths emblazoned with the character of their destiny. Some of these are developed in the *Myth* section later in this book. The essence of the King Arthur tale is that only by divine grace can one fulfill the highest destiny of her Dharma Type, whether she is a Warrior, Merchant, Educator, Laborer, or Outsider type. What it comes down to is a type of dispensation, a blessing for the worthy and virtuous that allows them to be the best they can be, and to have Justice, Prosperity, Truth, Security, and Freedom according to their Dharma Type, respectively. Living Myths that illustrate these principles tell us the same thing: **live your dharma, and dharma will live in you!**

Homework

As your homework, take some time to look at governments around the world, as well as your own society, to decide which Dharma Type fits them best. It doesn't matter if you've been born and raised in one place all your life, for even in America different states and regions have individual personalities. Though the USA is collectively a Merchant nation, there is wide variation between the West and East coast, between the north and the south, between Hawai'i and the Pacific Northwest. Take a look at your genetic and national heritage to see if you can find which Dharma Type pertains to your culture, family, or state.

Be creative! Use whatever sources of information you can find. For example, you can deduce a lot from the styles of entertainment found in different countries. England and Germany, both Warrior nations, run more austere, professional television programs than say, Italian TV, which is more Merchant-like and lively. American TV often portrays Disintegrated Merchant images of violence and terror, while Mexican entertainment runs to more Integrated Labor programs that involve dancing, singing, soap operas, and family-based specials. Think about how a country's type affects its image across the globe as well as with its neighbors. Canada, for example, as an Educator nation, has a reputation for politeness, diplomacy, and wide cultural views, though they are also sometimes portrayed as effete, wishy-washy, and indecisive. Think of everything you've learned so far to determine how your culture can benefit from knowledge of its Dharma Type. If you're more ambitions, you may even wish to ponder how to improve your government using the Dharma Type tools provided in this chapter.

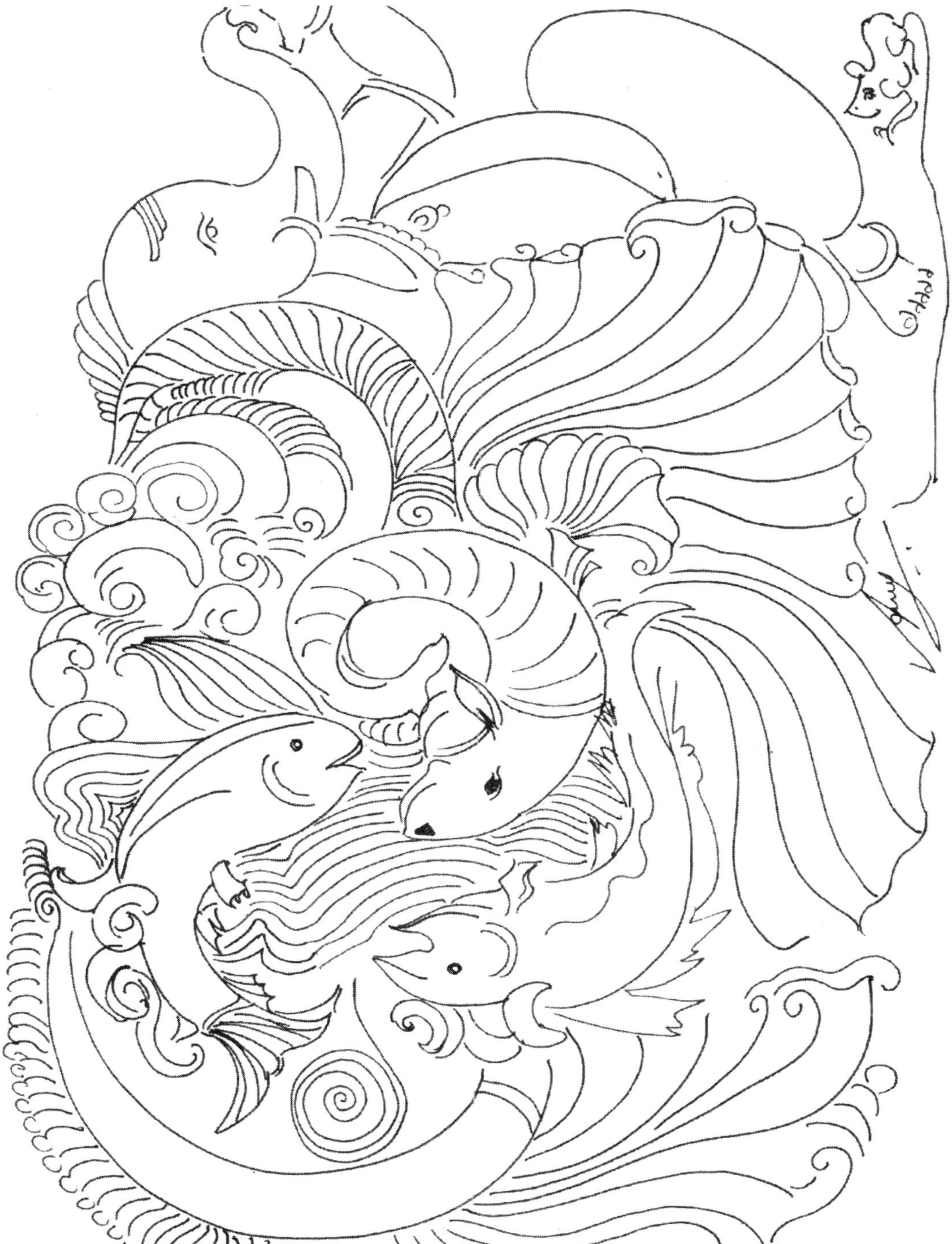

9
ELEMENT, TASTE, AND SEASON

Element

In Chapter 1 we looked at the 5 Elements and their corresponding Dharma Types. Now we shall discuss them in more detail. Element theory is the foundation of Vedic cosmology (Samkhya) and permeates practically every facet of the Vedic sciences, from *Ayurveda*, *Jyotisha*, and *Yoga* to *Vastu Shastra* and more. The five Elements can even be used as stand-alone personality-type proformas, but work best when understood side by side with their Dharma Type. Here is a summary of how the Elements and Dharma Types work together.

EARTH

Summary: Labor Type. 1st Chakra. Instincts of survival and self-preservation. Fixed, durable, and reliable, but also slow, heavy, and materialistic. Densest of the Elements, the most visible manifestation of reality.

Subtle Meaning: Dense objects create the most gravity. Spiritually, gravity correlates to Love, the all-attractive force. When its growth is unchecked, gravity turns into a black hole, a force beyond time and space, seeding galaxies that in turn bring forth new life. Black holes are the organizing principles around which other stars revolve; in the same way, the Labor type is the core of his community. And just as black holes are conduits to realms beyond time and space, spiritually speaking, love and loyalty, or *Bhakti Yoga*, is the Laborer's portal out of the temporal world of suffering. There is nothing that a Labor type cannot absorb and transmute through the power of Love and Devotion. A black hole is termed such because it is difficult to perceive and its immense gravity allows no light to escape. Similarly, Laborers may appear unremarkable on the surface, while being resplendent with gravity and light within. Such persons may only show their light by serving others, without need for gratitude or recognition. The densest Element has the potential to become the most potent force in the universe, and it is up to Labor types to transmute the "stuff" of their petty natures into the power of Nature Herself. In Vedic philosophy, Ganesha represents this force of the Earth Element and the root chakra.

Usefulness Here and Now: Integrated Laborers have a high *emotional IQs*, (explored in the next chapter), for they are patient, strong, and learn from experience. Grounded in the depths of their being they can take everything the world throws at them and still open their arms in devotion. Indefatigueable, undefeatable, the Earth Element is the ground of our being, the dust of our bodies, without which nothing can establish a firm foundation. Society is based on the Labor type without whom there would be nothing to hold people together. Without the Laborer's skill in engineering the material world, there would be no cities, machines, or tools to nourish our communities. In brief, we are all nomads without the Labor type's ingenuity to harness the Earth's resources and settle us down. Civilization is impossible without the Laborer's homemaking and communal instinct. He feeds us, weaves the cloth that warms us, and builds the homes that shelter us. He is the very fabric of our material existence.

> *We are all nomads without the Labor type's skill and ingenuity to harness the earth's resources and settle us down*

Precautions: Because Earth is fixed and solid, Labor Types can get too set in their ways. They become rough and immovable, or coarse, gruff, and difficult. They need **Water** to soften and mould them into a pliable clay that is adaptable to many uses. Water and Earth mix easily and their combination brings forth new life when properly harnessed. Agriculture, the foundation of settled society, is a good example, for it represents the cooperation of the Labor and Merchant types. In fact, it is easy to illustrate Integration and Disintegration points using the Elements. As we shall see below, Air (Educator) also shapes and moulds the Earth, but in a harsh and erosive way. A stone blasted by wind over time becomes rough, porous, and brittle. Thus, while culture and philosophy can also hone the Labor type, he is happier learning from Merchants, whose approach is better-suited to his style of learning.

Earth also relates to smell. Laborers have a good sense of smell and can pick up 'chemistry,' which is why they sometimes like or dislike others for no obvious reason. It is this sense that allows them to love a less than perfect partner. We'll learn in Volume II, *Sex, Love, & Dharma*, that Laborers do not value looks as highly as *utility* and *chemical attraction* in a mate. They prefer a partner who *feels* and *smells* good to one who only *looks* or *sounds* good. Because of the preponderance of Earth Element, tangible experiences like food and physical affection are more immediate and real to Laborers. Their communication style is also different. They do not communicate in linguistic concepts so much as in the subtle language of the body. It is well known that a majority of interpersonal communication is non-verbal, especially between the sexes. Labor types understand this well and have a good 'sense' about people even without knowing anything about them. Of course, when Disintegrated, this natural gift can turn into prejudice and bias, and Laborers need to take the time to get to know someone before making final judgments. They must back up their first impressions with first-hand experience and give people the benefit of doubt, something they are more likely to do when Integrated.

WATER

Summary: Merchant type. 2nd Chakra. Desire, creation and creativity, wealth, pleasure, possessions, enjoyment. Water is the most **sensual** of the Elements. Without water we cannot *taste* the food we eat, or enjoy life. *Joie de vivre* is based on the French verb *jouir*, which means *to enjoy*, but also *to spring forth* (as of water), and *to sexually climax* (ejaculate). The French intuitively knew that without *juice*, there is no joy in life. In Sanskrit, the word is *rasa*, the juice and joy that lubricates existence and makes life palatable to the embodied soul— a word particularly delectable to Merchant types.

Subtle Meaning: Water provides for the fluidity and continuity of life. It is the seat of sensual enjoyment and the primordial soup of all creation. Where the Earth is rigid, water moves sinuously and seamlessly to join and harmonize disparate entities with each other, just as the Merchant harmonizes and brings people together. Water is the glue of life that makes humans stick around and desire to experience material existence. It does this by creating relationships and attachments, most notably through sexual union. While Laborers are more concerned with the *function* of sex (procreation), Merchants are interested in its *enjoyment*.

Like the depths of the ocean, Water rules forces that are both unfathomable and irresistible, and correlates to all forms of desire and attachment. Water is also sacred in any ritual, spiritual or secular, especially those seeking to evoke the qualities of sacred union, of *shakti* and *shiva*, the indelible mystery of the feminine and masculine divine. As an example, wine can be the blood of Christ, connecting us to the supernal divine, or the drug of Dionysus for a carnal good time.

By itself Water has no fixed structure, and needs a vessel to hold it and give it shape. The Labor type and her Earth Element provide this vessel and give the Merchant meaning and value. Water roams aimlessly without two banks carved in the earth to guide its course. Also, random water is free, but water that has been bottled and contained has a price. This Integration between Merchant and Labor types provides the link between production and commerce, and runs the economic machine of human society.

Like Water, the Merchant type can also be a little too 'slippery' in her moral or fiduciary Duty to others. Therefore, it is incumbent on Educators to provide laws, and on Warriors to enforce them if the Merchant type is to be made accountable. Water also mirrors the Merchant's general lack of shape and rigidity, physically, emotionally, and spiritually:

1. **Physically**, Merchants may be challenged with weight accumulation, water retention, and an overall lack of physical fitness. It may be difficult for them to stay in good physical condition due to their strong taste for indulgence. Merchants love to taste life, and anything that interferes with this (like diets) gets second billing.
2. **Emotionally**, Merchants can be all over the place. Just as water swells and recedes, so the tides of Merchant emotions, while they run deep, can also wreak havoc when not controlled. Disintegrated Merchants are passionate, impulsive, and prone to bouts of depression and elation, with little real provocation.
3. **Spiritually**, Merchants are the least secure, which is ironic since their path is the clearest and easiest to follow. It suffices for the Merchant to let her abundant Water flow in order to walk the path of spiritual fulfillment. Merchants may take a lifetime to learn how to fill their inner void, but it is no more difficult than this: *share your abundance with and shelter others, and the universe will share its own and shelter you!*

Recalling the Circle of Life, one can see the Merchant's Duty is primarily to the Labor class, as the Laborer's gratitude provides Merchants blessings twofold—

first by nourishing them spiritually, and next by creating return customers for future business. The Labor type's Earth Element is best at providing healthy structure for the Merchant's Water. Just as earth mixed with water turns into clay that can be molded into infinite shapes, *when the Merchant is stabilized by the Labor type, there is infinite potential for utility, creativity, and prosperity.*

> **Merchants are the least secure among the Dharma Types, which is ironic since their path is the clearest and easiest to follow**

Usefulness Here and Now: If Laborers provides the means, Merchants give us the reason to live. Where the Labor type makes a cloth, the Merchant makes it soft, comfortable, and flattering; where Labor makes a shelter, Merchant makes it airy, hospitable, and decorated. That is why Merchants rule wealth and commerce, and feel at home in the marketplaces of the world, because humans are willing to pay a premium to obtain the good things in life, and where there is movement of people, there is circulation of prosperity. The Merchant's role is to grease the gears of society and make them work to the benefit of its members. Without Merchants, predominating in Water Element, we are unable to taste life's goodness, or know refinement and grace. Embodied life carries little appetite without Water, which is the primary conveyance of *Maya's* (Nature's) grasp on the world, holding us as She does, 'twixt the dual talons of Aversion and Desire.

Precautions: Because Water spreads and is absorbed into every space and cranny, Merchant types can become spread out, both physically and emotionally. In the physical matrix, too much water can lead to indulgence in luxury, gadgets, even drugs. They are into too much *stuff*. Emotionally, it makes them greedy, pompous, and enslaved to the desire for more experience, pleasure, and stimulation. Merchants need the Laborer's to ground them in reality. Earth's *astringency* absorbs excess water, and contact with Labor types can help control a Merchant's weight problems and emotional excesses. In nature, the earth also guides the direction and flow of water through the channels of its rivers and streams. This is good for Merchants to remember, who must stay ever vigilant and guided by the boundaries provided by their fellow types. Management must listen to Labor in order to be effective. When it doesn't, strikes and revolutions result. In addition, by associating with Labor types and doing Labor activities, the Merchant is reminded of the simple pleasures of community, food, and shelter.

The most extravagant meal is lonely without company, and Merchants feel hollow when they cannot share their good fortune. Water by itself has no taste or color; only when it is mixed with *substance* does it take on the color and quality of that substance. In return, it gives a medium for any material it contacts to fully express itself. That is how Merchants grease the gears of civilization: they allow people to contribute their gifts by providing the matrix for them to do so. They build stadiums for athletes to showcase their skills; they open restaurants for chefs to wow the world; they build museums, libraries, and universities to allow scholars access to the wisdom of the ages, and they build financial institutions that promote the continued development of Merchant society.

FIRE

Summary: Warrior. 3rd Chakra. Power, transformation, expansion, penetration, protection. The Fire Element represents change. It is raw, unfocused power that can harm or heal according to its use. The Warrior type has the greatest potential to transform self and others—most drastically through death. Warriors hold the power to kill and to heal, forces represented severally in their most typical professions: military and medicine. Like Fire, Warriors have potential that must be harnessed if it is to be useful. This takes wisdom and learning, which is why Educators are required to shape a Warrior's evolution.

Subtle Meaning: Agni is the first word of the *Rk Samhita,* the first Veda— the most ancient compendium of continuously-practiced spiritual precepts in the world. Recall from the Introduction that the first word of any Vedic text is meaningful, giving an account of what is to follow. As the Vedas are divine insights into the spirituality and practicality of human life, *Agni*—Fire— represents the medium between our two worlds; the worlds of spirit and matter. *Agni* also indicates that at our core we are all made of light. Beyond the illusion of solid matter, on the smallest scale imaginable, lie the basic building blocks of our existence, which are nothing but energy. And on the cosmic scale the entire universe came to being through explosion and Fire—a Fire that disseminated the Elements of life. In our solar system, we are the products of hydrogen's fusion in the sun. More locally, our planet with its fiery core is the source, sustenance, and protector of humankind. Dead planets have exhausted their Fire, and exist in a state of inertia that cannot support life, while our planet is still evolving, growing, and very much alive.

Chapter 9: Element, Taste, and Season

Even at the level of our cells, the chemical processes of life are ruled by Fire. *Chemistry* and *electricity* galvanize the flesh, transforming food into intelligent tissue, experience into memory, and toxins into waste. Indeed, such was its importance to the ancients that Fire was worshipped as the link between spirit and matter, the bridge across forever that has been used from the mists of antiquity to modern day to interface with the divine. In the candles of the church or the yogi's *havan* (fire pot), Fire makes sacred our most sacred places.

Just as Warriors sanction the Merchant's actions in the Circle of Duty, so Fire sanctions ritual, a Merchant activity. In Volume III we will explore the spiritual practices particular to each type and see that *penance* is the Warrior's domain, while *ritual observance* belongs to the Merchant. *Tapas*, a word that can mean both *Penance* and *heat*, inaugurates the great Vedic epic, *The Ramayana*, the story of Rama, which details the sacrifices Rama endured as part of his Warrior dharma. Fire exemplifies both the physiological processes of transformation (of food, thought, and experience) as well as spiritual penance and the soul's process of en-*light*-enment. Fire also relates to protection. In hunter-gatherer societies fire protects man from the dangers of the wild, while in agrarian societies it serves a more domesticated purpose, protecting the health of its members through cooking our food, heating our homes, and powering our machinery.

Usefulness here and now: Fire is at the same time the most useful and destructive tool. Its ability to heal and kill, harm and protect, illustrates the Warrior's double-edged gift. When used indiscriminately, Fire burns and wreaks devastation. When channeled conscientiously it can bring mankind to the ultra-modern edge of civilization. Warriors are the most skilled type because Fire represents technology. All machines and computers run on Fire— electricity, combustion, and chemistry— which drives the sciences of the 21st century. In an internal combustion engine, heat is both the propelling as well as the deceleration and degeneration force generated by friction. A nuclear reaction can create energy to heat our homes, or burn our bodies. Thus, Fire represents both progress and destruction.

For Warriors to get the most out of their Element they need to channel their energies intelligently, to think like a laser beam, not a forest fire. To do so, they must pick their battles, focus their energy, and when their task is met, move on to the next goal. When Warriors disperse their energies or have no useful goal, their life force becomes scattered and ineffectual.

Precautions: Just as the Warrior Disintegrates into the Merchant type, so Water puts out Fire, and dampens the Warrior's spirit. The goal is not to put out Fire, but to channel it constructively. That is why Educators, whose Air Element gently stokes and feeds Fire, are most useful to the Warrior. Although the Warrior has duties to the Merchant (see Circle of Life above), these at best maintain the status quo. The most optimistic combination of Water and Fire may be cooking and feeding people. This is a noble cause, but it belongs to other types: Warriors can grow irritable if they are forced to cook and clean all day. They need the high and mighty cause to fight for, obstacles to struggle against, and a goal to win. Fire and Earth paired together fare no better, though not as poorly as Fire and Water. These Elemental dynamics also enliven compatibility analysis, which is discussed in Chapter 10, and detailed in Volume II, *Sex, Love, & Dharma*.

AIR

Summary: Educator. 4th Chakra. Subtlety, movement, and travel. Dryness and intellectuality. Liberality, transparency, and high mindedness, but also fragility, fickleness, and indecision. Any material that becomes infused with Air becomes more brittle, and Educator bodies are less resilient than those of other types. Because Air relates to ideas, communication, and the transmission of knowledge, these are essential Educator qualities.

Subtle Meaning: Air travels over the surface of other Elements, though unlike Space, does not perfuse them. Similarly, Educators may travel to many places, and skim the surface of many cultures, but essentially remain themselves. Just Air may become colored by Earth in a dust storm, or obscured by Water in a downpour, it eventually returns to its original state after the dust settles and the clouds disappear. Like the Air Element, Educators can take on qualities of other types and sympathize with them, learning and growing thereby, but they stay themselves. Outsiders, on the other hand, like Space, become infused with other Elements to such a point that it is impossible to separate them. We know from physics that matter is mostly empty space; this is how the Outsider pervades the other types, because every Element contains and is contained by Space, and the Outsider is in everyone, and everyone in the Outsider.

The Educator is the Renaissance man or woman for the very same reason that Air travels around to interface with the other Elements. Educators may travel in their minds by reading books and newspapers, or by actually exploring other countries and continents, driven as they are by intellectual curiosity. However, though they may be touched by their experiences, Educators are rarely changed the way an Outsider is transformed by her explorations. One is a tourist on Safari, the other has settled down in the bush to become one with its people and customs. This does not mean that Educators cannot immerse themselves, but that such immersion is only likely to happen during Outsider Life Cycles, which many Educators indeed see during the course of their lives.[40]

Precautions: What does the mountain appreciate of the sky? Not his storms or furies, but his high nature, his ability to move above the lowly common world and inspire it. The same is true of the other types in relation to Educators. What can harm the air? Nothing. Air forgives all, even creatures who devour it, for it cannot be destroyed. An Educator established in wisdom knows that he cannot be harmed, unless it is the will of Spirit. He is protected by truth and dharma, just as he helps to protect truth and dharma in turn. His compassion and forbearance make the Educator laudable, and set an example for other types. It is not his great gusts or erosive chafing that endear an Educator to the world, but his ability to be above it all, to soar nobly above the petty cares of everyday entanglements. Educators must take care to rein in their tempestuous tempers, and learn to understand why they are valued by others. They must control their passions so they do not become a source of harm to the world, but a source of inspiration... a wind in the sails of every Dharma Type.

Without the earth's atmosphere to protect us, we would be subject to the whims and blasts of cosmic radiation, meteors, and random space junk. Though the atmosphere is nothing but Air, it prevents destructive foreign bodies from annihilating life on the planet. Likewise, Educators help to secure us by teaching us to understand and live in harmony with our world, from deciphering the will of God, to understanding plate tectonics. Though they are less useful in everyday matters~ Air cannot shield you from a hammer— Educators help us understand *why* things happen, and ensure our safety by creating the invisible blanket of laws and values that protect us. Most people take these for granted, but just as the loss of our atmosphere would spell annihilation for life on the planet, so the loss of these laws and values devastates society.

In today's world *Business* and *Entertainment* have greater value than *Education* and *Spirituality*, just as *gold* (Earth) and *oil* (Water) are more prized than *knowledge* and *wisdom* (Air). Is it a wonder that in the modern age our atmosphere has eroded, due to a Merchant society's values that put material

---
[40] Refer to Chapter 14 for more on Life Cycles and their effects on the Dharma Types.

gain over personal fulfillment? Physical reality reflects the evolution of humanity: during the Golden Age, material advancement was simple enough to promote a clean and harmonious life with the Elements. In modern times, the heavy emphasis on material production (oil, plastics, metals, and even food overabundance) destroys our relationship with the Elements, and disturbs the balance between Nature and mankind.

The Iron Age bias is towards Iron Age technology. We assume that advanced civilization is built around machines, metal, and electricity. Not finding these in our excavations of ancient cultures, we assume they were primitive, less advanced than ours. This may be true for societies in the Iron Age of the past 4,000 years, but when we go further back we run into astounding contradictions to this view. We find ancients possessing knowledge of precession, a complex astronomical reality that takes 26,000 years to detail. We find them capable of moving massive monoliths that only our heaviest cranes can wield, and placing them with computer precision relative to geological and heavenly coordinates. We find them capable of astounding feats of memory and mathematics, all without recourse to books or calculators.

According to sacred history, metal and machines actually represent crude tools of a *devolved* culture. According to *shastra*, spiritual literature, in previous Silver and Golden Ages manipulation of the mind superseded mastery over metal; rather than writing software, ancients wrote mantras to access the technology of the soul. If sacred rituals could produce food and rain, of what use a tractor? If mental communication connected people, of what use the cell phone, and that bane of Merchant society, the phone bill? We assume that we represent the most advanced version of our species, where in fact we are shorter-lived, smaller, duller, and less 'technologically' advanced than our predecessors in the Bronze, Silver, and Golden ages, according to *shastra* that has survived these periods.

It is not to lament our fate but to help us become aware of it that this is highlighted. These are the times we live in. It is not to overvalue Educators or Outsiders, but to give every Dharma Type *equal* rank. Vedic tradition states that spiritual advancement is actually *easier* in the material modern age. Because the world is starving for it, our slightest effort to know the Self yields fruit; our every desire to find Purpose is supported. Any alignment with or knowledge of Natural Law immediately puts us ahead in the race, for the converse of Kali Yuga's detriments is that God is more likely to take our call, because the line is rarely busy. People are more concerned with the temporary constructs of material identity than their eternal selves. Concordantly, those who do strive to realize their undying nature have less traffic to contend with, and their 'highway to heaven' is clear and uncluttered. Self-cultivation in the Kali Yuga is like driving on Sunday; because no one is doing it, there's no traffic, the ride is fast, and we get to our destinations without accident or mishap!

SPACE

Summary: Outsider. Fifth Chakra. Empty spaces, speech and hearing. Spreading, invisible, both black as well as transparent, empathic and universal. The darkness of Space makes its natives unable to see their own failings, which is why they need guides, teachers, and counselors to lean on. The transparency of Space makes its natives uncertain about who they are and how to find themselves. Their empathy allows them to blend with others; their universality can make them see social customs, laws, and morals as limiting structures and lead them to create their own.

Subtle Meaning: The subtlest of all Elements, Space is everywhere and nowhere. Each of the other four are discernible to the senses: we can see Fire, smell Earth, taste Water, and feel the movement of Air on our skin— but Space is invisible, just as the Outsider can be invisible to society. The other types have pre-set paths to follow in fulfilling their dharmas— even air currents travel in discernible patterns— but there are no paths in Space; the Outsider's path is everywhere and nowhere. This makes him at once the most populous type... and the most overlooked.

Usefulness Here and Now: The fifth chakra covers speech, and although Space is associated with the organs of hearing and sound, Outsiders have a special relationship to speech and words. Words express truth, but truth and language are relative. Outsiders are most familiar with this paradox of symbol and reality. As a result, they have the loosest conceptions of literal truth, and can become great liars or great actors. They can reinvent language, or simply spoil it. Outsiders plunge into the unknown to find truth, beyond the artifice of speech, and fulfillment in life comes when they bring that truth back and tie it to speech. Their challenge is to be relevant: when they tie their self-expression to the language of society, they become understandable to others. When Outsiders find a way to express their complex destinies, they become rewarded according to the quality of that expression. We said before that the Outsider's purpose is to find his purpose, but that's only half the battle. The other half lies in expressing that purpose *intelligibly* to others. When the Outsider coherently integrates *purpose* and *expression*, great forces reward him in turn.

Outsiders emerge from the shadows to pronounce the plight of humanity and offer it solutions. The outcast from society comes back to save it. This is the real meaning of *avatar*,[41] which comes from the Sanskrit prefix *ava*, and root *tri*, that literally means *"to cross (down) over."* Avatars are the ultimate embodiment of the Outsider virtue of returning back to society in order to save it. That is, *crossing over* into the world to offer the gifts of his transcendence is the Outsider's ultimate journey.

But we don't have to rise to the exalted level of avatars or saints to be effective Outsiders. Since Outsiders are the most populous type, and true exceptional beings come along only once in a generation—or millennium—what are the rest of us supposed to do? The fact is that every Outsider has a unique gift. There is something *you* do better than anyone else in the world... find it, and express it to the world! How refined this expression becomes depends on your personal evolution, but every Outsider is a revolutionary in his or her own way, just as the feral tiger roars even in the hearts of the tamest kitten.

In the final analysis, Outsiders are not builders, but destroyers; it takes other types to implement their suggestions into effective solutions, which is why Outsiders should work with Educators to record these ideas, and make them socially tenable. Then, Warriors can execute, while Merchants may put them to use in growing society. Finally, Laborers can build the housing and infrastructure to make them last. This model is apparent in everything from the establishment of a religion to building and running a business.

Four Seasons

One of the oldest concepts of Vedic society is the institution of *ashrama*, or Stages of Life. In the West these four life stages correspond to Childhood, Adulthood, Retirement, and Old Age. Childhood ends about the time kids graduate from college and move out into the world. Adulthood ends about the time male/female menopause signals a change in the priorities of men and women. A man's so-called 'mid-life crisis' is Nature's way of redirecting him into new territory, in which he releases his obsession with achievement and security, and begins to share his wisdom with the world. The Retirement stage is completed about the time most Americans finish sharing their lessons and

---

[41] Avatars in Vedic cosmology are holy incarnations of the divine who take birth on earth in order to restore dharma. Among the orthodox avatars like Rama and Krishna, most also consider the Buddha and Jesus as incarnations of the divine, or at least avatar-like.

retire from the world, usually by age 65. Finally, the stage of Old Age is completed by death.

In Sanskrit, the four stages of life are called *1. brahmacharya, 2. grihastha, 3. vanaprastha,* and *4. sannyasa.* They are represented here by Nature's four seasons. Like the four great ages of the world and Nature's seasons, time is cyclical in the ancient worldview. In Chapter 1 we saw that over thousands of years, the world ages come and go as civilizations die and are reborn, and that great world-changes occur at the junctures between one age and the next. Likewise, the human soul evolves with the seasons of the body, changing direction at each stage, until it drops the body and takes birth again, beginning the cycle anew. This view of time singles out life's crucial transitions and teaches us to gracefully flow with them. Not knowing what we're supposed to do during each stage of our lives leads to identity crises, stress, and other psycho-social problems. Our ancestors advised us to follow the cycle of life seasons in order to ensure the proper discharge of our dharma and karma.

The four life stages or seasons cover each about a fourth of our lives. Depending on our definition of an optimal lifespan, this could mean 20 to 25 years each, for an 80 or 100 year duration of life. Like the bible, sacred texts which treat on lifespan allot man about 108 to 120 years in this age, in accordance with natural and cosmic rhythms. By modern standards, these may seem ambitious figures, but if we average an 88 year life span, the stages break down into segments of 22 years each, marking the ages where most people experience transitions in Western society: completion of education, completion of family and security, retirement, and death. Nature, of course, reflects these stages by the four seasons, and each season has a special affinity with a Dharma Type. Let's take a look at them now.

SEASON	Spring	Summer	Fall	Winter
UP TO AGE	22-25	44-50	66-75	67/75+
DHARMA TYPE	Laborer	Warrior/Merchant	Educator	Outsider

Spring

Spring is the season for birth, growth, and optimism. It is when we discover the earth and begin to enjoy the fullness of its bounty. The springtime of our lives is our youth, in which our duties are simple: to *grow* and to *learn*. This is the time we attend school, develop our bodies, and obey our parents. It is not yet the season to enjoy the world in its fullest sense because we are still dependent on others. It *is* the time for simple pleasures and tastes, before the mind and senses have developed enough sophistication to fully discriminate 'good' from 'bad,' desirable from undesirable.

It is a plentiful season that shares its foremost quality with the Labor type. Although education is an aspect of youth, *growth* is Nature's primary concern during the first season, and a hale and vital physical body are core attributes of the Labor type. Physical development is more important to Mother Nature than how many facts can be stored in your head, because physical vitality allows you to procreate and continue the species. Besides, early education is more about discipline and social training than real learning. It is the time during which we discipline our brains with rote memorization and rudimentary knowledge that in later years, if we're lucky, turn to wisdom. In the Vedic view, we are not truly capable of attaining 'higher knowledge' until our minds have a) fully matured, and b) become tempered by experience. The first step happens by the end of Spring, the second by the end of Summer. Thus, wisdom usually dawns during the Autumn season of our lives.

Western medicine seems to agree, affirming that our brains do not complete their 'wiring' until our early to mid twenties. Our anatomies mirror the sacred cycles of the four seasons, just as do our social customs: in the West, the formal end of education (four years of college) at about age 22 coincides with the end of Spring and the beginning of Summer, during which basic training is left behind for real-world applications. Summer is the time we put all the education and social skills we learned in Spring to use.

Like children during Spring season, Labor types enjoy being 'trained.' They respond to firm, loving authority and right influence. And whether 'training' a spouse, or molding an employee, the same strategies that keep kids in line also work to keep Laborers Integrated: repetitive tasks, constructive distraction, and a healthy respect for authority keep Laborers on the right path. From singing a song to poring over spreadsheets, keeping busy keeps Laborers' minds from obsessing on negative thoughts and moving towards constructive uses. Going to

> *People live according to the laws of Nature whether they are aware of them or no, and savvy observers can advantage themselves and others by understanding this.*

a movie, or even taking a coffee break can distract Laborers and put them in a positive state, reminding them of just how enjoyable simple pleasures can be; reminding them of the Spring season when time has no meaning. That is why smart employers allow breaks for their workers, especially Labor types.

But distraction can also be dangerous, and one way that Laborers pick up addictions to cigarettes, coffee, and alcohol. What begins as an innocuous habit can become an addiction. It is well-known that habits we pick up in the Spring season tend to stay with us for the rest of our lives, and this is one reason tobacco advertising actively targets kids and adolescents. Whether we know it or not, the savvy world of Madison Avenue is well-aware of Spring's sticky quality, and is quick to take advantage of the impressionable nature of those in it, whether it is directly cognizant of the four seasons and the brain's wiring or not. People naturally live according to the laws of Nature whether they are aware of them or no, and savvy observers can advantage themselves and others by understanding this.

Summer

Summer is the season of the Merchant and Warrior. It is the time to earn a living and make a mark on the world. It is the season to be outside and active. Those who live in colder climates can appreciate the gift of summer for the paucity of its days and the blessing of its warmth. The summer heat compels us to Warrior activities like competition, physical exertion, and work. Why waste a perfect day by staying inside? This is the time to go out and experience the natural world for all its challenges, surprises, and rewards. School ends for the summer for just this reason. The Warrior, though benefited by knowledge, is usually not hell-bent on acquiring it, especially when there are other, more immediate tasks to be done. Thus, during the second portion of our lives, we are not concerned with education, but in putting that education to use. This is the time for cultivating family and social dharmas and building the pillars of society. Between ages 22 and 44 our bodies are mature and hale, and able to perform the tasks we require of them. We are all Warriors at these times, carving out a niche for ourselves, dealing with the competition, and building a reserve for those who will follow.

This is also a Merchant period, during which men and women work to secure a future for their families. **Prosperity**, **progeny**, and **profession** are the focus, and Summer is not the time to withdraw from the world, unless becoming a monk is one's chosen path. But even then, monasticism becomes the *profession*, one's fellow monks the *family*, and one's students the *progeny*. Thus, even for spiritual aspirants, the Summer years are the time to interface most with the world and fight for realization of one's aspirations.

> *If children in the Summer of life do not reproduce, they bear the burden of attachment to their parents, and must replace the role that grandchildren play*

Fall

Fall teaches non-attachment. Just as leaves begin to detach from trees, between ages 44 to 66 our own grown-up children, now in the Summer of their lives, begin to leave home and start their careers and families. Men and women in Summer season do not have time to spend with their parents, as Nature pulls them to fulfill their own dharmas, and people in the Fall season of life are left alone. This is their first test in detachment. They may also lose their jobs, their hair, their memory, and in the case of women, their ability to reproduce. The loss of these and other non-vital functions begins to teach them the difference between what is permanent and what is fleeting, and to value the essential in life. This quality of *viveka*, discernment, and the transition to full detachment becomes complete when they enter into the final stage of life, where, tired of the entanglements and attachments of family, society, and even their spouses, the elderly take off into the wilds of Winter to hibernate until the coming of the next thaw. This hibernation takes the form of meditation and making peace with their spiritual selves, until sleep comes in the form of death to take them to a new body and a new Spring. But to make the transition easier for people in the Fall season, Nature provides them grandchildren to look after. In this way, though grandparents do not see their own kids much anymore, they still have someone to care for and teach.

It is the role of men and women in the Summer of life to produce children, and to enlist their parents' help in raising them. Procreation is part of the dharma of an adult human body, and an important duty to one's family, because it replaces the attachment that an aging parent has for a child with another, more needy being in the Springtime of its life. This releases people in their Summer periods to fully actuate their dharmas, and gives the grandparent a new perspective and appreciation for the innocence of Spring. If children in the Summer of life do not reproduce, they bear the burden of attachment to their parents, and must replace the role that grandchildren play. This can be difficult, for adults in Summer season are more interested in diving into the world than being doted on. Nonetheless, it is a child's duty to look after her parents, especially if there are no grandkids to replace her.

Autumn brings an end to the fiery race for self actualization, as the competitive juices of the Warrior subside, and the Merchant's desire for wealth and experience is gratified. We begin to slow down and appreciate our exploits, relishing more the passing of days and caring less about their outcome. This is a time to observe the change in the cycles of Nature. Leaves begin to turn red, even as our hair turns white. The weather is cooler and our bodies stiffer, and we are no longer able to dive into the waters of the wild. Our ability to interface with the physical world becomes more and more restricted. This is the time to take stock of our accomplishments and everything we have done in Summer and Spring. This third season is characterized by wisdom. It is incumbent on those in their Fall periods to consolidate their experiences and share what they have learned with the world. Will or no, we all become Educators in the Fall, as the younger generation looks up to us for guidance.

Educators by their nature are not as hearty and hale as the other types, but they command respect by their self-control and the example they set. No matter what their Dharma Type, everyone has something to teach during this time. Grandparents now, we can lend our wisdom to the rearing of our grandchildren, and allow our grown children to experience their Summer time unimpaired. Grandkids and others in their Labor (Spring) season are the worthiest recipients of our knowledge, and we must associate with them as much as possible, as it feeds our souls while nourishing their minds.

Traditionally, it 'took a village' to raise a child, especially the elders in a community, because these were at an optimal time to share their gifts. Grown in patience and diminished in ambition, they have the best interests of their pupils and progeny in mind. More on the important role of Grandparents is discussed in Volume II: *Sex, Love, & Dharma.*

Winter

In America, retirement officially starts at about age 65, which coincides with the beginning of Winter season, though for some Winter may start sooner or later. Some people may work well beyond their retirement years, effectively extending their Autumn period, while others may retire early, ready to settle into the warm shelter of solitude and self-reflection. Whatever the variance, there is a natural transition around this age that affects people in specific ways.

This period is characterized by isolation and change, qualities that befit the Outsider type. In Western societies, the elderly are sent off to nursing homes or hospitals, sequestered away from the mainstream world. For the average Westerner, the thought of death is oppressive, and we do all we can to sanitize ourselves from it. Despite the fact that it is the only certainty in life, we vainly screen ourselves from its reality, hoping it will go away. The elderly or sick who have death upon them are a reminder of that ultimate change, when the physical body gives way to the spirit self. Thus, people in the Winter of life become Outsiders, shunned by others, not because of any lack of virtue, but for the same reason we shun other Outsiders: we do not understand them, what they represent; they threaten the status quo of our daily existence.

> *"This kind of retirement plan requires no social security, only the maturity to walk out as a renunciate. Since the Indian society respects the Sannyasa [Winter] stage of life and the Veda enjoins it, naturally the basic needs of a sannyasi are taken care of by the society. Although some people postpone this stage of life, every one is expected to become a sannyasi in the end."*
> --Swami Dayananda, *from his commentary on the Bhagavad Gita*

The old man is less concerned with propriety: he has earned the right to speak his mind, to burp and do as he wills, to hell with the consequences! He is an Outsider because he cares little for the ordinary decrees of social decorum, aware that he can be snatched from the game of life without warning.

But Winter doesn't have to be laden with the hoary frost of bitterness. Nor, in the words of a famous dub poet,

> *"how, passions spent, we droop like sapless vines/ in the winter of our minds."*[42]

It is the happy redemption of our immortal soul, for the pledge of our mortality. It is a time of bitterness indeed, but such bitterness that makes the

---

[42] Linton Kwesi Johnson, from *Seasons of the Heart*

sweet taste sweeter. It is here that we understand what the Vedic saint Shankaracharya meant by 'throwing off the world with disgust.' Men have lost their *shukra*, their juice, their seed, and women their *shakti*, the feminine power, and all that's left is a dry shell that once harbored the flames of passion, but is now home to the light of the spirit. The fire of youth that burned so strong must now be transmuted into the steady light of wisdom, wisdom gone beyond the mundane world of time and space into the far realm of the spirit. Whose mortal eyes fail, now has the faraway look of one who beholds a distant shore. Whose mortal eyes fail, now looks upon the inner spaces of the mind. Nature, in Her ever-present goodness, trades one gift for another. If we have the wisdom to exchange our expired tools for the new set that She gives us, we can continue to enjoy the protection of Natural Law, the dharma of life's final stage.

The person in the Winter of life, like any Outsider, must be honest with herself and face the truth of her immanent reality. She must own the present, and prepare for what Nature has in store for her. This whole book is about following the Natural laws of the universe, the dharmas of body, mind, and soul. Having reached Winter, we can't stop now. In fact, this is the most important time to heed the call of Natural Law, for here it promises to take us to its highest fulfillment, the realization of our true Self. Whereas the dharmas of the lower world offer temporal returns: Health, Wealth, Name and Fame, the dharma of the spirit holds eternal rewards for us such as cannot be fully redeemed in the body.

We should remember that the Four Seasons are not only religious or philosophical designations, but have real and practical correlations. Research shows that between ages 50-75 health declines relatively slowly. But after age 75 physical ability drops off more drastically, reflecting the transition between Autumn and Winter seasons. During Autumn one still makes use of the body to share wisdom and experience with younger generations. But with the onset of the final season our duties to others come to an end, and our bodies begin to withdraw from the world in preparation for their final transition. This does not mean that we have to go meekly into the night. In fact, people in Winter season are encouraged to exercise and remain active both mentally and physically. However, the emphasis here is not on creating more attachments to the world, such as having a beautiful body or a glowing reputation, but in relinquishing them. One can remain hale until one's dying days so long as one is also aware that the body and all of its connections are impermanent expressions of a permanent Self. During the Winter phase, Nature encourages us to get to know that Self by shaking and even breaking our attachments to anything that stands in the way of that knowledge.

Special Applications

The Four Seasons of Life are well-known to most Indians. However, most people do not make the connection between the seasons and Dharma Types. Understanding the permutations of these connections can open up our world in new ways. For example, Laborers love to reminisce and wax eloquent about their 'good 'ol days,' when they were young and strong, and the world seemed to shine with the brightness of Spring. Older Labor types may disparage the present, and things associated with it, and drone on about how things were better in the past. Since Spring is the Laborer's season, the time between birth and age 22, can you see why Laborers would have a fondness for their youthful years? It is not about a particular time in history, but about *when they were young.* And because Autumn represents the time of the Educator, a Laborer's Disintegration point, is it a wonder that Laborers get cranky between ages 44-66, when their bodies no longer move the way they should, and their ability to be good nurturers and providers begins to wane?

On the other hand, Educators do not mature until their 40s, 50s, and 60s. Since wisdom does not fully ripen until Autumn, Educators may spend their early years in painful but gradual learning. Spring is hard for them because they Disintegrate into the Labor type, and Educators are often teased or pushed around, or feel clumsy and awkward during this time. They begin to hit their stride and shine in the Summer season, an Integration time for them, though they do not really come into their own until their later years. Summer is both a Merchant and a Warrior period during which Educators look to get ahead (Warrior) and profit from their knowledge (Merchant). From software engineers to astronomers, teachers, and professors, they make their mark in the world and profit from it best in Summer season. But since the Educator's priority in life is not profit, she does not find full satisfaction until Autumn.

For their part, Warriors shine during Summer. Since they have to use their bodies and life energy (prana) in order to be successful, these are at their peak between ages 22-44. For athletes, this is the season of greatest accomplishment, and, with a few exceptions (like gymnastics), when most world records are broken and money is made. Since Summer is also a Merchant period, it can be a time of stress and overwork, which is why Warrior types can die from heart attacks and strokes in their Summer years. Warriors Disintegrate into the

Merchant, and should watch out for pushing too hard during this time. In their zeal to achieve and be somebody, they must be guided by wisdom to know how much is too much, and what boundaries must be respected.

We can also use the Four Seasons to look at how people relate with each other. Educators, for example, are sometimes awkward with children, since kids represent the Spring season, their Disintegration point. Much better are Laborers, who enjoy being parents, caretakers, and nurses, because the freshness of Spring that is still on children rubs off on them, reminding them of their youth. Or, like Bruce Springsteen or Kid Rock (an Outsider playing a Laborer), they may use memories of their 'Glory Days' to inspire them in their careers.

A quality of the naturally devotional Labor type is to sit and learn at the feet of her parents and mentors. Be it life skills and morals, or athletics and arithmetic, the devotional spirit of children is cultivated in the first Stage of Life as they are taught to obey and serve their elders and follow social standards. We do not judge our children to be inferior or 'lesser citizens.' In fact, this is when we love them most, when they are brimming with innocence and the freshness of life. The same is true of the Labor Type, who is also beloved of the Dharma Types when she is Integrated. A Laborer in line with her dharma has the innocence and freshness of Spring ever about her, even into her Winter season. For the same reason, Educators tend to look or feel *older* than they are, because they represent Autumn, while Warriors seem to always have an air of energy and danger, be they eight or eighty!

The Seasons of Life, along with the Elements (and the Tastes which follow) are tools to help guide our life transitions, understand our psychologies, and pattern our behaviors. We can use them in new and innovative ways to shed light on our professions, relationships, as well as our spiritual lives. The remainder of this book and the volumes to come cover these topics in depth, but really the only limit how we use the Dharma Types is our own imagination... the permutations are endless.

TASTE	Dharma Type and SEASON
Sweet is a taste of Heaven. It is anabolic, relating to growth, optimism, and everything that is good in life. It is the reward for good deeds or a job well done. Yet too much Sweet promotes fantasy and immaturity. It represents the baby stage of life, and of all stages, this is when we need the most sweetness from our environment, food, and relationships. This is when we need to be nurtured and cared for by the world.	LABORER SPRING
Sour whets our appetites for other tastes. It represents the school-age when kids are forced to learn, which though unpleasant, opens their minds up to other possibilities, and makes them hungry for life experience. An excess of sour turns to 'sour grapes;' when we want things so much for ourselves that we cannot enjoy sharing them with others.	LABORER SPRING
The **Salty** taste makes us thirsty and kindles our appetites in a different way than the Sour taste. Sour is slow to work: salty makes us want food immediately, which is why we can't get enough of salty snacks or treats. It represents the middle of life in which we desire to improve ourselves. Too much salty taste leads to water retention, and represents greed and accumulation.	MERCHANT SUMMER
Pungent is the spicy hot taste that drives us to compete and gives us energy, passion, and desire. It clears our heads and makes us push to achieve. It also represents adult life when we are at the height of our power and most able to affect the world. The Pungent taste is the most 'dangerous,' in that a little bit goes a long way, and too much can be painful!	WARRIOR SUMMER
The **Bitter** taste makes us appreciate the sweet. It shrinks our tissues and repulses us from food. Like the Autumn stage of life, the bitter taste sets limits on how much we can ingest, and makes us turn our minds to other things. It sometimes makes us long for sweetness. Bitter is catabolic, beginning the breakdown process that encourages our 'fasting' from the everyday menu of worldly life, and looking to other forms of sustenance.	EDUCATOR AUTUMN
The **Astringent** taste is like an unripe banana: it dries up the tongue and sucks out the juice from the tissues. Astringent, like Winter time, is catabolic, breaking down and purifying the body further, until little excess remains.	OUTSIDER WINTER

Taste

In Ayurveda, the Vedic science of life, six tastes are classed according to their effects on the body and mind. The six tastes each represent a discreet part of our existence, and taken together mirror the totality of the human experience. They are: Sweet, Sour, Salty, Pungent, Bitter, Astringent. Their effects are indicated on the preceding page.

Too much or too little of any taste can spell too much or too little of its qualities in our lives. For example, let's say Joseph eats too much sweet taste. He is compelled to reach for a candy bar or soda at the slightest sense of uneasiness or hunger. This demonstrates an immature mentality that lacks impulse control and cannot *grow up*. Joe needs some bitter taste to balance out the sweetness, as Bitter relates to maturity and realism, whereas Sweet represents idealism, fantasy, and puerile behavior. People who overeat sweets are hooked on the fantasy of the short-term high, but ignore the reality of the long-term deleterious effects of sugar.

Another example is Jane, who can't get enough salty snacks: potato chips, French fries, you name it, she can't stop eating it. The more she eats, the more she buys. Salty taste relates to greed, and our desire for more things in life. It is appropriate at a certain age and in judicious quantities, but our culture is inundated with sweet and salty tastes, thereby addicting people to *Fantasy* and *Greed*: we spend more and more on goodies and objects, and think that everything will pay for itself, as we get deeper and deeper into debt. This mix of naïveté and desire spells disaster for our bodies and pocketbooks alike, and eventually the economy itself.

What is needed is a healthy helping of Bitter and Astringent tastes to balance sweet and salty. Dark, leafy greens are great sources of bitter, and in the words of Dr. Vasant Lad, *'Bitter is better for the liver.'* The liver is our primary detoxifier, and benefits from generous servings of salads and leafy vegetables. The fiscal equivalent of leafy greens is *self-restraint*. Restraint and Contentment are especially healthy for Merchant types, and Merchant society itself, though they may be an acquired taste, like dandelion and sprout salad. Contentment is also one of the observances of the Yogic path particularly useful to the Merchant, as illustrated in the table below.

Though the Yoga Sutras tell us that *all* of these codes of self-regulation or restraint *become a great vow when they become universal and are not restricted by any consideration of the nature of the kind of living being to whom one is related, nor in any place, time or situation,*[43] in practice it is useful to focus on one or two of these, especially as they pertain to our Dharma Type.

DHARMA TYPE	YAMA	NIYAMA
Educator	Ahimsa/ Non-Violence	Svadhyaya/ Self-Study
Warrior	Satya/ Truthfulness	Tapas/ Austerity
Merchant	Asteya/ Non-Stealing	Santosha/ Contentment
Laborer	Brahmacharya/ Continence	Shaucha/ Cleanliness
Outsider	Aparigraha/ Non-Grasping	Ishvara Pranidhana/ Surrender to God

For example, Warriors sometimes have dilemmas about non-violence because this may appear to interfere with their dharma of protecting others, or clash with other lifestyle choices, such as eating meat, that otherwise promote their well-being. But for Warriors, Truthfulness, or doing what they say and saying what they do, is *the first and foremost vow* they must master. In fact, this alone can take them to enlightenment, because going deep enough into any one discipline can lead a type to the other side.

Likewise, Continence is the vow particularly useful to Laborers. For householders Continence does not mean abstaining from sex, but using sex for procreation in the crucible of one's marriage. Laborers thrive on their communities, and building a big family goes along with their dharma. Saving their sexual ardor for their loved one and sharing it in this context, rather than wasting it frivolously, bears great fruit for a Laborer type.

For Outsiders, who have harder times finding their dharmas, it is tempting to *grasp* and try to be somebody else. Though this is useful for a while, ultimately every Outsider must come up with her own Unique Expression and share it with the world. Therefore, Non-Grasping becomes the vow best suited to their

---

[43] Translation of verse 2.31 of the *Yoga Sutras of Patanjali* by Swami JnaneshwaraBharati, available at www.swamiji.com.

highest purpose. In the same way, special attention to *Cleanliness* for Laborers, *Contentment* for Merchants, *Self-Study* for Educators, *Austerity* for Warriors, and *Surrender to God* (Acceptance of their life circumstances— which leads to Responsibility, Ruth, and Respect) for Outsiders leads to an optimal life experience. These, along with the 18 classic Vedic disciplines are developed in detail in Volume III: *The Spiritual Types.*

Special Applications

As we grow older, we appreciate bitter tastes more: adults learn to enjoy drinking beer or eating salads as a natural mark of an evolving maturity. Yet *too much* Bitter or Astringent curtails our enjoyment of life. These tastes relate to people who willingly or unwillingly throw off the world, like ascetics and mendicants. Too much of anything is unhealthful. Balance is necessary to obtain satisfaction in life. Vedic wisdom encourages the skilful use of ***all six*** tastes to promote a unique rasa, or sense of enjoyment in the degustator. Likewise, Vedic philosophy encourages knowledge and skillful use of its many disciplines— Ayurveda (Self-care) Jyotisha (Astrology), Vastu (Home Arrangement), Samkhya (Cosmology) and the Yoga principles previewed above, to create a superb rasa in the totality of one's life experience.

As we saw with the Four Seasons above, these six Tastes lend themselves to different applications. They are used in Ayurveda to treat disease and restore balance to the body. But leaving aside their health implications, we can see again why Educators are more *serious* than other types, for their affinity to the Bitter Taste and Autumn season. We can find a physical correlation to the Laborer's jealousy in the Sour Taste. Laborers are the most jealous types, one of their few shortcomings. The Sour taste predominating in them can describe character traits like jealousy and sour grapes, as much as actual taste preferences.

Warriors can be harsh and unyielding, and of all the Tastes, Pungent is the most potentially harmful. While other Tastes can kill you slowly, the effects of Pungent are immediate and acute. Pepper spray is concentrated Pungent Taste, and whether defending against charging bears or attacking criminals, it has direct uses for self-defense and law enforcement. Not surprisingly, Pungent Taste in the form of cayenne pepper improves blood flow in the body and is good for the heart. Recall from the Wellness chapter that the heart and blood are Warrior organs, circulating energy and courage to every system in the body. Thus, the links between the types and the various categories enumerated in these chapters go on forever. Ultimately, we cannot describe every nuance of embodied life as it relates to the Dharma Types. It is up to you, as a reader, to form ever new correlations that benefit you and others!

Dharma Type (Technology)	Category (Interface)	Your World (Health, Relationships, etc.)
Educator	Element, Taste, Season	⟶
Laborer	Circle of Duty	⟶
Warrior	Five Bodies	⟶
Outsider	Anatomy	⟶
Merchant	Brain Systems	⟶

Homework

Your homework in this chapter is to start making connections between the Dharma Types and your world, using the categories we have learned so far. These categories are interface mechanisms for applying the Dharma Type technology to our lives. You may ask yourself, *"If I'm an Outsider and linked to the Astringent Taste, what does that say about my food preferences?"* Since the Astringent Taste is rare and unusual, you may like interesting food, or have diet and lifestyle preferences that are different from your society's. You may be Vegan, while living in a small town in Texas. You may love Indian curry, though hailing from Minnesota. Combining this with the connotations of *death* in Winter season, we may find that Outsiders eat canned or leftover food. Canned food is considered 'dead' in that many of its nutrients are robbed from it. Furthermore, Astringent taste breaks down tissue, which is again why Outsiders make good troubleshooters, but not necessarily builders: they can break down and critique what's wrong, but not necessarily know how to build it up. Try using the **Elements, Tastes, Season, Circle of Duty, Five Bodies, Brain Systems, Anatomy** and other categories to interface with your life. Even the tables on the preceding pages describing long-term vs. short-term effects can be profoundly useful once you know your type. Are you generally ruled by Emotion or Intellect, Objects or Ideas? How does this affect your relationships, or work performance? Consider these categories, as well as the ones to follow (Intelligence, Speech, & Secret Fear) on a regular basis, and your world will open up to you in new and fresh perspectives!

Chapter 9: Element, Taste, and Season

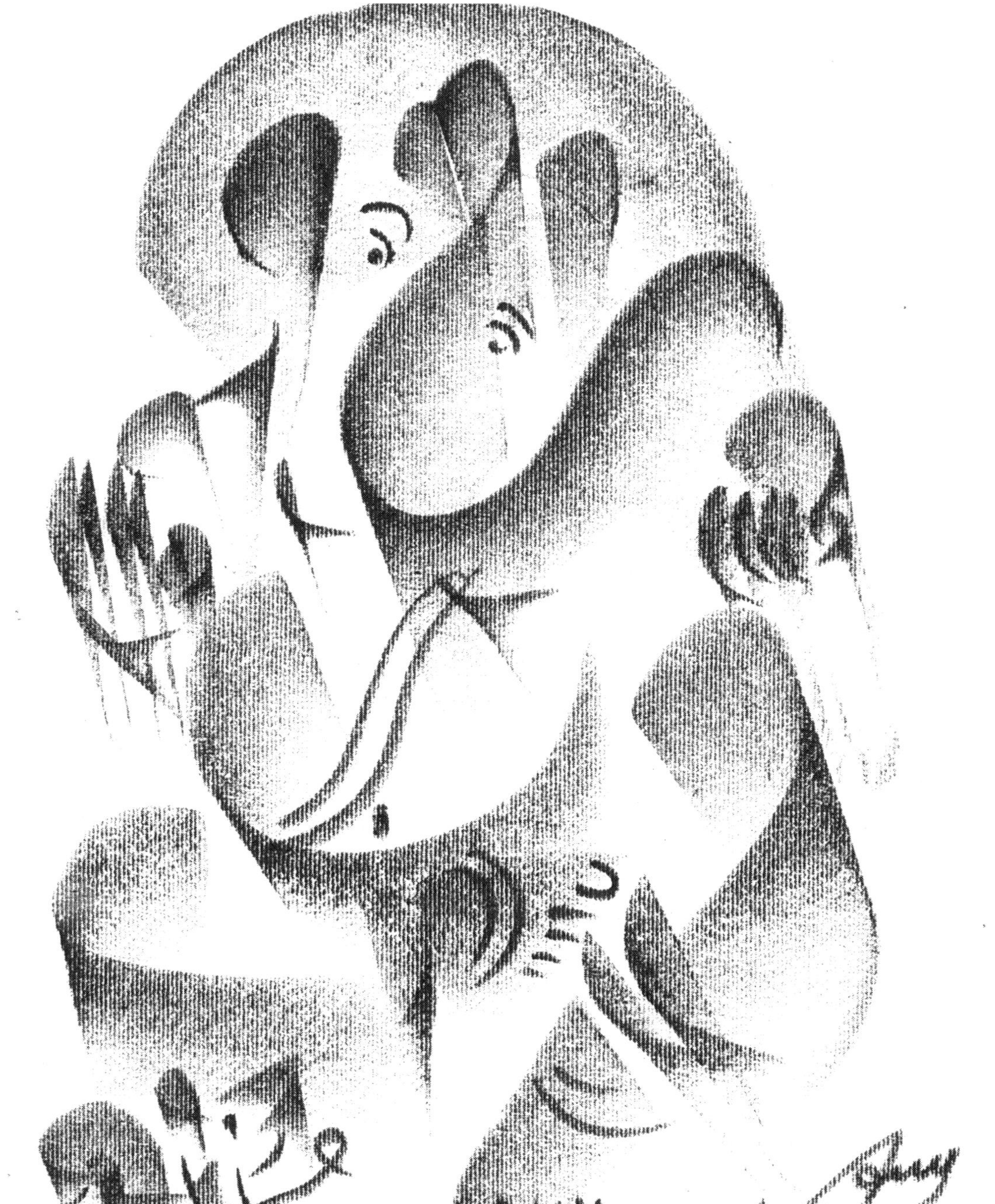

10
INTELLIGENCE, SPEECH, AND SECRET FEAR

Intelligence comes from the Latin *inter-legere*, to *read between the lines*, to understand the underlying dynamics of a given situation. Each of the five Yoga Bodies discussed in previous sections has a specific Intelligence. Let us take a look at these here, with some of their keywords:

Laborer	Outsider	Warrior	Merchant	Educator
Food/ Flesh Body	Bliss Body	Vital/ Breath/ Energy Body	Sensate Body	Wisdom Body
Emotional Intelligence	Mystic Intelligence	Energetic Intelligence	Aesthetic Intelligence	Intellectual Intelligence
Capable Practical Intuitive	*Iconoclastic Experimental Empathic*	*Ambitious Skillful Coordinated*	*Convivial Clever Sensitive*	*Sophisticated Ideological Wise*

Intelligence denotes sophistication of an Emotional, Energetic, Sensate, Intellectual, or Mystic nature, according to the 5 Yoga Bodies. Thus, while one person may have Intellectual sophistication, they may possess a paucity of Emotional or Energetic Intelligence. Likewise, some persons who are physically skilled, may possess little openness to the Mystery of life.

Laborers, for example, have the highest *Emotional* IQ, as they are better able to grasp and deal with the emotional currents in the human body. We should not wonder why *emotional* Intelligence is associated with the Flesh Body, since science tells us that emotions are carried and catalyzed by our neurochemistry and hormones. Long before modern medicine, the ancients knew that emotions were *physical* things, which is why can be manipulated with drugs, food, exercise, and touch.

Laborers make the best caregivers. They are grounded, down to earth, and not easily shaken. Their deep reserves allow them to cope with a crying child, a complaining mother, or a dying patient with dignity and compassion. No other type has the potential for emotional maturity that Laborers are capable of, which is why they are perceived as practical, stoic, and nurturing. And even though Merchants rule the Sensate Body, they can be emotionally immature because they are not grounded in the Flesh Body like Laborers.

> *You can't solve an illogical problem by thinking about it logically. Outsiders offer new solutions to old problems using their Radical Intelligence.*

In the same way, Educators have *Intellectual,* or *Philosophical* Intelligence, the kind most commonly measured with an Intelligence Quotient. But IQ tests ignore the other four human Intelligences. Only in the Educator type is this rational, linguistic intellect emphasized. Other Intelligences are non-verbal. When a baseball player sights a ball rapidly traveling towards his body, for example, his Energy Body allows him to correctly adjust the vector and timing of his bat to produce the intended outcome—hitting the ball out of the park. This is a non-linguistic Intelligence particularly useful for survival, in which the brain and nervous system fire electrical and neurochemical impulses to coordinate movement for a specific purpose. Warriors possess this type of *Energetic* Intelligence.

For their part, Merchants have a high *Sensual,* or *Aesthetic IQ.* They know how to value things such as art and manufactured goods, which is why they are the primary producers and consumers of *luxury.* From Godiva chocolates to Aston Martin sports cars, Merchants tend to enjoy things more for their glamour and style than for their usefulness, as discussed in the Merchant section of Part One. Their affinity with the Sensate body can also refine their senses and make them sensitive to emotional slights, which may lead Merchants to create great music and art... or to simply act out.

Finally, Outsiders are the mystery seekers and explorers of the Dharma Type family. They possess a Mystic, or Radical Intelligence that allows them to probe the hidden aspects of life. Another word for *hidden* is *occult*, and from UFOlogists and conspiracy theorists to theoretical physicists, their ability to sense and experiment with the *extra sensory* is unmatched. You can't solve an illogical problem by thinking about it logically. Outsiders offer new solutions to old problems using their Radical Intelligence.

It is not the *quantity*, but the *quality* of Intelligence that separates one archetype from another. It is not *how much* Intelligence someone has, but *what type* predominates in them. A martial artist possesses Intelligence, though not the type we think of when we consider someone 'smart.' A finely-tuned athlete is in fact supremely Intelligent at the Energetic level, where they can make their bodies move with a degree of sophistication unavailable to those who do not possess such Intelligence. The Warrior's Energy, or Prana Body is tied to the breath, and the movement of electrical and neuro-chemical impulses that coordinate mind and body functions for a specific outcome, such as scoring a goal or killing an enemy. Prana is also termed *chi, ki,* or *vital breath* in different disciplines. Contrast this with the Laborer's Physical Body, which is more typical of muscle, sinew, and flesh, and less concerned with the goals and achievements of the Warrior type but with what can be touched, felt, and manipulated with the hands.

These distinctions have practical applications in daily life. Being tied to the thinking power of the body, Laborers have stronger 'gut feelings' and hunches, and learn kinesthetically, through touch and movement. Laborers must *feel* a person before they can like them. That's one reason Educator politicians like Barack Obama have difficulties connecting to their Labor-type constituents, because they fundamentally speak different languages and think with different Intelligences.

A genius who probes the unfathomable mysteries of space but cannot balance his checkbook may possess Intelligence of the Mystic Body, but little savvy or street Intelligence, which is the domain of the Sensate Body and the Merchant Type. In fact, few are gifted with Intelligence in all 5 areas. Most people operate on one or two levels of competence, with less development in the other three. Knowing your Intelligence can help you obtain success in life by singling out your strengths, so that, for example, you can get a job that best suits your high points, while de-emphasizing your 'dummy' areas. Of course it is important to develop a well-rounded personality, and this map also helps us distinguish which areas we need to shore up. Learning the Intelligence of our Integration point, as we shall see below, is vital to making us well-rounded human beings.

Mastering at least two Intelligences gives us two legs to stand on and the ability to actualize our talents while hedging against our vulnerabilities.

Language

To *read between the lines* implies such a facility for understanding that one is able to discern implied, hidden meaning not overtly expressed. It is truly the ability to *speak a language*. In such a way, each of the 5 Bodies speaks a different language that only those versed in it can fully appreciate. When a Warrior learns a tennis stroke, she learns it faster and masters it more quickly than the other types, because she *speaks the language* of coordination and skill. Her body and mind are wired to naturally figure out the nuances of energy and control. On the other hand, when the Merchant learns a card game or a sales pitch, he is better at it than his fellow Dharma Types because of the inner Intelligence that steers him to the most powerful way to affect people, and the most profitable strategy to make money. In addition, those who speak *the same language* are more at home with each other than those who don't, which has repercussions on Compatibility between the types.

It is in the Integration point of the types that we find the most useful 'second languages' to learn. The Educator, for example, must learn the Warrior's ability to express *prana*; while Warriors must learn the Educator's linguistic skill. For Merchants and Laborers it is again reciprocal. **Each type should learn the language of its Integration point to improve its own capacity to communicate.** Just as a child born to Mexican and American parents learns to speak both Spanish and English, we must ideally learn two languages and **master two Intelligences** if we wish to fully express our talents: those of our original Dharma Type and those of our Integration point.

Ultimately, it is also useful to learn a third language, that of the Life Cycle we are in, when this is different from our Dharma Type. Like it or not, we have to speak the language of our Life Cycle, just as the English and Spanish speaking child must learn German if she moves to Germany. Life Cycles can last years, even whole lifetimes, and the more languages we speak, the better our ability to navigate through them with ease. The more Intelligences we understand, the more we are able to relate with others clearly, rather than through the stained glass of our own perceptions.

The 5 Bodies

The Food Body (Laborer)

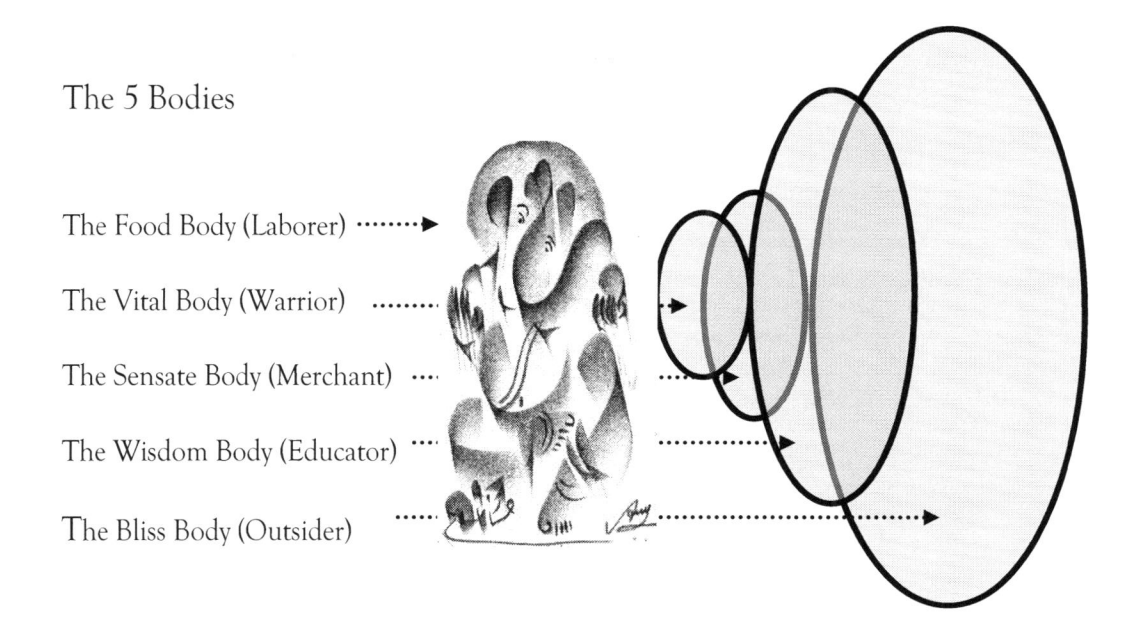

The Vital Body (Warrior)

The Sensate Body (Merchant)

The Wisdom Body (Educator)

The Bliss Body (Outsider)

Looking back to Chapter 7, we saw what every type has to do in order to obtain **fitness**, allowing for optimal vitality to experience life, health, and longevity. This was based on the affinity between the Dharma Types and their Yoga Bodies. Recall that Warriors have to master the first two Bodies to have health, while Merchants had to master three, Educators four, and Outsiders all five Bodies. Like Russian nesting dolls, each sheath 'fits' within and is encapsulated by another. In the same way, Outsiders must learn to speak and understand all 5 of the body's languages and Intelligences, a skill they are particularly good at.

To translate this into real world applications, Outsiders are best at learning second, third, and fourth foreign tongues,[44] like Spanish or Italian, because they are able to blend and assimilate better than any other type. This explains their affinity for strange customs, foreign relations, and the other Outsider categories, from Government to Profession, covered throughout this book. On the other hand, Laborers are usually not required to learn many of the body's other Intelligences, except perhaps that of their Integration point, because their Food Body does not require them to. Their dharma is such that they are quite happy speaking one or two of the body's languages, obtaining fulfillment therefrom. As a result, they do not learn and assimilate foreign tongues well: whereas an Outsider may roll her 'r's with a perfect Spanish or Italian accent, a

---

[44] The word *tongue* in this section is used to refer to foreign languages, like Italian or Spanish; the word *language* refers to the Intelligence and skill of a specific Yoga Body

Laborer will struggle to grok proper pronunciation, bedeviled by the limitations of her type.

That does not mean that Laborers should not study foreign tongues. Though they may not come easy, learning new tongues and skills, like *Jyotisha, Sanskrit,* or *Vastu Shastra*[45], can do wonders for the health, wealth, and personal development of a hard-working Labor Type. Laborers *appreciate* these skills more than anyone else, because they've had to *work harder* than anyone else to acquire them! Outsiders may take their talents for granted, but a Laborer cherishes everything she's learned by the sweat of her brow. Learning a foreign tongue can change a Laborer's life forever, while for the Outsider such a skill may be less earth-shattering. Even Educators, when they acquire foreign tongues, are less moved than Laborers. These Educators will also retain more of an accent and sound 'scholarly' when speaking, for as subtle as Air is, it cannot blend near as perfectly as the Outsider's Space Element, unless, of course, those Educators are living in Outsider Life Cycles.

The *potential* to speak many of the body's languages is why Educators can make good teachers and why Outsiders may have good perspective and problem-solving acumen. When Integrated, they are able to see the world through different lenses and relate to people on many levels. They are able to make laws that are inclusive, or abolish practices that are restrictive, because they understand the plight of other types. But when Disintegrated, they may never realize this potential, and be as narrow-minded as any other Disintegrated type. The key is that they have the gift: it is up to them to use it.

When types Disintegrate, they become oblivious to other Intelligences, unable to speak languages other than their own. This is tragic on the interpersonal as well as global levels— in relations between people as well as countries, who also have Dharma Types, and are ruled by the Natural Laws that govern individuals. Throughout history, some of the unfortunate venues for misunderstood Intelligence have been **religion** and **male-female relations**. Since religion is a topic for Volume III, let us look at how Intelligence relates to and can improve gender dynamics.

---

[45]Jyotisha and VastuShastra, like many classical subjects, are languages that allow us to interface with the world in specific ways, and employ similar learning pathways in the brain..

Men and Women

	MEN	WOMEN
YOGA BODY	VITAL BODY WISDOM BODY	FOOD BODY SENSATE BODY
ELEMENT	FIRE/AIR	EARTH/WATER
BRAIN HEMISPHERE	LEFT	RIGHT
DHARMA TYPE	WARRIOR (primarily) EDUCATOR	LABORER (primarily) MERCHANT
INTELLIGENCE	ENERGETIC/ LINGUISTIC	KINESTHETIC/ SENSATE-EMOTIONAL

Archetypally, women have a greater affinity to their Flesh and Sensate Bodies and men with the Vital and Intellect Bodies. The Flesh and Sensate Bodies are closely tied to the Earth and Water Elements and physical chemistry, which is why women are attributed higher emotional Intelligence than men. Men for their part relate better to the Vital and Intellect Bodies and their corresponding Fire and Air Elements. Fire relates to sight, goal-setting, and the transformation of other Elements, which is why men have stronger needs to manipulate their environment, make and use tools and set goals. This is reflected in our anatomies, where men possess greater physical strength while women have superior emotional integration via more sophisticated anatomical structures, such as the corpus collosa and their complex hormonal systems. Thus, one is able to *do*, the other to *feel* and *express*, more adeptly. This also relates to a goal-oriented, 'left-brain,' rational, problem-solving mentality for men, and a holistic, 'right-brain,' visceral, emotionally-integrated Intelligence for women.[46]

---

[46] While the Food Body represents muscle and flesh, it is the *Energetic* impulses from the brain that actually generate *strength;* thus, men are generally stronger than women, even though women are more closely allied with the Flesh Body. On the other hand, women have

The Flesh and Sensate bodies relate to the Labor and Merchant types, who are characterized by Earth and Water. These Elements are usually, though not always, represented with feminine traits in mythology, like *Mother Earth* and *Mother Nature*. Nature's life-giving qualities are most conspicuous in the water we drink and the food (Earth) we eat. On the other hand, Fire and Air tend to be Masculine. The Sun (Fire) is male and paternal, as is *Father Sky*. In this way, our ancestors related the macrocosm of the universe to the microcosm of our bodies. Without a key, we lose the relevance between the eternal nature of these myths and our momentary existence. Understanding the Intelligence of the five Bodies, Elements, and Dharma Types allows us to link ourselves to our environment in the fluid, intuitive, and holistic manner of our ancestors.

Practically, this means that men need to learn the Labor and Merchant languages if they are to have success communicating with women. Men who are already Labor or Merchant types have an advantage, whereas Educator and Warrior men are not as handily equipped to deal with the opposite sex. Take a look at the list of Labor and Merchant type men from Part 1 and you will find that many have reputations for being 'good' with women: *Warren Beatty, Bill Clinton, Muhammad Ali, Elvis Presley, Frank Sinatra,* and *Sean Connery* among the Merchants, and *Harrison Ford, Kevin Kostner, Dean Martin, and Marlon Brando* among the Laborers.

Now take a sample from the Educator side: *Woody Allen, Billy Graham, Bob Dylan,* and *George Lucas* don't exactly invoke raw sex appeal. Though there are some Educators like *Barack Obama* who have charisma and charm, Educators are usually beloved for other qualities. Warriors, on the other hand, though they do not naturally speak the Merchant or Labor tongues, tend to embody raw masculinity, making them sexy despite this failing. Thus, though they may not *communicate* perfectly with women, Warriors usually do not have a problem *getting* them. Not many women would kick *Paul Newman* or *Robert Redford* out of bed, given the chance.

For their part, women need to learn to speak "Warrior" and "Educator" to better communicate with their male counterparts. Unfortunately, however,

---

greater pain tolerance, affinity to touch, and better 'gut instincts' than men, all qualities of the Flesh Body and the Labor Type. The corpus collosum mediates between the left and right hemispheres of the brain, allowing them to communicate. Being more integrated in women and homosexual men, it allows them to *express* (left brain) what they *feel* (right brain) more effectively than straight men. In the end, it is not that men do not feel, but that their intellectual, rational brain is not *in touch* with these feelings.

Chapter 10: Intelligence, Speech, and Secret Fear

> *For women, a handsome man is one thing, but he must also possess good scent, or chemistry, and know how to move her emotionally, if he is to generate powerful attraction...*

Warrior and Educator women, though better-equipped to communicate with and understand men, are not necessarily the most desirable *to* men. This is because for men the rules change. Just as Warriors embody masculinity, Merchants and Laborers embody femininity, so men prefer a Merchant type woman regardless of whether she can communicate, because men are more fixated on *physical looks*, whereas women may prefer other intangible qualities, like charisma, self-control, power, leadership ability, and success. Take a look at *Marilyn Monroe, Paris Hilton, or Michelle Pfeiffer* from the Merchant pool and you will find some of the most desired women on the planet. Being Warriors, men are ruled predominantly by the Fire Element. Fire relates to sight, and men respond better to *visual stimulation*, which is why they crane their necks and use their eyes to suss out a potential mate. Hip-to-waist ratio, breast size, and other biological, visually-discernible factors dictate female attractiveness for a man.

Women, like Labor types, use other senses to *feel out* a man. For women, a handsome man is one thing, but he must also possess good scent, or chemistry, and know how to move a woman emotionally if he is to generate powerful attraction. We will discuss male/female matters in greater depth in Volume II: *Sex, Love, & Dharma*.

Secret Fear

The Educator's secret fear is for survival. Because she lacks physical skills to fully care for herself, the Educator is often the most physically vulnerable. Her antidote is to Surrender to the forces of Nature, and allow Nature to take care of her. This is difficult, but an Educator surrendered to the greater Will becomes invincible. Gandhi is an example of an Educator who harnessed the forces of Surrender to achieve superhuman results.

The Laborer's secret fear is being ridiculed. Laborers fear being perceived as stupid or not knowing enough. Their antidote is love and devotion. Linguistic behavior, facts, and information do not stand up to pure, unalloyed love. Oprah Winfrey and Mother Teresa are example of Laborers whose ability to love transcended their secret fears of ridicule.

The Merchant's secret fear is that he is worthless. There is an emptiness inside Merchants that is only filled by giving. This is the spiritual paradox of the hungry ghost: no matter how much he eats, he cannot be fulfilled. External things cannot rid him of this feeling. The antidote is to give the very thing you crave, and in doing so, to be released from the desire for it, which is the cause of suffering.

The Warrior secretly fears God. Warriors are masters of the material plane, where they can control themselves and their environment. They fear that which they cannot control, which is the spiritual. Right knowledge protects the Warrior, and assures him of his just place in the world. It also sanctions his actions when they are performed with the proper intent. This type of right understanding is the central theme of Krishna's teaching in the Bhagavad Gita.

Ironically, though he is the most willing to give his life for another, the Warrior type also secretly fears Death, or what lies beyond Death, because it is an enemy he does not know how to conquer. Death and God are things he does not easily understand, and he may devote his entire life to doing so. People who understand Death and what lies beyond are revered by Warriors, which is another reason Educators and Warriors share a bond of need. The first has the theory, the second the power and patience to make it work. The Buddha was a Warrior who transcended Death by his intense practices, many of which he learned from his Educator comrades in the forest.

The Outsider fears being caught and restrained. As a result, he tends to hide himself or conceal his intentions. The answer is to be plain and honest with people. Freedom comes not from skulking in the dark, but in turning the light on to yourself. Outsiders can only be restrained when they deceive themselves and society: therefore for Outsiders THE TRUTH WILL SET YOU FREE is not a cliché, but a mantra for personal emancipation.

Speech

Speech is life energy organized and expressed with the intent to communicate. Communication can be achieved through bodily movement (dance), symbol, (writing and art), sound (music & speech), and more... but in this section we will focus particularly on the language of the spoken word. In bygone days adherence to one's word was vital, as speech was perceived an extension of one's self. When a person spoke, she not only exhaled *prana*, life energy, but her very soul— life energy combined with intention and intelligence. Though modern attitudes to speech are less rigorous, what you say and how you say it is important, and every type has special injunctions that govern how they should speak.

For example, words can be weapons for Warriors. They can be tools to protect people or cut them down. As it is the Warrior's task to protect dharma, she must craft words to suit her purpose. A knife in the hands of a surgeon can be used to cut out disease, in the hands of a butcher to separate meat from entrails and bone, and in the hands of a soldier, to destroy an enemy. But whether coming from a lawyer or a soldier, words on the Warrior's lips should reflect the Warrior ideal: incisive insight, accurate judgment, and uncompromised truth. Warriors can be brutally honest, though experience usually teaches them that tact can be just as useful as force.

Warriors are by no means always outspoken, however. *"The Warrior's speech is soft, but his heart is sharp"* is a Vedic adage that attests to the Warrior's ability to speak softly and carry a big stick. A Hero speaks kindly from a place of strength, though he may not always have the well-wishing nature of the Educator type. Warriors are wary and on the lookout for a fight, so they keep their senses about them. They know all too well the craftiness and exploitive nature of the human beast, and are quick to pounce and punish others when they step out of line. A Warrior's politeness and civility is not to be mistaken for weakness, as her tongue can turn razor sharp as the need arises.

When they lash out, Warriors can be severe, especially those hardened by the crush of humanity, using words that penetrate to the quick. Such an approach becomes useful for law enforcement officers and people who need to cut through lies and deceit to get at the truth. But whatever their profession, Warriors can be recognized by their ability to communicate a strong presence, even without saying a word. When they Integrate into the Educator, they become soft-spoken, humble, and forthright, the ideal of the perfect leader who commands others not with bluster, but with quiet respect earned of actions instead of words.

For his part, *"The Educator's tongue is sharp, but his heart is soft."* This second part of the Vedic adage applies to many Educators whose crusty, gruff exterior belies their inner tenderness. The Priestly class ultimately want the best for all beings, and endeavor to bring it to them, however well or ill-conceived their methods. In the action-flick extremes of hero and villain, we sometimes find Disintegrated Educator masterminds explaining to no end the devious

> *The Educator's ability to give hope is not based on encouragement (Warrior), hype (Merchant), devotion and zeal (Laborer), or profound inspiration (Outsider); it comes out of his ability to see all sides of a story and offer solutions that are both morally and intellectually satisfying.*

machinations of their plots, leading of course to their ultimate demise. Such comical scenarios illustrate the Educator's motivations: the mastermind must inform *everyone* of his brilliance and derring-do, out of conceit, but also from a sincere desire to *educate* and *enlighten* those who have not been blessed with his vision! He has conceived that by his twisted intrigues he can create a new utopia, and that no matter how destructive, the results of his actions must ultimately benefit the world.

Mythic caricatures in TV and comic books sketch out strengths and flaws in the basic archetypes, and can be ingenious at showing the Circle of Duty in operation, if we have eyes to see and decode these dynamics. For example, it takes a Hero in his Priority to foil the plot, by striking at the heart of the Educator's well-conceived but impractical plans. Recall from the Circle of Duty that in times of extreme stress, one type can rise up to thwart its type of Priority, as in, say, Laborers striking against unfair Merchants, or Educators outwitting Outsider terrorists. This way, the Warrior-Hero thwarts an Educator-Villain's plans, while teaching him a lesson in the process. That is how the types help each other, especially those which Integrate together. In this case, the Educator learns from the Warrior that his bullshit cannot fly, and that he needs to return to the Surrender and Benevolence that are his basic traits, rather than trying to become a master of the universe. He learns that, despite his wild dreams and passions, in practice he must be true to his essence, which is wise and compassionate, not dark and scheming. Reprimands from the Warrior work wonders to keep him honest.

An Educator's words must serve to enlighten and brighten, to encourage and counsel. An Educator's words must fill one with hope and goodness— that joy born not of objects, but of good deeds: like the feeling you get when helping a friend in need, or someone stuck on the side of the road. With their speech, Educators can have a calming effect upon others. Barack Obama was noted by supporters and critics alike for having a reassuring, soothing influence on his staff as well as his opponents. His *speech* as an Educator was one reason he was elected, because it embodied the composure, learning, and non-judgment that are hallmarks of Integrated Educators. The Educator's ability to give hope is not based on encouragement (Warrior), hype (Merchant), devotion and zeal (Laborer), or profound inspiration (Outsider); it comes out of his ability to see all sides of a story and offer solutions that are both morally and intellectually satisfying.

Yet while some Educators are eloquent, others can be stiff and pedantic, especially when Disintegrated. Others still are mild and withdrawn, reticent even to speak, as if the effort were draining to their energy. Though they have much to say, some Educators cannot find the best ways to say it, or their words fall on deaf ears, so they prefer to say nothing at all. In such cases, art, music, or their professions become outlets for these Educators, who express themselves through their work rather than small talk or social graces. These Educators must find their passion and speak it— then they can be heard, as much for their enthusiasm of expression as for what they have to say.

As for enthusiasm, none can match the Merchant's zest, whose speech is the sweetest of all. The most voluble, clever, and glib of the Dharma Types, Merchants are never at a loss for words, and know how to use them to affect others. Even if they are not educated, Merchants know how to paint pictures in the minds of an audience, and have the best appreciation for *shakti*. They are able to link words and speech with intention in such a way as to persuade people to align their life energy with theirs. Because they can make friends and convert people to their cause easily, they are the best sales men and women, for people prefer to give their money to a friend, not an enemy. The Merchant's speech greases the grooves of everyday conversation, and at its best, can soar to become the highest music and art.

Whereas Laborers under-promise and over-deliver, Merchants talk a good game, but rarely deliver in full on their promises. The mantra when dealing with Merchants is 'don't hold your breath' – learn to expect less to not be disappointed. This is not because Merchants are intentionally deceptive, but that their exuberance is difficult to rein in. Recall from Chapter 7 that Merchants are ruled by *short term, acute* passions, which can make it challenging for them to follow through on their ambitions. Unlike Laborers, who are more *long-term* oriented, Merchants are quick to shine, and quick to burn out.

Sometimes they have a hard time containing their enthusiasm, and whether telling a story or selling cars, they may exaggerate in order to make vivid pictures in the listener's mind. Other types should not hold them to the fire for this tendency, unless it is specifically intended to deceive or swindle. Then, Merchants must be made accountable so they do not repeat their mistakes. This constitutes the Warrior's Duty and the Laborer's social Priority to the Merchant. When Warriors fail to keep Merchants in line in their daily Duty, Laborers must rise up in Priority to censure the Merchant class, as we saw with the Warrior's Priority to the Educator in the comic book example. In recent times, the world witnessed just such an outcry during the global economic crisis of this decade. Where Warriors failed to uphold the laws that prevented plundering by Merchant institutions, an uproar from the general populace demanded that lawmakers do something about Wall Street, and a complete overhaul of the commerce system was proposed, with purported greater transparency and accountability.

Educator-Laborer Speech Dynamic

The Laborer's words can be square and heavy, economical and earnest. The Laborer's language is kinesthetic, with the power to move people and make them feel. The Laborer's speech is direct and true, even laconic. It is plain, practical, and delivered in a 'take it or leave it' manner that can make a Labor type appear gruff or insensitive. But Labor types are quite the contrary. They feel deeply, but may not necessarily possess the words to convey their emotions. And they don't need to, because their actions communicate better than words. Consider Labor-style music. One doesn't listen to the Blues for its lyrics— it is the emotional power of the Blues that affects its listeners. It is sufficient just to be around a Labor type to understand *who* they are and what they're about. There is little need for words or explanations.

Laborers prefer plainness in their speech and in that of others. That is why Educators have difficulties relating to the Labor type, for they tend to be spacey and elliptical, whereas Laborers are direct. Each party can feel misunderstood and misrepresented. On the one hand, Educators feel invalidated because despite their efforts, they cannot make themselves understood to Laborers. This feels like a major failing as Educators are supposed to be the teachers of the Dharma Types! On the other hand, the Labor type may fall into the trap of 'I'm stupid; I don't understand enough; I have no value.' **Both of these attitudes are illusions created by each type's inability to understand the relating process of the other**. It is important for Educators to know that Laborers understand *actions* better than words, and it is through their *behavior* that they can reach the Labor type, not through their sermons. On the other hand, Laborers should appreciate the complexity of the Educator's task, which is to learn, absorb, and transmit knowledge, and to cut them a break when they slip up and fall on their faces.

This is in line with the Laborer's basic instinct, which is to nurture and feed others. A handshake and a smile, a shared meal and a drink— these can promote better understanding between Laborers and Educators than debate and argument. In fact, this method of sharing Love is efficient in communicating with every type. Though they may not word it that way, it is essentially Love that Laborers share with the world when they devote their time, energy, and emotion to others. And Love is a language without nations, without borders. It is understood by black and white, young and old, Muslim and Jew, and for this reason makes Laborers the best communicators of all!

Laborers and Preachiness

Laborers, however, love to preach, even when they are not qualified to do so. Preaching is for Educators, and as we know, Laborers Disintegrate into Educators. The problem is that when types Disintegrate, they begin to look and act like each other, so that it may be tough to tell them apart. When you see a Laborer look and act like an Educator, watch out— something is wrong! The same holds true for Educators who behave like Laborers—they are not in line with their dharmas, and will not have satisfaction. They need to look to their point of Integration to actualize themselves. Of course, when types Integrate they also begin to look like their Integration points, as discussed in Part I: Merchants resemble Laborers when they Integrate, and Educators look Warrior-like when in the flow of their dharmas. Refer to Part One for more on Integration and Disintegration.

With the Laborer's narrow and parochial attitudes to knowledge, preaching can be a dangerous road. On the one hand, the Laborer's focus on personal experience and 'walking the walk' makes him passionate and convincing on topics he believes in. Laborers experience a truth and believe that everyone should have the same experience. Insofar as this comes from a genuine desire to benefit others it can be nurturing and satisfying to those who partake in the Labor type's causes. Here we have the impassioned pastor, sweating it out on the stage in an ecstatic swoon, singing praises to the almighty. On the other hand, when the Laborer's narrow focus prevents him from acknowledging other ways of doing things, an ugly type of bigotry and pettiness can rear its head. Racism, fanaticism, jingoism, and other forms of intolerance spoil the Laborer's genuine zeal. Far beyond religion and politics, this form of small-mindedness can insinuate itself into his very lifestyle and become a hallmark of his personality.

Few can stir up tears or pluck the heartstrings of emotion like an impassioned Laborer. In his pathos lies his nobility, and in his earnest devotion the Labor type stands above all others in inviting the heart to feel. But in his pettiness and smallness, none is more reviled and despised. When they speak it with a heart intent on teaching and open to be taught, there is no force more rootsy, passionate, and moving than the Labor type. Be it in daily life or on the stage— in work or politics, music or religion— the Labor type can reach and grab our hearts and send us into ecstatic union. Bruce Springsteen is an example of an entertainer whose Labor-roots run deep through his music.

On the other hand, corrupted Labor types have used this ability to connect deeply to take advantage of people on massive scales. Communism (a Labor type system) had the appeal of uniting the underprivileged classes into solidarity, but in practice was perverted by Stalin and other communist leaders, who used their Labor appeal to preach peace to the masses, while stabbing them in the backs. From the corner bible thumper to the next-door politician, the road is narrow and fraught with peril when the Laborer takes to impose his views onto others.

Here are some rules to follow in order to get the most out of the Labor type's advice, and some pointers if you are a Labor type intent on sharing your wisdom:
1. Labor types are qualified to give advice mainly to other Laborers, Merchants, and Outsiders. When they dispense wisdom to **Warriors and Educators, it is not as effective, for these types think with different Intelligences,** and have methods of obtaining knowledge unavailable to the Laborer.
2. Laborers understand the POWER of their emotion, and assume that it carries with it TRUTH. *'If I feel it then it must be right!'* is the mantra in this type of thinking. A little education and experience, however, can contextualize the Laborer's emotions and help her temper her passion with knowledge. This is what Martin Luther King endeavored to bring to the black church, which he felt disempowered its members by stressing *emotionalism* over *education*[47].

---

[47] "I wondered whether religion, with its emotionalism in Negro churches, could be intellectually respectable as well as emotionally satisfying." —Martin Luther King reflecting on his early life in the ministry.

Chapter 10: Intelligence, Speech, and Secret Fear

Instead, he sought to feed people's minds—as well as their souls—and give them power through knowledge. In this way, Laborers must be open to being wrong, and to constant re-education.

Here is the table from Chapter 7 to remind us about the two basic camps among the Dharma Type family. Outsiders are excluded because they take on qualities of the type they are emulating. Thus, Outsiders playing Warriors move to the *Thinking* duo, while those playing Laborers will be in the *Feeling* group.

DHARMA TYPE	RULED BY	TYPE OF STRESS	NATURE	EXAMPLES
Laborer	Feeling	Long-term emotional	Chronic	Worry, low level anxiety
Merchant	Feeling	Short-term emotional	Acute	Anxiety, panic attacks
Warrior	Thinking	Short-term mental	Acute	Post-traumatic stress*
Educator	Thinking	Long-term mental	Chronic	Spaciness, Dementia

* Post-Traumatic Stress Disorder is further detailed in Chapter 12.

Warriors and Harshness

We may think of Warriors as harsh and unyielding, but they can be remarkably polished and polite. Observe how professional adversaries like politicians, athletes, and businesspeople communicate. They can be complimentary and courteous on camera, but ready to pounce on their enemies when need be. This is because Warriors respect the rules of a game and are ready to play it.

Publically, they may observe social etiquette— but when it is time to play, they play to win. When not constrained by the conventions of proper conduct, the Warrior's speech is often direct, to the point, and rarely superfluous.

Take Warrior doctors, who may look cold and professional to the point of seeming hard-hearted. They treat people as 'cases,' and their bedside manner may appear uncaring, even cruel. This type of doctor gets into medicine to battle disease, not interact with patients. His goal is to effect a cure and prevent suffering. Educator types, on the other hand, may be more sympathetic to the personal issues of the patient, depending on their theoretical outlook; if there is something to learn from, or to teach them, Educators will interact with patients readily, just as Laborers may commiserate with the suffering by virtue of their human touch and sensitivity.

Yet it is not because they are hard-hearted, but because they are *conscientious* that Warriors assume a role of professionalism, and wear it like armor. It is to keep their hearts from being broken by every terminal case that the Warrior surgeon girds herself with protection. The Warrior's challenge is to protect herself without shutting others out. When she becomes blinded and desensitized to suffering, she begins to lose her life purpose, which is to ease that suffering. Therefore, she must strike a balance between too much and too little. For the intense and excess-prone personality of the Warrior, however, this remains a lifelong challenge.

This is where some find help in Eastern traditions, like Buddhism, Taoism, Hinduism, and other philosophies that stress a type of ease and harmony with Nature. The Buddha did not hesitate to push the envelope on human endurance and potential, but ultimately found value in a middle ground of *effort* combined with *surrender*. *Wind too tight, you break the string; too lax, and it will never sing.* From Shaolin monks to Samurai swordsmen, Eastern spiritual traditions are famous for producing warriors of legendary mien. Such Warriors achieved their mythic status not by the *number* of armies they conquered, as do

Warriors in the West, but by the *quality* of their interactions and degree of skill they exhibited in the dispensation of their duties.

Supernormal powers and hair-splitting skill are attributed to such masters. These feats do not come out of an excessive physicality or blood-thirsty rage, but from an even-tempered *zone* of stillness in action, like the eye of a hurricane. Warriors attain this by integrating qualities of the Educator into their nature.

Here are some of the traits they can absorb from the Priestly class, and how they are benefited thereby.

1. Knowledge— grows their strength and influence. Knowledge is power for the Warrior, and can be used as leverage to intelligently navigate through her duties.
2. Diplomacy— helps them win battles they need to win, and avoid battles they don't need to fight.
3. Compassion— drives them to justice and fans the desire to fulfill their destiny.
4. Surrender— Surrender to *what is* balances the Warrior flame. In balance, they become conscientious and skillful, and *skillfulness in action* is one of the definitions of Yoga.

When Yoga is achieved, the Warrior's speech becomes gentle, yet firm, direct, but all-embracing. It says little, but intends a lot. His tone conveys compassion tempered with accountability, and like fire, used to heal as well as to kill, his words become instruments of *progress* and *evolution*.

Outsiders

Speech is a marker of identity; it tells people who you are. You cannot understand someone unless you speak their language. Outsiders are adept at learning new accents, tongues, and identities. However, this ability also keeps them from finding themselves. They must eventually learn the language of *their own* souls to discover who they are. Outsiders must discover their Unique Expression and share it with the world if they are to find a place and feel understood by others. They cannot expect to be heard by society unless they teach the world to sing *their* song, thereby refreshing the social harmony in revolutionary new refrains.

Outsiders have the loosest concept of self-expression. Nothing is off-limits, and they express themselves in unique ways from the most vulgar to the most profound. In Latin, *vulgar* means *of the people*, and referred to the *proletariat*, the working class, the largest section of society. While in other ages the proletariat idea was associated with Labor types, in the Iron Age the Outsider's numbers outstrip other classes. The Roman Empire effectively created whole nations of Outsiders by conquering tribes and assimilating their cultures under the aegis of Roman rule. Their speech and customs, being different from that of their conquerors, relegated them to lower ranks in society as slaves or workers, because it is impossible to access the higher echelons of a culture without being fluent in its language and traditions. The same is true of our global economy today, where industrialized societies assimilate migrations of Outsiders on massive scales, making it easier to be an Outsider, but harder to find yourself in the fray.

Jewish Educators need to learn Hebrew to understand the roots of their culture. Educators who meditate, do yoga, or otherwise study the Vedic tradition that this book is based on, should study Sanskrit.

One result of the Roman Empire's conquests was that as a group, Outsiders contributed their Unique Expression by creating the Romance Languages— French, Italian, Spanish, Romanian, and others that emerged from the vulgar vernacular of a society in which Latin was spoken by the elite. English is another such mélange, a product of the linguistic melding of conquering influences in the British Isles. Today, English is the language of worldwide currency and diplomacy, which underscores the influence Outsiders have had on the Iron Age. Outsiders as a group literally found their *Unique Expression* in the many languages they left behind.

Just as Outsiders do this collectively on a global scale, Outsider individuals must also find and add their voices to the chorus of society. By adapting to it, Outsiders change society, so much so that it begins to sing their song. After all, the Romance languages today resonate all over the world, while Latin, their progenitor, is relegated to the stained-glass halls of academia and ecclesia.

Language and the Educator

This Outsider influence over the fourth age of man has also had negative effects. As mentioned, there are very few 'pure' languages left in the world, and where these exist, they are mostly used for sacred purposes, such as maintaining the myths and lore of a tradition. Examples of such languages include Hebrew and Sanskrit, or Greek and Latin for Westerners. Other less well-known linguistic traditions, like Gaelic or Finnish dialects, are also notable keepers of lore. Because linguistic Intelligence is specific to Educators, learning the sacred language of a tradition is particularly important for them. Jewish Educators need to learn Hebrew to understand the roots of their culture; Educators who meditate, do yoga, or otherwise study the Vedic culture this book is based on, should study Sanskrit. That is because reading second-hand interpretations is not sufficient for Educator types. They must access lore *directly* if they are to teach it to others.

Even on a practical level, going to the source is always useful for Educators. Politically-minded Educator types do better to source their news from C-Span rather than the plumy late-night politicasters on the local news or CNN. Science-minded Educators get more out of reputable scientific journals than glossy magazines, because to get **to the truth they must go to the root**. A mathematician's 'language' may be Calculus; for computer programmers it may be HTML or Java. For students of the sacred sciences, getting at the core of their field requires plunging into the lake of sacred dialects that remain in this age.

Language changes the structure of thought and how we see the world. In the words of Outsider-playing-Educator Gabriel Byrne, *"to be robbed of your language is to be robbed of the way you think."*[48] The language we speak affects our reality, and every type should endeavor to learn its own 'tongue,' as discussed in the *Intelligence* section above. And while Laborers learn through touch and Warriors through movement, Educators learn through reading, discussing, and listening to *words*.

One drawback of English as the world vernacular is that English as we know it has no sacred history or literature. China has the Tao Te Ching, Hebrew the Torah, Greek the New Testament and Plato, Sanskrit has the Vedas and Upanishads, Latin has Virgil and Augustine... but what does English have? The greatest English writers, like Shakespeare and Milton, drew wisdom from Greek and Latin. They sourced what they could from the wellspring that was ancient even in their time. The spiritual traditions of the English language pale next to those of the more ancient languages of the world. Therefore, to truly understand ancient thought, one must learn the language in which it was transmitted. Reading in translation is seeing the world through a muslin screen. We must have first-hand experience of a thing for it to be real to us. We must speak the language of a place to interface with its customs, for in the words of Nobel laureate Czeslaw Milosz, *"language is the only homeland."*

---

[48] Radio interview, *Fresh Air, NPR* 2009.

230

11
MUSIC, MYTH, AND POODLES

Music

Every musician plays or sings according to the characteristic of her Dharma Type. Warriors sing of struggle, Laborers of drama and suffering. Outsiders rebel, Merchants revel, and Educators contemplate the nature of their world. When Outsider-playing-Educator Alanis Morissette sings,

"Thank you Frailty, thank you Consequence, thank you, thank you Silence."[49]

she expresses the Educator's vulnerability (*frailty*, Chapter 7: Body Type), propensity to instant karma (*consequence*, Chapter 2: Educator), and love of quiet self-reflection (*silence*, Volume III: *The Spiritual Types*). The same is true of Pavarotti when he sings from Tosca,

> *O dolci baci, o languid carezze...*
> *(O! sweet kisses! O! languid caresses!)*

Awaiting execution, reliving the taste and feel of his passionate lover, his Laborer heart pours out the drama of the moment. Labor music is gutsy and devotional. It relies on instinct and emotion to hook its listeners, not on the refinement of its content. Being also 'workingman's music' it can be sung in the neighborhood tavern or in the army foxhole to boost morale and build camaraderie. Because its roots run deep, it is passed down from generation to generation. Patriotic, Traditional, Blues, Gospel, Religious, and other styles that share the above qualities exemplify Labor-Style music.

Like the Merchant's easygoing nature, Merchant music makes you feel good. It is foot-tapping, hand-clapping, light-hearted entertainment. And like their music, Merchants have a knack for raising spirits. That is why they are successful at making money, and the reason pop music sells millions of records.

---

[49] *Thank You,* from the album *Supposed Former Infatuation Junkie,* 1998.

People pay to be reminded of their precious joy as human beings, and Merchants are the beneficiaries of that need. Because they have a gift for ornamentation and embellishment, Merchants' music is also flashy and trend-setting, inspiring fashion movements, hairstyles, and the like. Though it may lack substance, it is catchy, hummable, and easy to digest. It is easy to market as it is quickly appreciated... and usually quickly forgotten.

Where Merchant music is designed to make you feel good, Warrior music often does the reverse: its intense, driving melodies come from the Warrior's need to fight. Where this fighting spirit is directed determines how the music comes across. From provocative, in-your-face attitudes, to fighting for justice and the rights of the underprivileged, Warrior music *carries a message* that highlights injustice. Here, Warriors walk hand in hand with Outsiders who have similar agendas. Because it evokes the ugliness in society, the hard times of personal relationships, or individual struggles and addictions, Warrior music does not carry the sing-songy, feel-good message that Merchant music does. Consequently, it is usually not as popular, though that is hardly a concern for Warriors. Like the Outsider who brings them up for society to look at, the Warrior's job is to redress social evils. This can take place on the personal (a battered wife), social (police brutality), and even global levels (war), and it serves the Warrior's deep-driven need to Correct and Control, as noted in Chapter 3.

Warrior music is hard-driving, intense, and powerful. Like Labor-type music it is also repetitive. Its hooks, rhythms, and melodies pound into us over and over until they conquer the senses and overwhelm the palate to bring the listener to an altered state of awareness. Hard Rock and Gangsta Rap are good examples, though it can span any style that has Force as its hallmark. **The Warrior's mind is constantly racing after a challenge and a goal, and Warrior music provides a track for that mind to follow. When the mind has been properly harnessed or overthrown, a sort of trance, peace, or equanimity emerges wherein the Warrior earns a moment of respite.**

When the Warrior is Integrated into the Educator type with knowledge and wisdom, he seeks to teach and show the world its shortcomings. Educators also do this, but their music comes across with less force and more subtlety than the Warrior's. Educator music is softer, has a lighter touch, and when understood can be profound. Though it may not be as melodic (Merchant), inspiring (Labor), or powerful (Warrior), it is seeded with the purity born of the Educator's heart, and can be a medium to our highest selves. However, poorly-made Educator music may just seem wishy-washy, spineless, and boring. Everything depends upon the skill and personal evolution of the composer.

Educators pursue their craft to express a higher truth through music, often with little recompense. They may not be recognized for their gifts, or at best, be appreciated by a select few (other Educators mostly). Nonetheless, when done right, Educator music can touch the hearts of the masses, stirring up echoes of the numinous self, and reminding us of who we are as spiritual beings.

Educator music is the most cerebral and socially conscious. Think Bob Dylan and Joni Mitchell. Not necessarily the easiest to understand or appreciate, it relies on its content to appeal to the public. Folk and classical are primary examples of this type of music. Not surprisingly, students scored higher on IQ tests after listening to ten minutes of Mozart, and babies responded positively when it was played during pregnancy, in a highly publicized study. It is not a stretch to believe that Educator music, like Educators themselves, can make you smarter!

Finally, Outsider music is always fresh, different, and sometimes shocking, offering new paradigms to its listeners. Also, one country's pop music can be another culture's Outsider fare. In Jamaica reggae is the norm, whereas in the U.S. it is Outsider music. In the same way, 'World,' and other musical imports are considered exotic. Outsider music is often an amalgamation of different styles, meshed together in the musician's soul and regurgitated as a totally different genre. From punk rock to jazz and World fusion, it is an eclectic, heterogeneous mix of cooky and cool, odd and audacious. It can come from left field to knock your socks off, redefining music standards— like Rock 'n Roll in the fifties— or it can simply degenerate into vulgarity and cacophony, and become untenable as music.

Living lore is passed down from person to person, and cannot survive on paper as a written word: like a living soul, it needs a body to give it proper shelter and expression, to translate its reality for a new generation.

Myths

Myths are archetypal images and stories that we use to generate, maintain, and transmit *lore*. Lore is knowledge with a living spiritual essence. Such knowledge has lasting, universal value, and appeals to different civilizations over the expanse of time. When its spiritual center is lost or forgotten, lore degenerates into fantasy or superstition. This deterioration is sometimes inevitable, especially as we move from age to age. It is almost impossible for people in the Iron age to understand the myths of the Bronze or Silver ages, no less the Golden age. As a result, modern storytellers must make do, and sometimes turn what was once living lore into a spectacle for the sake of money, or to satisfy their misguided desires. It is difficult for one age to understand the myths of another, particularly because the spiritual reality behind them is no longer apparent. Living lore is passed down from person to person, and cannot survive on paper as a written word: like a living soul, it needs a body to give it proper shelter and expression, to translate its reality for a new generation.

> *The king's crown is the earthly counterpart of the saint's halo*

The written word is so often misinterpreted that it engenders more entropy than enlightenment; but living breath gives direction and meaning to the dry and lifeless page. That is why ancient societies cherished oral tradition over its written counterpart, *shruti* over *smriti*.[50] But in movies and TV, in our books and media and in the way we live our lives, the current Merchant culture does not place a high value on hidden spiritual realities, but on their manifest, gross appearance. An example is the way we value gold for its surface quality rather than its intrinsic meaning.

Before gold became sacred to Merchants as a mark of wealth, it was sacred to Warriors as a sign of higher authority. Ancient kings wore gold crowns as symbols of their divine right to rule. Gold was considered solidified light, representing *sattva*,[51] the 'anointed' halo of purity, truth, and divine radiance. The king's crown is the earthly counterpart of the saint's halo. Just as the poet's laurel wreath marks his favor with the lesser gods of poetry and art, the king's crown designates him as favored of the One, the central Sun around whom all great bodies are but planets, revolving according to His will.

---

[50] Sacred wisdom over secular knowledge.

[51] Purity, the radiance of the holy, *sattva* is discussed in detail in Volume III.

From Egypt to the Americas, from Vedic to Nordic lands, this link to our divine origins was vital to our ancestors. The king's right to rule was given and taken away by God. Its symbol in heaven was the sun; on earth it was gold. Yet everything degenerates over time. Yesterday's spiritual truth becomes today's cult and superstition. The lore and learning of previous ages become the lies and legends of our age. From Astrology to Religion, the insights of previous epochs have dimmed into dark superstitions. The same is true of gold in the Iron Age, which is precious less for its intrinsic value than for the remnant cachè of its supposed allure.

Merchant society has appropriated it as a marker of value, not understanding or caring about its original significance to the kings of previous ages. As a result, world leaders grab at gold and other so-called *precious* metals as sources of wealth and power, rather than symbols of divine mandate. But a king must be equal in valor as in wisdom, in justice as in judgment. Leaders who take power only to feed their coffers, who fail to recognize the connection of their exalted position to the exalted source of their authority, fail to bring positive change to their kingdoms and ultimately suffer their karmic hells for doing so. That is why Warriors make the best rulers. Even if it is subconscious and forgotten, inherent in the Warrior is an abiding respect for the divine source of his power, represented and interpreted as that is by the Educator type.

Outsider Heroes

From James Bond to Beowulf, the most common Heroes are Warriors, populating myth and legend from the beginning of time to our modern era. Whether folk legends or super-spies, Warriors are famed for rising up to save the day from the endless evils that beset the world. They are also today's sports superstars, conferring honor to their teams and nations through their exploits. In times of peace, sports rivalries substitute for real conflicts, and Warrior champions shine on the playing field rather than the battlefield.

But as this is no longer a Warrior age (see Chapter 1), Warrior myths have been given a spin, and Outsiders *playing* Warriors have become archetypes of the modern protagonist. From Spider man to the X Men, today's Outsider heroes are freaks of nature who are as valuable to society as they are different from it. The Iron Age reflects the lower instincts of every Dharma Type, and Outsiders are the heroes who emerge to redress evil in the Kali Yuga. The stagnation of the Iron Age is impossible to overcome unless one adopts radical measures. The world's *avatars* and holy incarnations, sources of great myth and lore, are all

Outsiders. Ironically, Outsiders are also the age's worst criminals. These two extremes, of hero and villain, represent juxtaposed Outsider types, each trying to escape the clutches of their age: one by wisdom, the other by selfish means; one by *releasing*, the other by *embracing* ego.

Ultimately, it takes the ingenuity of both types to redress the calamities of the world. It takes one Outsider to destroy the status quo while another offers solutions to rebuild it. Destruction precedes renovation, and for Outsiders, the lines between right and wrong, good and evil are rarely clean and clear. The sacred and profane have little meaning for a person who is an amalgamation of both. In fact, the only way for superheroes to defeat their villain foes is to really understand them, by being part of them. Spider Man knows how to defeat his nemesis because he understands his strengths and weaknesses. He understands them because he has them himself. It is only a matter of choice that separates one from the other. It is only a matter of spiritual evolution that marks the hero from the villain.

In ages past, that line was clearer. In the Silver Age when the Vedic avatar Rama walked the earth, the guise of evil was embodied in his counterpart Ravana. As an incarnation of the divine, Rama stood for all that was good and just, while Ravana was his opposite. Today it is harder to tell good from bad, partly because the standards have loosened. *Tapas*, the first word of Rama's epic, the *Ramayana*, recounts the *austerity, discipline,* and *self sacrifice* he endured to save his people, with little thought for himself. These words, which summarize *tapas*, also embody the ethic of the Silver Age. While these ideals remain with us, modern mores are more flexible and less demanding. It is impossible to be that good and virtuous in the modern era. Modern myths emphasize this struggle to become the best we can be, regardless of our social standing, gender, race, or economic status. This makes the Dharma Types all the more important for this age, where people have lost sight of their inner archetypes, and have no personal myths to guide them to fulfillment.

Every age has its heroes. In a Golden Age, Educators are revered as exemplars of evolved humanity. Seers and sages are the champions who remind us of our spiritual essence. In the next age, Warriors become emblems of Truth and Justice alongside Educators. Then, in a corruption of the Silver Age ideal, Warriors take over as sole heroes of the Bronze Age, only not for Truth and Justice but for Power and Dominion. Finally, in the Dark Age, Merchants and Outsiders become the heroes of our time. Merchants are the 'real-life' idols, while Outsiders become the larger than life, mythic icons of the world.

Entrepreneurs and entertainers are today's royalty, the dream of teenage boys and girls and the envy of the working classes. They epitomize the glories of wealth and fame, and are hailed by the Merchant media. On the other hand, our sports heroes, the long-haired soccer geniuses and tattooed basketball mavens, who travel around the world wowing audiences, tend to be Outsiders. There is something about Outsiders that makes them appeal to a wide audience, on the one hand, and to seem untouchable, on the other. It is no wonder they are called *"Untouchables"* in Indian society. They are a source of awe and inspiration, as well as fear and disgust.

Modern Myths

Mythology is the language of the Dharma Types. Myths and archetypes live deep inside our collective consciousness, transcending surface values of mode and fashion. In modern times, movies and comic books have replaced ancient epics as conveyors of archetypal images, and when well-conceived, are as powerful as any of the myths born of ancient Greece, India, Scandinavia, or Rome. If anything, they are more pertinent than their antiquated counterparts, for the gods of Greece and Rome are dead, or lie embalmed in heavy tomes on dusty shelves, nevermore to feel the cleric's ardent breath. But our TVs crackle every day with electric life to feed us the fast-food imagery of modern mythology.

> *A coward is a hero with a wife, kids, and a mortgage*
> --Marvin Kitman

Today, myths exist under our noses. The original pin-up girl, Venus, is replaced by Marilyn Monroe and Angelina Jolie in modern culture's equivalent of the femme goddess. Sylvester Stallone and Arnold Schwarzenegger have exhumed Hercules, while Johnny Depp dubs as Apollo. But the best myths are the Dharma Types, and we can see them hard at work in pop culture from the silver screen to our favorite sit-coms.

Laborer

In Chapter 5 we saw that Laborers make the best sleuths and detectives. Because of their dogged determination they can persevere to get to the bottom of practically any case. Laborers are also thick-skinned and naturally ingenuous types, so they don't mind asking questions that other types might cringe at for fear of looking stupid. The detective Columbo in the eponymous seventies television program embodied this archetype. Patient, rough around the edges, and seemingly facile, he was also a master sleuth, capable of following his instincts and sniffing out malfeasance. Laborers think with their bodily Intelligence, using their gut feelings and nose to lead them, and these rarely fail to steer them in the right direction.

It is difficult to lie to a Laborer. Unless they choose to ignore their instincts, they, like Warriors, have a nose for deception. The only time their senses become scrambled is when they have strong feelings for someone. Laborers will allow love to override their basic instincts, because their communal and family spirit is stronger even than their own sense of self-preservation! They would rather believe the lie their lover tells than trust in what they know is true, just to keep a relationship going, This is why Laborers are unreliable 'lie detectors' when they have a personal stake in the matter, and why Warriors are ultimately better at ferreting out truth. Warriors can separate emotion and logic and proceed based on rationality rather than romanticism. This spells the difference between police and private detectives: the former being Warriors, the latter Laborers. The first need a structure and rules to work within, the latter prefer to work for themselves, use their own tools, set their own hours, and turn down cases they don't like. These qualities come out in the Professions preferred by each type, as discussed later.

> *The gods of Greece and Rome are dead, or lie embalmed in heavy tomes on dusty shelves, nevermore to feel the cleric's ardent breath.*

Rocky Balboa is another tough-as-grit Labor character. He is all heart, and despite what people think about him, is not dumb, but carries an inner intelligence that is usually foolproof. He is beloved for his plain-speak, has simple tastes and needs, and unscrupulous people try to profit from his sincerity and popularity. He knows everybody on the block, is great with kids, and supports his neighbors. He has to work tooth and nail for everything he gets, and earns his bread by the sweat of his brow. Typical of Laborers, he is self-deprecating, but inwardly confident— a confidence not born of egotism, but of intimate self-awareness: he knows his limits and what he is capable of. Laborers know their inner strengths, which makes them able to withstand the blows the world throws at them. He does not try to go where it's not his business to go, but sticks to what he knows... though that never keeps him from dreaming big!

There are real-life Laborers who have little in common with the trappings of Rocky's life, but all Laborers share certain inner qualities. Real-world Laborers like Harrison Ford, Bruce Springsteen, and Oprah Winfrey are living embodiments of the Laborer myth. What they have in common is the practical, loyal, rough-necked and raw-wristed spirit that lives in every Labor type.

Another iconic Laborer personality is Cling Eastwood, who embodies this spirit in his movies as in real life. From the early days of Dirty Harry and spaghetti Westerns to the last decade in his attempt to preserve the memory of war veterans in movies such as *Flags of Our Fathers,* Eastwood stuck to his guns in detailing the outwardly tough, inwardly sensitive Laborer persona, especially evident in the patriotic and emotional reminisces of his World War II biopics. Clint's journey from Dirty Harry to Walt Kowalski (in the movie *Gran Torino*) hallmarks the evolution of this Labor-Hero on the silver screen.

> ***Itzhak Stern****: "Let me understand. They put up all the money. I do all the work. What, if you don't mind my asking, would you do?"*
>
> ***Oskar Schindler****: "I'd make sure it's known the company's in business. I'd see that it had a certain panache. That's what I'm good at. Not the work, not the work... the presentation!"*
>
> --dialogue encapsulating the Merchant-Laborer dynamic from Steven Spielberg's, *Schindler's List.*

Merchant

Schindler's List exemplifies the Merchant myth of caring for others. Oskar Schindler's story, as popularized in the 1982 book by Thomas Kenneally[52] and the 1993 motion picture by Steven Spielberg, shows the extraordinary things Merchants can accomplish with their wit and panache, on one hand, and their compassion on the other.

Scrooge is another Merchant myth that teaches an unrepentant hero the true value of wealth late in his life. More light-hearted popular myths that typify the

---

[52]Thomas Keneally, *Schindler's Ark*. New York: Simon and Schuster, 1982

Merchant's social ease and gift for gab are the *Ocean's Eleven* series, as well as their real-life counterparts, the original 'Rat Pack,' that featured Frank Sinatra, Dean Martin, Peter Lawford, Joey Bishop, and Sammy Davis Jr. among its male members, and Marilyn Monroe, Angie Dickinson, and Shirley MacLaine among its female 'mascots.' Though not all of them are Merchant types, they together embodied the Merchant ethic of high-spirited hedonism.

Outsider and Warrior

The Outsider Hero is the most prevalent in today's myths, because one has to effectively buck the system to express one's true nature, as Merchant society is not built to support heroic self-fulfillment. Therefore, Outsiders assume roles and personas to hide their true selves from the world. Clark Kent is the Educator mask of an Outsider Superman. He can never fit into society because he is physically and intellectually different. Stories like Batman, Spiderman, and even Indiana Jones, in which our hero has a public persona radically different from his private face, illustrate the Outsider archetype. And from burly, tattooed basketball millionaires, to extreme and exotic illusionists, real-life Outsider heroes have captured the attention of society, while keeping their private faces hidden.

Like superhero costumes, the Dharma Types embody five distinct Myths that teach us to harness our special powers. People do this every day when they go to war in the name of *God* and *Country,* as the *Martyr* or *Patriot* archetype allow them for good or ill to put aside their normal lives and do extraordinary things in the name of their ideals. Imagine what you can do when you don the costume of your Dharma Type, and custom-tailor it to a perfect fit using the Four Seasons, the Circle of Duty, your Language and Intelligence, and coming later, your particular Life Cycle! Imagine becoming larger than life when you tap into the ready source of strength and inspiration that is your Dharma Type!

Hollywood regularly employs archetypes to create successful blockbusters and memorable characters on the big screen. The *'Disney Formula'* works over and again because its characters are archetypes that audiences intuitively connect to, often without knowing why. Talented artists attain success when they link their subject matter to such characters. Archetypes exist within us, with or without our conscious knowledge. When we link ourselves to their subtle power, we *as people* become successful and memorable, just like the movies and stories that use them for the same reason.

Now let us take a look at the Educator. Since Outsider and Hero myths prevail in popular culture's movie, book, and TV landscape, let us move on to an archetype that does not get as much press, but is just as important.

Educator

Educators are unlikely heroes. Harry Potter from the popular children's book series, and Gandalf of *Lord of the Rings* fame typify the Educator in popular myth. In fact, the Lord of the Rings, though an Educator tale, portrays all of the Dharma Types with an equal mastery of execution. There we find the Circle of Duty demonstrated over and again; Labor to Educator (in Sam's loving service to Frodo), Educator to Warrior (in Gandalf's dutiful service to Aragorn and other worthy heroes), Merchant to Labor and Outsider (in Pippin and Merry's service to Sam and all of the Outsiders they encounter, from *Ents* to *Elves*) and Warrior to Merchant (in the lords of Gondor and Rohan's protection of Pippin and Merry). Disintegration is shown in Boromir's fall to greed (Warrior to Merchant) just as Integration is demonstrated by the king to be, in Aragorn's service to Gandalf, and his embrace of wisdom and lore (Warrior to Educator). These and other relationship dynamics consistently permeate the trilogy, as well as *The Silmarillion*, its predecessor. It is testament to the author's deep understanding of myth and archetype, and one reason his work has endeared itself to readers through the years.

Practically every myth demonstrates archetypal dynamics between the classes, from the simplest fairy tales, to our most complex and modern legends, like those of Middle Earth. Tolkien understood the value of sacred lore, and worked to bring it into popular culture through the vehicle of 'fantasy fiction.' As a creation myth, his *Ainulindale* is as beautiful and stirring as anything extant among the world's spiritual epics. Though Christian, he populated his works with divine and semi-divine beings co-existent with man in a world similar yet categorically different from our own, a world that moved in cyclical time through Four Great Ages, rather than in linear history.

> *Just as love is lost in the mechanical act of sex for hire, so the essence of myth is lost in its mechanical replication through the Merchant media machine.*

Unfortunately, the movies that brought his works to wide acclaim could not convey this lore, the real life essence of Tolkien's world. This is a trenchant example of a

Merchant ethic unable to understand Educator values. Not surprisingly, they were still wildly acclaimed by the Merchant culture, too distracted as it was by the gross spectacle to miss the subtle force Tolkien worked painstakingly to create.

The purpose of myth is to teach. Every tale has at its core the lore that enlivens and gives it its essence. At its worst, consumerism has turned lore into a whore, prostituting it for profit. Just as love is lost in the mechanical act of sex for hire, so the essence of myth is lost in its mechanical replication through the Merchant media machine. We have seen tales imbued with lore become mere 'action flicks,' built to satisfy a temporary desire for distraction and be forgotten, until the next myth is chopped up and served to us again, a fast-food rehashing of the same unsubstantial and unfulfilling fare.

Real myths fill us, live in us, and inform our souls for life. They teach us by inspiring, frightening, and stirring us to action. Some movie critics give 5 stars only to those movies that readily pass the *re-watch test*: films they would gladly watch a second and third time. Really great movies, like great myths, reveal more and more layers upon every viewing, and become part of our lives by changing the way we *speak*, *act*, and *see* the world. Outsider-cum-Educator George Lucas accomplished this with his first *Star Wars* trilogy, just as Tolkien did with his books, plumbing the riches of ancient lore to bring out myths for their generation. Both of these Educators' epics depict journeys into darkness to confront the depths of fear and pain... only to fail and be saved by grace. **This is the essence of good myth— that alone we are doomed to fail, but for the supernal favor of grace**. That in the world evil is always stronger than good, that the path is perilous and fraught with obstacles... and that all these are as nothing to the hand of divine grace.

Grace saves the person living out the essence of their archetype

Grace saves the person living the essence of their archetype. In *The Lord of the Rings* trilogy, it is the Educator's compassion that ultimately redeems him. When Educator types Frodo and Gandalf spare the wretched Gollum, their redemption comes from Gollum in the end. It is the Warrior's self-sacrifice that saves him: not for his own glory but for the highest cause does he fight and stake his life. For the Merchant, grace comes from feeding, supporting, and cheering others, even when he has no food nor strength nor cheer for himself. Grace follows the unquestioned faith and devotion of the Laborer, the unheralded backbone of any story, to whom accrue the rich spoils of his duty in the end.

The popular Harry Potter books show us another Educator hero. Unlike the august Middle-Earth epics, the Harry Potter series is more plainly an adolescent Educator story. Wizards are, after all, pagan priests, ministering to the world and communing with Nature's hidden powers. The Educator's dilemmas and sticking points are illustrated here, from Dumbledore's lust for power, to Harry's anger and longing for something he cannot have. Dumbledore sums up the Educator's need to control his senses and resist temptation: *"...power was my weakness and my temptation. It is a curious thing, Harry, but perhaps those who are best suited to power are those who have never sought it."*[53] How appropriate a lesson this, for Educators who grasp at Power when they should be reaching for Providence. We have seen this throughout history, as when the pope's reach exceeded that of the state, and he imposed the terror of excommunication, as well as execution, upon the bewildered masses. Harry Potter is a cautionary tale against such perversions of power directly aimed at young Educators.

But the series also shows the flipside— Harry's deep surrender to his destiny, his sincerity and solicitousness for his comrades, and his acceptance of his fate, demonstrating the Educator's indomitability of spirit once his destiny is embraced. When the Educator/Wizard surrenders to his fortune, and accepts *what is* as Nature's reality, he becomes part of and supported by Nature, and a force so powerful that it cannot be defeated, only surrendered to in turn. That is also what separates a *wizard* from a *sorcerer*: one is bent on protecting Natural law, the other on bending and breaking it.

TV Homework

These examples from movies and books illustrate how powerful modern mythic images can be. From *Scrubs* and *Seinfeld* to reality programs, archetypes exist in the ensembles of the most popular T.V. shows. A mix of every type makes for great drama, and viewers who understand the Dharma Type model are treated to extra insights. Let us take the cast of characters from *Friends* as a case study, including their fictional professions:

---

[53] *Harry Potter and the Deathly Hallows,* J.K. Rowling. Bloomsbury/Scholastic, 2007.

Character	Type	Profession
Joey	Warrior	Actor, playing a Doctor
Rachel	Merchant	Mass Media
Ross	Educator	Teacher
Chandler	Merchant	Business
Monica	Laborer	Catering (feeding others, hospitality)
Phoebe	Outsider	Music/Other

Perhaps one reason for *Friends'* popularity is the accuracy with which characters represented their Dharma Types, right down to their professions, a credit to writers who were able to tap into the strengths and weaknesses, the dark and light spots of each Dharma Type and bring them to the screen. As viewers, we pick up on these archetypal images and resonate with them on a primal level. Any writer or producer who can do this is ahead of the game when it comes to ensuring a successful program. On the other hand, programs with an incomplete ensemble of Dharma Types find themselves weighted towards the types they use, and against the missing types.

For example, the show *Lie to Me* incorporated a cast of characters that included Educators, a Laborer, an Outsider, and a late-addition Warrior. With prominent Educator personalities, the show appealed to Educators, but had some or little allure for Merchants, who were not represented in the cast. This is a dangerous strategy, for Merchants are synonymous with entertainment, and successful, entertaining shows need to have them represented. That is why *Friends* attracted America's Merchant culture with massive appeal, for it had *two* Merchant main characters, Chandler and Rachel!

PBS (the Public Broadcasting Station) is less-known for its entertainment value than its educational programs, like Sesame Street, which is appropriate since it is patently an Educator station. For the same reason, however, it relies on pledge drives rather than Nielsen ratings and commercials to stay on the air.

Chapter 11: Music, Myth, and Poodles

As your homework assignment, take some time to discover who is who on your favorite TV shows. Ensemble casts make for great television and allow us to view the evolution of the Dharma Types in real time. Some shows with 5 main characters, like *Entourage*, are easy to decipher: others may take a little more time. List the characters by Dharma Type and include reasons why you think they embody that archetype. What mannerisms, quirks, and other telling qualities give them away? What type was Carrie, from *Sex and the City*, or Cliff, from *Cheers*? Good luck!

The Value of Myth

Without lore, there is only action without accountability, hijinks without heart, metal without meaning.

It was reported recently that a piece of Star Trek memorabilia sold for half a million dollars at auction. A trivial item with no real, intrinsic value, it was nonetheless instilled with the aura of myth. Like gold, whose mythic value was discussed at the beginning of this section, *we cherish things that represent the sacred*, things imbued with lore. We are so moved by the meaning that heroes and myths bring to our lives that we pay anything to keep them around, as if losing them could mean our deaths. And perhaps it could. Perhaps a life lived without meaning is empty, and tantamount to death itself!

Inventive, resourceful idea-gogues have profited by providing people a semblance of meaning and associating their products with myth and lore. George Lucas re-cast the Hero myth into a likeness comely to the modern eye, in the guise of Luke Skywalker and Han Solo, and created a billion-dollar empire based on the dreams and ideals of viewers. He transposed mythic messages to give meaning to a new generation. Ironically, when he abandoned mythic images, as in the later Star-Wars trilogy, he also failed miserably. Without the masculinity and magnetism of the Warrior, there is no real hero. Without the idealism and wisdom of the Educator, there is no lore. And without lore, there is only action without accountability, hijinks without heart, metal without meaning.

> *Only she who courts her death becomes fully engaged in life; who flirts with disaster marries sweet success, and to the Hero go the spoils, while to the layman, daily tribulations.*

It is the role of Educators to provide that meaning, Warriors to live it out, Merchants to glorify it, Laborers to preserve and enjoy it, and Outsiders to inspire and redefine it. Every class has its role, every class has its place. It is no more the part of an Educator to profit from memorabilia, than for the Warrior to rest on his laurels. The Warrior fights, and does not have time to sit back and enjoy his work. Like a doctor who has cured a patient, or a lawyer who has won his case, these types cannot rest on yesterday's triumphs; they must seek them out ever anew. Laborers for their part are the spectators, the audience that recounts and records the Hero myths of their generation. They are the great storytellers, helping to preserve the essence of a culture's myths, while the Merchants propagate them with fanfare and panache.

Ultimately, Heroes are important because they are precious and few. Today, Heroes are people who stand up to the Merchant society assembly line to make their voices heard. They do not have to be Warriors or Outsiders; every type has a heroic gift. The Hero is a man or woman who undertakes to fully embody the highest aspects of her Dharma Type, for only she who courts her death becomes fully engaged in life; who flirts with disaster marries sweet success, and to the Hero go the spoils, while to the layman, daily tribulations.

We cheer those who break from bondage to pull away from the crowd, but we also jeer when they fall under the grind of the Merchant machine. Stories of fallen Heroes serve as cautionary tales to keep us in line. As a result, most people don't get to live up to the silver-screen ideal. Instead of persevering on the quest for self-fulfillment, they are left slaving away to stay out of debt and fulfill their financial obligations to the world.

Nonetheless, aware of mankind's need for good and true role models, the Merchant machine still tries to fill that void, even while cashing in on the process. From video games and movies to books and comics, modern myths still make their way to the starving public, though they are often outnumbered by inferior fare. The pop-star imbroglios and bubble-gum fairy tales fabricated by modern storytellers have monetary gain, not moral instruction as their incentive, and these pseudo myths and images are not the same as the flesh and blood of real people and living heroes. As a result, we are left unsatisfied and must turn to other sources that temporarily fulfill our need for wholeness, like shopping, sex, food, drugs, and even pets.

Pets

Merchant society's fascination with pets comes from the Merchant's natural instinct to shelter and care for others. It also arises from her loneliness and need for company. Merchants use pets as substitutes for partnerships to help fill the void that people often can't. In this respect, pets are a blessing to Merchant cultures like the U.S.A, for they teach responsibility and care for others. But they can also become a negative fixation that leads people away from real human interaction.

It is not surprising that we dote so much on our pets; after all, they are human creations designed to augment our lives and keep us company. The breeding of dogs and cats into customized human companions has taken millennia; we can even trace the history of our relationship with animals to the cycle of the ages. In a Golden age, man coexists with creatures of the wild in a way consistent with Educator values. He adopts a *live and let live* attitude to Nature and uses his superior spiritual development to communicate with animals on their level. In a Warrior period, tired of being attacked and ravaged by certain beasts of the wild, man begins to hunt, capture, and domesticate them for the good of society. These animals become valued as hunters and warriors themselves, and rewarded for their service to mankind. In such a Silver Age, they are treated with respect and honor, securing a role in the tales and myths of the time.[54]

In the next age, dominated by lower Warrior instincts and conflicting Merchant values, animals become man's *tools* and *commodities*, rather than sentient equals. Because it is still a Warrior age, beasts of strength and power continue to be respected and feared, but they become less our allies, and more our tools, bearing the yokes of the farmer, and packing our larders with milk, cheese, and their own flesh. As society grows, animals become more and more sources of food, not company. Our ability to communicate with them becomes

---

[54] The *Ramayana* provides a good example of man's relationship to animals in a Silver Age, presenting animals that coexist with humans in a time dominated by Warrior virtues. Bears, monkeys and other creatures of the wild fight side by side with humans, winning laurels and infamy according to their deeds. Warriors judge *actions*, not *appearances* and in the Silver Age creatures are judged by their valor and character, not their outer appearance. Accordingly, many are depicted possessing character flaws and virtues just like humans, and like people, shown capable of both good and evil deeds.

lost by the end of this age, and the gap between man and beast is permanently widened. This is also the time when mythical creatures depopulate earth. The faery folk and their lore begin to leave us, as man becomes increasingly deaf and blind to the subtleties of their existence. By the onset of the Iron Age, they are almost completely gone, and their legends become nothing more than 'fairy tales.'

In the present age, the Kali Yuga, as societies and populations exponentially increase, animals become a 100% commodity. From the abattoir to the zoo, their use becomes restricted mostly to our sustenance and entertainment. This is also where manipulation of their genes becomes an art form. Consider man's domestication of the dog over the last 4,000 years, which surpasses every other animal in the shape, size, color, and variety of its breeds. Consider the journey from wolf to Chihuahua to see the progression of man's fascination with pets over the years and through modern day.

It is no wonder that our pets are so dependent on us. They rely on us for food, grooming, exercise, and entertainment. It is up to us not only to walk them, but to keep them clean, well-nourished, and happy. This is a burden we take on when we manipulate their genetic structure to our ends. It is also a burden that takes significant time and energy. Another downside of having pets is that sometimes we forget they are animals and that their consciousness is different from ours. Excessive emotional investment in them can tie us down and prevent us from living out our own destinies. It is one thing to love a pet, but quite another to smother it with sentimentality to such a degree that it substitutes for our own experience of life.

But the mantra for the Age of Kali is to *use what you've got*. We can use the values of the Merchant age to evolve out of ignorance. Our pets can be conduits to a better understanding of ourselves, teaching us to relate with others by generating greater authenticity, warmth, and compassion in our relationships. How much of a leap is it to care for another human being or do something nice for our neighbors when we find that they are also animals, and require the same warmth, food, shelter, and exercise as our pets? How difficult is it to say *'Hi!'* to someone when you know that they also share your passion for Labradors, and spend the same troubles in caring for, grooming, and loving them as you? The beauty of living in an Iron Age is that by opening our eyes to the tools life gives us, we can use anything to rise up from the droning darkness of routine existence to harmonize with the light around us.

Chapter 11: Music, Myth, and Poodles

A Memorable Fancy

As I walked with my teacher along the streets of our city, it was impossible not to notice people with their animals. The conversation naturally turned in their direction.

What do you think about people's obsession with pets in America?

"People feed their poodles designer baked biscuits, but turn their noses at volunteering at a shelter to feed their fellow human beings. Engrossed in vanity these people congratulate themselves on being a 'good person' though there is nothing in their actions to account for this self-image. Actions must be judged by the objective barometer of shastra *(scripture) to correctly calibrate the inner gauges of the subjective account.*

"They say the road to hell is paved with good intentions, and most people walk that road every day, unable or unwilling to change their trajectory. But shastra *tells us what each type must do to reverse their steps and walk the road of heaven. There is little excuse for ignorance, much less for those who know the right path, and fail to walk it still.*

But isn't the attention people give to animals a type of blessing?

"It's a fact of life that what you give your attention to rewards you in like kind. Devote your time to insentience and dullness, like sitting on the couch, drinking beer, and watching TV, and sure enough next lifetime you'll make a fine rock, that even the animals of the wild will enjoy sitting on! Mind you, it's great for the pets—they're practicing being human, and next lifetime they'll be holding the leash!"

He laughed and continued.

"But the best way to handle pets is to let them be animals: respect them, feed them, take care of their survival… and let them live their lives. One of the problems with owning pets is the responsibility you have to them. They become like children, and in a place like NYC you can't let your dog run loose like he wants to, so you have to walk him, groom him, give him love and attention… it teaches selfless service… if only people could treat each other the same way!

A Memorable Fancy, continued

It's okay, you know, in the midst of selfless service come those mindless moments while walking 'Buster' or grooming 'Fluffy' during which you can turn your mind to spiritual things, while the body and senses are distracted by their habitual duties..."

He paused and laghed—

"Ha! So you have the Yoga of Cat Grooming and the Tao of Doggie Doo... only in America!"

So, what do you tell students who have pets?

"It is okay to love your animals, you see. We need to learn to love this way, at this level. We need the comfort of a fellow soul. But we need to take it to the next stage too. That is the hard part. We snuggle Fluffy, but bite the husband's head off when he comes home. The problem is that Fluffy might become the husband in the next life!"

He turned to me, as if in warning. *"Don't forget that!"* and we both laughed.

Homework

Part One

A revealing exercise I used to give fitness seminar attendees was to have them go home and find their totem, or spirit animal. This is the creature in nature that best resembles you on a material, psychological, and spiritual level. The next day many people who had done their homework would come back with a glint in their eye, ready to share.

"So, what's your spirit animal?" I once asked a lively woman in the back.
"I'm some type of bird, for sure," she replied.

After a brief discussion, I asked her, "So, what do you like to eat?"
"Well, I like bread and cereals... and I really like nuts and seeds."
I smiled, paused, and then, "What type of foods do birds like to eat...?"
She opened her eyes big and laughed—apparently she hadn't put it together.

Your totem animal can give you new insight into matters as diverse as diet, appearance, physical habits, even psychology. Another man raised his hand and volunteered his results.

"Well, I meditated all night on it, and the only thing that kept showing up was... a coyote!"

Of course, when it came down to his favorite snack, he gave a wily grin and said, "Just give me a good steak and I'm set for the night. You know, I don't like to eat much during the day, but give me a steak dinner and I'm happy!

Everyone murmured as they began to appreciate the correlations between their spirit animal and eating habits. Those who had flaked out on the exercise swore to do it that night and come up with their totem animal the next day.

Finally, a burly guy from the back volunteered, "I'm a bear. And it's funny, I always thought my diet was all over the place... I mean, I love fish— tuna and salmon, actually— but I also eat a lot of bread, candy and sweets, and I've had a hard time figuring out what to feed myself to be healthy."

Another class member then piped up, adding that bears love to forage, but eating sweets, especially refined sugars and alcohol, was terrible for them, and made them fat and listless.

He laughed, "Yeah, I can relate to that!"

Diet is just the beginning of discovering the secrets your spirit animal has for you. Along with types of exercise (fast, explosive for cats; slow and studied for elephants, for example), we can discover social habits, appearance, haunts, and even the Dharma Type that goes along with your animal. How well an animal matches you depends on your ability to imagine the correlations and make the connections.

Totem animals carry a personal meaning for every individual; my totem bear and yours might mean different things. They may describe features about us that range from the spiritual to the mundane. Take time to research and meditate, and find out what animal best fits your personality, and remember that in many traditions the totem animal is not shared with anyone- it is for your personal evolution only. Also they do not have to be your favorite animals— in the beginning you might not even like them! But there is nothing wrong with pigs and rats and snakes, if we understand their motivations and how they resonate with our deeper sensibilities. The rat, for example, is associated with luck, charisma, wealth and intelligence in China. Representing the first year of the Chinese zodiac, rats hold a place of honor, and are said to have first introduced rice to mankind. And though the *black* rat was the harbinger of the flea that caused the plague in Europe, his bigger *brown* rat cousin is believed to have ended the plague by kicking him out and taking over. Take time to research the deeper meaning of your totem animal and you might discover that even the lowliest creatures have noble virtues worthy of guiding us on our paths!

Having a friend's help in this process is also helpful, as friends are more objective about us than we are. Don't be too literal in trying to make everything 'fit:' not everything has to match precisely. It is the essence and spirit of the animal that you are looking for, not every one of its habits... though many habits do reflect that essence. Use your totem animal as a guide to help you tune in to Nature and how it connects to you. After all, the Dharma Types were designed to work *with* other systems, not as an exclusive technology.

Part Two

Perhaps the reason we as a culture love pets is that they remind us of the stripped-down essence of our Dharma Type, teaching us to be good Merchants, Laborers, Educators, and such. Sometimes the qualities of the Dharma Types are displayed most purely in animals. For example, dogs are archetypal Warriors. They can be trained and disciplined, and make good, trustworthy companions. They are thoughtful and goal oriented, learning from past mistakes. Cats on the other hand are Merchant creatures. They become more affectionate when they want something, and though they are concerned primarily with their own survival, can be irresistible nonetheless, with a grace and charm that makes us happy to provide for them. Unlike dogs, who have a significant prefrontal cortex, cats have none at all. They do not reflect on actions or possess self-control. Recall that the prefrontal cortex is the 'Warrior' part of the brain, and it is fitting that dogs have it well-developed, while cats are completely lacking in it. Cats are more representative of the limbic system that governs primal emotions and libido, which is why cats are more leisurely and affection-seeking, while dogs are more rigid and loyal.[55]

As a homework exercise, try listing animals according to their Dharma Type. Consider how the world treats them, what they give or take from the environment, and their role to humans. For example, turtles could be Educators because they are generally harmless creatures, benevolent and honored for their wisdom in many cultures. The Labor-type cow, on the other hand, is the only animal that freely gives of its milk to other species, and loves all equally. Sweet and doe-eyed, cows sustain communities with the work and food they provide. It is a shame that we treat the animal responsible for nurturing and sustaining humankind for millennia, with the least care, affection, and courtesy. Could it be that for the last 5,000 years we have also treated Laborers this way, basing our society on their hard work and selfless service, while keeping them down as second-class citizens? There are countless implications between an animal, its Dharma Type, and our relationship with it. Cows will never be as sexy as Chihuahuas or kittens, which is precisely why Laborers must Integrate into Merchants if they are to get their due. We have to give Labor-type animals an 'image makeover' if they are to receive recognition for their contributions, and if we want to align our culture with the tenets of an enlightened, sacred society.

---

[55] Cat owners, retract your claws: I am the proud and happy owner of two cats myself!

Mistreating the animals that give us the most with torture, punishment, and little more regard than 'objects' is a reflection on our own humanity, the low values of the 'human' animal. What type of animal are we, who do these things? Humans must certainly be Outsiders, as evidenced in the extremes of our behavior— in our ability to do enormous good and terrible evil— as in the mystery of our origins and the complexity of our evolution.

Serpents are also Outsiders, maligned and misunderstood though holding powerful medicine for society. Their sheer mystery inspires terror and panic, earning them a bad reputation. Tigers are often represented as Warriors, but how about canines, whose values are loyalty, hierarchy, leadership, and efficiency? When he locks his eyes on a target, there is no stopping the wolf from attaining his goal. And can we see the Merchant type in parrots, lovable for their loudness, temper, and mimicry? Or how about the ludic dolphin,[56] for his carefree, charming nature?

Fundamentally, all animals are Outsiders on this planet. Biologists tell us with some certainty that the seeds of our existence, the amino acids and peptides responsible for creating life on this planet, were carried to earth by meteorites and comets crashing down from outer space. We are stardust, nomads from afar, a fact on which both our spiritual as well as secular texts agree!

> *We are stardust, nomads from afar, a fact on which both our spiritual as well as secular texts agree!*

In these chapters we have classified much of Nature into Dharma Type categories, as our ancient ancestors did before us. From the Elements and Seasons, to the Music and Sports we play, the Dharma Types inform our everyday reality. As an extra-credit spin on this exercise, try taking a look at the different breeds of your pets through the lens of the Dharma Types. Though dogs are Warriors, are some breeds Merchants, or others clearly Laborers? Can you come up with a way to relate with them that befits their Dharma Type? Does your Warrior shepherd benefit from discipline and exercise? Does your Educator retriever seem almost human at times, how smart she is? Or does your

---

[56] Dolphins are said to be the only species other than humans to engage in sex just for pleasure! Closely tied to the Water Element, they seem to share the playful, pleasure-seeking qualities of the Merchant personality.

Persian cat have different needs from the Russian Blue? Can you use this to figure out your pet's *dharma* and what behaviors are best suited to its type, just as you would with humans? When you begin to see the world through the lens of dharma, you may come to recognize the supreme order and variety in the universe, while enjoying your own place in it.

Enjoy!

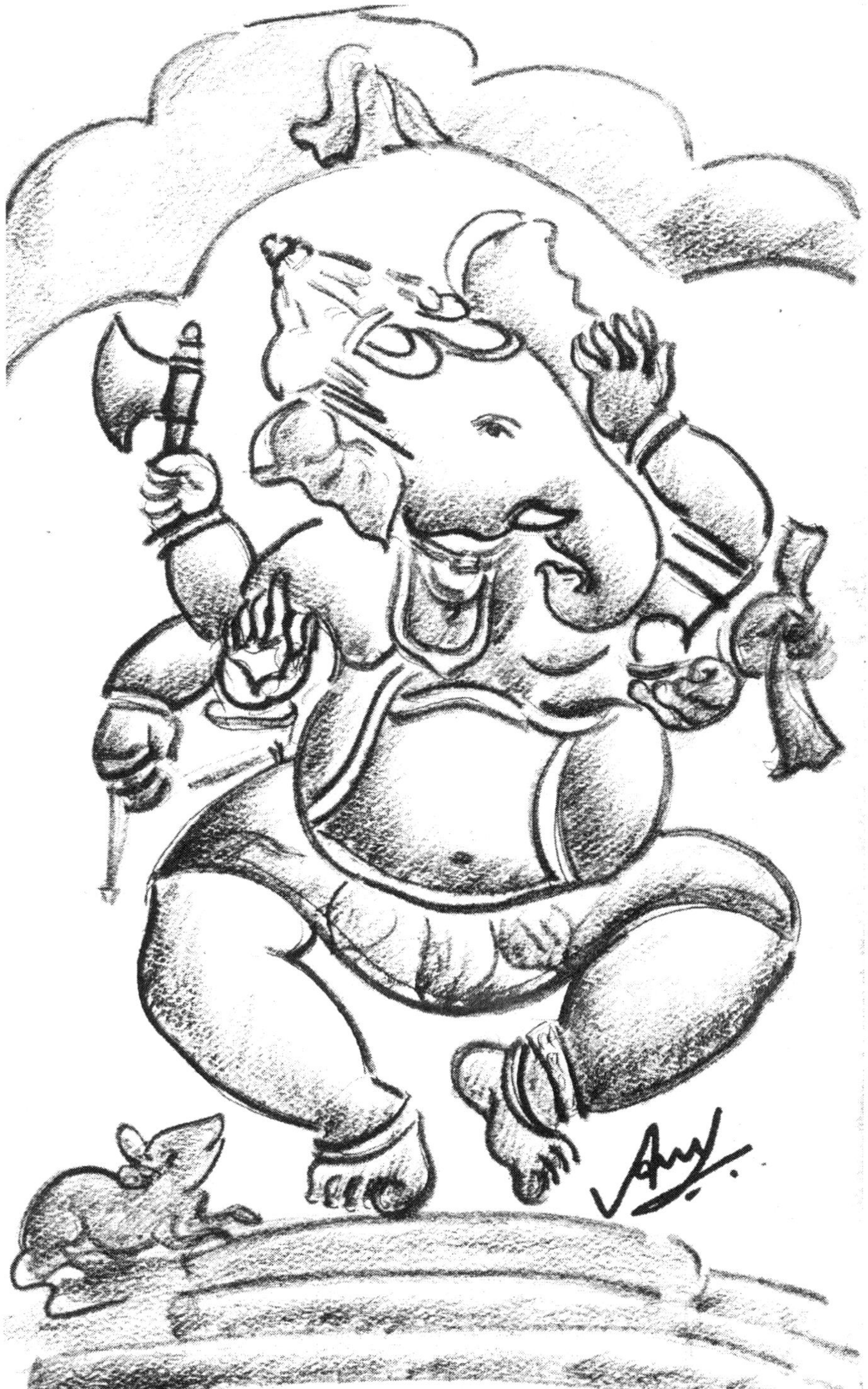

12
SPORT, WAR, AND WARRIORS

SPORT

Sport involves the concerted movement of body and mind, force and intention, to obtain a specific goal. It is the creative expression of *prana* for play and recreation. Recall that *prana* is the *breath* of the Vital Body. It is what in some cultures is called *ki*, or *chi*. It is the *life force* and breath that animates our flesh.[57] As any athlete knows, it is difficult to express your talents without proper conditioning, for conditioning is up to 90 percent of athletics. In Western sports, *prana* is harnessed for the purpose of obtaining some goal; in the East, harnessing *prana* is the goal itself, as in practices like t'ai chi or *pranayama*. However, one cannot excel at sport unless the Energy Body has been mastered to some degree, in conjunction with the muscles, bones and fascia of the Food Body, and this mastery means that sport has wider applications than putting a ball through a hoop or conquering an opponent.

Sport as Metaphor

Old-time fitness guru Jack LaLane used to say that training was his penance. Sport and training are ways to get out physical toxins, to express and release pent-up emotions, and to discipline our mind and spirit. In ancient societies, sport was a spiritual event, especially for Warrior types. From the ancient Maya to African tribes, it was a metaphor for perfecting the self by surpassing the limitations of the human body. Few historians remember that the sports events of the Olympic games were originally an adjunct to a grand religious festival that also included poetry, singing, dancing, and religious worship. The ancient Greeks believed Olympia, a city on the Peloponnesian peninsula, to be the center of the world, and Mount Olympus home of the gods. Olympia was a place of sanctuary and worship, and even warring cities would postpone their

---

[57] *"And the Lord God formed man of the dust of the ground, and breathed into his nostrils the breath of life; and man became a living being."* Genesis 2:7 NKJV

> *While we idolize the Greeks for their gifts of **logic** and **democracy**, we have a long way to go to understand their embrace of natural spirituality*

conflicts in order to partake in its religious festivals. Consider how far the modern Olympic spectacle has strayed from this ideal, and you will notice that, while we idolize the Greeks for their gifts of *logic* and *democracy*, we have a long way to go to understand their embrace of natural spirituality. Today's sports festivals are more famous for **advertising goods** than **admiring gods**, and closer aligned to Merchant values than to Educator or Warrior virtues.

Sport is a natural outflow of spiritual worship, and many athletes have had their religious experiences on the playing field rather than in church. Professor and author Joseph Campbell relates that he felt his first epiphany while running track. When the field becomes your altar, and your breath the offering, the heat and sweat of your body can represent your purification, a transformation into something more refined. The mechanics of this become clear when we look closer at how skill and mastery are acquired.

Sport in Practice

Mastery of sports skill begins with theory. One must first learn the rules of a game, understand its concepts and history, and logically analyze its movements. A tennis stroke is broken down intellectually into its component parts. Next, physical training takes center stage. At this middle step, one begins more *doing* than *thinking*. Reflexes become automatic by assiduous repetition and disciplined practice. Doing requires a different intelligence, synchronizing the Food and Breath Bodies in movement. Here, intellectual concepts are subordinated to the body's physical intelligence. Thinking is buried at this stage, because it is a hindrance. If you are thinking, "now I must flex my wrist and jump and push my hand in order to make the ball drop into the hoop" you will probably not only miss the shot, but never really master the skill. This second level of learning is kinesthetic, and must rely on the *pranic* intelligence of the body to impose its will on the ball and make it go where it needs. This requires present moment awareness.

Being in the present is crucial for any sport. An athlete who is in the Now, the "Zone" of witnessing awareness, is capable of astounding feats. This state allows one's *prana* to coordinate movement without egoic or intellectual interference.

Chapter 12: Sport, War, and Warriors

Intention unchecked by thinking is a powerful force. It has the capacity to orchestrate muscle, sinew, and bone into a symphony of movement that achieves its end without effort, without thought, without attachment to an outcome. In the Zone, to Michael Jordan the hoop looked enormous; the path through the lane appeared obvious, and missing a shot seemed a ridiculous concept. There was no thinking, only action, for at the second level of learning, intention produces its desired result without interference of rational thought.

Finally, at the third level, subtle thought comes back into the equation to guide our intention, without overburdening or blocking the flow of *prana*. At this point, Roger Federer can guide the ball to the baseline corner with astounding precision; Tiger Woods can align his shot with the hole from 20 ft. away and sink an unmakeable putt. This is the third and final level of learning, the level of mastery. When skill has become second nature, through learning and then doing, it is refined at the third level by guided intention, thought and action working together.

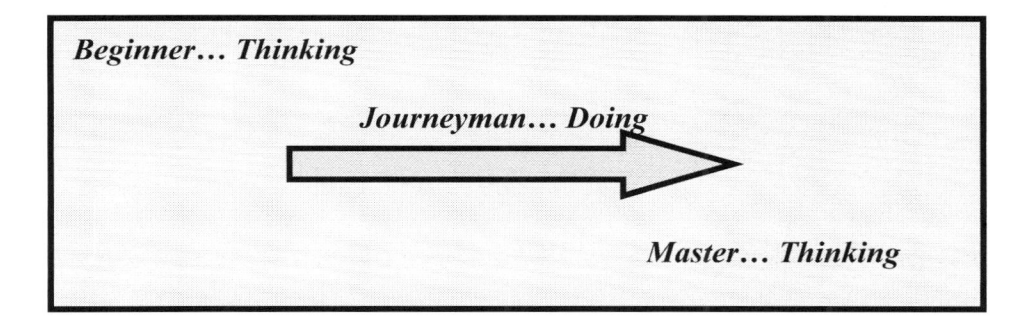

> *Beginner... Thinking*
>
> *Journeyman... Doing* →
>
> *Master... Thinking*

These three stages of skill acquisition have correlations to other parts of Dharma Type philosophy. They represent the three seasons of life, where we begin life by *learning* in Spring time, *doing* in Summer time, and applying *wisdom* to doing in the Fall. As students, our job is to acquire theory during our formative years. In the next season, as we strike out in the world, we become doers, learning by experience and leaving behind our studious ways. Finally, in the Autumn of our lives, we start to learn again and apply our wisdom back into the world, this time tempered by experience. The final, or Winter stage of life, represents retirement, giving up all that has been learned for rest and emptiness, freedom from the rules and requirements of the game. This is not the Disintegrated Merchant's emptiness, but the Outsider's void of experience, the blissful absence of *vritti* (fluctuation), also known as nirvana, the absence of suffering and agitation.

A lesson for the Warrior type, for whom Sport is a metaphor, is that in order to Integrate himself, he must begin by acquiring knowledge. In the middle stage, he is himself responsible for developing skill through the intense application of his Intention. Then, in the final stage he must return to using his mind, so that he does not curtail his evolution at the second level. Integration thus begins and ends with coaching, and Educators and their concepts are integral to a Warrior's development.

Play

In the animal world, play is a natural component of growing up. It hones and sharpens a young animal's physical repertoire while building valuable social skills in a pressure-free environment. For a cub, chasing its mother's tail is fun, but it also develops agility and timing necessary for the hunt, qualities she'll need for survival later in life. It is through play that a baby evolves and learns to become an adult. And unlike animals, who stop their evolution as their bodies reach maturity, humans have the potential to continuously evolve even into their waning years. One of the common ways we do this, as with animals, is through play. Sport is the elision of *play* and *exercise*, an activity that involves skill, coordination, and discipline along with a feeling of enjoyment. It is through the sports we play that we become stronger, healthier, and wiser individuals.

Sport can be an avenue for our evolution, as the skills we put into hitting a good topspin forehand can serve us equally well in our daily relationships with others. Unfortunately, most of us don't regard athletics this way. We step off the court a more tired, but essentially the same version of ourselves that we were before we stepped on. But as we have seen from the animal kingdom, there are valuable life lessons to be learned from leisure physical activity. Aside from the physical implications, there is an opportunity for psychological and spiritual self-inquiry when we engage in any rigorous practice and challenge our minds and bodies to excel. It is through this challenge that we can find aspects of ourselves hitherto untapped, to see who we really are when put under the gun. For its part the military, another side of the Warrior coin, makes it a point to emphasize that its personnel be trained to parlay their skills and discipline into everyday life. When this actually works, it makes better people and citizens; when it doesn't, it can create monsters instead of men, or traumatic situations like PTSD, which can scar a Warrior for life, as we shall see below.

> *"Playing sports, or even just watching, builds a stronger understanding of language"*
>
> -University of Chicago. *"Playing, And Even Watching Sports Improves Brain function"* Science Daily September 2008

Sport and Dharma Type

Educators are benefited by sport because they Integrate into Warriors, and sport is a Warrior activity. Not surprisingly, movement and sport are shown to have direct correlations to enhanced cognitive skills. Thus, just as meditation and self-study produce better Warriors, movement and sport enhance an Educator's intelligence by moving his life force and inspiring new ideas.

Tennis, hiking, and horseback riding are some Educator sports. Activities that have more the upliftment of the spirit, and less the dominion of the body as their aim are Educator pursuits. We do not find Educators well-suited to brutal sports, such as rugby or wrestling, because Educators are essentially harmless. They may, however, take up the martial arts for the philosophy of self-cultivation and self-defense. They also participate in sports for their own sake, the sake of the game. They enjoy being challenged to learn the techniques and nuances of a new endeavor. And the challenge of the game is more fun than beating an opponent at it. Therefore, games of skill that require a lifetime to learn, like chess or tennis, are beloved of Educators.

Warriors can excel at any sport. From Archery to Weightlifting, Warriors can be champions at anything, though they prefer activities that stress competition and, to a lesser degree, recognition of achievement. Horseback riding is fine... as long as you are riding against someone. Hiking is great, so long as you reach the summit first. This is the challenge of the Warrior, who prefers the glory of achievement to the quiet exaltation of the spirit that is the Educator's reward, even when this achievement is only recognized by himself.

Merchants on the other hand are often interested in sport for tangible rewards, such as money, fame, and popularity. Or, they may prefer the aesthetics of sport, the subtle pleasures of 'juking' an opponent, or refining their motor skills to such a degree that they become art in motion. Some of the most memorable athletes of the last century have been Merchants, for their showmanship flair and fun personalities.

Merchants' interests run along lines of profit, and they may also become team owners, agents, or otherwise benefit from the *business* of sport rather than its *practice,* finding the same fulfillment, the same tests and challenges in the economic marketplace, as an athlete finds on the playing field or a soldier on the battlefield.

Laborers prefer sports that emphasize teamwork and community. They also make good boxers and weightlifters because of their hardy constitutions, and can excel at any sport that requires heavy work. In addition, they do well at endurance events that challenge their physical as well as mental toughness, such as marathons. Outsiders, by contrast, have different reasons for going into sport. Unlike Warriors, who want to challenge themselves and be #1, or Merchants who crave aesthetic refinement or financial reward, Outsiders go into sport to expresses something unique, or to escape from their status quo.

Snowboarding or MMA fighting are examples Outsider sports. MMA (Mixed Martial Arts) in particular is an example of a popular Outsider sport, because it *blends* different fighting styles into one amalgam, something Outsiders excel at doing. Outsiders may also be attracted to sports that are not as well-known, like Parkour or Louge, though that does not mean that every louger is an Outsider. It does mean that Outsiders gravitate to things that are different, edgy, and slightly subversive.

That basketball is the sport perhaps most synonymous with African American inner-city youth culture is no coincidence, since the black experience in America is tantamount to the Outsider's experience of the world. As a form of personal expression, culture, and even community, basketball has done more to bring Outsiders together than perhaps any sport in America. One cannot distinguish, say, a basbeball player or a golfer in a crowd. But basketball players cut a swath much different from their surroundings. Because of their height, basketball players are Outsiders, and basketball an Outsider sport, one designed for persons otherwise ill-suited to other activities.

Because he likes to fly and is ruled by the Space Element, the Outsider also favors aviation as a hobby or sport. Because of that Element's unpredictability, his interests are also impossible to define. From X Games to Aviation, Outsider activities favor the underdog in society, or the loner, or the individualist who does not otherwise integrate into mainstream culture. Because Outsider sports are a vast genre, it is impossible to describe them in one breath. However, it is

Chapter 12: Sport, War, and Warriors

WARRIOR	LABORER	OUTSIDER	EDUCATOR	MERCHANT
Archery Auto Racing Boxing Dance Diving Equine sports Football Gymnastics Hunting Martial Arts* (Weapons, Grappling, Striking, Mixed) Motorcycle racing Rowing Running (esp. short to medium distance) Speed Skating Surfing Track and Field (esp. Running)	Animal Sports (rodeo, horse racing, angling) Auto Racing Baseball Bodybuilding Boules Bowling Boxing Fishing Football Hockey Motorboat racing Rowing Rugby Running (esp. long-distance) Track and Field (esp. Throwing – Shot Put) Soccer Weightlifting	Aerobatics Auto Racing Basketball Cycling Dance Diving Gymnastics Motorcycle racing Parachuting Rock climbing/ Mountaineering Soccer Surfing Track and Field (esp. Jumping — Pole Vault)	Aikido Archery Chess Dressage Golf Hiking Polo Rowing Running Skiing T'ai Chi Tennis Volleyball Yachting	Cue Sports Figure Skating Golf Soccer Skiing Swimming

* All combat sports generally belong to the Warrior type, though specific martial arts that also befit other types, such as T'ai Chi or Boxing, are listed accordingly.

Note that some sports fit more than one Dharma Type.

easy to spot them when they take place, because they are different, and like MMA, often incorporate elements of various other disciplines. Let us take a look at some individual sports and the Dharma Types they relate to most.

Golf doubles as a Merchant and Educator game, and soccer as a Merchant/Laborer sport. It is not surprising that soccer is the world's #1 sport, since Merchant society recognizes Merchant values and aesthetics above all others. It is, however, strange that soccer is not more popular in the U.S., the prototypical Merchant country, where we are crazy about Warrior spectacles like American football, instead. This speaks perhaps to the Disintegration of our society, which favors Warrior instead of Labor values, which are more representative of its Integration point. In the last century, baseball's popularity in America has been eclipsed by other sports, perhaps to the detriment of the best values of the country.

That basketball is the sport most synonymous with African American inner-city culture is no coincidence, since the black experience in America is tantamount to the Outsider's experience of the world.

Baseball is a Laborer game as it emphasizes many qualities of this type. Baseball players are superstitious, and sometimes have elaborate pre-game rituals they perform to help them win. Baseball is also a slow game that is family-oriented and grounded in down-home earthy values. There is a relaxed sweetness, a youthful wonder that draws Labor and Merchant types to play and watch it. That is perhaps why it has lasted so long as 'America's Game,' especially during the Labor-era of the mid 20th century. With the coming of the sixties and seventies, America entered an Outsider period, during which sports like Basketball and others became more prominent.

Laborer sports have one thing in common: they are simple, require little equipment, and serve to gather community together. They can be practiced at any age and are accessible to everyone. Unlike sports that require special terrains and equipment, like polo or tennis, which are aristocratic, Educator pastimes, baseball needs a stick and a ball, while soccer goes one step simpler, and eliminates the stick. Even sports like weightlifting, which do require special equipment, begin as Laborer activities, like lifting and carrying large workloads.

Team and Community

It is safe to say that in interpersonal relationships—in love and sex— Merchant society exalts the virtues of *variety* while sacrificing *intimacy*. Lasting profundity is traded for temporary excitement, a trend that encourages less satisfaction and increased desire to consume more. It promotes the sense of emptiness that Merchants are prone to, and ironically reduces their ability to really enjoy themselves. The antidote is the Laborer's loyalty and stick-to-it-ness. As in daily life, in sport we need to *marry* our athletes to their teams in order to gain the benefits of a lasting union: longer life, better prosperity, and greater professional success, benefits that accrue to married couples, and which can accrue to loyal athletes as well.

> *Merchant society exalts the virtues of variety while sacrificing intimacy. Lasting profundity is traded for temporary excitement, a trend that encourages less satisfaction and increased desire to consume more.*

Loyalty to team and community is part of a team's success—not just in the stadium but in the real world. An athlete's effect on his city can be more important than his success on the playing field. From modeling good behavior to actively contributing time and money to social causes, players with roots are likely to feel more grounded in their professional and personal lives. This is especially crucial for Outsider sports and their athletes, who are prone to feeling left out, judged, and even discriminated against.

In the 70s and 80s, sport became big business as it teamed up with TV and other media to become *Sports-Entertainment*. The unfortunate spawn of this union has been the destabilization of teams and communities by the marketing of players to the highest bidder. Nowadays it is rare for a team to stay the same for more than a year, as players and coaches are traded back and forth to build the best 'organization.' As a result, fans are left with little to cheer about as the athletes they just learned to love are scuttled off to another team, and they are left grasping to fill a void. This kind of impersonal business-first atmosphere is neither good for fans nor athletes. Spectators become more critical and demanding of players in order to compensate for the constant manipulation of their emotions, while players withdraw and learn to play for money, rather than love, as their loyalties to place and team are replaced by the bottom line.

In the final picture, what does it mean to be a Phoenix Sun, or a New York Met, when the players that make up a team are neither raised in Phoenix or New York, nor spend enough time there to even learn the street names, no less get to know the local culture? What does it really mean when *'your'* team wins? Is it really Phoenix or New York triumphing, or an eponymous business that has no devotion to place or player? We must understand how we spend our energy, and where we devote our attention. Do the sports we follow really reward us and uplift our community, or do they suck our resources and attention, while leaving us with fluffy hometown souvenirs as keepsakes… souvenirs that have themselves been outsourced to China?

Ultimately, the value of sport comes from the amateur level, where athletes play for love of the game, rather than financial remuneration. College teams tend to stick together and play with more heart and passion than their professional counterparts. It also lies in individual participation. We don't have to be Kobe Bryant or Roger Federer to enjoy a game of hoops or tennis. In fact, games are more enjoyable when there is less pressure to succeed. Sport is about cultivating *perfection*, not *profit*, as per the Warrior's credo, and the challenge and reward of perfect execution is a lifetime pursuit that has lessons for every type.

A Memorable Fancy

Athletes and soldiers are both Warriors, but one builds his body and plays for a living, while the other brutalizes his body and kills for a living. I asked a teacher about these differences as we sat watching a game on TV. Here's what he said:

"Athletes are reincarnated soldiers. When a soldier has given himself for God, Honor, and Country, shouldn't he get to play? Doesn't he deserve to enjoy the benefits of his good karma? And the more valorous he has been as a soldier, the greater his reward in heaven and the next life."

Muslims believe strongly in heaven for death in a righteous war

"Yes, and so did the Scandinavian, Germanic... actually all of the ancient peoples believed it, because it was true. It still is true. But this heaven is not just a place somewhere in the atmosphere; the rewards of good and bad deeds are also enjoyed right here on earth!"

So you're saying that Michael Jordan was a war hero in a past life??

"Ha! Who can tell? The ways of karma are mysterious. Nadi readers* and gurus sometimes reveal such things. But for every good deed there is reward; for every misdeed there is penance. The secret is to know the difference. It is all about viveka—*discriminating between actions which lead to happiness, and those that drag you down to more experience and suffering. The ultimate end is freedom from bondage. And even though these sports players are enjoying their time, they are still in bondage.* Viveka *is* discernment, *and discernment leads to action that is free from any suffering... and then one goes beyond the short-lived heaven of good deed..."*

What's that like?

"Go see for yourself!"

We laughed together. Later, I asked his definition of Yoga.

"Long ago, yoga was designed to dismantle the body, mind, and soul structures that limit the self. To demolish limitations of the body, asanas *[postures—disciplined physical activity] are practiced. To destroy negative patterns of the mind and emotions,* pranayama, yama, *and* niyama *[disciplined breath control, moral restraints and observances] are cultivated.*

continued...

"To develop the spiritual self, starting with the moral restraints and observances, the higher practices of dharana *[one-pointed focus],* dhyana *[meditation], and* Samadhi *[concentration, full absorption] are cultivated. Ultimately, yoga is about freedom from the things that bind you. Freedom is the ability to express yourself limitlessly."*

What about Warriors who are not part of the formal school of Yoga, not on the spiritual path?

"Every Warrior is doing yoga, even if they are learning a sport, or just studying a skill. Warriors know the hard work, self-sacrifice, and one-pointed focus necessary to be successful at anything. This is yoga in action. They understand Sacrifice, *just as the Brahmin [Educator] understands* Surrender. *Vyasa says, 'Yoga is available in all states of mind.'** The difference is that in our [Vedic] tradition, these skills were codified not for the sake of reaching a worldly goal—like becoming a doctor or an athlete—but for the sake of the skills themselves; greatness is a* side effect *of yoga... not its aim!*

"But practicing yoga helps you in anything you do. Becoming detached from winning a game usually helps you win the game! That's the paradox of life. Being detached means not being afraid to lose. When the fear is gone, you let go. And when you let go, your creativity is channeled so you can do great things. Haven't you noticed that when you really want to impress a girl, she pulls back, because she feels your desperation? But when you don't have anxiety about the outcome, you're detached, she feels your 'coolness' and pulls in towards you? That's the real definition of being 'cool!'"

I chuckled to myself, remembering the too many times in life I had pushed girls away because I wasn't 'cool' enough. So I asked the smart-ass question

So, yoga can help me pick up chicks?

"Ha ha! Yes, Warriors should practice yoga philosophy to be happy in everyday life. Real wisdom never goes out of style. Let them read Sun Tsu's Art of War *to be great at battle; let them study the* Gita *and* Yoga Sutras *to be effective on the internal battlefield of the soul!"*

*Nadi readers are a sect of astrologers in India who use proprietary techniques to determine past-life karmas

** Vyasa is the foremost commentator on the *Yoga Sutras of Patanjali,* one of the seminal texts on yoga philosophy.

War and Warriors: Post-Traumatic Stress Disorder

Let us now examine another type of Warrior, the soldier. According to statistics, as many Vietnam vets have committed suicide as died in Vietnam itself. In 2007, 12,000 American Iraq-war soldiers attempted suicide—1,000 attempts per month. This deadly cult of guilt and shame can be stopped if Warriors and those acting as Warriors understand what it means to be a protector of dharma. When Warriors cultivate the skills they need most—not strength and killing techniques, but *good judgment* and a *Just Cause*— they can re-integrate into society without suffering the fallout of Post-Traumatic Stress Disorder (PTSD).

> *Merchant Society is more interested in proliferating automatons than nurturing informed and thoughtful Warriors who are masters of themselves and their surroundings. This is because automatons are expendable, predictable, and therefore easily controlled.*

PTSD and similar afflictions can follow when a Warrior doubts his life purpose and the cause he is defending. When the Warrior's inner conscience cannot reconcile the actions he has performed, dis-ease is the result. On the one hand, Warriors believe in the code and camaraderie of the armed services, which turn them into refined instruments of law enforcement. However, when they are thrown into situations that are ill conceived by their superiors, or when their ethical and moral compass contradicts the actions they are forced to take, a powerful rift develops, like tectonic plates moving in different directions inside them. It may not be apparent on the surface until the stress builds up to a breaking level, and their world shakes with the power of released violence and emotion.

Warriors have no problem with violence or extreme situations. It is when these are undertaken for ignoble purposes—for profit and dominion—that Warriors suffer. They are willing to kill and be killed to defend their sons and daughters, their loved ones, their country and their faith; but when Warriors become instruments of profit for a Merchant society, their inherent Noble Cause is lost, and the inner compass that guides them with such certainty becomes turned around. They begin to wander, half-pulled to the thing they love and hate, the armed service, and half-repelled by its egregious misapplication in world affairs.

In the words of one soldier, **"I love being a soldier; the only bad thing about the army is you can't pick your war."**[58]

Sometimes Warriors defend the blunders of their leaders, even to the point of violence, because to contradict these would be to implicate themselves in those very blunders. This dissociation is evident when talking to Warriors whose brains have been disciplined to believe in something their hearts cannot conceive. Again, such a powerful juxtaposition of conscious and unconscious attitudes is strongly divisive, both to the Warrior's inner self as well as his relationships. There is nothing more stress-releasing, enjoyable, and healing to a Warrior than to invest himself fully, totally, 100% into a noble effort. There is nothing as stressful and eviscerating as uncertainty and doubt about his cause. Therefore a Warrior can empower himself with knowledge in order to find a Just Cause, or plunge into complete denial so he can never be blamed for actions he undertakes.

The first option offers a way out for Warriors who have lost their compass, the magnetic charge that inspires their lives and guides their destinies. The second option creates a Mercenary, an automaton who marches himself and others to spiritual annihilation. Sadly, Merchant society is more interested in proliferating automatons than nurturing informed and thoughtful Warriors who are masters of themselves and their surroundings. This is because automatons are expendable, predictable, and therefore easily controlled. The offer of a bit of money and the illusion of security and happiness for family and country is enough to get some Warriors hooked. It is ironic that the leaders who offer these incentives have no real regard for their soldiers, though they are eloquent at paying them lip service when necessary— at enlistments and funerals.

At its worst, Merchant society betrays the faith of its fallen by prostituting itself to the highest bidder. It creates wars that make murderers of men, and corrupts its children because it does not know how to raise them. That is because Education is compromised to favor earning potential rather than general wisdom. For a boy to become a man he must be inspired and taught by his tribal elders. But when his tribe and leaders are only after gold and profit, because they themselves were never trained to be men, boys become incomplete creations of an imperfect society. It is up to us in the 21st century to reintroduce proper values to our children and even our government in order to herald a new era. Recall from the Four Seasons that for the first 22-25 years of age,

---

[58] From the documentary, *The War Tapes,* 2006

children are in their Spring season. At this time they are learning, growing, and obeying their elders. Unless we find something integral to teach them, inspired by Educator, Warrior, Outsider, Laborer *as well as* Merchant values, they will become the next generation of imbalanced citizens and leaders in the Summer of their lives. If it is too late for ourselves, who lacked complete upbringing, it is not too late for those who are still fresh and ready to learn, because the lessons we teach them now shall temper the world for 50 years to come.[59]

Teaching boys to become men does not mean purging and brutalizing the female essence within them, though this is exactly what the armed forces do in order to create killers. That essence is inside every male. Jung called it the *anima*, just as the *animus* is the male counterpart inside every female. These must not be eliminated but *brought into balance*, and the only way to do it is to be taught by someone who has already done it, a leader who exemplifies this balance within. In Eastern traditions great Warriors are marked by this dynamic equilibrium of yin and yang. The *anima* in men gives them compassion and caring. Without it they more easily become mercenary killers and automatons. The attempt by certain sectors of the armed forces to erase compassion and caring is one of the causes of PTSD— they do enough to get boys to kill and even perform atrocities, but after killing, these same boys become tortured by their conscience, which has not been wholly destroyed. The only way to prevent this is by educating Warriors about their Purpose, and how to protect it.

> *"Remember that Education gives you not only knowledge, which is power, but wisdom, which is control."*
>
> *"It is possible to affirm the existence of God with your lips and deny his existence with your life.*
>
> -Martin Luther King Jr.

---

[59] It is little wonder that the most brilliant mathematical minds of this decade went to work on *Wall Street* rather than Main Street, resulting in the greatest world economic catastrophe since the Great Depression. In a Merchant society, the short-term lure of money sometimes overwhelms the long-term rewards of your Dharma Type.

Real Warriors are conscientious. The Integrated Warrior takes qualities of the Educator into his personality, like consideration and tactfulness, and uses them to become a better Warrior. Recall from the Anatomy section that the Pre-Frontal-Cortex of the brain is concerned with thoughtfulness, planning, and learning from mistakes. Since Warriors are strongly led by this part of the brain, they cannot count on *forgetting* things they've done: their bodies and minds simply will not allow them to.

PTSD— Prevention

Many soldiers have dreams that haunt them after war. The brutal deeds of the battlefield are replayed upon the movie screen of their minds, often for years on end. This happens when they are forced to perform or have witnessed acts that are not consistent with their normal reality. That is why it is vital for a soldier to have proper ideals and personal integrity in place before he goes to war, so that he can sleep at night *after* war. When soldiers are made to deviate from their moral purpose, they must search their hearts and ask themselves, 'will I be able to sleep at night if I do this?' Usually, the answer is instantaneous, as it should be, for excessive thinking can get you killed on the battlefield. Answers come quickly, especially to a Warrior who has been trained in proper discrimination, judgment, and personal morality. The decisions he makes on the war front can have telling consequences for the rest of his life.

War is hell. It is brutality and the carnage of man on man. To survive it, a base instinct is sufficient. However, to survive the *consequences* that follow takes a moral purpose and understanding that support a soldier in his toughest battles on the field, and give him good account off the field. Everyone wants to live, but Warriors can just as easily override this animal instinct in order to save a life. It's a curious trait— they are ready to sacrifice themselves for their brother or their cause. The decision of *when*, and *how*, and for *whom* is up to them, and usually instantaneous, but when Warriors give themselves for another, they fulfill an essential part of their dharma: self-sacrifice. Putting another before yourself is the greatest penance a human can perform, and Warriors are ready to do it. Living in this spirit of sacrifice takes an inner compass that is specially tuned by proper physical training, moral education, and spiritual orientation.

Warriors who suffer PTSD have lost their orientation. They either resign themselves to brutality as the reality of life, and take a 'if you don't kill them, they kill you' attitude, or they suffer from the conflict of values that creates a rift in their being, as described above. The way to deal with these is to understand that we live in an imperfect world, and that few actions will be neat and clear-cut, especially in war. The important thing is that we nonetheless *strive for perfection*. Knowing that we will never achieve it and yet trying our best is the hero's journey. The more dire the situation, the more heroic the deed; the more hopeless the battle, the greater shines your struggle for victory. *Heroes are not great because they live in a perfect world—it is because they* don't *that their deeds carry weight and meaning!*

So what to do? Sometimes the best fight is not to fight; insubordination, or peaceful refusal to cooperate with a regime of wrongdoing is sometimes enough. Imagine if enough German soldiers sat out or stood up against the atrocities at Dachau and Auschwitz. They may have been killed for their actions, but dying to defend dharma is better than killing in opposition to it. Sometimes Warriors can embrace a better fight, and battle evil in a way that upholds their dharma. Even after battle, they can to attempt to redress wrongs perpetrated during the fog of war. These are difficult choices and every soldier must consult his or her inner compass for support. Every Warrior must use skillful judgment to obtain a perfect report of himself from the greatest commander there is, the inner Self. In sports we know that every generation breaks the records of its predecessors. Perfection is constantly redefined. But the Warrior's secret is that perfection is not an external benchmark, but an internal event. In Sanskrit, this type of personal perfection is called Yoga.

Yoga

In hatha yoga, it is not how well you twist yourself into a pretzel that determines a good *asana*, but how fixed and rooted one is, and how well one embodies that asana. Sometimes an inflexible everyman can have greater integrity in her yoga practice than a veteran of thousands of backbends and downward dogs. In fact, if flexibility and strength were the only benchmark of yogic excellence, gymnasts would be the supreme yogis of our world, as they are unsurpassed in these. But strength and flexibility are not the barometers of yogic mastery—they are its *side effect*. In just the same way, it is the Warrior's *struggle* for perfection not its *attainment* that is the ultimate heroic deed, and the Warrior's highest yoga.

Yoga means '*union*.' Union creates wholeness, and wholeness is the root of *health*. Healing comes when the Warrior reconciles his deeds with the fact that it is impossible to be 100% right, especially in the modern age. Healing comes when a Warrior is united, joined to his Purpose, and never wavers from it, and even when he does slip, strives to reunite with it. It is a special knack, nay a need, for Warriors to get themselves into perilous situations. How they handle these determines their excellence, *not* whether they are victorious. The Bhagavad Gita relates the counsel Krishna gave to his Warrior friend Arjuna as he was about to undertake the battle of his life:

Both of them are ignorant, he who knows the soul to be capable of killing and he who takes it as killed; for verily the soul neither kills, nor is killed

The soul is never born nor dies; nor does it come about only after being born. For it is unborn, eternal, everlasting and ancient; even though the body is slain, the soul is not.
Weapons cannot cut it nor can fire burn it; water cannot wet it nor can wind dry it... therefore you should not grieve.

Your right is to work only, never to the fruits thereof. Do not be attached to making your actions bear fruit, nor let your attachment be to inaction...

And whatever fight the Warrior chooses, be it non-violent protest or a righteous war, Warriors must remember their Duty:

There is nothing more welcome for a Warrior than a righteous war... but if you refuse to fight then, shirking your duty and losing your reputation, you will incur sin, nay, people will pour unending infamy on you...

Die, and you will win heaven; conquer, and you enjoy sovereignty of the earth; therefore, stand up, ready to fight!

Treating alike victory and defeat, gain and loss, pleasure and pain, get ready for the fight, then fighting thus you will not incur sin.

Perform your duties established in equanimity, renounce attachment and be even-tempered in both success and failure; this equanimity is called Yoga.

Action with a selfish motive is far inferior to this Yoga of equanimity... for endowed with equanimity one sheds in this life both good and evil. Therefore, strive for the practice of this Yoga of equanimity, for Yoga is skillfulness in action.[60]

---

[60] Selections from *The Bhagavad Gita,* Chapter 2. Gita Press, 1996.

This equanimity, whether in war or non-violent resistance, is key to the Warrior's ultimate survival and sanity. Learning to cultivate it takes steady practice and study, the path of Integration for the Warrior type.

Homework: Winning the War

Another way to support Warriors is to understand that it takes more than Warriors to win at war. It takes Educators to dictate the ideological battle, with diplomacy, negotiation, and moral integrity. It takes Laborers to erect the infrastructures that build good will in lands ravaged by conflict. Building wells, housing the poor, and caring for the sick wins more hearts and minds than guns and tanks. It takes Merchants to create incentives for peace. Peaceful environments allow for the full enjoyment of life's luxuries, and this is impossible in a dog-eat-dog world of survival. It takes Outsiders to create understanding between warring parties, understanding that comes from Intelligence gatherers (spies), translators, and cultural attaches.

Today's military leaders acknowledge that modern wars are not winnable by military strategy alone. They are ideological battles that involve complex variables including economic, religious, demographic, technological, and social factors. Each of these implicate the Dharma Types in specific ways that are beyond the scope of this book to detail. Ultimately it is up to the reader to express the grandeur and complexity of her Dharma Type in everything from making love to making war. Taking what you have learned from this book, living your dharma, and bringing dharma to people who are lost and confused can effectuate real global change.

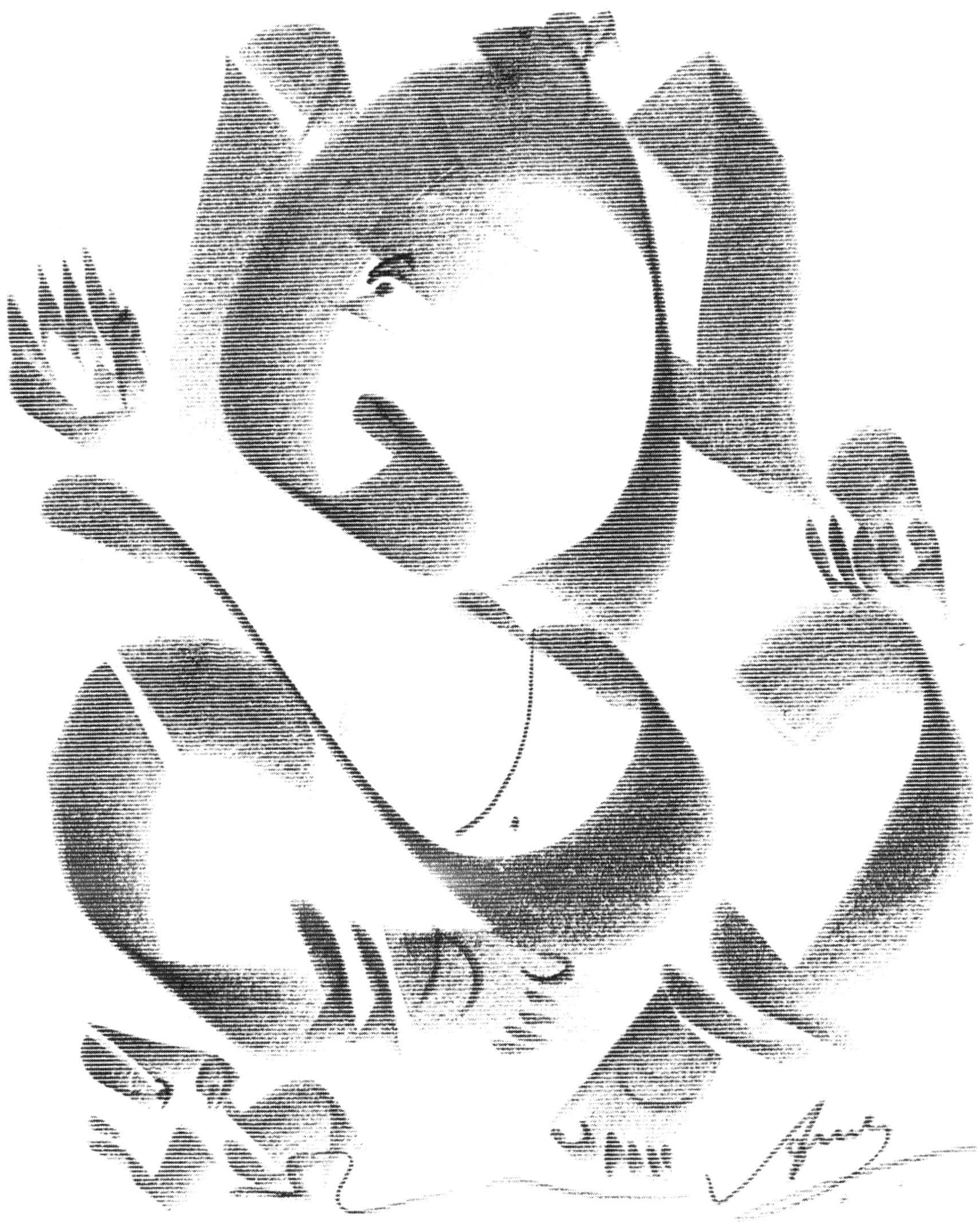

13
MONEY & PROFESSION

One way to understand your purpose is to ask, "What would I do even if I weren't getting paid? In a perfect world, would I continue to do what I am doing, or would I take up something else? What do I love?" In some way, Outsiders would still seek to untangle the mysteries of the world, and blend different disciplines to create something new. Educators would continue to pursue knowledge and counsel others. Warriors would tackle obstacles, challenge themselves, and fight for a Just Cause. Merchants would still involve themselves in commerce and social intercourse, while Laborers would build, work and serve, for the pleasure of the work itself, not its reward. *Reward is one type's gratitude for another's contribution.* What one Dharma Type can do, others cannot do as well, and every type is rewarded by its fellow Dharma Types in a reciprocal fashion, which creates social equality in a society that recognizes everyone's talents. Vivekananda, who at the turn of the century single-handedly brought Yoga to the West, said:

> *"Caste is a natural order. I can perform one duty in social life, and you another; you can govern a country, and I can mend a pair of old shoes, but there is no reason why you are greater than I, for can you mend my shoes? Can I govern the country? I am clever in mending shoes, you are clever in reading Vedas, but there is no reason why you should trample on my head..."*
> (The Complete Works of the Swami Vivekananda, III 245)

We all give and earn reward by the natural operation of our dharmas. Money and Profession are therefore closely tied together.

Each of the two pairs of Integrating types (Educator-Warrior, Merchant-Labor) share qualities that make them compatible. Among these qualities is the attitude towards money. Educators and Warriors require less in order to live happy, fulfilled lives. Merchants and Laborers on the other hand, are blessed to enjoy more of the material 'good things' in life, especially those that money can buy. Remember from Chapter 1 that Merchants are associated with *Kama*, desire, and Laborers with *Artha*, survival and nourishment, among the four drives of life. While every type can *survive* with very little, we are considering what each type perceives as necessary for full enjoyment of life. *Artha* relates to security, and the land, houses, food, money, and family that provide this. *Kama* relates to enjoyment and luxury, which require the same things in abundance. As we shall see, every type has different ideas about what is necessary.

Educator

Educators require the least amount of money and luxury of all the types. This does not mean that they do not have expensive tastes, however. What an Educator deems necessary may seem wasteful to another. A $150 dictionary and a mountain-top retreat may be indispensable to an Educator who makes her living writing books, though these would hardly seem *necessary* to a Merchant type who doesn't. Organic greens and costly dietary supplements may be *de rigeur* for another health-conscious Educator, where McDonalds would do for a Labor type who is less concerned with the delicate machine that is the Educator body.. Nonetheless, despite their specialized tastes, Educators still require less in the way of material resources than their Dharma Type brethren.

It is sufficient to supply them what they *need* to keep Educators happy: a functioning vehicle, a roof over their heads, the tools necessary for their livelihood, and enough paid leave to keep them balanced. (Time spent in contemplation needs to be funded so that Educators can enjoy collecting their thoughts without thinking about their survival.)

Educators do not need to own material property, though they should control their *intellectual* property, because when this becomes valued by Merchant culture it can lead to tremendous wealth, as in the case of Bill Gates, an Outsider playing an Educator.

> *Food, shelter, and necessities should never be an issue for Educators; a society that cannot provide these for them is seriously deficient in priorities, and teeters on the brink of moral corruption.*

In the everyday world, school teachers who drive respectable cars, have decent houses and the wherewithal to care for their students, have abundant means with which to lead happy lives. Food, shelter, and necessities should never be an issue for Educators, and societies that cannot provide these for them are seriously deficient in priorities, teetering on the brink of moral corruption.

Chapter 13: Money & Profession

Classically, Priestly/Educator types begged for their daily food and wage. Today, this is not much different. Consider how often Teachers, Scientists, Priests, and Philosophers have to petition for funding from private and state institutions to support their continued pursuit of truth and enlightenment. We must not forget that this pursuit ultimately benefits society. Without advances in medicine and science, we cannot promote health. Without improved social consciousness, we cannot encourage peace and global understanding. Without increased awareness of the environment, we cannot live harmoniously in the world. And without spiritual understanding, we cannot truly fulfill our purpose in the cosmos. It is the Educator's role to provide these for us, just as a tree gives its shade equally to all who seek it. Educators are a Natural Resource, and should be treated as such. Their fragile, complex natures require a dignified but simple upkeep; in return they freely offer their majestic insights and inspiration to all.

> *"Those of you who uphold the pure precepts should not buy, sell or trade. You should not covet fields or buildings, or keep servants or raise animals. You should stay far away from all kinds of agriculture and wealth as you would avoid a pit of fire."*
> --Sutra on the Buddha's bequeathed teaching (for Educators)

One of the problems Westerners have with the Indian caste system is that Brahmin (Educator class) families tend to command the respect and resources in their societies, generally leaving others owning little and slaving away at low-class jobs. This situation reflects the ***devolution*** and ***perversion*** of the archetype system. It is true that Educators/Priests should command respect in their culture— not for their power or economic influence, but for their abstinence from the same. Evolved Educators shy away from money and power because they are more concerned with ideas and ideals than with material resources. That is why they, the Brahmin caste, are traditionally the beggars in society, *not* the working classes! Merchants, Laborers, and Warriors are assured of home and hearth because they have jobs. Educators have to rely on the goodwill of others, especially Laborers and Outsiders, who have a Duty to take care of them. When they cannot produce this good will by making themselves useful in some way, they may starve. This sets up Educators to inspire their societies in the best ways they know how, by teaching, ministering, and enlightening others, whatever their actual professions. The Educator's reward for this may be money, but it may also be a bowl of rice, a *"Thank you!"* and a lifelong respect from the other types, who each give what they can.

When they are spared the need to compete for money, goods, and shelter, Educators become fit to make laws and precepts, as they have little personal gain from the exercise of such laws. *Educators have nothing to gain, and everything to lose, by setting themselves up as material masters of culture.* Such positions are ill-suited for them, unless an Educator happens to be in a Life Cycle that sanctions these actions for a time. (See the next chapter for more on the Life Cycles). Educators earn the esteem of their fellow classes by soaring like the Air Element above the influence of greed and gluttony. They require little in the way of wealth save what is necessary for the purposes of their dharma, because Educators in any capacity are basically *monks*.

Be they scientists or teachers, Educators, like monks, should ideally wend their way in the world with the humility befitting their role as ambassadors of higher values. An Educator in government may hold up *social justice* as her Truth, while a scientist may venerate the sanctity of *ecological sustainability*, but their dedication to these causes is no less austere and committed than a priest's devotion to God— the only difference is the subject matter they pursue.

When Educators follow their truth they are provided for by the powers they serve. When they do not, when they look with lustful or greedy eyes upon a person or object, they squeeze integrity out of their systems. When they seek to use their intellect for selfish gain rather than benefiting the world, and introduce the oppressive caste structures that advantage them over others, their special dispensation dries up.

Educators do not need to maneuver and contrive to find financial freedom. Though neutral to the Merchant type, they essentially Disintegrate when adopting Merchant values, because these lead them away from their ideal of *surrender*. When they strive exclusively for money, power and fame, they never attain satisfaction and end up losing these things in the end. Such temptations for the Educator, who thinks he can profit from the world using his intellect to *scheme* rather than to *dream*, lead him down the wrong road, and eventually to self-destruction.

Warrior

Like his Educator partner, the Warrior requires little in the way of luxury or comfort to be happy. Warriors can go for stretches in extreme privation from food, shelter, and other necessities. However, because Money is Power in today's world, Warriors also gravitate to money as a way to secure their interests. It is inevitable that where power goes, Warriors follow. But as we can see from the cycle of the ages in the first chapter, Warriors who resort to any means to secure power lose their inherent purpose, which is to protect others. Thus, in a competitive free-market economy where Merchants rule the yard, Warriors can become hard-pressed to succeed, breaking the rules or taking short-cuts to get to the top. This, again, goes against their primordial instinct to *uphold* the rules, and as a result, Warriors become shamed, often to the point of suicide, when they are caught compromising their principles in the name of profit. Many are the examples and cautionary tales of lost Warriors in the Merchant society.[61]

In the truest sense, Warriors should be rewarded by money as an afterthought, or an embellishment to their primary work. The actual value of a gold medal does not define the worth of an athlete's achievement. Anyone can buy a gold medal on E-bay or at some specialty store. What matters is the accomplishment it represents, and the skill and work it took to get it. For Warriors, *that* is the true reward; everything else is icing on the cake. Warriors should seek a worthy cause and let the rewards *follow*, rather than plunging after the reward itself, which becomes meaningless when pruned of its real value. Fortunately for many Warriors today, great prize money *does* go along with many of their achievements, from sports to medicine to the military, and they are taken care of by a society that values these. However, many heroes die penniless and unknown because their gifts are not as valued by the Merchant culture. Nonetheless, it is the inner pride and satisfaction of having lived your life with a purpose that sustains a Warrior type. Nothing else can provide that same rush, that feeling of aliveness, and the sense of a life lived to its fullest.

In the **Government** section of Chapter 8, we examined why Warriors are more suited to public service than Merchants, looking particularly at their devotion to *ideas*, such as Truth and Justice, rather than material benefits. We discussed that running a country is not the same as running a business, because business has material wealth as its raison d'etre, while a country has the health and

---

[61] Refer to the next chapter, The Life Cycles, *Warrior in Merchant Period*

welfare of its citizens as its primary goal. Thus, we observed a basic division between Warriors and Educators, on one side, and Merchants and Laborers on the other, a division that has far-reaching applications, from Government, Health Care, and Money, to Religion and Spirituality, which we will cover in later Volumes.

Educators and Warriors enjoy a bond on the level of ideas and concepts, which is why when dealing with Money, Warriors and Educators tend to sell *ideas*, while Merchants and Laborers sell *products*. Where the enterprising Merchant type may make millions by inventing the paper clip or the bobble-head, savvy Warriors promote themselves and what they can *do* for people, not what they can *give* people. Laborers and Merchants are better at working with *materials* to produce something useful: Educators and Warriors are better at organizing how such products fit into the social scheme.

TYPE	RULED BY	DURATION	REALM	WEALTH AS GOAL	SPIRITUAL SKILL*
Laborer	Emotion	Long-term	Objects	Yes	Works (Service)
Merchant	Emotion	Short-term	Objects	Yes	Works (Charity)
Warrior	Intellect	Short-term	Ideas	No	Wisdom (Judgment)
Educator	Intellect	Long-term	Ideas	No	Wisdom (Knowledge)

* The spiritual skills, or *Yogas*, prescribed for each type in the Gita and other Vedic sources, are detailed in Volume III: *The Spiritual Types*.

The attitudes of *Thinking* (Educator/Warrior) and *Feeling* (Merchant/Laborer) extend to almost every area of everyday experience, from helping us choose a profession, to picking what to wear for the job interview. '*I feel like you should wear that dress*' is not an intellectual opinion, but an observation that wearing a certain dress will *feel* right for the speaker. Merchant/Labor types start sentences with 'I feel...' while Educators/Warriors might say 'I believe,' or 'I think.' Even when they *say* 'I think,' Merchant/Labor types really mean 'I feel,' reflecting the two different ways these groups relate to the world.

> *Only Warriors are allowed to make life and death judgments... Educators are too far separated from reality to make practical decisions, while Laborers are not broad and inclusive enough in their scope to make good political authorities.*

As related in previous sections, every human being has multiple Intelligences, which in this case break down into two camps: the body and the mind; the gut and the brain. The *Feeling* group is better at listening to their gut, while the *Thinking* group pays more attention to their head. One is not smarter than the other— they have different functions and different modes of communicating.

Merchants, famous for their street smarts and savvy, rely on their gut to make instinctual decisions. Warriors, on the other hand, must balance gut instincts with their principles if they are going to live up to the Warrior code. *That is why Warriors are allowed to make life and death judgments, because they are in the middle of the Feeling/Thinking continuum that goes from Laborers (very kinesthetic) to Educators (very cerebral).* Being in the middle, Warriors are designed to use both brains—the head and the gut— to make equitable, just decisions. That is also why they make ideal leaders, for they have both the idealist's acumen and the realist's practicality. Educators are too far separated from reality to make practical decisions, while Laborers are not broad and inclusive enough in their scope to make good political authorities.

Interestingly, other sacred sciences make similar divisions. In hand analysis, this is tantamount to the difference between short and long fingers, long fingers connoting deliberation and cognitive understanding, while short fingers connote action and visceral understanding.[62] If we look at the Four Elements,

---

[62] In *hasta samudrika shastra,* the Vedic art & science of hand analysis, every finger is attributed to an Element, beginning with the thumb (Space) on down. From the standpoint of biology and palmistry, it is the thumb that makes humans unique among mammals. We are Outsiders because of our opposable thumbs, our use of sex for recreation and pleasure, and our spiritual search for freedom—all qualities of the Outsider type. In this way, every finger

which are used in practically every esoteric ancient science, we see that Water and Earth mix well, just as do Air and Fire. There is compatibility between the types in each group, and incompatibility, or at best neutrality, between the opposite camps.

However, these camps are not always clear-cut. The short-term/long-term duality has Warriors and Merchants together on one side and Educators and Laborers on the other. This short-term/long-term classification has several implications, including Health and Fitness, as discussed in Chapter 7. For example, the short-term duo are susceptible to acute-onset illnesses, while long-term types are more prone to chronic disorders. Since this basic division can be used for diagnosis, it is also useful for recommending lifestyle modifications. The short-term group respond to 'quick fixes,' more intense and focused exercise and diet regimens, while the long-term group are better off with longer treatment and exercise regimens. In Money terms, Laborers and Educators are better-suited to long-term strategies for wealth accumulation, all other factors being equal. Warriors and Merchants, however, tend to be more risk-taking (Warriors) and temperamental (Merchants), which leads them to explore more lucrative but dangerous profit strategies.

Merchant

While Educators have to rely on the good will of their peers for sustenance, Merchants are blessed with greater potential for prosperity. This does not mean, however, that they are never poor. Because of their volatile personalities, they may go through periods of success and privation in their lives, though the fear of loss and hope for gain tend to drive them back to find security. This propensity has prompted one Merchant to quip, *"I have lost more money in my life than most people have made."*

Because by nature they are given to wealth, they more than anyone can share their prosperity with others. Their charity serves them in turn, for they receive back the gratitude and karmic merit of their giving. Investing in charity is no different than investing in the stock market, save that the returns are not as easily discernible: they are *adrishta*, invisible to the unaided eye. When you give to a cause, be it social or spiritual, you get a return on your investment, especially if the giving is done without unreasonable attachments and conditions. Merchants benefit from the very fact of giving, but like investing in

---

relates to a Dharma Type; it is not for nothing that hand analysts look at the ring finger (Merchant, Water) to discuss business, money, art, and creativity in a person's life.

> *There is a difference between a **special interest** and the **common good**. Merchants need to learn what seeds offer up fruit to feed the multitudes, and what seeds grow a thorny, selfish tree*

the stock market, when Merchants put money into irreputable ventures— knowingly or unknowingly— they do not reap the generous fruit that watering a good tree yields. Therefore, they need to be smart and learn to help causes that uplift mankind, rather than serve the petty concerns that benefit a select, unworthy few. There is a difference between a *special interest* and the *common good*. They need to learn what seeds offer up fruit to feed the multitudes, and what seeds grow a thorny, selfish tree. Otherwise they might as well keep their money and resources for their own families.

Charity does not just mean handouts. It is giving opportunities to those who don't have them. It is giving others the chance for education, a dignified living standard, and self-help through entrepreneurship. Nobel Laureate Muhammad Yunus is an example of a Merchant's ingenuity and generosity when applied to the good of the world. He popularized micro-finance, the practice of private lending to poor entrepreneurs in developing countries, which led Bill Clinton, Oprah Winfrey, and news organizations around the world to hail this type of peer-to-peer lending as an easy and revolutionary way to help people help themselves. With a 99% payback rate, microloans are safer investments for Merchant types than the stock market or other financial gambles, for the return is more than monetary: the ability to change a family's fortunes, for the price of a dinner for two, can be priceless. [63]

Dr. Yunus believes that micro-lending is one of the steps to the eradication of poverty, as he says on his website, *"a programme for putting homelessness and destitution in a museum so that one day our children will visit it and ask how we could have allowed such a terrible thing to go on for so long"*

Such an inclusive, optimistic vision typifies the Integrated Merchant's worldview, for the Merchant's growth comes through widening her familial net to see *all people* as her extended family. Having done this, a Merchant does not need much else to invite grace into her life. Educators have to sit for hours memorizing and cogitating, Laborers working and serving, Warriors practicing

---

[63] Typically, a micro-loan ranges from $20 to $200 and can be done from home. For more information visit www.kiva.org. For information on Dr. Yunus, visit www.muhammadyunus.org.

> *"Poverty in the world is an artificial creation. It does not belong to the human civilization"*
>
> --2006 Nobel Prize winner, Dr. Muhammad Yunus

and perfecting, Outsiders roaming and seeking... but the Merchant need only extend a hand. Good works, good energy, and 'writing the check' are the deeds that ensure a Merchant type's continued success!

When they have made all the money they can make, what's next for a Merchant type? They can go on trying to fill their void in vain with *things,* or they can give their things away. A dramatic example is Oskar Schindler, who upon making millions from war profiteering turned a corner and used his charm, popularity, and money to save 1200 Jews from certain annihilation. His generosity is remembered to this day by the more than 7,000 grateful descendents of 'his Jews.' Such stories typify the Merchant's ability to change the world for good. He does not have to be a saint or live a monastic life, but to use his God-given abilities to create new opportunities for those who have none!

Bill Clinton is another Merchant who worked to share his talents with the world, having perhaps done more after his presidencies than he did during his tenure in the oval office to bring countries without clean water, food, education, and other opportunities into the 21st century. Such undertakings task all of a Merchant's resourcefulness, skill, and optimism, but also deliver priceless rewards.

When Merchants fail to reinvest in their society, seeking power and wealth for themselves, they blight the Merchant name and condemn themselves to a lonely life, isolated from the community they are meant to support. As the Merchant moves towards Warrior values of Power and Ambition, she Disintegrates. Wealth is not a substitute for power. Real strength and authority are best evinced in Warriors, who have these as their birthright just as the Educator has Wisdom and the Laborer Love. Real power cannot be bought, though that is exactly what the short-cut leaders of Merchant society attempt to do. This grabbing at power and resources leaves society more vulnerable, less secure, and eventually impoverishes both the Merchant herself and her community.

Even Merchants lacking prosperity must understand this concept. They need to evaluate their behaviors and attitudes towards others, and ask themselves, *'do I have charity in my heart?'* Merchants who are poor may not have money to offer up, but can still give of themselves— they can share their energy, skills and time to reap the rewards of karmic merit. In the Vedic tradition, this is known as *karma yoga,* the path of right action and good deeds. An Integrated Merchant cannot help but become wealthy, for in sharing her energy with the world, she inevitably receives the world's energy back many times over. Just as Nature nurtures the other types, She supports Merchants in their giving.

And once they flourish, Merchants need to avoid becoming arrogant and extravagant in their wealth. They must eschew the desire to lord it over others and demand unusual respect from subordinates and anyone who appears to have less than them. This is a clear case of Disintegration, which eventually spirals into destruction. When they are selfish, they become poor in spirit and in wit and eventually end up losing both. A lesson for poor Merchant types is not to repeat the mistakes that lead them to this fate, but to embrace, as difficult as it may be, their path of Integration, in which Nature and the universe support their prosperity.

Outsider

Since Outsiders value *Freedom* above most things, they are likely to spend money to achieve it. From buying loose-fitting clothes to secluded island retreats, they spend money to achieve the isolation and expansion that their Space Element requires.[64] Freedom also motivates them to make money and work at professions that allow them maximal gain with minimal restriction to their time and liberty.

Outsiders may discover new ways of making money, or have ambivalent attitudes towards money. Since historically they have operated on the fringes of society, they do not have established attitudes to money, and need to let other types like Merchants or Laborers help them manage their wealth. Every other type understands the power and value of money—even Educators, though they are less concerned with it. But for many Outsiders money is a strange commodity. It is easy come and easy go. In Outsider professions money flows in unpredictable ways. A male stripper may make $1,000 one night, and only $50 the next. An astronaut may make nothing while he is training, but end up on a government stipend for the rest of his life. Taxi drivers, independent

---

[64] A sartorial note: Outsiders often prefer to wear black, the color of the Space element. Not surprisingly, Outsiders of all stripes through history have embraced black as a way to rebel, blend, and hide from others, as in their biker, businessman, and ninja personae.

contractors, musicians, inventors— all rely on an uneven or sporadic flow of income, and duly attract Outsiders to such professions.

Not surprisingly, Outsider attitudes towards money can run to the extremes. They may be shockingly lax or conservative with their wealth. They may prefer to earn money in unusual ways; they may also prefer spending it on unusual things. On the one hand, an Outsider bank robber might feel justified in stealing because of having gotten a raw deal in life. On the other, like Robin Hood, this Outsider may have little qualms in giving that money away, illustrating both the negative and positive traits of his persona: the ability to self-justify anything, and the gift of empathy with the suffering of others. Such unconventional attitudes are Outsider calling cards.

Outsiders may take on attitudes of the other Dharma Types when they are playing a particular character, or living through another Life Cycle. Much of what we can say about Outsiders and money has to be in the context of the persona they take on. An Outsider playing an Educator will deal with money as an Educator, and an Outsider playing a Merchant will behave as a Merchant, with the notable exception that they can at any time revert to playing another role, or no role at all; in matters of money as in everything else, Outsiders are unpredictable.

Outsiders may deal in foreign, mysterious, or even forbidden things to earn wealth. Being the most populous type, and because it is their dharma to bring new ideas to the world, the last 200 years has seen an explosion of invention and new opportunities arising from enterprising Outsiders in every walk of life. From aviation and electricity, to nuclear power and the internet, Outsiders have pioneered new sources of wealth and opportunity for millions, even billions of people. This explosion has led some Vedic thinkers to speculate that we are coming to the end of the Iron Age of darkness into a new world age of light and wisdom. It is not clear whether these thinkers have also considered that the coming of a new age is always accompanied by great catastrophe— catastrophe brought on by the instruments which serve that very age!

Laborer

Classically, Labor types worked the land to produce goods and services for the community. In today's world, Laborers can work in any profession, but their affinity for land and property remains unchanged. Therefore, it is important for them to own their land as well as the tools and equipment they use in their daily work. Laborers are fond of their own 'things,' and society, particularly Merchant types, must provide these for them. Since Laborers use their bodies to produce income they must also have security when they grow old. Being the longest-lived of the Dharma Types, they require some type of social assurance to ensure that they are cared for even in their 80s 90s and 100s, when their bodies are no longer able to produce for them. The best security is having an extended family, with children and grandchildren to care for them, as well as free and clear property and possessions.

Laborers who own their land and provide for themselves are thus able to feed the masses, and provide for others, especially Educator types, which is their Duty (see Chapter 8: Circle of Duty). They can do this with no loss to themselves because they produce more than enough to feed their community. In ancient days a farmer would bring milk to the local hermit to drink when his own family needs were taken care of. Because cows, trees, and crops produced an abundance of food, there would always be enough to go around. In another instance, a landowner would allow a solitary Educator or Outsider to use a lonely plot of land to live on. These days, the Laborer's hospitality is still legendary, as they make the best restauranteurs, chefs, and hoteliers. While modern professions have taken them away from the land, the mores and values of the Labor type remain unchanged.

Time and seniority play a crucial role in how the Labor type is perceived in society. The longer his tenure at his job, the better pay and benefits he receives. Thus, Laborers tend to be loyal to their bosses and value long-lasting work relationships. Of course, they also don't mind working long hours and overtime to earn that respect. Time being the all-important measure of a Laborer's worth, elders are respected for their wisdom and experience. Thus, Labor types tend to take care of their elders better than others, knowing that they will be cared for in turn when their time comes.

Lessons from the Labor Type

Laborers are naturally devotional types and have special lessons to teach the other classes, like how to value the good things in life. Laborers have an attachment to things that define them, like their *country*, their *house*, their favorite *chair*, and the *shirt* they have worn since high school for good luck. A car need not be just an inanimate object for them, but a personal, cherished part of their lives, especially if it reflects their personalities. Some people like trucks, others like sports cars; the vehicle a person drives can say as much about them as the clothes they wear and the words they say.

Laborers can teach an Educator to name his favorite telescope, or the dog-eared dictionary on his desk, and hold on to these as anchors to his dharma. Educators do not usually identify with inanimate objects, and can find investing their personalities into some *thing* a useful way to hold fast to their purpose... even when they have forgotten it themselves. Educators can all too soon forget the people, places, and things that have touched their lives, feeling alone and cold like the Air Element that rules them. But when they recall the people they have known, and the lives they have changed, they begin to warm up and remember their contribution to society. They must cherish their inner pictures, and build an album of precious memories— not as a source of sentimental attachment, but as a way of remembering their own value to the world.

Laborers teach Merchants stability. In return, by the mutual interplay between Integration points, Laborers receive valuable input from the Merchant type. Laborers are sentimental, while Merchants are excitable. These two types share an emotional nature: one attached to long-term emotional value, the other to short-term excitement. A Merchant may be dazzled by the newest BMW or stereo on the market, while the Labor type cherishes his 1959 pickup and turntable. They are both deeply tied to the emotions that pull them to these things, but in different ways. For one, the novelty may pass when the next model comes out; for the other, his attachment is so comfortable that it becomes an unconscious part of his life. This can play out in all sorts of ways, but in the final picture, both benefit from a shot of the other's medicine to keep them emotionally balanced. For example, Merchants may find the prettiest spouse only to trade her in for another four years later when the excitement has worn away. Likewise, Laborers may become so inured to married life that they treat their spouse like a piece of furniture: something they love and ignore at the same time. The Merchant has to learn emotional stability and devotion, while the Laborer has to find the spark of excitement in his life.

Laborers teach Outsiders how to be relevant. By imparting the value of a good day's work, of honest self-reflection, and the simple pleasures in life, Laborers show Outsiders how to be present with themselves and their reality. They also show that there is strength in solidarity, and that sharing life with like-minded people makes its pleasures more precious, and its pains more tolerable. Community is a refuge for the furtive Outsider, who may seek all her life to find people who think like her. Laborers show her that the door is open and she is welcome inside.

Finally, Laborers teach Warriors the value of work for its own sake. Warriors, who are busy with high-minded goals, perfecting themselves, and living for the Just Cause sometimes miss the obvious satisfaction of ordinary work and a job well done. Warriors share the Laborer's love of physical work, save that they are not inspired unless their efforts amount to some greater purpose. For Labor types, on the other hand, work is its own reward. This is a valuable lesson for the Warrior, who may be too busy *planning* her life, to actually get down in the mud and start building it.

Cautions for the Merchant

Because we live in a Merchant society, the Merchant ethic is widespread, which is why every type must be aware of the dangers as well as the glories that go with living in a Merchant world.

At their worst, Merchant types can be mean and heartless. They can take advantage of the unwitting with their superior cleverness. Sacha Baron Cohen, in his two movies *Borat* and *Bruno*, illustrated how inventively funny and excruciatingly heartless a Merchant can be, at the expense of his less-clever, less articulate victims.

Usury, swindling, meanness, mockery, and other forms of belittling people form a dark streak in the Merchant personality. This is nowhere more evident than on Labor types. Though they should Integrate into one another, Laborers often bear the brunt of the fallen Merchant's scheming tactics. From corporate treatment of employees, to one-on-one relationships, Merchants sometimes cannot resist taking advantage of Labor types, simply because *they can*. A famous example is the relationship between Joe Frazier and Muhammad Ali.

> *"In the ring Joe Frazier and Muhammad Ali were the equal of each other. Yet today, Ali has sold an 80% interest in the use of his name and likeness for commercial purposes for 50 million dollars... and Joe is living in a room above his gym in Philadelphia."*
> --Thomas Hauser, Muhammad Ali's Biographer

Friends at first, the Merchant Ali later turned on Frazier after losing to him in their first fight, resorting to excoriating diatribes and insults that caused a permanent rift between the two fighters. With his gift for gab, the otherwise elegant Ali smeared Frazier, ultimately tarnishing both of their reputations. The naïve Frazier believed that his boxing in the ring would do the talking for him, but he was proven wrong, and their legacy to this day bears the bitter taste of hatred and regret.

Like Ali and Frazier, Merchants and Laborers need each other. Neither boxer would have been as great without the other. Their personal differences were based only on ego fixations; at the core the Merchant needs the Laborer's down to earth stability and heart, while the Laborer benefits from the Merchant's self-promotion and vivacity. Nobody has more heart and more common sense than the Labor type. Merchants, who think they have an abundance of both, are usually proved wrong by life itself, and that is when they need to lean upon the Labor type for assistance. For their part, Laborers, who can be wrongheaded and stubborn, need to be cracked out of their shells by the eclectic and vibrant Merchant. Together, they better the world in unfathomable ways.

Earning Power and Consumption of Luxury

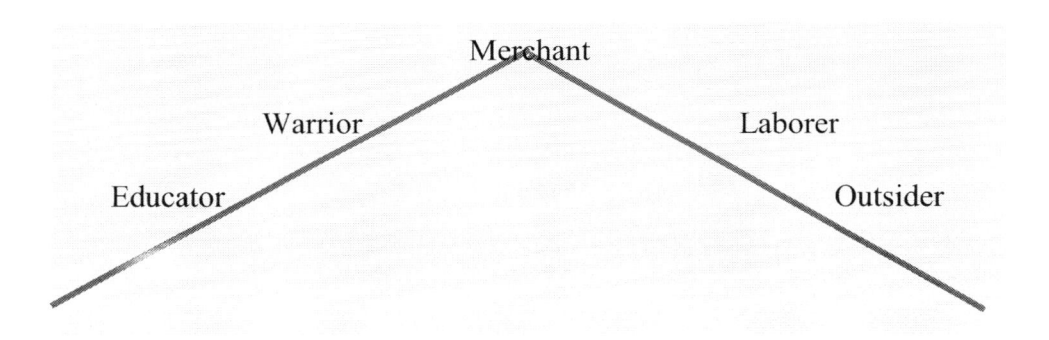

In a just society this figure reflects the earning power of the different types, though Outsiders can vary from top to bottom depending on which type they are emulating. That is, Educators tend to earn least, while Merchants earn the most. But money and earning power must be examined together with the Circle of Duty to form a more accurate picture, and set aright the obligations of one type to the next. Recall that Educators have a Duty to Warriors, who have a Duty to Merchants, who have a Duty to Laborers and Outsiders both— *Merchants are the only type with double duty to two classes.* We can now see why: since they are afforded the highest earning power and consumption of luxury, they are best suited to share it with the largest demographic. By contrast, Educators, who require the most support, are the only type who *receives* two Duties, from Outsiders and Laborers (see Chapter 8, *The Social Conscience of the Types*).

> *"Pure, unencumbered, raw capitalism is never the answer for anything that involves a public mission..."*
> **David Simon, *Baltimore Sun* reporter and creator of "*The Wire*"**

Another way to term this is according to production output, the idea that labor output should cover the consumption of luxury. Educators have humble needs; they neither consume nor work to create much luxury. Accordingly, they have little control over the means of production. Warriors have more of a hand in the work of production since they are the overseers, managers, and executives, and are afforded more luxury than Educators. But the Merchant has the highest use *and* production of luxury, and he disposes of most of society's money and resources. Laborers, while intimately involved in the actual production, have less of a role to play in managing corporations and running the infrastructures of capitalist society. Therefore, like Warriors they are allowed less than the Merchant, though more than the Educator. Though they do more actual *work* than any other type, Laborers are not afforded as much *wealth* in the Dharma Type model, because inordinate wealth can actually backfire on the Laborer, who needs to take time out from working to manage her money. Managing money is no easy matter. Money is *shakti*, energy, and like raw plutonium, it is difficult to handle when you don't have the tools and training to do so. It can become a hazard to people emotionally unequipped to deal with it, and many are the messes in society born out of the mismanagement of wealth.

Rules of the Game

Special rules govern how money moves—*out* of whose hands and *into* whose pockets it flows. Those who do not understand the rules are at a disadvantage in a capitalist global economy. A recent study showed that over the last century, suicide rates across the globe skyrocketed during the tenure of conservative governments and decreased under liberal regimes. This occurred because conservative governments allowed so-called 'market forces' to control economies, while liberal governments typically favored interventionist policies, like public welfare programs and other forms of social security. Under

> *Values and ethics in the Vedic system are based on the tripod of **karma**, **dharma**, and **duhkha**: principles stating namely that a) what goes around comes around, b) there is a purpose to life—live by yours—and c) when you lose sight of a. and b. you inevitably suffer.*

conservative regimes, those who understand the rules of the game necessitate less intervention than those who do not, a process that favors the Merchant type, but disadvantages others who do not know how to play the Merchant game. Merchants are equipped to play the money game by both design and desire: they have more interest in and intuitive feel for how *shakti* moves and how to accumulate it. As a result, Merchant governments are more likely to write free-market policies that suit their needs, leaving other types to either play their game, or suck it up, whence the inevitable rise in dissatisfaction among the rest of the population, as reflected by the sharp rise in suicide rates.

The result of such free market policies is that those without a grasp on money mechanics are disadvantaged. We have only to consider the global economic meltdown of the previous decade to see the side effects of people trying to play the Merchant game without proper training and knowledge. People sold on the capitalist dream learned to overextend themselves, so much so that as they fell off the branch, they took everyone else with them. While they have a share in the responsibility, ultimately those to blame are the masters of the money machine who lured them out on a limb in the first place. One cannot make the rules and then blame others for trying to play by them. The global economic disaster was not caused by renegades outside of the system, but by those who played within the corrupt rules of the game itself, which means that we must either change the rules... or teach everyone else how to play.

Consider the example of buying a car. Those who know how to negotiate, who also understand the wholesale value of a vehicle and its real market value, are better-equipped to get a good deal than those who walk into a dealership without an idea of what they want, how much it is worth, or how to go about getting it. Regular folks do not usually have the bargaining acumen of trained salesmen, or inside knowledge on financing, interest, and the real price of other add-ons. They need to know how to access such information if they are to avoid being ripped off. It is almost an American ritual for parents to take their grown-up son or daughter to the auto lot and teach them how to bargain. But how is a parent to do this when they never really learned it themselves? How is one to obtain this information if it is only available to the Merchant elite? The internet

> *Educators abuse with knowledge, Warriors with force, Laborers with strength of numbers, Merchants with cleverness, and Outsiders with deception.*

has helped greatly, but ultimately it falls on Merchants to teach the other types how to prosper themselves and play the game, for the sustained benefit of both society and themselves.

It is not just Merchant types who take advantage of others when the rules are stacked in their favor. A salesman is as likely to fleece a naïve buyer as a trained boxer is to beat up an out-of-shape contender. When you are trained in the rules of your game, you can take advantage of others who are not, unless within those rules is some form of ethic and moral integrity that protects the less advantaged. Values and ethics in the Vedic system are based on the tripod of *Karma, Dharma,* and *Duhkha*: principles stating namely that *a)* what goes around comes around, *b)* there is a purpose to life—live by yours—and *c)* when you lose sight of *a* and *b* you inevitably suffer. By suffering, you learn that the only way to attain durable fulfillment is to treat others as yourself, and to live the dharma of your type to the best of your ability. These three legs of the Vedic value system have survived for millennia, particularly because they underscore something basic and true to the human experience. This is that, no matter the government, legislation, or religious regime, without an inner understanding of these three concepts, all three— government, law, and religion— are bound to crumble from the inside.

Educators abuse with knowledge, Warriors with force, Laborers with strength of numbers, Merchants with cleverness, and Outsiders with deception. Corruption is not endemic to one Dharma Type, though it is apparent in Merchants today because of the abuses that have plagued money dynamics since the advent of Merchant society, and the Kali Yuga itself. Merchant training is essential for people who live in modern Western societies and capitalist countries. Understanding *compound interest*, *lending*, and *credit* is essential to building security and social status in a free-market economy, because the rules of the game will always favor those who do, and disadvantage others who don't. Once one understands the game, it can be enjoyed for what it is. Once you get that the game is not personal, emotional hang ups can be taken out of the equation: when you understand that sales people are punished for not getting the most out of customers, you can have compassion for both parties in a sales negotiation. In fact, once you get that a salesman is trained to leverage the most money out of you, you can begin to leverage the salesman. Knowing the rules can help people turn the tables, and leverage the Merchant's own need to sell against him, in order to make deals that benefit both buyer and seller.

Dangers of the Game

Aside from the obvious dangers of financial ruin and even suicide, the subtle entanglements of the Merchant game are more insidious. Learning how to handle and invest money is key to getting ahead in capitalist societies. Merchants do their communities a service when they share the secrets of financial success with their fellow Dharma Types, freely, openly, and without agendas. For many, such education is a lifesaver, and in little time can help a poor to middle-income family become more secure and self-sufficient. The danger is that once Merchant training replaces Educator principles, learning tends to stop there. Once people become wealthy enough, secure enough, and fat enough, they may be lulled into believing that is all there is to life, and to pay nominal, if any, interest to learning the secrets *other* types have to teach, especially their own. This is because there is a lacuna in the Merchant mentality that cannot be filled by material security alone. It takes the Educator's ideals, the Warrior's discipline, the Laborer's faith, and the Outsider's sense of wonder to complete society. A society perfused with only Merchant philosophy cannot remain happy for long. When the spiritual underpinnings of the human experience are forgotten or put away, such as when people begin to pay more attention to the size and shape of their car than what it is used for in the first place, people lose sight of their destination as human beings, which is not obtaining *things*, but *self-attainment*.

Though the rules are simple, Merchant training *can* be complicated. From getting a real estate license to investing in the markets, proper training can take months or years, requiring time and energy that could be devoted to other pursuits. For Merchants, such investments of time ultimately prove useful to their quest for self-attainment, for they lead to Enjoyment and Personal Growth for them, as we shall see in the Profession section below. But for others, Enjoyment and Personal growth come from different avenues, and it can be daunting to chase the Merchant's life while trying to be faithful to your own dharma. Recall from the Bhagavad Gita, that *it is better to be bad at your own dharma, than to be good at that of another...* The danger of the Merchant game is that one can become lost in its intricacies and forget one's own path. Staying true to your course, in spite of the power of money to steer you to places you do not really want to go, is crucial for surviving the Merchant age!

Profession

Without *passion* and *drive* we cannot be successful at our Professions. Each type naturally has passion for its own dharma: Educators for knowledge, Warriors for justice, Laborers for security, Merchants for prosperity, and Outsiders for variety and mystery. Dharma is the road we follow even when there is no monetary reward. It is what each type does naturally with its talents. To determine a likely Profession, we ask the same question above for Money: "What would I continue to do even if I didn't earn money doing it?"

Whatever we devote our attention to, grows. Whatever we spend the most time on becomes who we are. Since in the West an average person's Profession is the mainstay of her day, it has the most to say about what kind of person she becomes. That is why one of the first questions people ask when they meet is, "*What do you do?*" What we do is synonymous with *who we are*, which is why professions like *Smith, Tanner, Porter, Chandler, Wainwright* and others became family names. Today, the name John Smith does not identify its bearer as a blacksmith, because we have lost the sense of dharma that goes with our professions, and most of us work at 'jobs' that have little to do with who we really are.

Profession is the activity whereby one gains a living by contributing to the community. A Profession is different from a 'job' in that it allows the widest avenue for *Personal Expression* and *Growth*. But how do we know if we have a 'job' or a Profession? How do we know if we are *growing*... or just decaying? Does our work afford maximal *personal expression*, or does it dictate someone else's rules for how we must express ourselves? The Dharma Types provide a key. Here is a summary of the ways that every class fulfills its needs for expression and growth through their Professions.

The Merchant class... express best and grow when making money. There is no other way around this; Merchants must make money, first for their own survival, then to nurture their families, and finally to care for their communities. This is the Purpose of the Merchant, to clothe, shelter, and connect her world. Her personal growth comes in commerce of goods, services, or even her own talents and skills. Her expression comes out in public performance, networking, social intercourse, and community service, such as volunteer, charity, and other philanthropic work. She finds fulfillment and enjoyment in various forms of entertainment.

The Labor class... express themselves through useful service. Laborers grow by growing something else in turn: by making or building things that are images of themselves. From erecting a building to raising children and family, their work is a creative expression of their dharma, and represents evolution and growth for a Labor Type.

The Warrior class... express and grow through competition and challenge. Warriors grow by testing their limits. They express themselves by completing feats and challenges. In proving equal to their challenges, Warriors find fulfillment in their Professions.

The Educator class... grow by learning and best express by teaching. An Educator's desire to learn is ultimately a quest for self-knowledge and personal growth. Whether studying the cosmos and the stars or the atoms they are made of, an Educator's quest ends with wisdom about the Self. This wisdom is ultimately the Educator's path of personal growth, and its transmission her greatest form of expression.

The Dharma Types can work any Profession they choose: a Labor type can be a teacher, an astronaut, or a farmer, but the way he does his job will be unmistakably stamped by his Dharma Type. Laborers will be more narrowly-focused, diligent, and careful about their work than other types. Outsiders will accentuate their uniqueness, and Merchants their cleverness. Educators will try to offer good counsel, and Warriors will try to complete a challenge or compete for a goal. Let's look at an example of this through the lens of some professions, examining the same type of work through the eyes of an *artist*, a *taxi driver*, and an *Ayurvedic doctor*.

As artists, Outsiders are inclined to push the envelope of accepted aesthetic values. They may shock the public or bring in new styles of artistic expression. Being *avant-garde*, literally the '*front line*', they experience the hits and the highs of new discovery first. Like Van Gogh, such discoveries may not be appreciated until well after their demise.

Educators, emphasizing *truth* and *purity*, will produce art for its own sake, without the imperative of recognition or reward. Merchants, on the other hand, *must* be recognized and remunerated if they are to have satisfaction and fulfill their role to the world. Consequently, Merchant art tends to be the most circulated and recognizable.

Laborer art has form and function as its mainstay, and can include everything from murals and stained-glass windows, to cabinetry and sculpture. It appeals to the practical mind, is well-made, and tends to be more lasting as a result. Finally, Warrior art is strong and has force, struggle, and character as themes, reflecting Warrior values, such as self-sacrifice, honor, and valor. Warriors work in the name of an ideal, regardless of whether that ideal is recognized by the world.

As cab drivers, Educators may point out landmarks and recite interesting trivia to their clients. They are less in it for the money than to meet and learn from interesting people and situations. Warriors in the same position would fight to get to their destination as fast as possible, even if they have to battle traffic with their accelerators, horns, and even their mouths!

Merchant cabbies, looking for the good fare, are happy to chat it up with their clients, taking a leisurely route to their destination, and making it a pleasant and enjoyable experience, if painful to the wallet. Labor types may not converse much, except to respond to direct queries. Having probably worked their seventh straight fifteen-hour shift, they are more concerned with their family, paying the bills, and getting home to a good meal, than any common courtesies their clients might expect!

Finally, the Outsider cab may look, smell, and feel exotic. Outsiders may play odd music, have varied decorations, or speak differently. Whether foreign immigrants or local locos, they will usually know uncommon and intriguing things about their city. Immigrants, who are either Outsiders or people in Outsider periods, stand out by their speech, mannerisms, and even what they eat, not to mention their personal expression through profession.

Each of the Dharma Types can work in any profession. How they do it and what they gain from it, however, varies. Ancient texts on Ayurveda tell us that the Science of Life is to be studied by Educators *for providing benefit* to all creatures, by Warriors *for protection*, and by Merchants *for earning livelihood*. Each excels at a specific branch of this discipline. Merchants may be masters at the alchemy of herbs and drugs, while Warriors may make the best surgeons. Educators do well in general medicine, theory, and education, while Laborers may excel at Rejuvenation, body therapies, and Pediatrics. Finally, Outsiders are challenged by diseases of the mind and disorders of unknown origin. Anything that is outside of the mainstream, from psychosis to possession to incurable diseases like AIDS and cancer, proves fertile ground for the Outsider's interest.

The Types And Their Professions

Outsider: Any profession that involves foreign influence, or fringe professions that are little understood. Foreign languages, anthropology, troubleshooting, pornography, mysticism, new discovery, and the paranormal. Professions that no one else wants to do. Professions involving profound research or self-sacrifice. Professions that involve lying, stealing, or cheating: thieves, illusionists, assassins, spies, etc.

Merchant: Entrepreneurship, sales, banking, pharmaceutical, business/commerce, investment, promotion/publicity. Advertisement, entertainment, performance, games and gambling, food and beverage, beauty, sex, fashion and luxury.

Laborer: *Building and creating things*: community building, construction, engineering, agriculture, obstetrics. *Specialized fields and trades*: detectives, massage therapists, plumbing, esthetics, make up, carpentry, mechanical, real estate, etc. *Care and public welfare*: crisis management, nursing, EMT. *Economics*: accounting, financial services, banking, bureaucratic government positions. *Service:* restaurant and hotel, manual labor. *Old things:* archaeology, geology, antiques, history.

Educator: Education and research, intellectual pursuits, the sciences, diplomacy, counseling, religion and spirituality, humanitarian professions, anthropology, literature, the humanities.

Warrior: *Protecting others:* Law, law enforcement, firefighting, medicine, military. *Competition and power:* executive corporate and government positions, athletics, martial arts, leadership and management posts.

Educators may teach Ayurveda and its philosophy, rather than actively practice it. They may focus on its spiritual components, where the Laborer would be more practical-minded and interested in its immediate use. Warriors may work for the government to protect others, by dictating health-care policy or performing emergency surgery on the battlefield. Outsiders may synthesize Ayurveda with other practices to form unique offshoots.

Merchants may grow wealthy by preparing and selling drugs and concoctions. We see this today: one of the most profitable industries in the world is the drug company that supplies everything from Aspirin to Zoloft to ease the pain and improve the pleasure of the American public— typically Merchant pursuits. Thus, while different types may choose the same profession, they do it with profoundly different orientations.

The 8 Limbs of Ayurveda and Corresponding Dharma Types

Internal Medicine	Educator
Eye, Nose, Throat	Educator
Surgery	Warrior
Poisons	Warrior/Outsider
Spiritual/Mental afflictions	Outsider
OB/GYN	Laborer
Rejuvenation	Laborer/Merchant
Aphrodisiac	Merchant/Laborer

Individual Types

Laborers tend to be specialists, and there is no one more diligent and devoted to their chosen profession than a Labor type. Whether a brain surgeon or an electrical engineer, the Laborer loves what he does and is particularly good in his niche. However, because of this narrow focus, he may not be as good in areas that require broad knowledge of diverse and varying subjects. As an engineer he may specialize in electrical, mechanical, or other forms of engineering, but do not ask him about Medicine or Law, because these are outside of his scope of expertise. **The Educator** on the other hand, being a Renaissance man or woman, knows a little bit about many things, in diverse

> *An Integrated Outsider can use deception to give energy rather than take it from the world*

and varying fields. What he does not know he is quick to *learn*, as intellect and understanding are his strengths. When Educators specialize, they remain well-rounded, retaining their intellectual curiosity about the universe. However, this too-liberal tendency to many interests can make them wishy washy and unable to focus on one thing. They are also the least manually-skilled type, and this impracticality can make them seem out of touch with ordinary reality.

Outsiders do not do well with a 9 to 5 schedule. They need freedom, variety, and independence. Outsiders gravitate to professions that allow them to make their own hours. Independent contractors, truck drivers, stuntmen, actors, artists, writers, and musicians are some such examples. The common thread uniting Outsiders is their need to retain their individuality and freedom.

Outsiders are also world changers. Whether they do this as revolutionaries or quiet agents for transformation depends upon individual circumstances; but Outsiders are put on this earth to reform and transform it. Just as Space is the most prevalent Element, Outsiders are the most influential type to history and society, though ordinary society is usually ignorant of their contributions. The Warrior's duty to protect, the Educator's call to counsel, the Laborer's obligation to work, and the Merchant's drive to prosper are directives that are clear-cut and easy to appreciate, but few realize the crucial role Outsiders play in our daily lives, and the extent of their influence on world events. Whether winning the Cold War as spies and counterintelligence agents, or World War II as codebreakers and atomic bomb makers, the Outsider's invisible footprint on history is staggering to contemplate. The cracking of the German code in WW II prompted Winston Churchill to say, *"Before Alamein we never had a victory; after Alamein we never had a defeat."* Whatever their professions, Outsiders are the secret-keepers of the world!

Each type has a positive and negative expression. The Outsider's negative emotion is Self-Deception. When this is turned around, an Integrated Outsider can use deception to *give energy* rather than *take it* from the world. They become illusionists or magicians, tricking observers for their pleasure. Many Outsiders also make great makeup artists, costume designers, or movie makers... anything that has to do with creating illusion and tricking the eyes of the observer. Outsiders bring new things to the world, like realms of fantasy and never-before-seen images, which makes them good fiction writers and storytellers. Anne Rice's vampire series and Isaac Asimov's outer space explorations are examples of groundbreaking ideas brought to the public through print.

	Negative Emotion	**Positive Emotion**
Outsider	Deception, Anxiety	Empathy/Wonder
Educator	Lust	Compassion
Laborer	Sloth, Jealousy	Love, Loyalty
Warrior	Anger, Pride	Generosity
Merchant	Greed	Conviviality, Enthusiasm

Warriors and Wellness

Warriors are the natural doctors and surgeons of the Dharma Types. If medicine is a war against disease, no one is more fit to tackle it than the Warrior type. Warriors can make crack decisions and life-and-death choices in order to cut through afflictions. They also have the physical fortitude to battle for patients, even to their own detriment. It is the dharma of Warriors to fight and protect the weak and innocent, and medicine and wellness are fields that allow them to do so on a regular basis. And when Warriors learn to Integrate Educator skills, their bedside manner improves and they become friendly and understanding towards their patients.

The desire to fight on behalf of the disadvantaged also makes them great lawyers. Some people equate lawyers with sharks, but one must remember that in many countries the accused have no rights and often await their fates in jail without recourse to comfort or counsel. In these cases, lawyers are the only protection the innocent— even the guilty — have. In this sense, the Warrior's obligation to help those who cannot help themselves, to fight for the rights of the underprivileged, and to give themselves for the cause of another are fully satisfied.

We can forgive lawyers who take the easy road to gain in Merchant society. If we can't forgive them, we can at least understand the pressure to conform to a system that promotes Profit, not Protection. In the long run, both the lawyer and his society suffer when he Disintegrates into a money-making machine. But as long as the Merchant train grinds on, such Disintegrations remain unnoticed, as those who fall are crushed under its wheels, and those who fail to stay aboard are left behind. At some point, though, as it loses its valuable members, its operators and conductors, the machine itself crashes and becomes irreparable. At such a time it becomes necessary to re-invent the system and allow everyone to re-board and participate in steering society in the right direction, each according to his or her Dharma Type.

Homework

Breaking down Professions according to Dharma Type is useful, but ultimately people can work in any field that provides fulfillment and allows freedom for *Personal Growth* and *Self-expression*. In the Government section we saw how the Armed Forces branch into five limbs according to Dharma Type, and how these further split into individual subcategories. For example, while the Army, Navy, Air Force, and Marines reflect the Laborer, Merchant, Educator, and Warrior personalities, duties like *tank operator, intelligence agent*, and *recruiter* relate specifically to Labor, Outsider, and Merchant types. We don't have to change our careers to find something that suits us; sometimes we just have to find the *niche* within our existing careers that befits our individual dharma.

Whatever your profession, there is usually something in it for every type. It is not only Warriors who make great doctors. While they have a talent for surgery, Laborers may be excellent pediatricians or nurses, and Educators might make great general practitioners. It is your homework today to think about your work— from agriculture to zoology— to discover how it expresses your Dharma Type, and ultimately the Life Cycle you are in, which we discuss next. *Enjoy!*

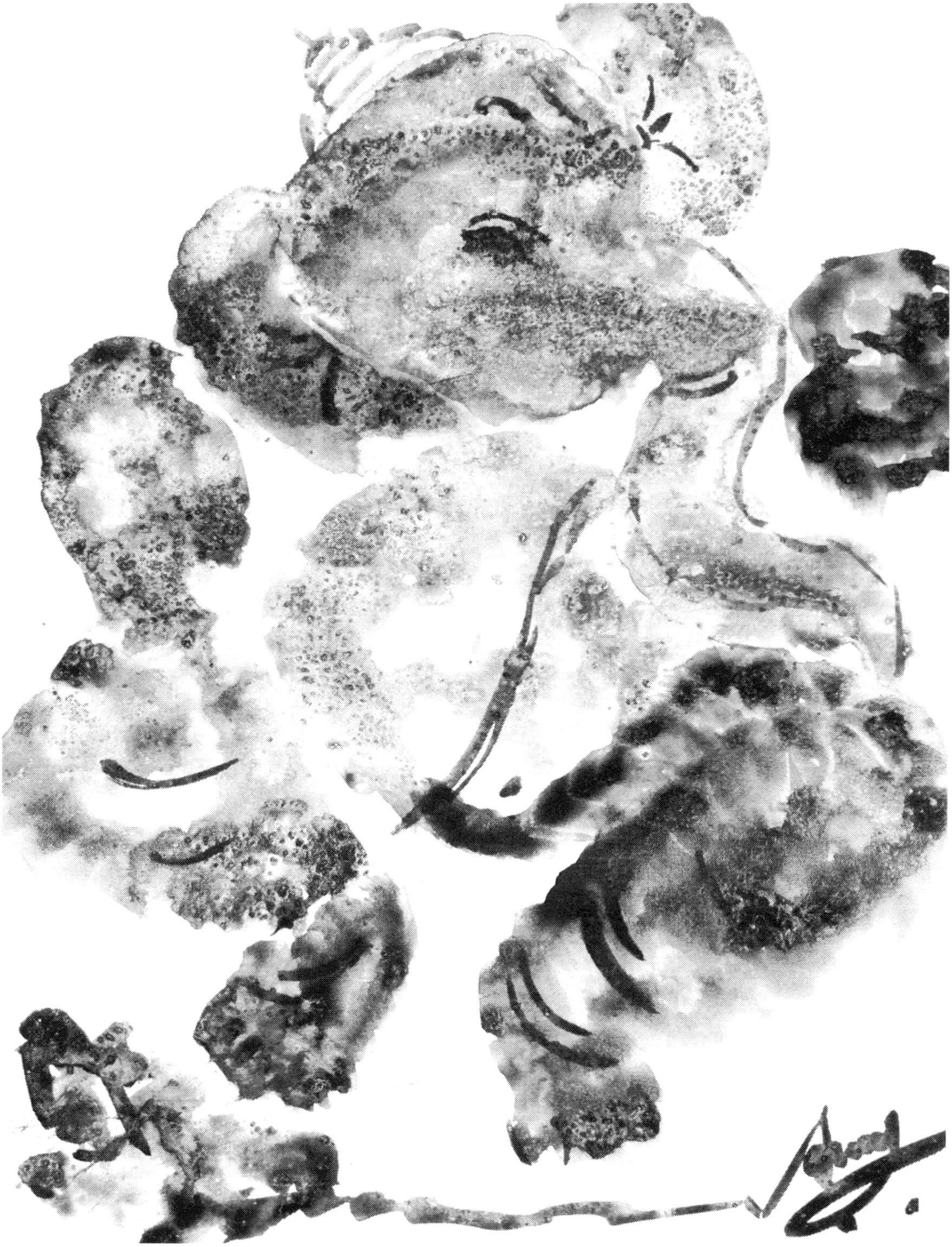

14
THE LIFE CYCLES

We end this volume with a discussion of the Life Cycles, not because they are less important, but because they are invaluable to getting the most from your Dharma Type. In the Vedic tradition, first and last chapters are special, because they create the first and last impressions in the reader. In Chapter 1 we began with a survey of the Dharma Types, the basic nature of every individual at birth. In this chapter we discuss how that basic nature takes shape over the course of a lifetime, as expressed by the Life Cycles. Practically speaking, your Life Cycle determines what's going on *right now* in your life, while the Dharma Type outlines your basic DNA print at birth. Who you are is the Dharma Type; how you express who you are is influenced by the Life Cycle you are in.

For example, every woman has the *potential* to give birth, but that potential is only *actualized* during a specific portion of a woman's life, between puberty and menopause. In addition, fertilization is only possible during narrow windows within her ovulation cycle every month. Nature works in cycles within cycles. Thus, we cannot help but follow Nature's rhythms if we are to obtain desirable results, from having a successful pregnancy to creating a successful life. Like Nature and Nurture, the Dharma Types and Life Cycles come together to give us a complete picture of who we are... and where we're going.

When people take the Self-Test at the beginning of this book, they usually select two types. One likely represents their Dharma Type, the other the Life Cycle they are in. Sometimes it can be difficult to separate *who we are* from *where we are in our lives*, our Nature from Nurture. This is especially true for people in Outsider periods, as these tend to be confusing to begin with. Outsiders, who can relate to every type, have a harder time finding themselves, and people in Outsider periods are particularly challenged. The good news is that there are ways to map out the Life Cycles with clarity and insight. The best of these requires an accurate birth time and is read using the Vedic Life Map, or horoscope, which provides a snapshot of a person's Dharma Type as well as the past, present and future Life Cycles she will experience.

> *"Not to know what happened before we were born is to remain perpetually a child. For what is the worth of a human life unless it is woven into the life of our ancestors by the records of history?"*
> *-Cicero*

Dr. Daniel Amen, whom we discussed in Chapter 7: *Health and Wellness*, uses SPECT imaging of the brain to determine which of its five systems are over or underactive, thereby facilitating diagnosis as well as treatment options. Though Dr. Amen recommends reading his books and taking his tests, the only way to really *see* your brain is to have its picture taken and interpreted by a professional. In much the same way, having a snapshot of your Dharma Type and Life Cycles, along with the questionnaires and tests in this book, is the best way to decipher the world of the Dharma Type.[65]

But even without Vedic techniques, we can look at our lives to determine our current Life Cycle. Are we in a money-making time, in which prosperity, social intercourse, and enjoyment of life are primary motives? If so, we might be in a **Merchant** period. Are we devoted to raising a family and the quiet comforts of home, working hard to earn money but not ambitiously craving it? Then we may be in a **Labor** time. Or are we ambitious, driven, physically active, and looking for promotion? This could signal a **Warrior** period. The **Educator** time is marked by self-cultivation, study, and an interest in humanistic concerns, while **Outsider** periods bring the unexpected. They put us in contact with the unknown, are unpredictable, and tend to keep us on the fringe of accepted social norms. Even people who gain fame and fortune in Outsider periods do so as rebels or distinct personalities. By looking at the karma we experience at any given time, we can judge the Life Cycle we are in, and when it changes. Let's take a look at some examples.

Joe was an Educator who loved to study and flourished early in school. At 18 he lost interest in academia and found himself rebelling against his teachers. He began to resent the boundaries that restricted his self-expression, and started to experiment with drugs and reckless behavior that eventually alienated people around him. When things at home began to feel stale, he dropped out of college and went abroad to discover other cultures, to which he adapted quickly and felt a special affinity. He adopted many of their customs, and when he returned home, found himself somewhat out of the loop with his friends and family...

---

[65] Visit www.spirittype.com for more information, and to find a professional near you.

Can you guess what Life Cycle Joe entered at age 18? If you said 'Outsider' you are on the mark!

...After roaming the world for a few years, Joe began to think to himself, "I'm tired of being poor and unsettled. I need to make money if I want to enjoy the good things in life!" He enrolled in several trade courses and became a successful design consultant to wealthy homeowners and businesses. Using his acquired language and cultural skills, as well as his natural ability to counsel and teach, he became a successful businessman for the next 17 years.

At this time it is clear that Joe entered into a Merchant period. Here, his focus shifted to making money. However, because our basic nature stays with us, he could not escape the need to *instruct* and *counsel* others, though he found lucrative ways to do it. This is how the Merchant Life Cycle colored his Educator Dharma Type.

Let's look at another example.

June was a Warrior Type who worked quietly to support her little girls. At a certain point in life she began to take an interest in self-improvement, and started reading books on health, diet, and spirituality. She discovered yoga, which led her to take classes and eventually complete a Teacher Training course. She began teaching yoga and loved it so much that she quit her old desk job to teach full time. Her renewed outlook and life philosophy started to rub off on her students, whom she taught by setting a strong example herself. Her main priority was to protect her children, and she often adopted this attitude towards her yoga students, helping them to grow and transform through discipline, hard work, and a 'never quit' attitude.

Can you guess what cycle this is? If you said Educator, you are correct. Our Warrior June's interests naturally turned to *education* and *self-improvement* as the habits of her old Cycle (perhaps a Laborer period) began to fall away. She became interested in knowledge and how to transmit it. She also began to empower herself, and because Warriors *Integrate* into Educators, her Educator period was particularly supportive for her, as we'll see below. Protecting people comes naturally to Warriors, who also like to practice what they preach, experimenting on themselves before subjecting others to their discipline. These were all hallmarks of her yoga teaching style.

The Life Cycle will not change your purpose, just its *expression*. Cycles different from your Dharma Type will express your virtues in different environments and

> *The Life Cycle will not change your purpose, just its **expression**.*

different ways. This is where an Educator goes to Africa to teach English in an Outsider period, or a Warrior begins building housing for the homeless, in his Labor time. It is where an Outsider opens an import-export shop, in her Merchant period, and where the Merchant enters politics to save the economy, in his Warrior cycle.

As you can see, it is not difficult to tell when you enter various Life Cycles because your interests reflect the changing seasons of your karma. Below is a summary of what you can expect in each Life Cycle.

Summary of the Life Cycles

Outsider

People in Outsider periods find it boring to live normal, everyday lives. They are keen on exploring the underbelly of existence, traveling, and discovering the unusual. Their education is interrupted, their living situation is in flux, and this period prevents their normal integration into the flow of society. This may cause suffering, but can also become their strength, molding them into a *vichitra purusha*, a creature unlike any other. Coming and going within the community, they can be disruptive, like a strange breeze. Whether that breeze wafts sweet scents or foul airs depends on their personal evolution, and what they have learned from life.

Outsiders often long to be normal. This is usually out of ignorance of their own gifts, and the fact that they would actually *hate* normalcy if they had it. If you are in an Outsider period and find yourself wanting the roller coaster to stop, remember that you are here for a reason, and consider that if you shut your eyes to the experience, you may never again see the sometimes strange and wonderful vistas that being on the roller coaster affords. That doesn't mean you have to become a carney to enjoy the ride: one does not need to be a rebel or an iconoclast to embrace Outsider virtues. Instead, one must make the most of what is available. Whatever the attitude, one thing is certain; no one is ever the same after a ride in an Outsider Life Cycle!

Chapter 14: The Life Cycles

Merchant

A person in a Merchant period becomes more interested in the finer things in life... and how to acquire them. A natural sense of financial opportunity arises, and one is able to take advantage of it during this period. Out of *fear of poverty* and *desire for success*, the person in a Merchant Life Cycle drives herself, working hard to attain financial security. Her web of friendships grows, as she begins to network and gets to know people outside her normal sphere, even if only superficially. She becomes more affable, attractive, and consequently better-known in her community. Money is a big deal, and the primary focus during this time. Everything revolves around the importance of financial security, and the shelter, clothing, and sustenance it provides. The Merchant time is a great period for advancing one's fiscal agenda.

Educator

A person in an Educator period becomes a role model for others, aspiring to truth and purity in their actions and beliefs. At this time they are interested in self-improvement, self-help, and the betterment of the world. They are more studious and open to learning both spiritual as well as practical, everyday matters. Knowledge becomes precious, as do ideas and ideals. They are likely to be attracted to intellectual people and pursuits.

Labor

A person in a Labor time is settled down and interested in work. Quiet service and a job well done become more important than self-promotion and deal-making. Such a person becomes more devoted to family, and his close attachments grow stronger. Life becomes uncomplicated and its goals clear-cut. The pleasures of working with your hands, sitting and eating, and existence itself become more deeply appreciated, as do hardships and tragedies. A Labor person's life is more keenly felt, and that is why having a close-knit community of friends and family becomes monumental during a Laborer Life Cycle.

Warrior

Anyone in a Warrior period becomes a leader. Even though leadership may not be part of their natural disposition, people in Warrior cycles are thrust into roles that require executive abilities. A person in a Warrior time becomes a doer. He cannot sit and just let things happen. He must be implicated in the flow of his destiny and instrumental in bringing about his desired outcome. He picks a cause and fights for it. The person in his Warrior time has definite opinions and is willing to defend them. He is a protector, sacrificing himself for others, and will take on missions that put him in the line of fire. This may simply mean working at two jobs to feed a family, or actually fighting on a battlefield. In either situation, an individual is not content with sitting still during his Warrior time, and will take action to ameliorate his circumstances, or the circumstances of others.

Integration/Disintegration

Mutually Disintegrate	Mutually Integrate
Warrior-Merchant	Warrior-Educator
Laborer-Educator	Merchant-Laborer
Outsider-All	Outsider-All

Now that we've surveyed each Life Cycle, let's take a look at how these periods affect the Dharma Types based on their Integration and Disintegration points. When a Dharma Type finds itself in a Life Cycle that is its Integration point, it will tend to find success in that period, while such a type will experience obstruction during the period of its Disintegration point. A Dharma Type in a Life Cycle that is neutral to it will find itself neither terribly obstructed nor particularly supported. Let's take a look at what this means.

A **Warrior** in a **Merchant** period is not likely to do as well as a **Warrior** in an **Educator** period, all factors being equal, because Warriors Disintegrate into Merchants, and Merchants into Warriors. Likewise, a Laborer is likely to find Educator cycles lonely and tough, just as Educators will feel unappreciated in their Labor cycles. That is because they Disintegrate into each other, and when a type sees its Disintegration period, it can spell obstacles and difficulties. Here are some examples:

John is a Laborer who spent his high school and college days in Outsider Life Cycles. After graduation he got a job at a bank and soon thereafter began an Educator Life Cycle. Although he felt at home in his department, he was promoted to corporate trainer. This new job allowed him to travel and meet new people, but he preferred his old position and friends to the revolving door of new faces and new ideas every day. Although he made more money, he felt lonely and isolated, unable to make permanent bonds with people, even feeling like an ascetic at times.

An Educator time holds some pitfalls for the Labor type. The *benefits* of this period include learning new things, obtaining training and being otherwise instructed. The dangers come when these Labor types are put into positions that require Educator tasks they would rather not perform. In such cases, they must excuse themselves from these positions if they want to keep their sanity and well-being, even if it means taking a financial hit.

Ultimately, Laborers do better without the headaches of having to deal with Educator issues. In fact, this may not be the most profitable time for Laborers, as they may spend money on school and learning and time away from the work that allows them to earn that money.

Conversely, Laborers entering a Merchant period will find the hustle and bustle of activity stimulating, not draining. Here, Laborers see their gifts appreciated rather than misunderstood. Here, they feel more at home, as opportunities allow them to fully express their talents and be remunerated for them.

Stacy is a schoolteacher, an Educator just finishing her Labor period. She is soft-spoken, overweight, and her life has been marked by quiet service to her ESL kids: students learning English as a second language. Though severely trying at times, this period has taught her that standard teaching protocols don't work, and she has worked hard to develop new, more successful techniques. Now, as she enters into her Warrior period, she feels compelled to share her discoveries so others can benefit from her work. She begins advocating for reform in teaching protocols, and the once quiet and unremarkable homeroom teacher now speaks with a voice that captivates thousands and demands appreciation. The new activity inspires her to renew her gym membership, and she finds that training her mind and training her body go hand in hand towards building a positive new image, for herself and for children around the world.

An Educator entering her Warrior Life Cycle is at the apex of her strength. This is a time when her wisdom may become particularly popular and valuable to others. During their Warrior period, Educators are encouraged to strike out boldly and put their ideas to the fore. They are disciplined, driven, and more likely to make their name than at any other time. Hence, this is a period for leadership, publication, and public acclaim.

Conversely, the Educator in a Labor period is typically more closed in and dedicated to her private work and the immediate affairs of her family.

Educators become more emotional and in touch with their feelings during this time. They also gain an added appreciation for the simple, concrete things in life, like a home-cooked meal, a well-crafted object, and good company in general. Though not as philosophical and lofty, their ideas will carry weight and have more material applications due to this influence. There is a quiet enjoyment during this period. Because the Educator Disintegrates into the Labor type, it is important to watch out for intellectual laziness, sloppiness, and unbalanced thinking.

One must remember that Life Cycles rarely last a lifetime, and if you find yourself in a Disintegration cycle, it does not have to be a negative experience. As an Educator, you cannot ever *be* a Labor personality. It is a time for research and investigation that will contribute to breakthroughs and insights in future periods. For Stacy, her Labor time gave her the experience and endurance to observe how kids learn. And though it took a toll on her, she used it to inspire a new chapter in her life as her next period rolled around.

Every Educator must *learn* in order to have something to *teach*. The Labor period is a time of learning, though often not by choice, or in the manner that one prefers. It is a time of humility and quiet submission to the cycles of life, as it may be difficult for the clumsy Educator to fit into the Laborer's world. But the rewards are also there. The lesson is not for the Educator to *fit* in, but to *learn* from her dharma, for her own benefit, and the benefit of others. This is a time to swallow your pride, put your head down, and accept with faith and devotion what Nature gives you. You may not be seen for all that you are, but what you are seen for will be enough.

Xu is a Warrior who has trained in Kung Fu since he first learned to walk. He spent his early days at his father's gym, eating, sleeping, and training. He cared little for talk, and always felt actions spoke louder than words. As Xu entered his Merchant period, his father gave him the responsibility of running the gym and making it profitable. Xu experimented with many different things, but found the headaches and worries of keeping his business fiscally solvent almost overwhelming. He began to cut corners and make mistakes, sometimes even cheating people. He began staying out late, drinking and carousing, leaving his training behind.

Several years later, as he began an Educator phase, Xu's mind started to turn back to Kung Fu; this time not as a martial art, but a philosophy to help him deal with his elevated blood pressure, restlessness, and anger issues. He began to take retreats to sacred sites where he reconnected to the essence of his tradition, eventually returning to his gym to become a teacher, offering his students classes on a donation, pay-as-you-can basis.

Because Warriors Integrate into Educators, Xu's Educator period was fruitful both spiritually and intellectually. He began to read and study, learning the theories behind many of the disciplines he took for granted: the *philosophy* behind the *practice*. Xu may end up writing books or teaching his skills at this time, and become honored by his students and readers. The emphasis here is on cultivating inner virtue and conscientiousness, not externally fighting for it. In fact, this is the stage in which Warriors learns the value of Peace. They may let their physical skills lapse, while developing other, more intangible attributes. Essentially, Warriors take on the characteristics of the Educator type, and, because the two are compatible, this is a most satisfying period. On the other hand, Warriors in Merchant periods tend to take on the negative qualities of the Merchant: loudness, instability, showiness, anger, and self-interest. Warriors can slip into egotism and pride when their Merchant periods roll around… attitudes they usually pay for later on, since the Warrior's dharma is about protecting others, not serving himself.

Homework

Take some time to think through how each Life Cycle affects the Dharma Types with special attention to yours. There are 25 possibilities. This chapter is not about enumerating every period for every type, but rather a guide to help you integrate how different periods fit your life using your own imagination and what you've learned of the Dharma Types so far. Outlined below are some paragraphs to get you started. We will look at Outsider cycles first, since no type Integrates or Disintegrates into them. Then we will observe the Merchant cycle as an example of how you can do this for yourself.

The Outsider Life Cycle

Educator

What does an Educator do in an Outsider cycle? He still writes books, but they are about the foreign and the unknown. He still studies, though his subjects may be arcane or esoteric. His mind is still occupied with self-improvement, though his route to it may circumvent the obvious, and delve into alternative methods. Looking for Atlantis? Researching the Kabbalah? No subject is outside the Educator's curiosity at this time, though his conclusions may differ from what established research has to say.

The Educator at this time perceives more keenly matters that may have long evaded investigation. His mind is freed from the shackles of rote and established thinking to roam the expanses of the unknown. He may partake in mind-altering substances, or go to excesses to obtain the object of his research. And in doing this he must be careful, for the limitlessness characteristic of the Outsider can also derange his mind's ability to stay rational, and therefore relevant.

People in Outsider periods become disaffected with the status quo. They need a break from the routine of their home and job, which is why many change professions and residences during this time. But relevance is the saving grace of Outsiders, who must construe their experiences into a model fit for public consumption if they are to be of use to themselves and society. Educators swimming in Outsider waters must take care not to drown in their depths, or be carried away by their strange currents, lest they fail to return and share the treasures they have found, and become adrift and alone, useless to themselves and others.

When they do return, they are likely to bring back things never-before seen. Their investigations and conclusions may bring about a paradigm shift to the world's consciousness, and instigate new modes of thinking. Educators who enter into the unknown either disappear forever in its depths, or, if they manage to reemerge, become permanently altered by their experience. From sexual escapades to psychedelic exploration, Outsider periods redefine an Educator's normally rigid boundaries, and permit him to experience life with a curious admixture of depravity and virtue.

To maximize his stay on the border of the known, the Educator must stay true to his Dharma Type and continue to seek wisdom and self-improvement. As long as he does this he achieves his goal and attains fulfillment, no matter where his future may take him in other cycles.

Special Conditioning: Educator

Sometimes Dharma Types spend their whole lives in one Life Cycle, becoming so conditioned by it that they permanently take on many of its qualities. This is a rare and special occurrence that deserves exploration. An example of an Educator whose life has been conditioned by Outsider Life Cycles is shock-rocker Marilyn Manson, whose has been mostly in one long Outsider period. Knowing this helps us to understand that, for all of his garish displays (Outsider), he is at his core *playing a role,* and teaching people (Educator), presumably to be non-judgmental and relax their inhibitions. His Outsider persona is pointing out the flaws in our morals by invoking strong reactions, while his softer, sometimes geeky Educator side is at the same time shining through to temper these displays with a moral subtext. In this way, understanding the Life Cycle of a person, and how their basic type orients to it can give us crucial insight into their psyche.

Alanis Morissette is an Outsider *playing* an Educator who has been in Outsider periods most of her life. She will not see another period until her seventies. Themes of sexual experimentation, drug use, anorexia, and general exploration of musical, social, and personal boundaries characterize this curious Outsider-playing-Educator's search for meaning in the world.

Merchant

The Merchant in an Outsider period may use his business skills in foreign or unknown markets. He may also take to dealing in drugs, crime, and other shadowy features of the Outsider element. He may himself become expatriated and begin life anew among different cultures. The Merchant type perennially suffers from a sense of uneasiness, a type of emptiness that causes him to question his self-worth. In this period he may set out to find its source, and fill that void with answers from the unknown.

Outsider periods temporarily dissolve the structures that bind a Merchant, allowing him to penetrate into vistas far removed from his usual haunts. He may travel to new locales and experience a variety of entertainments, pleasures, and curiosities. In the end, these may serve him as he brings back his experiences to the normal world. He may find profit in new markets or by new strategies gained from his 'walk on the wild side.'

There is one danger for the Merchant in an Outsider period. With his already loosely-defined moral structure, he may be tempted to throw ethical considerations to the wind and cross the line of legal/moral decency at this time. As noted above, experimenting with drugs and sex may be too enticing to pass up. The Merchant's willpower is usually poor (except when it pertains to generating wealth, where it is unrivaled), and this may cause him to slip into behaviors he would not perform under normal circumstances. But in an

Outsider period, he is temporarily out of sight of the Warrior's vigilance (see Circle of Duty), cruising under the radar, as it were. This allows him to do things he wouldn't normally consider.

Special Conditioning: Merchant

An example of a Merchant conditioned by her Life Cycle is Marilyn Monroe. Born a charismatic Merchant type, she spent her *entire life* in Outsider Life Cycles, thereby injecting a sense of the misfit (she was raised in foster homes), iconoclast (she never settled for what Hollywood gave her), and the libertine (she sought freedom from and pushed the boundaries of sexual expression). In her desire for freedom, she functionally became an Outsider to most everyone in her life, from the Kennedys to her Hollywood cohorts, and ultimately to herself, as she sought to liberate herself from limitations to the point of committing suicide. Even her death was tinged with the mystery and suspense of the Outsider personality, and the spectacle and notoriety of her Merchant archetype.

Elvis Presley is another charismatic Merchant who never saw another Life Cycle. Elvis came out of left field to redefine Country/Blues into something totally fresh, new, and dangerous— he was the face of Rock 'n Roll. Thus, two of the most charismatic (Merchant) and eccentric (Outsider) personalities of the 20th century, Marilyn and Elvis, both won peerless glory as well as infamy by spending their entire lives in Outsider periods.

Consider the parallels of Elvis and Marilyn's lives with that of Kurt Cobain, another Merchant who spent his life in Outsider periods. The dangers and the laurels are many. For Merchants equipped with a working knowledge of the Dharma Type, and a map to their Integration into the Laborer, the Outsider period can be most fruitful. But for those who lack the wisdom and support to point themselves in the right direction, the Freedom of the Outsider period can prove confusing, delusional, and even deadly.

By contrast, most people will see at least two different Life Cycles in their lives, and many may pass through all five. In Madonna's life we witness a cornucopia of change as she dances through Outsider, Warrior, Educator and back to Outsider periods, hitting the height of her career during her Educator period and sustaining it over her lengthy Outsider cycle through the nineties and today. This brings us back to the insight that each type will experience its most desirable effects during the Life Cycle of its Integration Point, and may undergo obstacles or difficulties during the Cycle of its Disintegration Point. As an

Chapter 14: The Life Cycles

Outsider functioning as a Warrior, Madonna found herself optimally set to enjoy success during her Educator period, and will never see a Merchant period in her life.

Warrior

The Warrior whose lord has been slain, or whose cause has been destroyed, must set out like a mercenary into unknown territory. This is the Warrior in the Outsider stage. Unrecognizable to his surroundings, his cause and credo may become foreign to the culture he lives in. His methods may become unorthodox or unpredictable. He begins to feel alone, to fight for different beliefs, adopting unorthodox values. Yet he must not forget that *knowledge* and *intelligence* remain his Integration points, and to let these guide him to a noble purpose in his life.

The Buddha is an example of a Warrior whose destiny was altered when he entered his Outsider period. Born a prince and intended for the throne, the Buddha's life dramatically turns when he leaves the kingdom in pursuit of Truth. Renouncing his former life, he becomes an Outsider, performing rigorous penance and living in poverty and isolation— conditions utterly juxtaposed to the regal title he was born into. This influence remains with him even after he assimilates back into society, for he remains a Warrior-Rebel, unaccepted by most in mainstream brahmanical society.

> *Outsiders have the power of surprise and innovation on their side, and, when they have earned it, moral superiority.*

His philosophy of *nirvana*, emptiness, clashes with the theistic view of the Brahmin culture current in India. Nonetheless, he becomes a champion of self-effort (Warrior) for those who wish to realize themselves, and rejects systems and authorities (Outsider) for guiding aspirants to that end. Only a Warrior could have performed the severe penance that the Buddha did, going to the extremes of fasting and asceticism. Only an Outsider could so re-frame the current system, as to bring about a total paradigm shift in religious thought. *There is no God! There is no soul!*— Indeed, only Outsiders, or those in Outsider cycles, know how to shock the establishment! Only Outsiders know how to create revolution. Compare, from Matthew 21, Jesus' radical invective on the temple priests: *"In truth I tell you, tax collectors and whores are entering God's reign before you!"* Outsiders have the power of surprise and innovation on their side, and, when they have earned it, moral superiority.

Special Conditioning: Warrior

James Dean is an example of a Warrior in a life-long Outsider period. His iconic role in *Rebel Without a Cause* was a fitting testament to the Warrior looking for his Just Cause. Remember that the Outsider's purpose is *to find his Purpose.* When he is unable to do so, he will push the envelope to connect to something bigger than himself. Combined with the Warrior's intensity and risk-taking nature, an Outsider Life Cycle can be a dangerous time if it is not harnessed to a Just Cause, a noble path to guide and channel his energies.

Contrast James Dean's demise with Marilyn Monroe's to find examples of failed coping strategies, one by a Warrior, the other by a Merchant. Finding themselves in Outsider periods, the Merchant Monroe turned to drugs and alcohol, while the Warrior Dean sought out intensity and thrills. When a Merchant cannot fill her emptiness by linking herself to charity and giving, she will seek to satiate herself in the quickest manner available. When the Warrior cannot give his life to a Just Cause, he will simply give his life… by taking increasing risks until they catch up to him. These are snares that await the unwary who enter Outsider Life Cycles. But just as the jungle is treacherous, it can also yield untold treasure. There is a wonder in the world's hidden places that you can't find on the paved roadways of cities and towns. The most powerful medicine and the wildest adventure lie in the unmapped jungle depths or the rugged plains. These are the domain of the Outsider Life Cycle.

Yet such cycles do not *have* to be exotic. Like the three layers of skin that correspond to the Outsider, (dermis, epidermis, hypodermis—see Chapter 7) there are degrees of experience when it comes to Outsider Life Cycles. The relatively insulated hypodermis remains close to the body of society—this could be a scientist working on an alternative cure for cancer, or a lawyer working with immigrants. They remain within society while brushing against the unknown. On the other hand, the dermis, the outside-most layer of the skin that is not connected to the life-giving capillaries of the body except by 'diffusion,' corresponds to a more radical experience of the Outsider Cycle. In such a time, our scientist may indeed depart for the jungle to seek alternative cures for cancer, all the while learning new languages and absorbing new cultures. Only a counselor trained in reading the Dharma Types can determine if your Outsider period will be one of extreme adventure, or quiet subversion from within... or something in between.

Laborer

Laborers may travel to foreign places for work during an Outsider period. This may be due to financial hardship or a promotion through their current profession, depending on their fortunes. During the Outsider time, they will experience an expansion of consciousness that is usually beneficial, as it opens them up to new ways of thinking, new cultures and traditions. The Laborer cannot help but be enriched by this, except where such new exposure costs him insurmountable difficulties, such as when he is exposed to ridicule, shame, or discrimination. In such cases, he is likely to develop a strong aversion towards the new, and close his mind up in order to endure such hardships.

But Laborers and Outsiders share a special bond. They are both cut from the same cloth, and have an affinity that helps the Labor type weather any changes with his typical hardiness. Laborers are handy and possess practical skills useful anywhere in the world, which makes it easier to adapt to working conditions. On the other hand, they are slow to take on new information, and this may detriment their introduction to societies that are radically different from their own. Whatever the situation, Laborers in an Outsider period generally do well, as a little change is always good for the soul of a Labor type!

> *Whatever your type, do not fear the Outsider time, for it may be the most memorable of your life!*

Special Conditioning: Laborer

Paul McCartney is an example of a Laborer who traversed Outsider periods during the formative years of his life. From early childhood until his early thirties, he entertained a Life Cycle that co-opted him and his fellow Beatles into a revolution that changed the world's musical landscape. Only Outsiders or those in Outsider periods can so alter the consciousness of society! Whatever your type, do not fear the Outsider time, for it may be the most memorable of your life. McCartney later went on to experience Laborer and Merchant periods, but none were as transformative to the world scene as his Outsider time.

Bruce Springsteen is another Laborer musician who spent a great deal of his life in an Outsider period. In fact, as we have seen in the sections on Money and Profession, Outsiders and those in Outsider periods tend to gravitate to jobs that offer just the kind of freedom, flexibility, and creative outlet that music affords, though one does not have to be in rock 'n roll to be a Rock Star in life. Learn how to harness your Outsider periods to express the unique gifts Nature gives you, whether for a day or a lifetime.

Outsider

The Outsider in an Outsider period is removed from the normal and mundane operations of life— he is in his own world. This may come about in undesirable ways, such as illness, during which he is forced to spend time in hospitals or at home recovering, or imprisonment, during which his actions are also extremely censured. Or it may occur in beneficial ways, like travel, exploration, spiritual study, research, or anything that takes us away from the humdrum, mundane reality of our lives. Outsiders in Outsider periods *rarely* settle for a nine to five existence. Instead, they leave to explore the wild, eventually bringing some of it back to their society if they are wise to their dharma. Remember, that an Outsider is never really fulfilled unless he digests, assimilates, and transmutes his experiences. This is equivalent to the three levels of Ruth, Responsibility, and Respect discussed in Part 1.

From the above example, this may be the person who beats his illness and writes a bestselling book about it. For the prisoner who does his time, it could be reaching out to his community and giving of himself to educate kids and help prevent crime. Or, it may be the escape artist/magician who scours the globe to hone his skills, and ends up with fame, fortune, and a show in Vegas.

Special Conditioning: Outsider

Many are the examples of Outsiders in Outsider periods, both glorious and tragic. Nicholas Cage spent his first thirty four years in Outsider Life Cycles, thereby permanently imbuing him with an oddball, Outsider persona in both his movies and personal life. While he used this to great benefit, Jimi Hendrix also wowed the world with his electric rock-god innovation, but was carried away by his Outsder Cycle's excesses. From age 17 to his death, Jimi both rose and fell in his Outsider period.

Bhagavan Rajneesh (Osho) is an example of an Outsider whose whole life was spent in Outsider periods. The ultimate iconoclast, this *double Outsider* even managed to piss off Ronald Reagan as he caught the attention of the American government with his lavish spending and anti-establishment message.

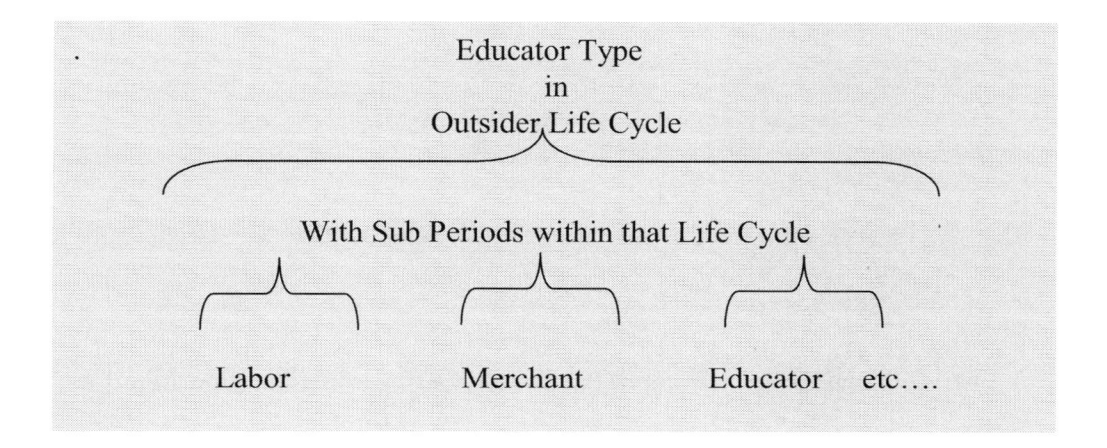

```
                    Educator Type
                         in
                  Outsider Life Cycle
        ⎧_____⎫
         With Sub Periods within that Life Cycle
         ⎧‾‾‾⎫      ⎧‾‾‾⎫      ⎧‾‾‾⎫
         Labor      Merchant    Educator    etc....
```

Cycles Within Cycles

During long stretches of one Life Cycle, there are invariably shorter-lived periods, or sub-cycles. Even for an Outsider in Outsider periods, there are times of Rest, Education, Goal-attainment, and Conviviality that correspond to Labor, Educator, Warrior, and Merchant sub-periods. Sub periods may last months or years, depending on the greater context of the main Life Cycle. In longer cycles, sub periods may indicate a temporary respite. For an actress in an Outsider period, a Labor sub cycle may find her giving birth and taking time away from acting to raise a family. Let's take a look at an example to illustrate the point.

Juliet is an Educator who enters a long Outsider period. During this time she becomes interested in Italy and its culture. What begins with a few language courses eventually turns into an extended stay in Florence. There, she takes a job at a coffee shop for a year to earn money and build roots, while drilling her Italian grammar at home. This is her Labor sub cycle, which though not very glamorous, lays the foundation and establishes her in her new home. After a while, she meets a boyfriend and through him begins to expand her social circle. Suddenly, she finds herself delighting in shopping for new clothes, wearing makeup, going out dancing, and living the high life of a twenty-something in Florence. Having done the work of learning the language and its customs,

> *Life Cycles are often, but not always, signaled by some event or change in life.*

she gives herself permission to have a good time and expand her network of friends. This is her Merchant sub cycle.

After a year and a half of dating and enjoying her time in Florence, she breaks up with her boyfriend, but is offered a teaching position at the same time, one that moves her to a university in Milan. There she takes a post as guest lecturer, as her Educator sub cycle begins to exert its influence within the context of her Outsider Life Cycle.

Here we have a complex picture of an individual who finds herself in an Outsider Life Cycle, as represented by her interest in Italy and her eventual move there. While in Italy, she sees various sub cycles that color the expression of her long stay. In this example, she goes from working to get by, to playing and enjoying herself, to settling down into a position suitable to her Dharma Type.

Life cycles and sub cycles do not negate each other. As we can see from Juliette's vignette, her Merchant sub period of fun and romance occurred *within the context* of her longer Outsider cycle, midst new friends and foreign surroundings. Life Cycles, Dharma Types, and sub cycles do not cancel out: instead, their energies blend to form a complete, fluid picture of one's life.

This example also illustrates that cycles often, but not always, are signaled by some event, or change in life. In this case, Juliette's study and move to Italy inaugurates her Outsider period. In Italy, her job as a waitress and quiet home study marks her Laborer sub cycle, while meeting her boyfriend and expanding her social circle initiates her Merchant sub period. Finally, moving to Milan to teach inaugurates an Educator sub cycle.

In looking at Life Cycles and sub cycles, a rule of thumb is to start where you are: consider the most immediate influence and work your way up. During her Merchant sub cycle, Juliette was most immediately experiencing the Merchant energy of fun and friends, which was happening *in a foreign country*. Like Russian nesting dolls, sub periods fit within the greater Life Cycle, just as the Life Cycle is subsumed by the Dharma Type.

Sub cycles should only be considered when you have an accurate depiction of your life map by a trained Dharma Type counselor. Practically speaking, simply knowing your Dharma Type and Life Cycle is enough to put you light years ahead of the curve in terms of self-knowledge and awareness of your life path. Adding the sub cycles is a fine-tuning of that knowledge that can be useful, but is not essential to getting the most from your Dharma Type.

The Merchant Life Cycle

Outsider

Now let us continue your homework by looking at the Merchant Life Cycle as an example of how we can break down and analyze any period. Because Outsiders Integrate into all four types, they can adjust to a Merchant role fairly easily, unless they are playing Warriors, in which case their Merchant period may pose some challenges. Knowing that Merchant qualities must be developed during this time can help an Outsider focus her energy and keep her from feeling 'lost' as many Outsiders can feel when they do not know their place.

This does not mean that the she will become a card-carrying Merchant just because she has entered a Merchant period, for a type's basic qualities always remain, though in the background, to color its personality. It does mean that her Outsider dharma will be served by embracing a Merchant role for a while. She may become more 'socialized' during this time, flowing smoothly with the culture stream, though this surface conviviality may come with an increased feeling of emptiness, as the Merchant's sometimes low self-worth can exacerbate an Outsider's already heightened anxiety. This can be countered by staying grounded in dharma. For the Outsider playing a Merchant, that means embracing charity— giving your energy and time to help others— and staying grounded in the Three Steps to Integration, as discussed in Chapter 6. Meditation and natural supplements like melatonin, valerian, and other calming herbs also work well.

During Merchant periods, Outsiders are interested in profiting themselves and may do so with novel ideas or products. They may become popular and well-liked, and during this time they have license to have fun, entertain, and enjoy the Merchant lifestyle. Neither Outsiders nor Merchants are particularly concerned with repressive morals, and the Outsider in this time is more interested in a good time, than in being 'good.' But she must be careful to maintain some moral order, lest she walk away with lasting reminders of her mistakes, which may include police records, diseases, or physical and emotional scars.

Educator

Because Educators neither Integrate nor Disintegrate into Merchants, this is a Neutral time for them; Educators are neither comfortable nor terribly bothered by the exigencies of the Merchant Life Cycle. This is a time to *sell* and *market* their knowledge. Like Outsiders, Educator types find it difficult to know when it is appropriate to market their ideas. In fact, they may prefer to teach, study, and do what they do, rather than actively promote themselves or worry about financial obligations. When Jesus sent out his disciples to teach and heal, he did so with the command to *take nothing for the journey except a staff— no bread, no bag, no money in your belts.* (Mark 6:37) This is very much an Educator sentiment. But a Merchant time affords them opportunities to harvest some rewards by using their smarts in different arenas. They may go into sales, investment, or find other ways to financially benefit themselves. This rest from Educator pursuits may in fact inspire fresh and new ideas when they move into different Life Cycles later, because Merchant periods are nothing if not motivating and exciting.

Warrior

The Warrior in a Merchant period is an instance of athleticism mixed with entertainment, a whirlwind mix of capitalism and pugilism that is at once brutal and exciting. In the best-case scenario, Warriors earn money through their valor, power, and/or reputation and their value is recognized by Merchant society. Yet this is also the most precarious stage for Warriors, for a Warrior in a Merchant period is also likely to lose his or her goal and purpose to Merchant temptations.

What does a Warrior do when there is no battle to fight? He finds a Just Cause to serve at home. This is what happens to athletes or soldiers when their glory days are over. They become businessmen, advisors, or workers, depending on their Life Cycles. Here is the athlete-turned sports commentator, franchise owner, or coach. Here, the retired boxer selling cookware to the multitudes. Whatever the case, for the Warrior in a Merchant period the flashing red light is 'don't sell out!' This is their only caveat.

Warriors entering into a Merchant time must therefore have an outlet for their skills— a just fight, a noble cause to embrace— in order to have inner satisfaction. If they fall into the trap of accumulating money and resources for their own sake, with no way to use them for a greater good, they risk descending into a Warrior hell. If, like the boxer selling cookware on TV they are blessed with good fortune, Warriors should inject their earnings into charities and noble causes of their choice, in order to leave behind a legacy worthy of them, and be *truly* honored for their achievements. Truly Integrated Warriors in a Merchant period give up to 50% of their check to help others, and are thus able to play the Merchant game to the max without being sullied in the process. That way, they can invest their total attention, energy, and skill into achieving fortune and fame, without the emptiness that hounds the Merchant and anyone traveling through a Merchant period.

> *"Yon Cassius has a lean and hungry look;*
> *He thinks too much: such men are dangerous."*
> -William Shakespeare, *Julius Caesar*

It is the nature of Merchants to give back, to feed and clothe others when they can. Thus, a Warrior in a Merchant time, while he may not be able to save the world and protect the innocent in a Warrior fashion, may yet do so in a Merchant way. Therefore, giving back sooner rather than later is imperative. Since not everyone will become a millionaire in their Merchant period, this does not have to take the form of extravagant philanthropy. From volunteering at the YMCA, to running a multi-million dollar charitable foundation— the gifts a Warrior gives are commensurate to his abilities. What matters is that he give them, **even if he has to do so in secret!** Part of playing the Merchant game and making it interesting is not letting others know what you are doing. Part of giving away his resources whets the Warrior's appetite for more, whereas hording them dulls the edge of his competitive spirit. It is good for Warriors to always stay a little hungry; even midst the feast of Merchant plenty.

It is the Warrior's nature to fight and die for a cause— in fact, he must always be ready to do so, for Death may take him at any moment. That is why Warrior cultures stress present-moment awareness and steady vigilance as tools for enlightenment. These are ways to keep Warriors centered in reality, and not get swept away by pride, lust, and anger, which are easy traps for Warriors in a Merchant time. Then, life has sanity and balance, and even should Death sneak up, He is faced in full readiness, rather than succumbed to in surprise. Then, a Warrior has the power to enter the next world on his own terms, with no regrets.

The collapse of Enron a few years ago gave us a tragic example of a Warrior corrupted by the Merchant system. A captain in the US air force, John Clifford Baxter was a top Enron executive, and, by all accounts, a man of utmost integrity. After the public debacle that followed Enron's bankruptcy, he killed himself, writing in his desperate suicide note, *'I've always tried to do the right thing, but where there was once great pride- now it's gone.'* A tragic example of a Warrior who lost his way. Warriors must remain centered during the Merchant period, and give away their earnings, time, and energy, not just to their families, which everyone does, but to benefit those who can't help themselves. This gives them a noble purpose, and prevents tragedies like this from happening.

Merchant and Laborer

Now take a moment to imagine how the Merchant will take to a Merchant cycle. Will this be a time of improvement or decline? Will Merchants and Laborers feel comfortable or awkward in this period, and if so, why? How will they express themselves? In fact, for Merchants and Laborers this period is one of opportunity and improvement. Merchants will find their skills expressed to the fullest and are likely to benefit through them, *just as any Dharma Type in a self-same cycle*. The wind is full in their sails and they should feel no compunction about being themselves, as the world is supportive to their self-expression. They should feel more charming, social, and involved with others. Money, goods, and opulence await them here, just as they do the Labor type, who will feel like he is on center stage, earning the deserved rewards of hard work.

> *For the Labor type, the reward of good work is more work!*

Neutral Dynamics

Let us now examine an instance of a Neutral Life Cycle. Since we have seen the Educator in a Merchant time, we will consider the period between Warriors and Laborers.

In his Labor Life Cycle, the Warrior puts down his sword and takes up the spade. Here his strength, skill, and leadership ability is put to use coordinating and build things, rather than to destroying them. He finds respect in working hard and in the camaraderie of being part of a group, though he is not always appreciated for his full worth as a Warrior. His skills and training may become rusty, and his weapons unnecessary. At such a time the Warrior's sword becomes a paper weight while his basic work ethic is put to use.

For the Labor type, the reward of good work is more work. But the Warrior seeks a definite goal, an end to achieve. She needs a mountain peak to scale; the slow journey of 10,000 miles is not as interesting for her. Therefore she may grow bored doing Labor type work and feel her talents are being wasted. Conversely, the Labor type in his Warrior time becomes an impassioned and fervent fighter for the rights of others. He is a civil rights, community activist whose voice finally gets heard. He defends the causes he believes in, whether environmental or social, and the immovable object becomes an irresistible force in his Warrior period.

The only danger here is that he may become a *politician* rather than an activist, and take the wrong road to betterment. That is because it is difficult to keep one's integrity when playing the politics game. It is not easy to enter the matrix without becoming affected by it. Some historians have proffered that George Washington was the only unsullied president, having never campaigned or even desired the office; everyone else had to play the game of government, and compromise himself thereby. Such are the caveats for Laborers in a Warrior time.

Laborers may also never find lasting contentment in a Warrior period. Like a boxer who must fight to defend his title, Laborers cannot sit back and enjoy their laurels during this time. Thus, there is ambivalence: great achievement mixed with some dissatisfaction. There is action without rest and recovery, which Laborers normally enjoy.

Conclusion

Have you ever noticed that your friends change over time, and the people you considered yourself inseparable from are now distant memories? Or are you the type of person who has had the same friends all of your life? Much of our compatibility with friends and lovers has to do with the Life Cycle we are in. People in the same Life Cycle share a common framework. People in different, incompatible cycles tend to drift apart. People we wouldn't normally speak with sometimes cross our paths because they are on the same journey we are. Sometimes we get to know people on planes, trains, or buses that we would never have met if it were not for sharing a space and a similar destination. The same is true for sharing Life Cycles.

In the next volume, we will explore Compatibility between the types. One of the methods for determining compatibility is the Life Cycles people share. A true Outsider will get along with other types in their Outsider cycles. They will enjoy the common ground of shared experience. On the other hand, two Educators who normally understand each other may not get along if one is in a Warrior period and the other in a Merchant time. Though Educators share similar values, the expression of those values will differ according to the energy of the cycle they are in.

This work has been the foundation, a stepping stone to understanding your dharma. In the volumes that follow, we will take what you have learned and use it to scrutinize two areas that perennially baffle mankind: Relationships and Religion. We will harness the technology of the Dharma Type to open up the heretofore mysterious avenues of romance and spirituality, two unique expressions of our humanity and the objects of multi-billion dollar industries. We will also explore dharma on the three levels of Self, World, and Cosmos, tying it to other Vedic principles for greater understanding.

What happens when a Dharma Type does not live out its dharma? There are examples everywhere of people not fulfilling their potential. Sometimes family responsibilities necessitate taking on any paying work to feed, clothe, and house one's family. Difficult economic conditions such as the "downturn" of 2008 also do not seem to promote free movement towards a dharmic lifestyle. However, these obligations are also a dharma, a duty we have to our families and society. Living your Dharma Type potential and carrying out your obligations to the world are not mutually exclusive: they go hand in hand. In fact, the current economic depression affords us an opportunity to step away from previous jobs and commitments to analyze our lives. Such times can be ripe opportunities to shed ourselves of superfluity, and ask the question: *"Who am I, and what am I here to do?"*

During good economic times, we tend to coast along, comfortably numbed by a good paycheck, even while working in areas that do not befit our optimal *self-expression* and *personal growth*. But we are more than just money-making machines. We all have a higher destiny that but for war, pestilence, or other conditions that bar us from expressing it, we must try to live up to. In fact, it is *during* crisis that we look most at ourselves. It is during times of distress that we have the opportunity to redirect our lives in the direction we wish them to go.

> *Great creations grow out of great conflict: this is true in art as in life*

During the Rwandan genocide, people were forced to either become Warriors, fighting to survive, or Outsiders, running for refuge. When basic survival needs are not met, there is little space for the dharma of your type to shine. But even in our hardest times, we in the Western world do not face such overwhelming challenges. Whatever our circumstances, we still have the opportunity to make our essence shine if we have the motivation, and more importantly, the tools to do so. It may take work, however.

Everyone has a duty to family, society, and their environment. The higher dharma of the Dharma Type can only express when these obligations have been satisfied and leave us time to pursue our individual destinies. There is no shame in working to feed our kids. But resourceful people will seek a way to do both: to live up to the potential of the Dharma Type while fulfilling duties to family and society. They will work at two jobs until they finish that novel or complete that business plan. They will juggle responsibilities to others, and find time to be responsible to *themselves*, even if it means temporary hardship and setbacks. Great creations grow out of great conflict: this is true in art as in life.

There are many reasons not to live up to your highest potential. In the worst extremes, we see cases of serial killers who cannot express their natural selves but in the darkest and most tortured ways. But for the most part, people "*live lives of quiet desperation,*" as per Thoreau, hiding their worth and covering it with platitudes and good excuses. It takes great courage to stand up and say, '*This is who I am!*' with dignity and pride, and to let the chips fall where they may. It takes a calm surrender to the Nature that made you to accept who you are and create the most of your opportunities. There is one thing that you do better than anyone else in the world, and your Dharma Type is the key to finding it!

PART III
APPENDICES

APPENDIX I

Figures and Tables

	Skills	Strengths	Weaknesses
Warrior	Both gross and fine motor skills; usually a combination of the two that allows for the achievement of a goal- i.e. a soccer player.	Generous and self-sacrificing. Can achieve anything in the name of a good cause.	Pessimistic, cynical, materialistic. Does not believe in saving grace, and becomes prone to a dog-eat-dog mentality.
Merchant	Fine motor skills. Less goal-oriented, more focused on refinement- i.e. a violinist.	Inspirational and charitable. Entertaining and funny. Can motivate people.	Insecurity. Needs constant validation from others to believe own worthiness.
Educator	Mental skills- possesses less motor skills than other types; often clumsy or uncoordinated.	High minded, pure, and noble. A source of wisdom and purpose to others.	Wishy-washy, feckless, no backbone. Schism between ideals and reality- especially as pertains to base emotions like Lust.
Laborer	Gross motor skills, usually applied for self-sustenance as in a trade or hobby.	Loyal and devoted. Hard working and unaffected. The backbone of functional society.	Intense jealousy. Attachment to people, things, or ideas to the point of irrationality.
Outsider	Can mimic any of the types. Usually has affinity with Labor type.	Born to free other beings. Instigates revolution, progress, and positive change.	Blame, Self-Deceit. Refuses to accept responsibility for own actions; blames the world for his problems. Cannot see own faults and shortcomings.

Appendix 1

	LABORER	MERCHANT	WARRIOR	EDUCATOR	OUTSIDER
SEASON	SPRING	SUMMER	SUMMER	AUTUMN	WINTER
YOGA BODY	FOOD BODY	SENSATE BODY	VITAL/ BREATH BODY*	WISDOM BODY	BLISS BODY
INTELLIGENCE	EMOTIONAL	AESTHETIC	ENERGETIC	INTELLECTUAL	RADICAL/ MYSTIC
ELEMENT	EARTH	WATER	FIRE	AIR	SPACE
DUTY TO	EDUCATOR	LABORER/ OUTSIDER**	MERCHANT	WARRIOR	EDUCATOR
PRIORITY TO	MERCHANT	WARRIOR	EDUCATOR	LABORER/ OUTSIDER	MERCHANT

* Note that the Breath Body corresponds to the Fire Element. Like oxygen in an internal combustion engine that helps ignite gasoline and create fire, *prana*, or *chi*, is responsible for creating the processes whereby the energy systems of the body create force and transformation.

** Merchants, who have the greatest capacity to provide support, are the only Dharma Type with Duties to *two* types, while Educators, who *need* the most support, are the only type to *receive* two Duties.

Sanyasa or Karma

	DHARMA TYPE	YAMA	NIYAMA
jñana	**Educator**	Ahimsa/ Non-Violence	Svadhyaya/ Self-Study
→ Austerity Karma	**Warrior**	Satya/ Truthfulness	Tapas/ Austerity
→ Charity	**Merchant**	Asteya/ Non-Stealing	Santosha/ Contentment
Bakti	**Laborer**	Brahmacharya/ Continence	Shaucha/ Cleanliness
No Path → create unique	**Outsider**	Aparigraha/ Non-Grasping	IshvaraPranidhana/ Surrender to God

SEASON:	**Spring**	**Summer**	**Fall**	**Winter**
UP TO AGE:	22-25	44-50	66-75	67/75+
DHARMA TYPE:	Laborer	Warrior/Merchant	Educator	Outsider

Gross Anatomy		Subtle Anatomy
Outsider —	**Skin**	**Bliss Body**
Educator—	Head and Face	Wisdom Body
Merchant—	Digestion, Legs	Sensate Body
Warrior—	Heart, Blood *Prana*, Muscles	Vital/Breath Body
Laborer—	Reproduction, Bones, Feet	Food/Flesh Body

Appendix 1

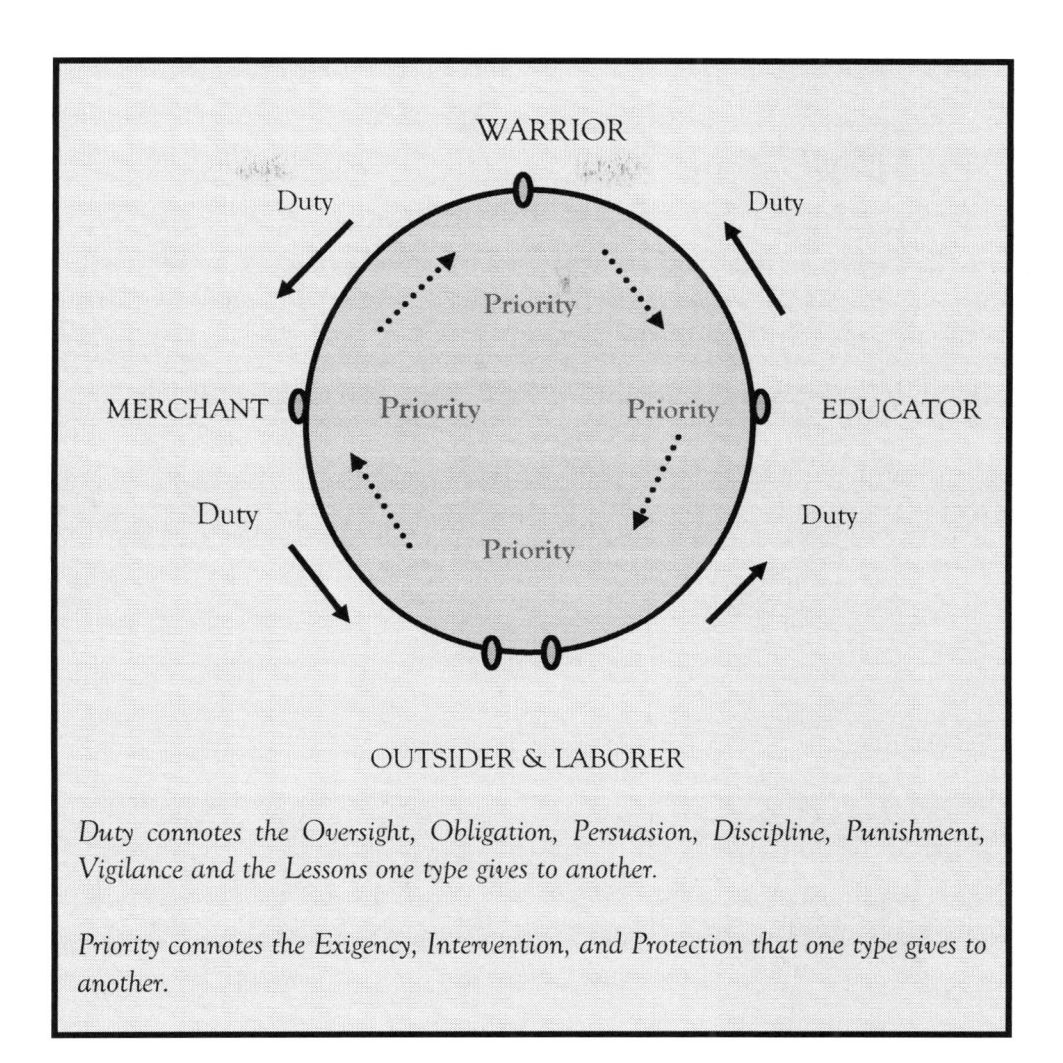

```
                    WARRIOR
         Duty                    Duty
              ↙              ↖
                  Priority
    MERCHANT  Priority  Priority  EDUCATOR
                  Priority
              ↘              ↗
         Duty                    Duty

              OUTSIDER & LABORER
```

Duty connotes the Oversight, Obligation, Persuasion, Discipline, Punishment, Vigilance and the Lessons one type gives to another.

Priority connotes the Exigency, Intervention, and Protection that one type gives to another.

	Negative Emotion	**Positive Emotion**
Outsider	Deception, Anxiety	Empathy/Wonder
Educator	Lust	Compassion
Laborer	Sloth, Jealousy	Love, Loyalty
Warrior	Anger, Pride	Generosity
Merchant	Greed	Conviviality, Enthusiasm

VEDA	UPAVEDA	DHARMA TYPE AND MODERN CONNOTATIONS
Rig Veda	Ayurveda (Healing)	Educator. Wellness and lifestyle. The founding principles of healthy living and society.
Yajur Veda	Dhanurveda (Warfare)	Warrior. Protecting people from threats to life and livelihood.
Sama Veda	Gandharva Veda (Music and Arts)	Merchant. Inspiring, entertaining, and distracting people. Enhancing the pleasure of living through music, trades, arts, and crafts.
Atharva Veda	ArthaShastra, Sthapatya Veda (Economics, Architecture)	Laborer. Securing people's moveable and immovable assets. Building structures and growing the wealth of society.

DHARMA TYPE	RULED BY	TYPE OF STRESS	NATURE	EXAMPLES
Laborer	Feeling	Long-term emotional	Chronic	Worry, low level anxiety
Merchant	Feeling	Short-term emotional	Acute	Anxiety, panic attacks
Warrior	Thinking	Short-term mental	Acute	Post-traumatic stress*
Educator	Thinking	Long-term mental	Chronic	Spaciness, Dementia

* Post-Traumatic Stress Disorder is further detailed in Chapter 12.

SUMMARY OF THE TYPES

Educator
Strongly idealistic, but not necessarily practical…
Noted for intelligence and grasp of abstruse concepts…
Generally not forceful, physically less resilient than other types…
Good counselor, but unable to follow his own counsel…
Motivated by truth, rather than money, but prone to indiscretions due to lack of control over his senses, i.e. anger, lust, greed.
Sanskrit terms: *jnana, dayaa, kshanti: wisdom, compassion, forbearance*

Outsider
Culture, beliefs, race, physicality, and other traits make her different from her immediate environment…
Travels to or lives in foreign lands and different or unusual places…
Absorbs and adopts foreign ideologies and concepts…
Incredibly adaptive—able to blend in and wear many hats…
Resents establishment and the 'normal' life of others…
Keenly aware of injustices in society, be they economic, educational, political, etc…
Values personal freedom over other things…
Sanskrit terms: *ananda, kaivalya, svatantriya: bliss, isolation/independence, freedom*

Warrior
Motivated by challenge to improve self and others…
Interested in protecting those who cannot protect themselves…
Responds to defiance and competition…
Values knowledge, wisdom, and innocence in others…
Sanskrit terms: *yukti, virya, viveka: skill, strength, judgement*

Merchant
Strongly motivated to secure personal and family interests…
Need to be around others, feels lonely or empty without company…
A smooth talker: likeable, glib, and socially active; highly entertaining …
Feels best when giving; at first to family, then community, and eventually the world.
Understands how the Merchant society functions and is good at taking advantage of it…
Sanskrit terms: *shakti, rasa, danam: energy, juiciness, charity*

Labor
Strong likes and dislikes…
Deep sense of community and belonging…
Emotional ties and loyalty to her 'own' things: her family, country, job, home team…
Good physical strength and endurance, and a powerful work ethic…
Capable of great service and self-sacrifice…
Strong intuition and specific intelligence, but not well-rounded…
Sanskrit terms: *bhakti, seva, dhriti: devotion/love, service, solidity/endurance*

APPENDIX II

EAST/WEST WISDOM: AUTHOR'S PICKS

Dr. Vasant Lad. Dr. Lad is perhaps single-handedly responsible for training more Westerners in authentic Ayurveda than any other teacher. His institute is a haven for all who thirst for Vedic wisdom, and a port to higher knowledge. He teaches with compassion and an uncanny understanding of a student's needs.
www.ayurveda.com

Robert Svoboda. The original Ayurvedic Westerner, Svoboda holds the distinction of truly honoring India's spiritual traditions in his books as well as in his life. A must-read for those wanting to explore Ayurvedic alchemy and the mysteries of sacred India.
www.drsvoboda.com

Hart deFouw. What Dr. Vasant Lad is to Ayurveda, deFouw is to Jyotisha— a living, breathing embodiment of the art and science of Vedic Astrology. The first Westerner to authentically imbibe and carry on a Vedic tradition normally inaccessible to Western students, his books and classes on Jyotisha make for tough reading, but set the standard in authentic instruction.
www.vedicvidyainstitute.com

Robin Gile. Author of *The Idiot's Guide to Palmistry*, Robin is a practicing palmist and Archetypal Symbolist in the Albuquerque, NM area. Few can match his talent and uncanny insight born of 40 years experience.
www.RobinGilePalmistry.com

Graham Hancock. This far-out journalist cum spiritual seeker has trekked the globe looking to uncover man's ancient civilizations and their connections to the modern world. Voracious in his thirst for knowledge and truth, here is an Outsider-Educator combination that makes us stand up and take notice. Even if you don't agree with his conclusions, his body of work cannot be ignored.
www.grahamhancock.com

Pavel Tsatsouline. Pavel is a Master of Sports, the title of highest achievement accorded in the old Soviet system—akin to a Ph.D in both athletic understanding *and* practice. Revolutionary in his approach, he transformed the Western fitness scene by introducing the kettlebell and other little-known training secrets to America. He makes difficult concepts simple to digest and is as compassionate in his delivery as he is brutal in his excoriation of what doesn't work. A true Warrior-Educator Integration. Check him out... or else!

www.dragondoor.com

John Douillard. John Douillard is a true admixture of East and West. A triathlete turned doctor turned Ayurvedic physician, his insights on modern Western integration of Ayurvedic principles, especially in athletics, are unique and enlightening. Buy his books.

www.lifespa.com

B.K.S. Iyengar. Well-known to the West, Iyengar is largely responsible for making yoga safe and understandable to the Western practitioner. All this, without diluting the essence of his tradition, Iyengar is one of few among the yoga multitude who has kept his Sincerity, Integrity, and Tradition intact over the years. For that, he remains a jewel to yoga culture.

www.bksiyengar.com

Krishna Das. Not an author, but a musician, KD is the East-West link to devotional Indian music and chanting. By the grace of his guru, he carries the spark of an ancient tradition in a modern Western voice that's guaranteed to make you sing along... just don't send him your speeding tickets.

www.krishandas.com

For more information, or to find a Dharma Type practitioner near you, visit www.spirittype.com, or write siddhadeva@yahoo.com

INDEX

adharma, 24
adrishta, 286
African American, 264
African Americans, 110
blacks, 114
Agni, 188
Ammachi, 82, 83
Animal Realm, 88, 131
apaurusheya, 5
archetype, 4, 10, 21, 25, 36, 37, 44, 71, 213, 239, 242, 243, 244, 247, 281, 320
avatar, 83, 162, 194, 238
avatars, 162, 194, 237
Ayurveda, 1, 5, 7, 43, 69, 128, 139, 150, 152, 165, 166, 178, 183, 205, 207, 301, 303, 340, 342
Ayurvedic, 27, 139, 300, 342, 343
Bhagavad, 3, 7, 65, 67, 108, 143, 149, 153, 220, 276, 298
Bhagavad Gita, 3, 7, 65, 67, 108, 143, 149, 220, 276, 298
Body Type, 233
Brahma, 44
brain, 43, 92, 123, 125, 127, 128, 129, 130, 131, 133, 142, 143, 157, 165, 197, 212, 216, 217, 254, 274, 285, 303, 310
Brain, 10, 128, 129, 148, 208
Buddha, 162, 163, 194, 220, 228, 321
Buddhism, 163
Buddha, 228
caste, 28, 35, 36, 113, 281, 282
chakra, 184, 193
Chakra, 183, 185, 188, 190, 193
Circle of Duty, 11, 155, 162, 163, 165, 208
Circle of Life, 11, 155, 158, 161, 189, 222, 242, 243, 291, 294, 320
Circle of Life, 11, 130, 135, 155, 161, 162, *See* Circle of Duty
Circle of Duty, 186, 190
Circle of Life, 80
diet, 62, 71, 73, 81, 128, 137, 138, 139, 144, 148, 208, 253, 286, 311
diets, 130, 148
diet, 21, 92, 138, 186
digestion, 69, 126
digestive organs, 127, 128
digestion, 127

drugs, 61, 70, 71, 72, 73, 76, 81, 124, 132, 149, 150, 152, 187, 212, 249, 301, 303, 310, 319, 322
duhkha, 5, 6, 64, 108
Duhkha, 5, 108, 297
Earning Power, 294
Element, 11, 23, 25, 26, 92, 95, 98, 107, 123, 132, 137, 142, 183, 184, 185, 186, 187, 188, 189, 190, 208, 216, 219, 256, 264, 282, 285, 289, 292, 304, 337
elements, 6, 95, 97, 128, 142, 146, 266
Elements, 22, 25, 26, 28, 144, 173, 183, 184, 185, 188, 190, 192, 193, 203, 208, 217, 218, 256, 285
Enneagram, 109
feet, 123, 126, 203
five 'Bodies, 123
five 'Bodies'
yoga bodies, 123
Four Aims of life, 22, *See* purushartha
Four Seasons
Season, 22, 194, 201, 202, 203, 207, 242, 272
Gandhi, 45, 52, 62, 97, 219
Gita, 3, 153, 276, 284
Bhagavad Gita, 3
Golden Age
Satya Yuga, 192
government, 8, 34, 94, 157, 164, 165, 166, 167, 168, 169, 174, 175, 176, 181, 272, 282, 289, 297, 303, 325, 331
Government, 11, 165
government, 11, 122, 164, 166, 215, 283, 284, 306
grace, 43, 106, 118, 177, 181, 187, 244, 254, 287, 318, 335, 343
heart, 52, 66, 73, 80, 81, 87, 88, 91, 125, 127, 128, 129, 148, 168, 180, 202, 207, 221, 222, 226, 233, 234, 240, 247, 268, 289, 294
heroes, 32, 127, 144, 177, 237, 238, 239, 242, 243, 247, 248, 275, 283
Homework, 10, 11, 116, 181, 208, 245, 252, 277, 306, 317
India, 3, 4, 6, 7, 28, 35, 36, 44, 74, 99, 105, 162, 176, 177, 239, 321, 342

343

Intelligence, 11, 83, 123, 142, 146, 208, 211, 212, 213, 214, 215, 216, 217, 218, 230, 231, 240, 242, 277
INTELLIGENCE Intelligence, 211, 217, 337
Iron age, 36, 123, 236
Jesus, 97, 98, 105, 111, 113, 134, 152, 161, 194, 321, 328
jnana, 63
Kali Yuga, 150
Iron age, dark age, 31, 33, 35, 192, 193, 237, 250, 297
karma, 3, 5, 6, 9, 10, 36, 44, 45, 64, 72, 73, 76, 91, 108, 109, 110, 133, 136, 163, 195, 233, 289, 310, 312
Karma, 10, 5, 37, 44, 107, 108, 297
Lad, 8, 205, 342
language, 4, 10, 42, 43, 44, 90, 132, 185, 193, 214, 215, 220, 224, 225, 229, 230, 231, 239, 311, 315, 325
Language, 11, 132, 214, 230, 231, 242
Life Cycle, 11, 97, 99, 100, 101, 164, 191, 214, 216, 242, 282, 283, 290, 306, 309, 310, 311, 312, 313, 314, 315, 316, 317, 318, 320, 322, 323, 324, 325, 326, 327, 328, 330, 331, 332
lore, 29, 101, 133, 230, 236, 237, 243, 244, 247, 250
Mahabharata, 32, 144, 177
Maya, 187, 259
Merchant society, 3, 8, 33, 47, 49, 50, 59, 66, 72, 86, 93, 166, 168, 175, 188, 191, 192, 205, 237, 242, 248, 249, 266, 267, 271, 272, 273, 283, 288, 293, 297, 305, 328
Merchant Society, 10
military, 82, 173, 176, 188, 262, 277, 283
Military, 173
money, 7, 8, 21, 33, 34, 41, 47, 48, 51, 66, 70, 73, 74, 75, 76, 77, 79, 86, 100, 117, 126, 134, 143, 144, 153, 157, 164, 174, 175, 202, 214, 223, 233, 236, 263, 267, 272, 273, 279, 280, 281, 282, 283, 286, 287, 288, 289, 290, 294, 295, 296, 297, 298, 299, 301,널306, 310, 311, 315, 325, 328, 332
Money, 10, 11, 4, 47, 52, 170, 279, 283, 284, 286, 295, 299, 313, 324, 330
Monroe, 219, 239, 242, 320, 322
Moses, 45, 135
music, 35, 42, 70, 75, 91, 92, 97, 133, 144, 166, 212, 220, 223, 224, 226, 233, 234, 235, 301, 324, 340, 343

Music, 11, 43, 92, 93, 166, 233, 246, 256, 340
myth, 4, 7, 32, 79, 101, 176, 237, 241, 243, 244, 247
Myths, 11, 4, 5, 79, 181, 236, 239, 242
Natural Law, 3, 9, 23, 24, 25, 36, 46, 125, 165, 167, 179, 192, 201
Neuro-Linguistic-Programming
NLP, 109
New Testament, 65, 105, 231
NLP, 9, 129, 131
pack, 92, 144
Persuasion, 11, 159, 161
pet, 250, 256
Pets, 11, 249
Plato, 27, 167, 231
Political Myths, 174
Post-Traumatic Stress Disorder, 11, 227, 271, 340
prana, 127, 137, 143, 202, 214, 220, 259, 260, 261, 337
Priority, 11, 155, 156, 157, 158, 159, 160, 161, 162, 163, 222, 224
Profession, 11, 33, 116, 122, 135, 215, 246, 279, 298, 299, 300, 324
PTSD, 11, 262
Post-Traumatic Stress Disorder, 65, 271, 273, 274
purusharthas, 23
Ramakrishna, 83
Ramayana, 107, 177, 179, 189, 238, 249
rat, 170, 254
relationship, 9, 10, 31, 48, 64, 92, 93, 123, 125, 126, 127, 129, 130, 159, 178, 192, 193, 240, 243, 249, 255, 293
Relationships, 8, 208, 332
ritual, 71, 75, 185, 189, 296
Ritual, 10, 71
sacred history, 29, 150, 192, 231
saint, 82, 108, 153, 201, 236, 288
samsara, 4, 5, 163
Sanskrit, 1, 4, 5, 23, 24, 29, 30, 31, 43, 63, 71, 73, 93, 116, 129, 142, 153, 162, 185, 194, 195, 216, 230, 231, 275
sattva, 236
Satya, 35, 206, 338
Season, 11, 208
Self Test, 10, 11
SELF-AWARENESS, 104, 106
Self-Improvement', 9
Seva, 93

344

sex, 4, 10, 29, 37, 73, 74, 104, 114, 126, 130, 134, 143, 178, 185, 206, 218, 244, 249, 256, 267, 285, 319
shakti, 59, 73, 74, 75, 178, 186, 201, 223, 295, 296
shruti, 25, 236
Sinatra, 218, 242
skin, 123, 124, 125, 193, 322
smriti, 25, 236
spirituality, 5, 6, 9, 30, 188, 260, 311, 332
Surrender, 10, 45, 46, 52, 54, 134, 135, 136, 206, 207, 219, 222, 229, 338
Taste, 11, 205, 207, 208
The Four Ages, 29
Thomas Jefferson, 24
Tithing, 158
totem animal, 253, 254
TV
television, 178, 181, 222, 236, 243, 245, 247, 267, 329
Unique Expression, 102, 103, 106, 123, 206, 229, 230
Unique Expression,, 103
UPAVEDA, 166, 340
Vasant, 8, 205, 342

Vastu Shastra, 183, 216
VastuShastra, 22, 216
Vedic, 10, 1, 3, 5, 6, 7, 9, 11, 21, 22, 23, 24, 25, 27, 28, 29, 30, 32, 34, 36, 43, 44, 64, 71, 78, 89, 96, 97, 107, 108, 109, 136, 139, 144, 149, 165, 183, 184, 188, 189, 192, 194, 196, 201, 205, 207, 221, 230, 237, 238, 284, 285, 289, 290, 297, 309, 310, 332, 342
Vedic Astrology, 6
Vedic', 6
Vidya, 7, 97
Viveka, 63, 64, 65, 180
Vivekananda, 25, 83, 279
YAMA
Niyama, 206, 338
yoga, 6, 7, 53, 72, 76, 83, 97, 139, 142, 230, 275, 289, 311, 343
Yoga, 11, 7, 43, 64, 116, 123, 139, 141, 142, 179, 183, 205, 206, 207, 211, 215, 229, 275, 276, 279
Yoga Bodies. *See* Five Bodies
Yogananda, 83
yugas, 35, *See* The Four Ages

Made in the USA
Charleston, SC
19 July 2013